Elliptic Curve Cryptography for Developers

Michael Rosing

MANNING

SHELTER ISLAND

For online information and ordering of this and other Manning books, please visit
www.manning.com. The publisher offers discounts on this book when ordered in quantity.
For more information, please contact

>   Special Sales Department
>   Manning Publications Co.
>   20 Baldwin Road
>   PO Box 761
>   Shelter Island, NY 11964
>   Email: orders@manning.com

Manning Publications Co.	Development editor:	Marina Michaels
20 Baldwin Road	Technical editor:	Mark Bissen
PO Box 761	Review editor:	Aleksandar Dragosavljević
Shelter Island, NY 11964	Production editor:	Keri Hales
	Copy editor:	Alisa Larson
	Proofreader:	Mike Beady
	Technical proofreader:	Gianluigi Spagnuolo
	Typesetter:	Ammar Taha Mohamedy
	Cover designer:	Marija Tudor

ISBN 9781633437944
Printed in the United States of America

Get the eBook FREE!
(PDF, ePub, Kindle, and liveBook all included)

We believe that once you buy a book from us, you should be able to read it in any format we have available. To get electronic versions of this book at no additional cost to you, purchase and then register this book at the Manning website.

Go to https://www.manning.com/freebook and follow the instructions to complete your pBook registration.

That's it!
Thanks from Manning!

To Katherine

contents

There are a great number of books on the subject of elliptic curve cryptography (ECC). Few of them have any code or explanations of how the code works. This book helps you understand both the mathematics and the code that implements that math. This book focuses on practical applications, so there are no mathematical proofs in this book. If the code works, the math is obviously correct. If the code fails, the code obviously has a bug. That's all the proof we need.

The mathematics of elliptic curves has been studied for over 300 years, and it's still an active area of research. This book cannot begin to present the depth of this field. We cover what we need to ensure solid cryptographic security can be implemented. While I found isogeny volcanoes a really cool name and fascinating topic, there's no need to go there.

Elliptic curve cryptography has been used for key exchange and digital signatures for over 30 years. In the past few years, it's been used for aggregated digital signatures on the blockchain, as well as for zero-knowledge proofs. The method of zero knowledge has been around for over 30 years as well. The use of zero-knowledge proofs on the blockchain to prove transactions without showing amounts is now possible with much less data using elliptic curve pairings of points.

In 2015, Professors Koblitz and Menezes published a paper that described the confusion around the National Security Agency's (NSA) statements concerning elliptic curve cryptography (see bibliography). The confusion stems from the NSA's comments about quantum computers' ability to break ECC. It seems highly premature to think quantum computers can break elliptic curve cryptography right now, and I want to take a moment to show why.

Quantum computers use qubits like normal (classical) computers use transistors. Unlike transistors which are either on or off, qubits are superpositions of on and off. It takes several qubits to create a gate just like it takes several transistors to create a NAND gate. For the past five years, the number of qubits in a unit area has doubled every year—this is better than Moore's law.

In 2017, Roetteler et al. published a paper on how to break ECC using quantum computers. The authors show how to create gates that will solve the discrete log problem on elliptic curves to find the key. After converting their values to powers of 2, their table of gates is shown in the third column of table 1. The first column describes the classical security level in bits and the second column describes the ECC prime number of bits required for this security level.

Table 1   Qubits to break ECC

security	prime	gates
80	160	1.7×2^{34}
128	256	1.8×2^{36}
256	512	1.0×2^{40}

This quantifies the confusion pointed out in Koblitz and Menez (2015). Today, there are 1.7×2^8 qubits in the largest reported device. That's about 2^6 gates. This means it will be at least 30 years before ECC is actually broken by quantum computers, assuming the doubling time of one year can be maintained for that entire time.

If you are younger than 40, you should start learning about how quantum computers work. They may well have an effect on your career. It's actually really amazing and fun stuff to learn! For at least the next 20 years, elliptic curve cryptography will be plenty secure and is clearly worth the effort to learn now.

Let's look at the first two columns of table 1. Security is related to a single secret key encryption method—for example, the advanced encryption standard (AES). To break AES, you need to try every possible key by brute force. On average, you need to try half the possible keys. So, the number of tries is $2^{(security-1)}$ attempts. Prime is the size of the prime number required to achieve this level of security with an elliptic curve. The factor of 2 comes from the method used to solve the discrete log problem over elliptic curves.

OK, I've used the phrase *discrete log problem over elliptic curves* a few times now, what does it actually mean? We'll get into the details in chapter 4, so for now I'll just say that if we have a point P on an elliptic curve, and we multiply that by some constant k, we get a new point Q on the curve. If you only know points P and Q, the discrete log problem is to find the constant k. The best algorithms today require the square root of the prime attempts to find k. If the prime has 256 bits, the square root of the prime has 128 bits, so, on average, it takes 2^{128} tries to find k. That's the same as 128 bits of security with AES.

There are an enormous number of ways to make the computations presented here more efficient and faster. It is more important to understand the basic operations first, and then if your situation requires it, you can dig into what options are available to improve your response time. The main emphasis of this book is security. What makes your code faster can make your adversary's life easier. To avoid toeholds for attacks, all the code presented in this book will use prime numbers for every level. While slow, it's very secure.

acknowledgments

When Troy Dreier contacted me about writing another elliptic curve cryptography book for Manning, I had just retired from full-time work. I spent a long time learning a lot of mathematics, most of which is not in this book. Fortunately for me, the original proposal I submitted for a book was reviewed by exceptionally knowledgeable people who pointed out that one of the main topics I wanted to discuss had been broken the week before I submitted the proposal. So, I reduced the scope and sent Troy a new proposal. This passed muster, and I spent quite a while writing code and text to make something readable.

I was also fortunate to have Marina Michaels, my developmental editor, edit the text and force me to be less terse. While many of our conversations included history, Marina spent most of our meetings covering better ways to write. Hopefully, I learned something.

Mark Bissen, the technical editor for this book and Emeritus Research Instrumentation Innovator at the University of Wisconsin–Madison, helped tremendously with the mathematical theory by asking lots of great questions. There are many ways to describe the same formula, but some are more clearly understood than others.

I want to thank Dr. Manu Drijvers, a researcher in cryptography at Dfinity Foundation, for explaining the notation used in his paper referenced in chapter 18 (Boneh et al., 2018). This definitely helped me write code with confidence.

The book was written using LaTeX. Benjamin Berg helped me a great deal getting started. He helped make the code annotations behave the way I wanted and was always ready with an answer for every question.

Gianluigi Spagnuolo, the technical proofreader, checked all my code and made many suggestions for improvements to both math description and code locations.

All the reviewers' comments were used to modify the book in some way. I really appreciate their time reading and commenting on draft versions of this text: Greg MacLean, Clifford T., Sergio Arbeo, Marco Massenzio, Adrian Cucoș, Rani Sharim, David Romano, Alain Couniot, Jürgen Hötzel, Maxim Volgin, Dautrey Mikael, Giampiero Granatella, Giuseppe Denora, Gregorio Piccoli, Tim van Deurzen, Rani Sharim, Peter Mahon, Roman Zhuzha, Ravi Kiran Bamidi, and Nick Decroos. Your suggestions helped make this a better book. The whole Manning team was really helpful in getting this book out in all the many formats available these days and ready for publicizing its existence.

A giant thanks to everyone—all the help is very much appreciated.

about this book

Elliptic curves over finite fields is a complicated subject. There are many possible routes one can take to understand pairings of points over elliptic curves. I think of this book as a path cut along the side of a mountain. It takes you to a nice lookout where you can see hundreds of other mountains to climb. Without getting to the lookout point, none of those other mountains are accessible, let alone visible. A few other paths will be pointed out with references, but the path to understanding pairings followed in this book is narrow.

Elliptic Curve Cryptography for Developers introduces elliptic curve pairing mathematics to cryptographic programmers. With a background of linear algebra and a year's experience with programming, a reader can understand the subroutines described here and translate them to their language of choice. Although knowledge of finite field mathematics is exceptionally helpful, the book goes step by step to teach this branch of math and its relationship to elliptic curves.

Unless you have a PhD in mathematics, it will be essential to read through the entire book to fully appreciate and understand the application examples described in the last two chapters. Every chapter uses information from the previous chapters to build code used in subsequent chapters.

How this book is organized: A road map

Chapter 1 gives a more detailed introduction to the whole book. Following this opening chapter, the book is divided into three parts.

Part 1 includes chapters 2 to 6. Starting from prime number fields in chapter 2, we'll write routines used in all the following chapters.

In chapter 3, I introduce elliptic curves over finite fields and discuss why slow code is better for security, especially on embedded systems. I also explain how arbitrary information can be converted to a point on an elliptic curve.

In chapters 4 and 5, we look at essential algorithms for key exchange and digital signatures.

In chapter 6, I describe the choice of curve and programs to find good curves. Most of these programs only need to be run once to set up a secure system. Once you have good curves, there is no need to change them.

Part 2 includes chapters 7 to 12. Each chapter introduces a specific mathematical topic with associated subroutines. These chapters build the background required to understand the mathematics of pairings. One of the main reasons pairings are not more widely used is because the math appears daunting. No question—the math is really deep. Since most of the deep stuff is tangential to what we need to know, we'll focus on what details help get the job done.

Part 3 includes chapters 13 to 19. In chapter 13 we head off into the subject of finite field extensions. From our perspective, these are just polynomials with a lot of useful properties. To get the ideas across, I use a minuscule prime to create a tiny curve and list all the points on the curve and its extension. A lot of terms that mathematicians take for granted will then be clear.

Normally we want the "embedding degree" to be a very high number to prevent attackers from translating an elliptic curve to a number theoretic discrete log problem. For pairing-friendly curves, we require curves with a low embedding degree. Chapter 14 goes into the mathematics of how low embedding degree field extensions can be created using the method of complex multiplication.

In chapter 15, we learn about the mathematics of pairing points on elliptic curves. A pairing takes two points from an elliptic curve to form a value that is not a point anymore. The value is actually an nth root of unity or n^{th} root of 1.

Chapters 16 and 17 then discuss the different kinds of pairings. The Weil pairing has properties that are both useful and problematic for different applications, which is true also of the Tate pairing. There are lots of other pairings that have efficiency applications, but once you know these two, getting into the other methods will be easy.

In chapter 18, we dive into one of the main blockchain uses of pairings: aggregated digital signatures. An aggregated digital signature is an extension of BLS signatures that allows a one-step verification of many signatures of a document.

Finally, chapter 19 examines the state-of-the-art use of pairings with zero-knowledge SNARK techniques. The acronym seems appropriate at first glance when compared to Lewis Carroll's poem "The Hunting of the Snark." The ability to prove knowledge of a transaction without showing who performed a transfer or what was transferred helps maintain anonymous blockchain validity. It's a very powerful mathematical tool.

The three appendixes explain how to obtain the software libraries used in this book as well as details on Hilbert class polynomials from chapter 14. All the code listed can be found on GitHub at https://github.com/drmike8888/Elliptic-curve-pairings. You can find additional programs and output included in the repository, especially from chapters 13 and 16, to help with understanding field extensions and pairings.

Why C?

One of the main uses of elliptic curve cryptographic protocols is embedded systems like smart cards and security dongles. While small powerful processors and field-programmable gate arrays (FPGAs) are low cost, they are also memory constrained. These devices are typically programmed in low-level languages like C and Verilog. Because my background is in embedded systems, I have a lot of experience with C. The C language has numerous advantages with bit manipulation and the ability to change the meaning of a pointer between integers and strings. In this book, many standard C tricks are used in various subroutines that involve pointers and arrays. I consider these to be advantages that allow control of computations in an efficient manner.

All the C code in this book can be compiled using GNU gcc. The version of the compiler does not matter. It was all written on Ubuntu Linux and should compile and link with any Linux gcc. Check that the version of GMP or PARI library you link with is compatible with your compiler. The code is very generic without any specialized system calls.

About the code

This book contains many examples of source code both in numbered listings and in line with normal text. In both cases, source code is formatted in a `fixed-width font like this` to separate it from ordinary text. Sometimes code is also **in bold** to highlight code that has changed from previous steps in the chapter, such as when a new feature adds to an existing line of code.

In many cases, the original source code has been reformatted; we've added line breaks and reworked indentation to accommodate the available page space in the book. In rare cases, even this was not enough, and listings include line-continuation markers (➥). Additionally, comments in the source code have often been removed from the listings when the code is described in the text. Code annotations accompany many of the listings, highlighting important concepts.

You can get executable snippets of code from the liveBook (online) version of this book at https://livebook.manning.com/book/elliptic-curve-cryptography-for-developers. The complete code for the examples in the book is available for download from the Manning website at https://www.manning.com/books/elliptic-curve-cryptography-for-developers, and from GitHub at https://github.com/drmike8888/Elliptic-curve-pairings.

liveBook discussion forum

Purchase of *Elliptic Curve Cryptography for Developers* includes free access to liveBook, Manning's online reading platform. Using liveBook's exclusive discussion features, you can attach comments to the book globally or to specific sections or paragraphs. It's a snap to make notes for yourself, ask and answer technical questions, and receive help from the author and other users. To access the forum, go to https://livebook .manning.com/book/elliptic-curve-cryptography-for-developers/discussion. You can also learn more about Manning's forums and the rules of conduct at https://livebook .manning.com/discussion.

Manning's commitment to our readers is to provide a venue where a meaningful dialogue between individual readers and between readers and the author can take place. It is not a commitment to any specific amount of participation on the part of the author, whose contribution to the forum remains voluntary (and unpaid). We suggest you try asking the author some challenging questions lest his interest stray! The forum and the archives of previous discussions will be accessible from the publisher's website as long as the book is in print.

about the author

MIKE ROSING's career spans high-energy physics to telephone-switch engineering. Working at Argonne National Lab as a high-energy physicist, he helped construct a Wakefield particle accelerator. For the past 20 years, he worked for several companies on various projects, including developing vision devices for the blind, radar for measuring heart rate in cattle, and modeling high-speed signaling on computer boards. He holds a patent on the passive method for controlling and correcting energy correlations in charged particle beams and has authored many articles in technical publications.

Rosing grew up in Colorado and earned his undergraduate degree in engineering physics from the University of Colorado in Boulder. He then earned a PhD in nuclear engineering from the University of Wisconsin–Madison. He lives in Madison, Wisconsin. He is the father of twin sons and is married to an artist. Newly retired, he now has too many projects and too little time to work on them. Some of his favorite hobbies include martial arts (Aikido) and meditation (Rinzai Zen). His wife is happy when he goes kayaking with her on Wisconsin's rivers and lakes. While rarer, bicycle riding is another activity when not sitting in front of a computer writing code.

about the cover

The figure on the cover of *Elliptic Curve Cryptography for Developers*, "Hacendado Propriétaire," or "Ranch Owner," is taken from a book by Claudio Linati published in 1828. Linati's book includes hand-colored lithographs depicting a variety of civil, military, and religious costumes of Mexican society at the time. In those days, it was easy to identify where people lived and what their trade or station in life was just by their dress. Manning celebrates the inventiveness and initiative of the computer business with book covers based on the rich diversity of regional culture centuries ago, brought back to life by pictures from collections such as this one.

Pairings over elliptic curves in cryptography

This chapter covers

- Defining elliptic curve cryptography (ECC)
- Where ECC is used
- Public key cryptography
- Who this book is for

I first became interested in elliptic curve cryptography (ECC) in the mid-1990s. I was involved with an activist organization working to legalize marijuana, and we wanted to ensure our member list was secure and that we could email each other with encrypted messages. While I was aware of pretty good privacy (PGP), as a scientist at Argonne National Laboratory, I wanted something more state of the art. So I dug into the papers and went to a few Cryptographic Hardware and Embedded Systems (CHES) conferences to learn how to write my own code.

Today, ECC is ubiquitous. For example, Europay, Mastercard, and Visa (EMVCo) support ECC in their cryptographic interface for credit card transactions. In addition to sharing secret keys as in an SSL/TLS handshake, it is also used for signing certificates to authenticate web pages and HIPAA documents. A blockchain holds globally accessible information shared among many peers.

The blockchain has found use for elliptic curve pairings to enable aggregate group signatures and zero-knowledge proofs. The impetus for blockchain may be cryptocurrency, but the technology has many more uses. Blockchain ledgers are used in healthcare and supply chain environments.

ECC has also been used for random number generation. However, this takes a lot more resources than linear feedback shift registers or hardware sources like zener diodes. So, there are a few places where ECC can be replaced by a better alternative.

Learning ECC math is still challenging, especially for those who do not have a PhD in mathematics. At first glance, the mathematics behind pairings appear exceptionally deep. Most developers find ways not to include pairings in their products. Once the basics are understood, pairing-based ECC will also become widespread. The learning curve is not steep if you know the right path. This book follows a very narrow path that is essential to adopt from beginning to end. You will understand how to compute elliptic curve pairings used in the last two chapters of the book by following each chapter one at a time.

1.1   What is elliptic curve cryptography?

First, there are no ellipses. Second, there are no curves. So why is it called an "elliptic curve"? The primary reason is history. Performing integrals of the elliptical orbits of planets gave rise to formulas labeled *elliptic curves*. These formulas were then used in other areas of mathematics, and the label stuck.

The areas of mathematics used in public key cryptography involve number theory (the properties of integers), combinatorics (the study of counting), and finite fields (sets with finite objects and specific rules). Elliptic curves are used in just about every area of mathematics. This makes studying elliptic curve math very difficult because it is hard to determine what you really need to know and what is just really interesting.

For example, elliptic curves have been used for factoring numbers and solving Fermat's Last Theorem. In chapter 3, I explain how elliptic curves on the complex plane are used to understand elliptic curves over finite fields. It's all interesting but not necessarily applicable to cryptography.

1.2   Why use elliptic curve cryptography?

Public key cryptography started with the RSA (Rivest–Shamir–Adleman) system, which uses exponentiation modulo very large primes. Algorithms for breaking RSA are subexponential, so several thousand-bit primes are needed for standard security. The advantage of using elliptic curve mathematics is the reduced size of the numbers involved for the same level of security. Larger numbers require more memory, more processing time, more gates on a field-programmable gate array (FPGA), and/or more processors in a GPU. That means the resources required (or the cost of the system) for other methods is higher. That reduced cost is one of the main drivers for the use of elliptic curve public key cryptography.

In the past decade, other properties of elliptic curves have allowed applications that are not even possible with other methods. Aggregate digital signatures are a primary example. And while zero-knowledge proofs were first introduced with other mathematics, the elliptic curve versions are much shorter to transmit, as we'll see in chapter 19.

Figure 1.1 is a conceptual view of an elliptic curve over a finite field. All the points are "on the curve." That means they all satisfy the elliptic curve equation. One point is shaped like a triangle, and one is shaped like a square. These points are mathematically related to each other using algorithms described in this book.

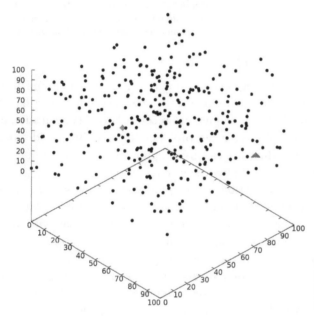

Figure 1.1 Conceptual elliptic curve over a finite field. Points are scattered in a multidimensional, astronomically large space.

Discovering the mathematical relationship is called "breaking the algorithm" or "cracking the code." For elliptic curves of high-enough field size and dimension, the cracking effort would take 10 million 4 GHz processors about 1 billion years to find the relationship. In part 3 of this book, I dive into the details of what high-enough field size and dimension mean.

Figure 1.2 is a hand-waving and purposely vague outline of elliptic curve pairings, which I will cover in part 3 of the book. The upper, larger circle represents an elliptic curve on a field extension. Buried within that are points on a base curve. A pairing of points on this curve results in a field extension value (technically, an nth root of unity). Only elliptic curve mathematics gives rise to cryptographically secure pairings. The relationship between pairing values and points on curves is more difficult to crack than the relationship between points alone. This is a fundamental reason for using elliptic curves in cryptography—it is very hard to break the algorithms.

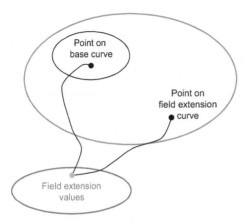

Figure 1.2   Schematic of elliptic curve pairing with one point on base curve, one point on field extension curve, and the result in field extension values.

1.3   *Elliptic curves come to public key cryptography*

The use of elliptic curves for cryptography is a very new development in the history of keeping secrets. From ancient Rome to the present day, secure messages have been sent using a secret key that both the sender and receiver know. Transmission of this secret key to both parties was always a major problem. In the 1970s, the idea of using one-way trapdoor functions, which are easy to compute and essentially impossible to unravel, introduced the concept of public key cryptography.

The fundamental idea behind public key cryptography is the use of a private key held by one person or organization and a public key transmitted openly by that person. Two people can create a shared secret using their private key with the other person's public key that no one else can determine, so encrypted messages can be exchanged. This is especially useful if the two people have never met.

Additional applications in the digital age have also been developed. A person can sign a document with their private key, and anyone can verify they signed it using the signer's public key. The combination of multiple signatures is also possible where many people or computer servers sign the same document. Zero-knowledge proofs allow transactions to be anonymous and verifiable at the same time, which also requires a private key to prove existence and a public key to verify. In the following sections, I will expand on these concepts, and the rest of the book will describe how to implement them in reality using elliptic curve mathematics.

1.3.1   *General description of key exchange*

To send messages securely over a public network, we want to use a very strong method of encryption. The National Institute of Standards and Technology (NIST) defined the Advanced Encryption Standard (AES) with several levels of security depending on the length of the secret key. A key exchange between two parties is performed using public key cryptography so that a shared secret can be created using open networks.

Suppose Alice and Bob want to exchange messages securely. They each create a private key they secretly hold so no one else can know it. Using the private key, they each create a public key, which they share with each other. In figure 1.3, we show how Alice and Bob can send their public keys over an open network. Alice combines her private key with Bob's public key to create a single secret key for a system like AES used to encrypt a message. The advantage of AES is that it is fast and can easily encrypt large amounts of data. The disadvantage is that it requires a single secret key.

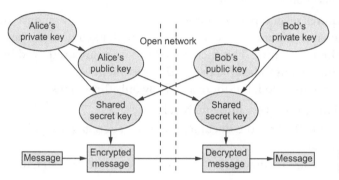

Figure 1.3 Creating a secret key by exchanging public keys

Bob uses Alice's public key along with his private key to create the same shared secret that Alice used to encrypt the message. Alice's public key, Bob's public key, and the encrypted message are what's seen on the public network.

The point of this system is that Alice and Bob don't have to agree on what secret key to use before they decide to communicate. As we'll see later, in addition to creating a shared secret, we can make the secret ephemeral so that even if someone could break the message key, they would not be able to break Alice's or Bob's public keys to discover their private key.

1.3.2 Digital signature algorithms explained

To prove that she created a document and to ensure that no one else can modify it, Alice can create a digital signature of the document. She uses her private key to sign the document, and anyone else can use her public key to verify that she signed it. If anyone changes even 1 bit in the document, the signature will not verify.

Figure 1.4 shows how digital signatures are signed, and figure 1.5 shows how they are verified. Alice uses her private key, along with a hash of the document, to create a digital signature that is posted along with the document in a public place.

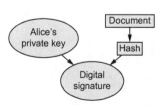

Figure 1.4 Processes involved with creating a digital signature

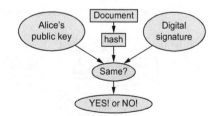

Figure 1.5 Process and data required to verify a digital signature

Anyone can then use Alice's public key, the document, and the digital signature to verify that Alice is indeed the person who created the document. Anyone else attempting to impersonate Alice would need to know her private key. As figure 1.5 shows, a valid document outputs a positive result for the correct public key.

1.3.3   *How multiple people can sign the same document*

If a document requires several people to sign it, a simple digital signature of each person signing the same document becomes complicated. Each person's key has to be used to verify their signature. This increases the storage area required because every digital signature needs to be attached to the document.

Figure 1.6 looks complicated, but there are really only three steps:

1 Aggregate all the public keys into one block.
2 Each person digitally signs the document plus the aggregated keys into their own signature data.
3 All the signatures are mathematically combined into one final signature.

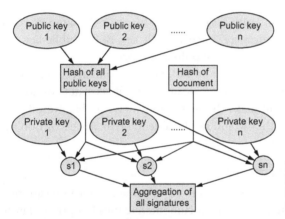

Figure 1.6   Aggregated digital signature signing combines multiple users' public keys and individual signatures to create a single signature.

Figure 1.7 shows how the aggregated signature is verified. The hash of the public keys can be re-created or saved with the document. That is a system-level time (processing power) versus space (storage size) argument, so we will assume it as an input. An elliptic curve pairing operation is done using the public keys, the document, and the combined final signature to determine whether everyone did, in fact, sign the same document. When the computations match each other (we'll get into the details in later chapters), the composite signature verifies.

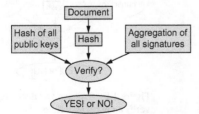

Figure 1.7   Aggregated digital signature verification process

The ability to verify an aggregated digital signature requires the use of elliptic curve pairings. Parts 2 and 3 of this book build up the mathematical background required to understand all the details of elliptic curve pairings.

1.3.4   *Zero knowledge, or how to keep a secret and prove you have one*

A digital certificate is used to verify data is authentic. An example is a web page that has been certified as genuine by some trusted authority. It can also contain personal data that someone may not wish to be exposed. The idea that we can prove an entity has some private information but not expose that information is called a zero-knowledge proof. For example, I can show I'm over 18 but not give away the fact that I'm 70.

A huge surveillance state was envisioned if every digital certificate was traceable to every issuer and owner. To eliminate this lack of privacy, a way was developed to verify that a prover knows what they claim without giving away any information. So, the prover knows what they want to keep private in the certificate, and the verifier wants to check whether the certificate is valid.

Today, we want transactions on a blockchain to be anonymous and keep the amounts of money transferred a secret. The original method of zero-knowledge proof was interactive, with the prover and verifier sending messages back and forth. If the probability of being correct was 50%, after 20 tries, the chances of the prover misleading the verifier would be less than 1 in 1 million.

The fundamental problem with an interactive method is the communication between prover and verifier. So, the next step in solving the problem was to introduce noninteractive zero-knowledge proofs. Figure 1.8 shows how a noninteractive proof is set up using public data and a public common reference string.

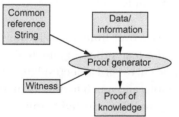

Figure 1.8   **Requirements involved to create zero-knowledge proof**

The public data is usually information contained on a blockchain. The common reference string refers to the elliptic curve parameters used to hide the data. The witness shown in the figure is private information, which can be a combination of public keys and coin data and/or address key information. The combined mathematical result is called a proof of knowledge.

The verification process uses the public information, the public common reference string, and the public proof of knowledge to verify that the information is correct. Figure 1.9 shows a zero-knowledge proof diagrammatically. If the data and proof are from the same blockchain, the verification will be a YES result; otherwise, one gets a NO result. The idea is to make the generation of the proof a time-consuming process (but not too long) and the verification to be a very short time. We also want the proof to be small and not take up too much space on the blockchain.

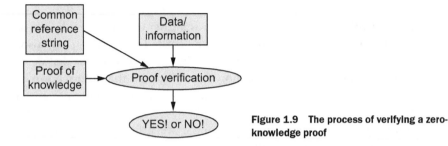

Figure 1.9   The process of verifying a zero-knowledge proof

The acronym developed for zero-knowledge proofs is SNARK, which stands for Succinct Noninteractive ARgument of Knowledge. After reading many mathematical papers on SNARKs, I found Lewis Carroll's "The Hunting of the SNARK" (Carroll, 2010) to make about as much sense. It was not a surprise to find a cryptographic article with the same title in Bitansky et al. (2014). These constructions use elliptic curve pairing operations, which allow the succinct part to happen.

1.4   Who this book is for

If you don't have an advanced degree in mathematics and you want to understand enough elliptic curve math to implement common algorithms, this book is for you. If you don't have a good grasp of linear algebra and are not familiar with the manipulation of polynomials, then this book might be too much. The learning process will be step by step, but the first step assumes you know how to manipulate equations with several variables.

This book will teach the basics of elliptic curves over finite fields to show how the math applies to cryptography. The book will also teach the fundamentals of elliptic curve pairing mathematics. Pairings on elliptic curves are a deep subject with many tangents that have nothing to do with cryptography and much to do with mathematics. Some topics were tried for cryptography and have been rejected because the system was "broken" by careful analysis.

By the time you finish this book, you will be able to implement the secure transfer of keys using elliptic curves of your own design and create pairing-based digital signature schemes for use on blockchain systems. You will have confidence in your ability to test the cryptographic underpinnings of your code.

So, let's get started!

Summary

- Finite fields are sets with specific rules and a finite number of objects. The mathematics of finite fields determines how we manipulate elliptic curves.
- Elliptic curves over finite fields are good for cryptography because they use smaller numbers for the same level of security compared with other public key methods.
- Key exchange and digital signatures are straightforward, using elliptic curve mathematics through simple formulas. This makes programming the mathematics easy.
- Aggregation of many digital signatures using pairings over elliptic curves allows for smaller storage on a blockchain than other methods. This reduces the amount of data transmitted between peers, which decreases over all transaction time.
- Zero-knowledge proofs can certify knowledge of information without exposing that information. Zero-knowledge proofs use reduced amounts of data compared with other methods when using elliptic curve pairing mathematics.

Part 1

Basics

The chapters in part 1 of the book cover finite field arithmetic, elliptic curve mathematics, and cryptographic primitives. Finite fields based on prime numbers are the essence of elliptic curve cryptography. They form the basis of everything else that follows.

Large integers consisting of 160 to more than 500 bits make up the finite fields used in cryptography. Large integer libraries have been around for a long time, and the one I chose for this book is called the GNU Multiple Precision Arithmetic Library or GMP. There are many routines not included within GMP that are required for elliptic curve implementations. These are discussed in chapter 2. One of the major routines covered includes taking square roots using a modulus. There are several routines that will be mentioned that use only a few calls to the GMP library. These routines are used throughout all the code in this book, so while they are simple, they are very important. Chapter 3 dives into elliptic curve mathematics. The idea of algebra on an elliptic curve is described along with some abstract pictures. The ideas are important and having some mental image can help you understand the mathematics. I'll discuss the idea of embedding values onto a curve and then describe code to add and multiply points.

This part includes two chapters on applications of elliptic curves over finite fields. Chapter 4 covers key exchange, and chapter 5 covers digital signatures. There are dozens of key exchange and signature algorithms to choose from. Each chapter only discusses two of the most commonly used algorithms. Once you understand how one algorithm works with elliptic curve cryptography, you will have no trouble implementing similar algorithms.

The last chapter in this part goes into the process of finding good curves. For the large prime fields this book is interested in, this process is not that difficult to do using the mathematical tools developed over the last few decades. I'll also have a short discussion on how to avoid bad curves. For all the methods shown in this part, the odds of finding a good curve are reasonably high if you search long enough (as in 24-hour computer runs).

Description of finite field mathematics

This chapter covers
- Fundamentals of finite fields
- Subroutines for modular operations
- Concept of quadratic residues
- Computing square roots mod n

Fields are mathematical objects that obey specific rules. Finite fields have a fixed number of objects. This chapter introduces finite fields over prime numbers and the code we will need in the rest of the book to manipulate these objects.

In this chapter, I'll start at the bottom of finite field mathematics by using prime numbers to define the core concept of a finite field. Every formula in this book depends on prime numbers to create a finite field. I'll first go over the rules of finite fields we need to know and then introduce simple subroutines that exploit the GNU Multiple Precision Arithmetic Library (GMP library) to implement some of those rules. The library is exceptionally useful for very large integers used in cryptographic protocols. You can learn about retrieving the GMP library and its documentation in appendix A.

The general equation of an elliptic curve is given by

$$y^2 + a_1xy + a_3y = x^3 + a_2x^2 + a_4x + a_6$$

Fortunately, we don't need the general curve because we work over finite fields. The ordinary equation used throughout this book has $a_1 = a_2 = a_3 = 0$:

$$y^2 = x^3 + a_4x + a_6$$

To find the y value from the equation of an elliptic curve, we need to compute square roots. After the simple code, I discuss a more complicated problem of taking square roots modulo a prime. This involves finding quadratic residues to determine whether a square root even exists for a number. GMP has a library routine to help with that. Then I will discuss the algorithm used to find square roots once we know it can be found. With that description, the code is straightforward to implement.

2.1   Basic mathematics of finite fields

In this section, I'll dive into the fundamentals of finite fields over prime numbers. A field is a very special term in mathematics. It describes objects that can be added, multiplied, and divided. Two special objects, **0** and **1**, are the identity elements for addition and multiplication, respectively. Identity just means $a + \mathbf{0} = a$ for addition and $b * \mathbf{1} = b$ for multiplication. We also have $a \cdot b = \mathbf{1}$, which implies that a and b are inverse of each other in the field.

The types of objects that make up fields include numbers, polynomials, and polynomials of polynomials! So, a field is a mathematical abstraction with very specific rules that apply to all these things.

A finite field has a finite number of objects. The field of integers is infinite. We can always add 1 and get the next number. Because objects in a field can multiply and add any object to any other object to get yet another object in the field, a finite field must be cyclic.

Your first introduction to a finite field was learning how to tell time on a clock. As shown in figure 2.1, adding 6 hours to 9 o'clock, you get 3 o'clock. On a 24-hour clock, you would get 15 o'clock. We say that 15 is congruent to 3 modulo 12. So, the size of the field determines what the results are. We say a 12-hour clock is modulo 12 and a 24-hour clock is modulo 24. The term *congruent* will also show up in many places, and it means "equal to" given the modulus.

Figure 2.1   Adding 6 + 9 modulo 12 and modulo 24

For cryptography, the size of the field is astronomical because a field size of 256 bits is a number 2^{256}, which is roughly the number of atoms in the observable universe. The problem with a clock is that the number 12 has three factors: $2 * 2 * 3$. We can create sets of numbers that are even, or factors of 4, 3, or 6. Each of those sets maintains a cyclic relationship. So, the set of numbers $\{2, 4, 6, 8, 10, 12\}$ forms a cyclic group. However, because it does not have the identity element, it is not technically a field.

Figure 2.2 illustrates the idea of a prime field using 43 as the prime number. It is drawn like a clock, so when counting to 43, we return to 0. Since both 0 and 1 are in the set of numbers, addition and multiplication are possible in this field. Computing an inverse modulo a prime number is also possible. That is what makes a prime number base into a field.

Figure 2.2 Finite field over prime numbers viewed as a clock ($p = 43$)

For cryptography, we want finite fields with really large prime numbers. For embedded systems, we want numbers that are easy to compute with. Later on, I'll give examples where I choose primes like $43 \times 2^{252} + 1$. Because this set of numbers contains both 0 and 1, it creates a finite field with $43 \times 2^{252} + 1$ numbers in it. A secret key will be one of those numbers. If code is written properly, good luck to an adversary finding it!

2.2 *Elliptic curves form groups of points over a finite field*

In this section, I'll cover how an elliptic curve over a finite field creates a new kind of finite field. The points on an elliptic curve over a finite field form cyclic sets. Sometimes, these sets are disjoint with two cyclic groups that do not overlap. I go over this type of curve in chapter 13 on field extensions. Sets of points in each cyclic group will have many subgroups that depend on the number of factors making up the number of points on the curve. The different possible combinations of factors create the number of groups that can be formed.

As an example, suppose the total number of points on the curve has three factors: $a \cdot b \cdot c$. The rules about these sets of points create seven total groups of cyclic points—one group for each combination of the factors. So, factors a, b, and c create group sizes a, b, c, $a \cdot b$, $a \cdot c$, $b \cdot c$, and $a \cdot b \cdot c$. Many of the points will be in multiple groups. The number of points in each group is called the order of the group.

Typically, if we pick a point at random, it will be in the largest group. We can move that point to a smaller subset group by multiplying by the other factors. For example, suppose c is a really large prime with $a = 2$ and $b = 5$. If we multiply the random point by 10, the result will be a point in group c. This is one of the finite field group rules we take advantage of with elliptic curve mathematics. Many more details will be spelled out in chapter 3.

Exercise 2.1
Given an elliptic curve with 86 points, list the orders of all the groups on this curve.

2.3   *Basic subroutines for finite field arithmetic*

In this section, I'll describe subroutines that make using the GMP library easier for the remainder of the book. See appendix A for details on acquiring the library. The fundamental, lowest-level routines are placed in a file called modulo.c. The header showing all the routines is given in listing 2.1. There are two groups of routines. The first group requires a modulus as part of the API. The second group assumes a local static variable has been set for the modulus.

Listing 2.1   Header: modulo.h

```
#include <stdio.h>
#include <stdlib.h>          Basic include for all
#include <gmp.h>             GMP polynomial functions

void mod_add(mpz_t a, mpz_t b, mpz_t c, mpz_t n);
void mod_sub(mpz_t a, mpz_t b, mpz_t c, mpz_t n);    Requires
void mod_mul(mpz_t a, mpz_t b, mpz_t c, mpz_t n);    modulus
void mod_div(mpz_t a, mpz_t b, mpz_t c, mpz_t n);    on
void mod_neg(mpz_t a, mpz_t b, mpz_t n);             Input

void minit(mpz_t m);         Setup for
void mget(mpz_t mod);        Internal modulus
void mset(mpz_t prm);

void madd(mpz_t a, mpz_t b, mpz_t c);
void msub(mpz_t a, mpz_t b, mpz_t c);
void mmul(mpz_t a, mpz_t b, mpz_t c);
void mdiv(mpz_t a, mpz_t b, mpz_t c);
void minv(mpz_t a, mpz_t b);
void mneg(mpz_t a, mpz_t b);             Requires
int msqrt(mpz_t x, mpz_t a);             modulus
void mrand(mpz_t rand);                  Initialized
int msqr(mpz_t x);
void mpowi(mpz_t a, mpz_t b, long i);
```

Since this header is included in all other files, the standard C includes are listed along with GMP. As you can see, all the subroutines begin with m, which means they belong to the modulo group of routines.

The GMP library has many types of functions. I exclusively use the mpz_* functions, which are for large integers. The type mpz_t is GMP's integer type. The majority of arguments used in listing 2.1 are type mpz_t.

The built-in routines to GMP include integer functions for add, subtract, multiply, and divide. There are many versions with a lot of different combinations of arguments. Chapter 5 of the GMP manual goes into this in detail. One of the GMP division routines is mpz_mod(). I combine this with add, subtract, multiply, and divide to get mod_*() routines. All my routines follow the same format as GMP. The output is listed first, and the input arguments to the function follow. This comes from thinking about the function as $a = b < op > c$ modulo n.

Let's take a look at the modulo division routine in listing 2.2. This has a few more lines than all the others because division by zero should never happen if your code is correct. If it does happen, we want to know about it so we can find the bug.

Listing 2.2   Modular division: `mod_div()`

```
void mod_div(mpz_t a, mpz_t b, mpz_t c, mpz_t n)
{
  mpz_t rslt;

  mpz_init(rslt);
  if(!mpz_invert(rslt, c, n))    ← Division by zero?
  {
    printf("division by zero in div_mod!\n");
    mpz_clear(rslt);
    exit(-1);
  }
  mpz_mul(rslt, b, rslt);
  mpz_mod(a, rslt, n);           Common to
  mpz_clear(rslt);               all m* routines
}
```

Because the result could be one of the input arguments, we need to create a place for the result to go so the inputs are not clobbered as we do computations (you can bet I learned that the hard way). The `mpz_init()` routine creates space for the variable. On an embedded system or a field-programmable gate array (FPGA), you may want to use fixed field sizes and your own specialized routines that take advantage of the modulus. These lowest-level routines are the best place to do this because all the number-crunching gets down to this level sooner or later.

The next function called is `mpz_invert()`. The inversion of c modulo n uses Euclid's algorithm, which we will get into later when we deal with polynomials. If c is zero, the function prints an error and kills the program. Division by zero implies a serious problem somewhere, and we need to find it.

The last three lines of the code are similar in all the `mod_*` routines—a call to `mpz_<op>()` followed by a call to `mpz_mod()` and then clearing the temporary variable space. Another efficiency step might be to set up the temporary space during initialization and just let it be global to all the routines. This saves a lot of `mpz_init()` and `mpz_clear()` calls.

Listing 2.3 is an example of one m* function taken from the `modulo.c` file. This is the `mod_add()` function that computes $a = b + c \bmod n$.

Listing 2.3   Modular addition routine

```
void mod_add(mpz_t a, mpz_t b, mpz_t c, mpz_t n)
```

```
{
    mpz_t rslt;                    Prevents overwriting
                                   when a is one of b or c

    mpz_init(rslt);
    mpz_add(rslt, b, c);           Output equals
    mpz_mod(a, rslt, n);           b + c mod n
    mpz_clear(rslt);
}
```

Most of the time, the modulus used in all the routines is the same prime number. Rather than having to list that with every call, we can store it as a static variable local to all the modulo routines. As we get higher up the chain, we sometimes need to know what that prime number is for different operations. So the routines `minit()` and `mget()`, respectively, initialize and get the modulus for all the `m*()` functions. At the top of the `modulo.c` file, I put the following globals:

```
static mpz_t modulus;
static gmp_randstate_t state;
```

The initialization routines are in the middle of the `modulo.c` file, as shown in the following listing.

Listing 2.4 Modular initialization routines

```
void minit(mpz_t m)
{
    mpz_init_set(modulus, m);      Set modulus
    gmp_randinit_mt(state);        and random state.
}

void mget(mpz_t mod)
{
    mpz_init_set(mod, modulus);    ← Return local modulus.
}
```

You'll notice there is no `mclear()` function. If your system needs to clear the modulus, it should be obvious how to just call `mpz_clear(modulus)` with a void function. The example code does not require this function, but real life might.

In addition to setting the local modulus value, the `mpz` random number generator is initialized. This is used to pick random values for probabilistic algorithms like the square root routine shown later.

There is a negate operation that simply performs $a = -b$ mod n. This is advantageous when b is larger than n (or could be) and we have the chance to reduce it in size before using it in other operations. As an example, take $b = 25$ mod 19 with $a = -25 \rightarrow -6 \rightarrow 13$.

2.4 Computing quadratic residues over a prime field

In this section, I'll describe testing whether a square root can be computed for a number in a finite field. Taking square roots of real numbers is easy. Newton's method has worked for hundreds of years. But taking square roots in a finite field is quite a bit different. The idea is simple: in $x^2 = a \bmod n$, we know a, and we want to find x. But some numbers will not have square roots mod n. Numbers that have square roots are called *quadratic residues*. All the remaining numbers are simply called *nonresidues*.

Number theory has been studied for a very long time. In 1640, Fermat wrote down what is now called Fermat's Little Theorem. It is one of the most fundamental properties of number theory and was used as the first attempt at finding square roots mod n. As seen in equation 2.1, we can paraphrase version I.3.2 in Koblitz (1994): for any prime p and any integer $a < p$, we have

$$a^{p-1} \cong 1 \bmod p \qquad (2.1)$$

More than 100 years later, Legendre wrote down a symbol for quadratic residues. Today we call this the Legendre symbol, which is defined in II.2.3 of Koblitz (1994) to be

$$\left(\frac{a}{p}\right) = \begin{cases} 0 & \text{if } p \text{ divides } a \\ 1 & \text{if } a \text{ is a quadratic residue mod } p \\ -1 & \text{if } a \text{ is a nonresidue mod } p \end{cases}$$

A number that is a nonresidue mod p will not have a square root with respect to p. As an example, the square root of 2 mod 23 is 5 because $5^2 \bmod 23 = 2$. The Legendre symbol is

$$\left(\frac{2}{23}\right) = 1$$

Similarly, the Legendre symbol

$$\left(\frac{17}{23}\right) = -1$$

says there is no square root of 17 mod 23.

Fortunately, GMP has a Legendre symbol routine, which we can use to check for residue or nonresidue as the case may be. Using the local `modulus` variable, we have the trivial routine shown in the following listing.

Listing 2.5 Legendre symbol

```
int msqr(mpz_t x)
{
    return mpz_legendre(x, modulus); ← Returns Legendre symbol of input
}
```

2.5   *Computing the square root mod p*

In this section, I'll go into the computation details of square roots over finite fields. The theory introduced here will also be used in chapter 12. Figure 2.3 is an overview of the process.

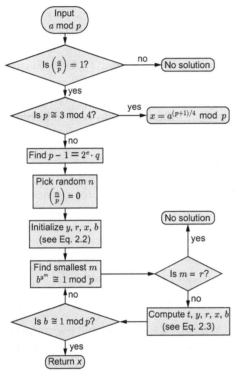

Figure 2.3   Compute square root mod p

After checking whether a number is a quadratic residue, we can compute the square root. We can use the last two bits of the modulus to determine how to take the square root. Since a modulus is odd, the last bit is always 1. The second to last bit can be 0 or 1, which means the modulus is congruent to 1 mod 4 or congruent to 3 mod 4, respectively.

If the modulus is congruent to 3 mod 4, we can use Fermat's Little Theorem (equation 2.1) to power our way to the result. The formula is found in section 1.5 of Cohen (2000):

$$x = a^{(p+1)/4} \bmod p$$

You can think about this as $p + 1$ converts the last two bits from 1 to 0, and then the divide-by-4 results in an exact power. Since $a^{p+1} \cong a^2 \bmod n$, when we divide by 4, we end up with $a^{1/2}$.

When the prime modulus p is congruent to 1 mod 4, life is a touch more complicated. The following description, called "The Algorithm of Tonelli and Shanks," is based on section 1.5.1 of Cohen (2000).

The first step is to determine how many zeros there are after we subtract 1 from the prime. We know there are at least two zero bits because the prime is congruent to 1 mod 4. But there could be a lot more zero bits in the binary representation of p. As we scan past the zero bits, eventually we get to a set bit. That becomes the least significant bit of a number, which is labeled q.

Therefore, we take

$$p - 1 = 2^e \cdot q$$

where q is odd and e is at least 2. We then choose a number n at random, which is a quadratic nonresidue. Since, on average, half the numbers modulo a prime p are in this group, that does not take very long.

The initialization process then proceeds with the setup shown in equation 2.2:

$$y \leftarrow n^q \bmod p$$
$$r \leftarrow e$$
$$x \leftarrow a^{(q-1)/2} \bmod p \qquad (2.2)$$
$$b \leftarrow ax^2 \bmod p$$
$$x \leftarrow ax \bmod p$$

where a is the number we are attempting to find the square root of, x is going to be our result, and b will go to 1 when we finish.

The loop process is: find the smallest m such that $b^{2^m} \cong 1 \bmod p$. If $m = r$, output a message that a is a nonresidue (which should not happen because we test for that to begin with).

We then perform the following operations mod p as shown in equation 2.3:

$$t \leftarrow y^{2^{r-m-1}}$$
$$y \leftarrow t^2$$
$$r \leftarrow m \qquad (2.3)$$
$$x \leftarrow xt$$
$$b \leftarrow by$$

We then test to see whether $b \cong 1 \bmod p$.

Exercise 2.2

Would taking square roots modulo 27213068317 use the power method or the Tonelli and Shanks method? (Hint: convert to hex and look at the last two bits.)

OK, now let's turn all this math into code. Listing 2.6 shows that I first check whether we can take a square root. If not, just bail without doing anything else.

Listing 2.6   Square root mod n: Entry

```
int msqrt(mpz_t x, mpz_t a)
{
  mpz_t n, q, z, y, b, t, t1;
  long e, i, r, cmp, m;

  if(!msqr(a))
    return 0;        | Exit immediately if nonresidue.
```

The second step is to check whether this is an easy calculation. If the last two bits of the modulus are set, we can use the direct power operation to compute the square root. This uses the GMP `mpz_tstbit()` function as shown in the following listing.

Listing 2.7   Square root mod n: $p \cong 3$ mod 4

```
if(mpz_tstbit(modulus, 0) && mpz_tstbit(modulus, 1))   | Last 2 bits set?
{
  mpz_init_set(q, modulus);
  mpz_add_ui(q, q, 1);
  mpz_divexact_ui(q, q, 4);          | Compute
  mpz_powm(x, a, q, modulus);        | a^(q+1)/4.
  mpz_clear(q),
  return 1;
}
```

If our modulus has bit 1 clear, we dive into the Tonelli and Shanks algorithm, shown in listing 2.8. After subtracting 1 from the modulus, I use the `mpz_scan1()` function to count the number of zeros at the end of q. I then brute-force divide by 2 for each clear bit to get q to be odd.

Listing 2.8   Square root mod n: Tonelli and Shanks

```
mpz_inits(n, q, y, b, t, t1, NULL);

mpz_sub_ui(q, modulus, 1);   ← q = p − 1
e = mpz_scan1(q, 0);         | Find number of       | Break down p − 1
i = e;                       | binary zeros.        | into 2^e * q.
while(i)
{                            | Remove one
                             | factor of
  mpz_divexact_ui(q, q, 2);  | two at a time.
  i--;
}

i = 1;     | Finds a generator
while(i >= 0)                | Randomly
{                           | search
  mrand(n);                 | for
  i = msqr(n);              | nonresidue.
}
```

```
  mpz_powm(y, n, q, modulus);  ← y=n^q                    | Initialize
  r = e;                                                  | working
  mpz_sub_ui(q, q, 1);            |                       | components.
  mpz_divexact_ui(q, q, 2);       | x=a^((q-1)/2)         |
  mpz_powm(x, a, q, modulus);     |                       |
  mmul(b, x, x);   | b=ax^2                               |
  mmul(b, b, a);   |                                      |
  mmul(x, x, a);   ← x=ax

  cmp = mpz_cmp_ui(b, 1);   ← Loops on algorithm until finished or failure
  while(cmp)   ← Terminate when b==1.
  {
    m = 1;
    mpz_set(t1, b);
    while(m < r)
    {
      mpowi(t1, t1, 2);
      if(!mpz_cmp_ui(t1, 1))    | Minimum m
        break;                  | such that
      m++;                      | b^(2^m) ≅ 1 mod p
    }
    if(r == m)        | Should never happen because
    {                 | a is quadratic residue
      mpz_clears(n, q, y, b, t, t1, NULL);
        return 0;
    }
    i = r - m - 1;         |
    mpz_set(t, y);         |
    while(i)               | t=y^(2^(r-m-1))
    {                      |
      mpowi(t, t, 2);      |
      i--;                 |
    }
    mmul(y, t, t);   ← y=t^2
    r = m;
    mmul(x, x, t);   ← x=xt
    mmul(b, b, y);        ← b=by
    cmp = mpz_cmp_ui(b, 1);   ← Is b == 1?
  }
  mpz_clears(n, q, y, b, t, t1, NULL);
  return 1;
}
```

This section of code looks for a quadratic nonresidue by starting with the assumption that the return value is 1. Once it finds a nonresidue, the value of `i` will be −1, and the loop will exit.

The initialization code follows the math step by step as previously outlined. There is no `mpow()` routine that uses the modulus because the only call for it outside `modulo.c` has not yet set the modulus when it is called. There is an `mpowi()` routine used outside `modulo.c` to take advantage of the `mpz_powm_ui()` routine, as shown in listing 2.8.

The final block of code performs the loop section described before listing 2.6. The first step is to find the minimal m such that $b^{2^m} \cong 1 \bmod p$. This means we square a temporary variable t1 until it goes to 1. If $r = m$ when we exit the loop, it means the input was a nonresidue. This should never happen because we check on entry to the subroutine. If it does, there is a serious problem somewhere that must be debugged.

Once I have m, I set the value t to y and compute $t = y^{2^{r-m-1}}$ using a squaring loop. Then y is set to t^2, x is set to $x \times t$, and b is set to $b \times y$. Finally, the loop end test variable cmp is evaluated to determine whether the routine is finished. When b equals 1, the variable x contains the square root of input a modulo the static prime modulus.

The final routine I want to show in the modulo.c file is the $b^i \bmod n$ routine in listing 2.9. This routine checks to see whether the input power is negative. If it is, I first invert the input and then raise that to a positive power. If the input power is zero, the return value is simply 1. Otherwise, it just computes the direct result with the modulus.

Listing 2.9   Small integer power mod n

```
void mpowi(mpz_t a, mpz_t b, long i)
{
  if(i < 0)
  {
    minv(a, b);                           Negative power
    mpz_powm_ui(a, a, -i, modulus);       is inverse
  }                                       to positive power.
  else if(!i)
    mpz_set_ui(a, 1);          b⁰ = 1
  else
    mpz_powm_ui(a, b, i, modulus);   a = bⁱ mod n
}
```

Answers to exercises

1   86 = 2 x 43, so all possible group sizes are 2, 43, and 86.

2   27213068317 decimal = 65606781D in hexadecimal. Since D = 1101 in binary, the last two bits are not both set. Therefore, the Tonelli and Shanks method is required to take square roots modulo 27213068317.

Summary

- A finite field allows addition, multiplication, and inversion with every element to another element in the field.
- Elliptic curve groups are finite fields consisting of points. The order of each point is some combination of the factors from the total number of points on the curve.
- Subroutines to compute over prime fields include addition, subtraction, multiplication, inversion, and division. These routines will be used throughout the book.
- A quadratic residue is an element in a finite field, which is a perfect square.
- Computing square roots uses a power function for primes congruent to 3 mod 4 and Tonelli and Shanks algorithm for primes congruent to 1 mod 4.

Explaining the core of elliptic curve mathematics

This chapter begins the journey into the mathematics of elliptic curves over finite fields. I'll start with elliptic curves over real numbers so we can visualize what the mathematics does. Then we'll see how elliptic curves on the complex plane map to elliptic curves over finite fields with very crude graphics. Then we'll dive into the detailed mathematics of how we can perform addition using two points on an elliptic curve and finally expand that to the concept of multiplication.

3.1 Elliptic curve algebra

In this section, I'll describe elliptic curves in a more visual way. It is useful to keep this visualization in mind when covering elliptic curves over finite fields because the formulas are the same. The plots over finite fields are not as pretty, so there are fewer of those.

To start, I want to show the standard plot of an elliptic curve in the (x, y) plane. The equation $y^2 = x^3 - 5x + 5$ is pretty when plotted using real numbers. Figure 3.1 shows a graph of this equation as an elliptic curve.

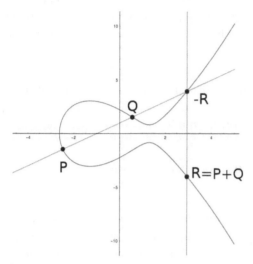

Figure 3.1   **Elliptic curve** $y^2 = x^3 - 5x + 5$

What makes elliptic curves so useful is the ability to do algebraic manipulation of points the same way we manipulate numbers. To add two points, P and Q, we draw a line through them and find the place where the line intersects the elliptic curve. As seen in figure 3.1, the result is actually taken as the point on the opposite side of the curve.

Using the vertical line between R and $-R$ for addition of those two points should give us the identity for addition. That is, $R - R = 0$. Clearly, point **0** is not on the graph. The identity element **0** is called the point at infinity. It is not on the curve but is essential for the points on an elliptic curve to be called a field. Different textbooks use different symbols. I will stick with **0** because the point at infinity acts like zero: any point plus zero is that point itself, and any point minus itself is zero. The point at infinity is special and will be treated as a special case in the code.

3.1.1   *Point representation*

In this section, I'll show how finite field elliptic curve points are stored in the computer. There are a few ways to represent points on an elliptic curve, which changes the formulas for point addition. These representations can reduce computation time. Chapter I of Silverman (2009) goes into these forms, and chapter IV of Blake et al. (1999) goes into details of a representation I won't cover here. In this book, a simple set of two values (x, y) will represent a point.

All the curves we are interested in are called *ordinary*. They are defined with equation 3.1:

$$y^2 = x^3 + a_4 x + a_6 \tag{3.1}$$

In chapter 2, I gave the complete equation for an elliptic curve. For ordinary curves over finite fields, we only need a_4 and a_6; the other coefficients in the general curve are 0.

Looking at figure 3.1, we can see that for every x value on the curve, there are two y values. Since a square root can have either a positive or negative result, that makes sense. The same is true over a finite field. The negative of a point from equation 3.1 always follows the rule:

$$-(x, y) = (x, -y)$$

For all the curves we are interested in, coefficient a_6 is never zero. This is exceptionally fortunate because y can never be 0. This gives us a way to represent **0** in the computer. Undefined is not "mathematically" correct, but for our purposes, it works really well:

$$\mathbf{0} = (0, 0)$$

That is, the point at infinity has $x = 0$ and $y = 0$, which is very easy to test for.

3.1.2   *Elliptic curves over finite fields*

This section goes into some esoteric math connecting finite fields and the complex plane. The idea is to show the depth and beauty of the mathematics. I also want to give a mental picture, which is useful with elliptic curves covered in part 3 (field extension curves).

One of the most fascinating aspects of elliptic curves is that we can map curves over finite fields to curves over the complex plane. This is both really cool and very important to keep in the back of your mind when we get into part 3 of the book.

In the process of doing a line integral over an elliptic curve on the complex plane, the complex plane is wrapped into a torus (to understand why, look at section VI.1 in Silverman [2009]). Figure 3.2 is a very crude attempt to get the idea across without diving into too much math. The elliptic curve function repeats along the drawn vectors. Since the torus is a surface, there are two independent vectors that mark out a range where the values do not repeat.

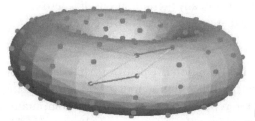

Figure 3.2   Elliptic curve over the complex plane

Figure 3.3 zooms in on the rectangle from figure 3.2. The points form a grid that repeats over the torus. The distance between the points perfectly divides the two vectors, so there is an integer number of points on the torus. This grid exactly maps to a finite field.

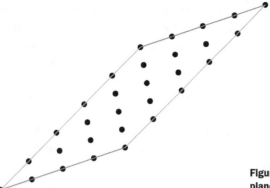

Figure 3.3   Points on a curve over a complex plane

Of fundamental importance here are the two cyclic vectors. The more horizontal lines represent one cyclic group, and the high angle lines, a second cyclic group. In the first part of this book, we will look at curves with just a single cycle. Part 3 of the book deals with curves composed of two cyclic groups, as this is what makes pairing of points possible.

Since a finite field is cyclic, it repeats similarly. This ability to map finite field math to complex plane math allows all the rules of calculus to be applied to the elliptic curves over finite fields. The rules for point addition are thus the same for real, complex, and finite fields. We are interested in finite fields based on large primes, not fields based on powers of 2 or 3. On very tiny processors with limited capabilities, finite fields over powers of 2 are exceptionally useful, so check out Rosing (1999) for those details.

3.1.3   Point addition

In this section, I'll cover the algebra of adding two points on an elliptic curve to get a third point on the same curve. The first step in adding points is finding the slope of the line between them. While we can come up with formulas for different points, we also need a formula for adding the same point to itself. That combination is a tangent to the curve, as shown in figure 3.4.

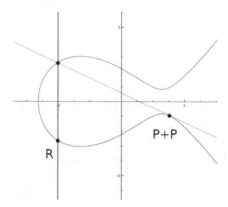

Figure 3.4   Adding a point to itself

Since the slope of a tangent is computed differently than the slope between two points, we normally have two different formulas. Unfortunately, this allows a side channel attack using power analysis, which can help an adversary determine the secret key. To avoid this problem, I will use the formula at the end of section III.3 in Silverman (2009) to compute the slope. This works for both tangents and different points equally. At best, an attacker can only learn the number of bits set (called Hamming weight in the literature) in the private key.

Let $P_1 = (x_1, y_1)$ and $P_2 = (x_2, y_2)$. It is OK for P_2 to equal P_1. Both points are on the curve (equation 3.1), so they satisfy that equation. We take the slope λ between the two points to be (equation 3.2)

$$\lambda = \frac{x_1^2 + x_1 x_2 + x_2^2 + a_4}{y_1 + y_2} \tag{3.2}$$

The resulting point $R = P_1 + P_2 = (x_3, y_3)$ is then found using the formulas in equations 3.3 and 3.4:

$$x_3 = \lambda^2 - x_1 - x_2 \tag{3.3}$$

$$y_3 = \lambda (x_1 - x_3) - y_1 \tag{3.4}$$

For the ordinary equation 3.1, the equations 3.2, 3.3, and 3.4 are the point addition formulas over an elliptic curve. There is a problem with this only when $y_1 + y_2 = 0$. This special case is rare and will be discussed in detail with the code implementation later.

Exercise 3.1

Why is $y_1 + y_2 = 0$ a problem in equations 3.3 and 3.4?

3.1.4 *Point multiplication*

In this section, I'll show how adding a point to itself multiple times is called multiplication. The next step in the mathematics of using elliptic curves is multiplication. We do this by adding a point to itself multiple times. For a point P and integer k, we write

$$Q = kP = \underbrace{P + P + \cdots + P}_{k}$$

with P added to itself k times.

Rather than actually perform this operation, we use the double and add formula. There are many ways to speed this up, as shown in section IV.2 of Blake et al. (1999). I paraphrase the method in figure 3.5 (which assumes $k > 1$).

The idea behind double and add is to expand k from most significant to a bit downward. Multiplying by 2 for every bit position is similar to a shift left, and then if the next bit is set, we add in the original point. This is a simple walk down every bit position. A side channel attack looks at power consumption to tell the difference between the double and the add routine. So, while it is a touch slower, using equation 3.2 is more secure on embedded systems.

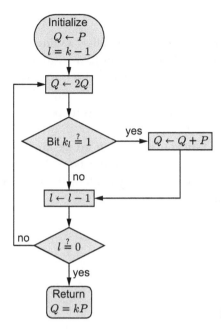

Figure 3.5 Double and add method

The points on an elliptic curve over a finite field are finite in number. When a point is added to itself enough times, you get back to where you started. This gives us a cyclic group to work with. Along the way, you will also hit the point at infinity. The number of times it takes to add a point to itself that gets to the point at infinity is called the order of the point.

As described in section 2.1, the points on elliptic curves form cyclic groups based on the combination of factors making up the number of points on the curve. We can determine what the order of a point is by multiplying each combination of those factors with the point to see whether we hit the point at infinity.

Using the example from section 2.1.1, we have two points belonging to a group with factor $a = 2$ and five points with factor $b = 5$. All the points on the curve that have order c are called the c-torsion subgroup. For security, we want c to be a very large prime. There will also be points of order $2 \cdot c$ and $10 \cdot c$, but they are not cryptographically useful because their order is not a prime.

Exercise 3.2

Show how the double and add method is similar to elementary school multiplication in binary using values 7 times 5.

Answer: $7 = 111b$ and $5 = 101b$. Using $k = 5$, start with answer = $111b$. Double this to get $1110b$. The second bit in 5 is clear, so no further addition is performed. Double again to get answer = $11,100b$. The last bit in 5 is set, so add in $111b$ to the answer which gives $10,011b = 35$.

3.1.5   *Embedding data on a curve*

In this section, I'll show how arbitrary data can be shifted to allow a value to become a point on an elliptic curve. Up to this point, all descriptions have assumed we have (x, y) pairs that satisfy equation 3.1. To choose a random point on the curve, we can start with a random x value. The odds that the value of x satisfies equation 3.1 are less than 50%. A look back at figure 3.1 shows half the plane has no points, so this is to be expected.

Elliptic curves over finite fields do not plot very well. What we see are individual points. Figure 3.6 shows an example curve used throughout this book. It is the curve $y^2 = x^3 + 23x - 1 \bmod 43$. It is easy to see some places have gaps along the x axis. Those x values do not satisfy the curve equation.

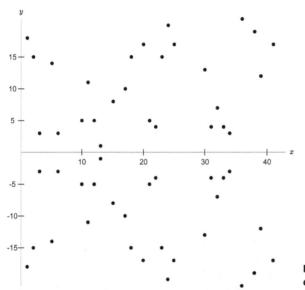

Figure 3.6   All points on tiny elliptic curve $y^2 = x^3 + 23x - 1 \bmod 43$

Figure 3.7 shows the process for embedding arbitrary data onto an elliptic curve. After computing the right-hand side of equation 3.1, the test in the diamond is the Legendre symbol from chapter 2 referenced to the field prime. If the value of $f(x)$ does not allow a square root, x is incremented by 1. This repeats until a value for x is found that is on the curve. The value of y is found from the square root of $f(x)$. More details will be developed with the code.

As an example, there is a gap on the right-hand side of figure 3.6 between 25 and 30. Suppose our random number generator picks an x value of 27. The routine computes $27^3 + 23 * 27 - 1 \bmod 43$ $(= 7)$ and then checks whether

$$\left(\frac{7}{43}\right) \overset{?}{=} 1$$

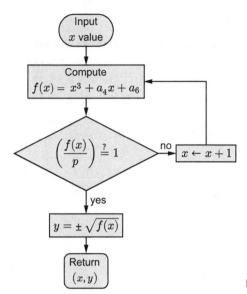

Figure 3.7 Embedding data on a curve

It does not, so the routine computes $28^3 + 23 * 28 - 1 \bmod 43$ (= 20), which also fails the Legendre symbol test; the same happens for $x = 29$. When $x = 30$, the Legendre symbol test does equal 1, and the y values turn out to be 4 and −4. While not every x value can be on the curve, there will be a nearby x value that is.

As an aside, note that the plot of figure 3.6 could have used all positive values of y. Instead of being mirrored around 0, it would be mirrored around 21. All negative values $-k$ can be replaced by adding the modulus p to get the equivalent value $p + k$. All the routines in this book will return positive values when a modulus operation is the last step, but they might return a negative value when subtraction is the last step.

Exercise 3.3

Will all values of x such that $\left(\dfrac{f(x)}{p}\right) = 1$ generate a point on an elliptic curve?

3.2 *Elliptic curve subroutines*

In the following sections, I'll show how finite field elliptic curve mathematics is implemented in code. Theory is great because it gives us an understanding of what we need to do. Reality requires a lot more detail. So, to turn all that math into code, I start with structures for curves and points and ways to manipulate those structures. Then I dive into the details of point addition and then use the point addition routine to cover point multiplication. Code for embedding data on a curve will be described as well, along with a few miscellaneous routines to create random points and help with debugging.

3.2.1 Code to represent curves and points

In this section, I'll define structures that are used in the rest of the book to help manipulate points and curves. Since both curves and points are used as objects, I'll start with a set of structures that are defined in a header. The file is `eliptic.h`, and it is obvious I can't spell. The structures are shown in the following listing.

Listing 3.1   Point and curve structures

```
typedef struct
{
    mpz_t    x;       The point is the (x, y) value.
    mpz_t    y;
} POINT;

typedef struct
{
    mpz_t    a4;      The curve is a₄, a₆ coefficients.
    mpz_t    a6;
} CURVE;
```

The point is the (x, y) value.

The curve is a_4, a_6 coefficients.

Since these are large integers in the GMP library, each component needs to be initialized. For some subroutines, we have temporary points, so these variables need to be cleared (`free()` in `malloc()` terms). These routines are shown in the following.

Listing 3.2   Point and curve initialization

```
void point_init(POINT *P)
{
    mpz_inits(P->x, P->y, NULL);    ← Initialize the point structure.
}

void point_clear(POINT *P)
{
    mpz_clears(P->x, P->y, NULL);   ← Clear the point structure.
}

void curve_init(CURVE *E)
{
    mpz_inits(E->a4, E->a6, NULL);  ← Initialize the curve structure.
}

void curve_clear(CURVE *E)
{
    mpz_clears(E->a4, E->a6, NULL); ← Clear the curve structure.
}
```

Two simple routines are used on points: (a) copy a point from variable *A* to variable *B*, and (b) test whether a point is the point at infinity. These routines are shown in the following listing.

Listing 3.3 Point copy and test

```
void point_copy(POINT *R, POINT P)
{
    mpz_set(R->x, P.x);        Copy both x and y values.
    mpz_set(R->y, P.y);
}


int test_point(POINT P)
{
    if(!mpz_cmp_ui(P.x, 0) && !mpz_cmp_ui(P.y, 0))    ← Both x == 0 and y == 0
      return 1;                                          for the point at infinity
    return 0;
}
```

3.2.2 Code for point addition

In this section, I'll describe the code that implements point addition for prime field elliptic curves. Adding two points is a major subroutine using equations 3.2, 3.3, and 3.4. Since any point added to **0** is the point itself, I first check to see whether any of the input points are the point at infinity, as shown in the following listing.

Listing 3.4 Point addition: Testing for 0

```
void elptic_sum(POINT *R, POINT P, POINT Q, CURVE E)
{
  mpz_t lmbda, ltp, lbt, t1, t2, t3;
  POINT rslt;

  if(test_point(P))
  {
    point_copy(R, Q);
    return;
  }                          If either point
  if(test_point(Q))          at infinity,
  {                          return other point.
    point_copy(R, P);
    return;
  }
```

After we determine that the points are not **0**, we compute the slope using equation 3.2. This is shown in listing 3.5. As seen in figure 3.1, points R and $-R$ have the same x values and opposite y values. So if we add two y values, we get 0, and equation 3.2 would then divide by 0.

Listing 3.5 Point addition: Computing λ

```
mpz_inits(t1, t2, t3, ltp, lbt, lmbda, NULL);
mmul(t1, P.x, P.x);
mmul(t2, P.x, Q.x);
mmul(t3, Q.x, Q.x);
madd(ltp, t1, t2);
madd(ltp, ltp, t3);
madd(ltp, ltp, E.a4);
madd(lbt, P.y, Q.y);
if(!mpz_cmp_ui(lbt, 0))
{
  msub(lbt, Q.x, P.x);
  if(!mpz_cmp_ui(lbt, 0))
  {
    mpz_set_ui(R->x, 0);
    mpz_set_ui(R->y, 0);
    mpz_clears(t1, t2, t3, ltp, lbt, lmbda, NULL);
    return;
  }
  msub(ltp, Q.y, P.y);
}
mdiv(lmbda, ltp, lbt);
```

$\text{Top} = x_1^2 + x_1 x_2 + x_2^2 + a_4$

Compute lambda using general form.

$\leftarrow$ **Bottom** $= y_1 + y_2$

$\leftarrow$ **Enter If** $y_1 + y_2 == 0$.

$\leftarrow$ **Compute** $x_2 - x_1$.

$\leftarrow$ **Enter If** $x_2 - x_1 == 0$.

$x_2 == x_1$ **results In point at infinity**

Special case $\lambda = \dfrac{y_2 - y_1}{x_2 - x_1}$

Either case $\lambda = \dfrac{\text{Top}}{\text{Bottom}}$

If we draw a horizontal line through point Q in figure 3.1, we would have three y values that are the same. That means there are three matching values on the negative half of the curve. While rare, it is possible that we have y value sums that cancel, but they are not at the same x value. Under this condition, we must compute the slope the old-fashioned way, using

$$\lambda = \frac{y_2 - y_1}{x_2 - x_1}$$

If $x_2 = x_1$, then this formula also goes to 0. The purpose of the two if() statements is to check

- $y_1 \overset{?}{=} -y_2$
- $x_1 \overset{?}{=} x_2$

The result is the point at infinity **0** if both conditions are true; otherwise, we can compute the third point.

Listing 3.6 is the calculation of equations 3.3 and 3.4. This is a straightforward use of the modular subroutines shown in chapter 2. Because we don't want to clobber old points while computing the new one (again, learned the hard way!), the temporary point rslt is used, so the final result can be copied back to the desired location.

Listing 3.6 Point addition: x_3 and y_3 calculation

**Finally compute
resulting point.**

```
point_init(&rslt);
mmul(t1, lmbda, lmbda);
madd(t2, P.x, Q.x);
msub(rslt.x, t1, t2);
msub(t1, P.x, rslt.x);
mmul(t2, t1, lmbda);
msub(rslt.y, t2, P.y);
point_copy(R, rslt);    ← Transfer result to output.
mpz_clears(t1, t2, t3, ltp, lbt, lmbda, NULL);
point_clear(&rslt);
}
```

$$x_3 = \lambda^2 - (x_1 + x_2)$$

$$y_3 = (x_1 - x_3)\lambda - y_1$$

3.2.3 Code for point multiplication

Multiplying points by a large number is the core of elliptic curve cryptography. The code to add two points is a bit complicated. But once we have that subroutine, the jump to point multiplication via figure 3.5 is easy. The point multiplication routine is shown in the following listing.

Listing 3.7 Point multiplication

```
void elptic_mul(POINT *Q, POINT P, mpz_t k, CURVE E)
{
  int bit, j;
  POINT R;

  point_init(&R);
  point_copy(&R, P);       Save input point.
  j = mpz_sizeinbase(k, 2) - 2;   ← Bit position index
  while(j >= 0)
  {
    elptic_sum(&R, R, R, E);   ← Double for each bit position.
    bit = mpz_tstbit(k, j);
    if(bit)
      elptic_sum(&R, R, P, E);   ← Add for each bit set.
    j--;
  }
  point_copy(Q, R);   ← Transfer result.
  point_clear(&R);
}
```

The GMP routines `mpz_sizeinbase()` and `mpz_tstbit()` are used to determine how many bits we need to work with and if a bit is set or not. The `sizeinbase` routine is used here to count bits. We subtract 2 from the return value because the starting offset is 1, and we skip the most significant bit. Every time through the loop, the result R is doubled, and if the bit k_j is set, the original point is added to the result.

3.3   *Code for embedding data on a curve*

In this section, I'll describe the detailed method of converting arbitrary data into a point on an elliptic curve. Suppose I want to use elliptic curves to transmit a short message. The first step is to convert the message into a point, (x, y). Unfortunately, not all x values have a point on the curve. We need to adjust the message to find some x' that is close to the message we want to send.

It turns out the odds of not finding an x' close to x are proportional to $\frac{1}{2^{2^n-1}}$ where n is the number of bits modified at the end of the message. There is a 50% chance with one bit. With 8 bits, the odds of not finding an x' on the curve are astronomically small (approximately 3×10^{-39}), and most likely, only 5 or 6 bits are needed.

The right-hand side of equation 3.1 is entirely a function of x. This makes a nice subroutine if we take

$$f(x) = x^3 + a_4 x + a_6$$

The following listing shows this calculation given an input value x and elliptic curve E.

Listing 3.8   Embedding data: Computing $f(x)$

```
void fofx(mpz_t f, mpz_t x, CURVE E)
{
  mpz_t t1, t2;

  mpz_inits(t1, t2, NULL);
  mmul(t1, x, x);        | t1 = x^3
  mmul(t1, t1, x);       |
  mmul(t2, E.a4, x);     |
  madd(f, t1, t2);       | f = x^3 + a_4 x + a_6
  madd(f, f, E.a6);      |
  mpz_clears(t1, t2, NULL);
}
```

To determine whether the value of x can be found on the curve, $f(x)$ must have a square root because $y^2 = f(x)$. If $f(x)$ is not a quadratic residue, $f(x)$ does not have a square root. As described in section 3.1.5, we can increment x and look to find an x value that is on the curve as shown in the algorithm of figure 3.7. Usually, this takes two to five tries, but sometimes it can take over 30. This is where the 5 or 6 bits of noise in x' are useful. I typically use the last byte in an x value as a spare when embedding specific data on a curve.

Listing 3.9 shows a way to embed data on a curve. To allow addition by 1 modulo the field prime, I create the constant one as an mpz_t integer. I copy the input value to the output x value of the point and then check whether $f(x)$ is a quadratic residue.

If it is, the value of x is used; if it is not a quadratic residue, then the point x value is incremented by 1, and the testing continues until a quadratic residue is found.

Because the square root has a positive and negative value, both points are returned. Since it is arbitrary, the first point is set to the smaller y value. With numbers modulo a prime, we can always take a negative value and add the modulus to get a positive result that is congruent to the original negative number. The GMP manual says the result of `mpz_mod()` is always nonnegative. For consistency's sake, I chose to put the point with the smaller y value first.

Listing 3.9 Embedding data: Finding points

```
void elptic_embed(POINT *P1, POINT *P2, mpz_t x, CURVE E)
{
  mpz_t f, one;
  int done;

  mpz_init(f);
  mpz_init_set_ui(one, 1);    ← mpz constant 1
  mpz_set(P1->x, x);
  done = 0;
  while(!done)
  {
    fofx(f, P1->x, E);
    if(msqr(f) > 0)          f(x) is quadratic residue
      done = 1;
    else
      madd(P1->x, P1->x, one);  ← increment x by 1.
  }
  mpz_set(P2->x, P1->x);
  msqrt(P1->y, f);           Two y values
  mneg(P2->y, P1->y);
  done = mpz_cmp(P2->y, P1->y);
  if(done < 0)               The smaller y value first
    mpz_swap(P2->y, P1->y);
  mpz_clears(f, one, NULL);
}
```

3.4 Miscellaneous routines

This section includes two routines that are useful in the rest of the book but do not fit a mathematical description.

There are two more routines in the `elliptic.c` file. One creates random points, and the other prints points to the console for debugging. The random point routine is shown in listing 3.10. This first finds a random value in the range of the modulus. It then checks the last bit of this random number and embeds the smaller y value to the point if the bit is clear and the larger y value if the bit is set.

Listing 3.10   Random point

```
void point_rand(POINT *P, CURVE E)
{
  mpz_t r;
  POINT mP;

  mpz_init(r);
  mrand(r);         ← Random value
  point_init(&mP);
  if(mpz_tstbit(r, 0))
    elptic_embed(P, &mP, r, E);  ← Last bit set returns smaller y
  else
    elptic_embed(&mP, P, r, E);  ← Last bit clear returns larger y
  mpz_clear(r);
  point_clear(&mP);
}
```

When debugging, it is very useful to know what intermediate values are. The point printing routine shown in the following listing requires a string to label the point and the point itself.

Listing 3.11   Printing a point

```
void point_printf(char *str, POINT P)
{
  printf("%s", str);
  gmp_printf(" (%Zd,  %Zd)\n", P.x, P.y);
}
```

The header file eliptic.h includes the structures in listing 3.1 as well as the function definitions described in this chapter. The following listing is a nice summary of all the code presented in this chapter.

Listing 3.12   Header function definitions

```
void point_init(POINT *P);
void point_clear(POINT *P);
void curve_init(CURVE *E);
void curve_clear(CURVE *E);
void point_copy(POINT *R, POINT P);
int test_point(POINT P);
void fofx(mpz_t f, mpz_t x, CURVE E);
void elptic_sum(POINT *R, POINT P, POINT Q, CURVE E);
void elptic_embed(POINT *P1, POINT *P2, mpz_t x, CURVE E);
void point_printf(char *str, POINT P);
void elptic_mul(POINT *Q, POINT P, mpz_t k, CURVE E);
void point_rand(POINT *P, CURVE E);
```

Answers to exercises

1 The variable λ is divided by $y_1 + y_2$. When $y_1 + y_2 = 0$, $\lambda = \infty$. Equations 3.3 and 3.4 are then useless.

3 Yes. In fact, it will have two matching points for $\pm y$.

Summary

- The fundamental formula for ordinary elliptic curves is

$$y^2 = x^3 + a_4 x + a_6$$

- The sum of two points on an elliptic curve is the negative point of the intersection point to the curve of a line drawn between them.
- The point at infinity is not on the curve. It is the identity element and, for ordinary curves, can be represented as $(0, 0)$ in code.
- Elliptic curves over finite fields have a 1-to-1 mapping to curves over the complex plane.
- The point addition formula has a special form for use in secure applications. Using a standard form can leak key information when side channel attacks are applied.
- Point multiplication uses a double and add algorithm to rapidly compute extremely large prime multipliers.
- When the point mP is the point at infinity $\mathbf{0}$, then P is order m and a member of the m-torsion subgroup.
- For coding, curves and points have simple structures, which include (a_4, a_6) and (x, y), respectively.
- The point addition routine must check for the point at infinity on input and output.
- Point multiplication code uses the same addition routine for doubling and adding to enhance security.
- To embed data on a curve the x value is incremented until $x^3 + a_4 x + a_6$ is a quadratic residue. When sending a message on a curve point, the last 6 to 8 bits should be considered noise.
- Random points are found by embedding random x values on the curve. This will be useful for many routines described throughout the book.

Key exchange using
elliptic curves

This chapter covers

- Creating a shared secret using private
  and public keys
- The Diffie-Hellman key exchange using
  elliptic curves
- Implementing the NIST Full ECC MQV algorithm

In this chapter, I'll describe two methods of secure key exchange. As described in chapter 1, elliptic curve cryptography is used to create a secret key for an efficient encryption algorithm. No one but the two parties exchanging public keys can compute the secret key.

Now that we have the basic elliptic curve mathematics routines for point addition and multiplication, we can begin to look at algorithms that use these techniques to implement public key cryptography. The private key is a large integer, and the public key is a point. Since the private key can be anything, a hash of a pass phrase, which is never stored, can be really secure. At the system level, this might be a problem if the phrase is forgotten, but there is nothing to be done about that here.

All key exchange algorithms are based on the Diffie-Hellman process. The process involves the sender's public key and the receiver's private key. For many peer-to-peer transactions that do not happen very often this is sufficient. For common transactions between two users (like an employee to their company), it might allow an attack on the shared secret. To prevent this, a more sophisticated method called the Menezes-Qu-Vanstone (MQV) key exchange algorithm can be used.

The following sections will describe the Diffie-Hellman key exchange algorithm, followed by the MQV key exchange algorithm. The MQV algorithm uses ephemeral keys that change every time two parties communicate in addition to the static public keys used in the Diffie-Hellman key exchange algorithm.

The use case for one over the other depends on your environment. If two systems communicate on a regular basis, then choosing MQV makes sense. If two systems will only rarely communicate (say, a customer registering a product), then using Diffie-Hellman makes sense.

4.1 Diffie-Hellman algorithm description

In this section, I'll describe the simplest algorithm for key exchange using elliptic curves. As pointed out in chapter 3, we can embed a message on a curve if the message size is less than the modulus used to hold an x value. If our modulus is 256 bits, our message size can be 250 bits or, at most, 31 bytes. This is not very useful for most communications.

If, instead, we use the x values to create a secret key for a symmetric encryption algorithm such as the Advanced Encryption Standard (AES; National Institute of Standards and Technology [NIST], 2001), our message can be as long as we want. This is the idea behind public key cryptography: two people send their public keys to each other and create a secret no one else can find. Figure 4.1 is a copy of figure 1.3 that shows how the Diffie-Hellman method works. Each person multiplies their private key with the other person's public key to create a shared secret. For a more in-depth description of Diffie-Hellman key exchange, see chapter 5 of Wong (2021).

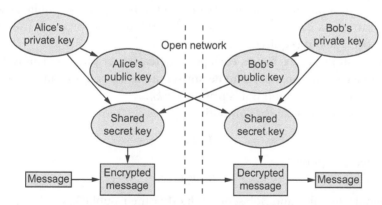

Figure 4.1   Creating a shared secret key by exchanging public keys

4.1.1 Elliptic curve math

In this section, the details of the elliptic curve Diffie-Hellman key exchange are described. In most books and papers, the number of points on the curve is called the cardinality of the curve and is written mathematically as $\#E$, where the curve E is the equation 3.1 repeated here:

$$E: y^2 = x^3 + a_4 x + a_6$$

Most curves over finite fields have a cardinality with many factors, but as we will see in chapter 6, it does not take too long with modern computers to find good secure curves that have prime cardinality with no cofactors. An adversary has no choice but to hunt over every point on the curve; there are no possible shortcuts.

We start a key exchange with a secure elliptic curve as described in chapter 3—a curve with a large prime factor in the cardinality. Since we are using ordinary curves over finite fields, it is possible to find curves that have a prime number of points as the finite number of points on the curve.

For the remainder of this book, capital variables will refer to points, and lowercase variables will refer to a field value. The point G has values (x, y), which satisfy the equation of the curve that the point G is on. This saves a lot of writing. It means we operate at a higher level of abstraction. So, the multiplication of a point by a value to get a new point must grind through all the equations of chapter 3.

Once we have a curve, we pick a base point G. G stands for generator. Since we are interested in curves with prime factor cardinality, every point on the curve can be a generator because the order of every point is the same prime number. When we get into field extension curves in chapter 13, prime factor cardinality is not possible, so we need to find curves with a very large prime as one of the factors in the cardinality. The remaining small factors are called a cofactor. For useful curves, I assume the size of the cofactor fits in a `long`, which implies it is very small compared to the large prime factor.

For simple key exchange, a secure curve over a finite field has prime order and, once chosen, is a public parameter. We make the base point G public as well, so everyone can use it. This public data is usually built into the program used for key exchange because it is required to create new keys.

To prepare for a key exchange, each person creates a private key. This is usually a hash of some pass phrase, but it can be any set of bits turned into an integer. We'll call Alice's private key k_A and Bob's private key k_B.

Alice creates a public key by computing

$$A = k_A G$$

and Bob creates a public key

$$B = k_B G$$

To communicate, Alice and Bob send each other their public keys.

The security comes from the inability to use the knowledge of points G and A to find the value of k_A. This is called the elliptic curve discrete log problem (ECDLP). Since the ability to solve this problem goes as the $\sqrt{\#E}$, we need twice as many bits in our prime factor as the level of security we are attempting to reach. That is, 128-bit AES level of security requires 256 bits of $\#E$ cardinality.

Once Alice and Bob have exchanged keys, they create a shared secret by multiplying the received public key with their own private key.

This gives us equation 4.1:

$$S = k_A B = k_B A = k_A k_B G = k_B k_A G \tag{4.1}$$

They each use the x component of point S (or some chunk of bits from it) as the secret key for a symmetric algorithm such as AES.

> **Exercise 4.1**
>
> Clare wants to securely message Alice and Bob. Can she create one secret key between all three of them?

4.1.2 Hash function

In this section, the important concept of hashing is described. This will be used in all example programs, including the routines in chapters 18 and 19. A hash function is an algorithm that takes an arbitrary length of bytes and smooshes out a fixed length of random-looking bytes. A secure hash function changes half its output bits if one single input bit changes. There are many secure hash functions available, so I chose one whose core was approved by NIST and has since been improved.

The chosen hash software is called KangarooTwelve and is available from http://mng.bz/jXgV, or you can use Git to download it from https://github.com/XKCP/K12.git. While there are many subroutines in this package, I only use one of them. If you want to know more details, you can check out the inventor's home page: https://keccak.team/kangarootwelve.html. Once downloaded, the source is straightforward to build into a library. I've added instructions to do so in appendix A.

The routine has two input strings and one output string. The lengths of each are a separate argument. While the internal core function is a fixed size, the routine I call creates an extendable output. NIST (2016) defines an extendable output function as a function on bit strings in which the output can be extended to any desired length. The reason we want extendable output is described in Faz-Hernandez et al. (2021).

That document describes how a problem occurs when we convert a hashed output down to a prime value using a modulus n. Since the modulus is less than a full power of 2, the odds are high our hashed output modulo n will be in a small range. To avoid this problem, IETF advises we add the number of bits we require for security to the output length.

Listing 4.1 takes an arbitrary length input string and outputs a value modulo an input prime, which should be the order of the base point. This routine has a fixed "customize" string used in KangarooTwelve. The IETF standard requires a domain separation tag (`dst`), which allows the use of the same hash function in different routines. By changing the `dst`, the same input string will output a unique result.

Listing 4.1   Hash to finite field

```
void hash(mpz_t hsh, unsigned char *dat, long len, mpz_t prm)
{
  unsigned char *outp, *dst;
  int m, k, b;

  dst = (char*)malloc(24);                         Set up domain separation tag.
  sprintf(dst, "Hash_b pring&sig");

  m = mpz_sizeinbase(prm, 2);
  if(m < 208)
    k = 80;
  else if(m < 320)
    k = 128;                                        Determine security level
  else if(m < 448)                                  and add appropriate
    k = 192;                                        extra bit length.
  else
    k = 256;
  b = m + k;
  if(b & 7)
    b = (b >> 3) + 1;   ← Round to next byte.
  else
    b >>= 3;
  outp = (unsigned char*)malloc(b + 2);
  KangarooTwelve(dat, len, outp, b, dst, 16);      Generate hash of input.

  mpz_import(hsh, b, -1, 1, 0, 0, outp);   ← Convert bits to an integer.
  mpz_mod(hsh, hsh, prm);        ← Force to be mod n.
  free(outp);
  free(dst);
}
```

The output length is first computed in bits. If any of the last three bits are set, the byte count is one more than a division by 8. The hash is then converted to an integer using the GMP `mpz_import()` function. The argument `-1` means little-endian input, the next `1` signifies b is in bytes, and the two zeros mean processor endianness output and no skipped bytes, respectively. Using `mpz_mod()` with p, the result is then the correct size.

4.1.3   *Key generation*

In this section, I'll show how an individual's keys can be created. The advantage of elliptic curve key exchange is that keys do not need to be stored; they can be computed every time they are needed. Once we have a hash function that converts a pass phrase to an integer mod p, generating the public key is easy. Assuming we use the random point function (listing 3.10) to create the base point, a nice structure to hold the public parameters is shown in the following listing.

Listing 4.2 Base key structure

```
typedef struct
{
   long  cofactor;  ← Assumes tiny cofactor
   mpz_t order;      Order of the base point
   POINT Base;       Base point (x, y) value
   CURVE E;          Curve (a4, a6) coefficients
}BASE_SYSTEM;
```

Note that this includes a cofactor. For our example curves, the cofactor will usually be 1, but for generality's sake, it needs to be included. I call this structure the BASE_SYSTEM because the curve and base point are field prime size. When we get to field extension points, curves will become polynomials with field prime coefficients.

Listing 4.3 shows that we don't need to do much to create a public key from a pass phrase. Tracking the private key is system dependent. The security of the entire system rests on the private key staying secret. That is, one advantage of going from a pass phrase directly to a key is that the private key never has to be placed in nonvolatile storage. I did not include string.h in the header, so the function strlen() is not available. Clearly, you can do that if you like.

Listing 4.3 Key generation

```
void gen_key(mpz_t sk, POINT *PK, unsigned char *phrase, BASE_SYSTEM bse)
{
   long np;

   np = 0;                       Could have used
   while(phrase[np]) np++;       np = strlen(phrase)
   hash(sk, phrase, np, bse.order);  ←── Private key modulo
   elptic_mul(PK, bse.Base, sk, bse.E);    base point order
}
```

4.1.4 Computing shared keys

In this section, I'll show the code for computing a secret shared key. I'm going to assume that both Alice and Bob have traded their public keys over an open network. Once that has been done, listing 4.4 shows how they both generate the same shared secret key. The output is the shared secret, and the inputs are their own private key and the other person's public key. The curve that the points are defined to be on is also an input, so the multiplication can take place.

Listing 4.4 Diffie-Hellman shared key

```
void diffie_hellman(mpz_t keyshare, mpz_t my_key, POINT Their_key, CURVE E)
{
   POINT Tmp;
```

```
    point_init(&Tmp);
    elptic_mul(&Tmp, Their_key, my_key, E);    ← ┐ Compute (their public key)*
    mpz_set(keyshare, Tmp.x);                     │ (my private key).
    point_clear(&Tmp);
}
```

Of course, they each have the other person's public key and their own private key. As shown in equation 4.1, they both compute the same shared secret.

4.2   MQV algorithm

In this section, I'll describe a more involved key exchange algorithm. Menezes et al. (1995) proposed a key agreement scheme that provided perfect forward security. That means even if you figured out the shared secret key for that message, you have no way of finding information about any other message. Over the past 25 years, the MQV algorithm has been studied and modified. In 2018, NIST published a document on all the various ways to implement MQV (NIST, 2018). I will go over one of those methods called Full ECC MQV.

What I really like about this method is the use of ephemeral public and private keys in addition to static public and private keys. Ephemeral keys are generated once per key agreement session. So while static public keys may be stored, the ephemeral keys must be transmitted by both sides before a shared secret can be computed.

4.2.1   Elliptic curve math for the MQV algorithm

This section goes into the details of the MQV method as described by NIST. For notation, I'll use subscript $_e$ for ephemeral and subscript $_s$ for static. As with Diffie-Helmann, the base point is G on the curve E. The order of the base point n and cofactor of the curve r are known. Alice has a static private key $k_{s,A}$ and ephemeral private key $k_{e,A}$. Similarly, Bob has static and ephemeral private keys $k_{s,B}$ and $k_{e,B}$ respectively. The public keys are

$$P_{s,A} = k_{s,A}G$$
$$P_{e,A} = k_{e,A}G$$
$$P_{s,B} = k_{s,B}G$$
$$P_{e,B} = k_{e,B}G$$

Alice sends Bob her public keys, and Bob sends Alice his public keys. The static keys could have been transferred prior to initial contact and the ephemeral keys when contact is initiated. This is system dependent. To prevent duplicating all the equations, I'm going to look at Alice's side of the calculation in the following description. The A and B subscripts swap for Bob's side.

Once both sides have each other's public keys, Alice computes what NIST calls an implicit signature with her own keys using the formula

$$s_A = k_{e,A} + avf(P_{e,A}.x)k_{s,A}$$

where $P_{e,A}.x$ is the x coordinate of the point $P_{e,A}$.

NIST defines the routine $avf()$ as the associate value function. This chops an x value in half and then sets a bit at the halfway point. Since the security of the system goes as $\sqrt{n}$, this sort of makes sense

$$avf(x) = x \bmod 2^{\lceil \log_2(n)/2 \rceil} + 2^{\lceil \log_2(n)/2 \rceil}$$

where the symbol $\lceil\ \rceil$ means next largest integer (i.e., round up), and n is the order of the base point G.

Next, each side computes a point using the other side's public keys. This formula is

$$U_B = P_{e,B} + avf(P_{e,B}.x)P_{s,B}$$

The shared secret is then computed as

$$z = (s_A U_B).x$$

and this value will be in the range $\{0 \cdots p-1\}$. The NIST standard also multiplies by the cofactor of the curve. That seems like a security overkill to me since all the points are in the prime order group. See section 5.7.2.3 of NIST (2018) for details.

To see how both sides get the same value, let's follow both sides through the previous description as in table 4.1. Alice's column duplicates the previous equations. Bob's column swaps the subscripts A and B because he has his private keys and Alice's public keys. The public keys are the private keys multiplied by the base point G. Expanding the middle line using the public key formulas, we see that the last line in each column shows the final result is identical.

Table 4.1 MQV expanded calculation

Alice	Bob
$s_A = k_{e,A} + \mathsf{avf}(P_{e,A}.x)k_{s,A}$	$s_B = k_{e,B} + \mathsf{avf}(P_{e,B}.x)k_{s,B}$
$U_B = P_{e,B} + \mathsf{avf}(P_{e,B}.x)P_{s,B}$	$U_A = P_{e,A} + \mathsf{avf}(P_{e,A}.x)P_{s,A}$
$s_A U_B = (k_{e,A} + \mathsf{avf}(P_{e,A}.x)k_{s,A})$	$s_B U_A = (k_{e,B} + \mathsf{avf}(P_{e,B}.x)k_{s,B})$
$\cdot(k_{e,B} + \mathsf{avf}(P_{e,B}.x)k_{s,B})G$	$\cdot(k_{e,A} + \mathsf{avf}(P_{e,A}.x)k_{s,A})G$

Since all the points are related to the base point G, the effective computation has both sides computing the same result. The impossible task of finding the private key values from the public information is what allows this to work.

Exercise 4.2

Assuming the static and ephemeral key points exist, how many point multiplications are required to compute the MQV algorithm for one person?

4.2.2   *MQV code*

In the following sections, the code to implement MQV is described. Now it is time to turn all that math into code. I'll start with the generation of ephemeral keys using pseudo random numbers. I'll then describe the simple associate value function. The full MQV code is shown after that. Converting the math into code is now simple because the hard part of summing and multiplying points is behind us.

EPHEMERAL KEYS

This section describes a routine to create a random ephemeral key for use with the MQV algorithm. In addition to the static key, the MQV algorithm uses an ephemeral key. These are randomly generated. A cryptographically secure random number generator should use hardware. Radioactive decay or thermal junction noise on a diode are typical sources available. For a really deep dive, check out https://csrc.nist .gov/projects/random-bit-generation. We'll just use the pseudo random generator from GMP, as shown in the following listing.

Listing 4.5   Ephemeral key generator

```
void mqv_ephem(mpz_t ephm, POINT *Eph, BASE_SYSTEM bse)
{
    mrand(ephm);    ← Random number for an ephemeral private key
    elptic_mul(Eph, bse.Base, ephm, bse.E);
}
```

The function takes the system parameters as input. The private and public keys are output. The private key is just a random number. The public key is that random number multiplied by the base point. While this function is cryptographically simple, making it secure in a system might be more challenging.

ASSOCIATE VALUE FUNCTION

This section describes the code which implements the NIST associate value function. The implementation of the avf() is shown in listing 4.6. The computation of $x \bmod 2^{\lceil \log_2(n)/2 \rceil}$ is a simple mask of the lower half of the number of bits in the order of the base point. Since the order is always prime, the ceiling function takes us to the next integer after dividing by 2. The mask is created by brute force. Setting one bit at a time is slow but obvious. Using lower-level routines, this can be accomplished far more quickly. After the input value is masked, the bit at the halfway point is set.

Listing 4.6   Associate value function

```
void avf(mpz_t z, mpz_t x, BASE_SYSTEM bse)
{
    long f, i;
    mpz_t mask;

    mpz_init(mask);
    f = (mpz_sizeinbase(bse.order, 2) >> 1) + 1;    ← f = n/2 + 1
```

```
  for(i=0; i<f; i++)
    mpz_setbit(mask, i);        │ The mask has f bits set.
  mpz_and(z, x, mask);          │ Apply mask to input.
  mpz_setbit(z, f);  ← Bit f is always set.
  mpz_clear(mask);
}
```

FULL ECC MQV

This section describes what NIST calls the Full ECC MQV algorithm. The NIST Full ECC MQV routine is shown in listing 4.7. There are basically two steps. The first is to compute the value *s* with the local side's private data modulo the order of the base point. The second is to compute the point *U* using the far side's public key values. The multiplication then acts like a Diffie-Hellman operation. The NIST requirement also adds the curve cofactor. Here, I check to see whether the cofactor is greater than 1 because there is no point doing the multiply unless it is.

Listing 4.7 Full ECC MQV

```
void mqv_share(mpz_t keyshare, mpz_t my_key, POINT MY_KEY,
               mpz_t my_ephm, POINT My_Ephm,
               POINT Their_key, POINT Their_Ephm,
               BASE_SYSTEM bse)
{
  POINT U;
  mpz_t s, z;

  mpz_inits(s, z, NULL);     │ Compute s.
  avf(z, My_Ephm.x, bse);
  mod_mul(s, z, my_key, bse.order);    │ s = k_e + avf(P_e.x)k_s
  mod_add(s, s, my_ephm, bse.order);   │

  point_init(&U);                  │ Compute U.
  avf(z, Their_Ephm.x, bse);
  elptic_mul(&U, Their_key, z, bse.E);   │ U = P_e + avf(P_e.x)P_s
  elptic_sum(&U, U, Their_Ephm, bse.E);  │

  elptic_mul(&U, U, s, bse.E);  ← Shared secret =sU  │ Compute key share value
  if(bse.cofactor > 1)                               │ (x component).
  {
    mpz_set_ui(z, bse.cofactor);    │ cofactor > 1
    elptic_mul(&U, U, z, bse.E);    │ requires multiply
  }
  mpz_set(keyshare, U.x);  ←┐
  point_clear(&U);          │ Return x component
  mpz_clears(s, z, NULL);    │ for a shared secret.
}
```

Using the Full MQV algorithm requires more communication than Diffie-Hellman. Both sides transmit their ephemeral public key to the other side in addition to their static public key. The other versions all require some communication of ephemeral keys, so even if you don't use the full version, some initial transfer of data is required. That is one reason this key-sharing method is so useful—you create a new key every time you connect. In terms of cryptographic security, an outside attack is essentially impossible. Just make sure your implementation deals with other problems, such as unknown key-share attacks.

4.3   Example test code

The following few sections present the example code to show how Diffie-Hellman and MQV algorithms can be used. To test the code, we first require curves to work with. The choice of curve depends on the prime chosen for the finite field. In chapter 6, I will explain the choice of primes. For now, I will use curve parameters found using methods I'll describe later. The obvious missing component in these tests is the actual transmission of the key data over the network.

In the following description, I first list all the curves and base point parameters that are input files to the test program. I wrote a trivial routine to skip text lines from the input file so I can easily convert numbers from a human-readable file. The test program uses both the Diffie-Hellman routines and the MQV routines, so the same private and public keys are used for each case. The two sides of the transmission are called "my side" and "their side." Private keys for my side are input phrases, and private keys for their side are fixed strings of random data.

4.3.1   Test curves

This section describes curves found using the method in chapter 6. It also describes an example program that executes the key exchange subroutines. Testing the above routines requires a curve and base point. One can use NIST-approved curves, or you can find your own, as shown in chapter 6. If you find your own, you should make sure they are not susceptible to various attacks. For these examples, I found four curves at different security levels and then checked that each subroutine worked at that level. The subroutines didn't work the first time!

Listings 4.8 through 4.11 show four different files with curve and point parameters. The following listing is a 160-bit curve using field prime $43 \cdot 2^{158} + 1$.

Listing 4.8   Test curve: Secure 160 bit

```
File: Curve_160_params.dat
prime
ac0000000000000000000000000000000000000001
order
ac00000000000000000006543ba11adf8eb6345c77
cofactor
1
curve(a4    a6)
1
```

```
782e
basepoint(x    y)
1680bbdc87647f3c382902d2f58d2754b39bca877
a08957b09764ae59da8fb3058efef9c428e497268
```

The following listing is a 256-bit curve using field prime $43 \cdot 2^{252} + 1$.

Listing 4.9   Test curve: Secure 256 bit

File: Curve_256_params.dat
```
prime
2b000000000000000000000000000000000000000000000000000000000000001
order
2b00000000000000000000000000000002e7f521c85bba055a6e2161b956a47f69
cofactor
1
curve(a4    a6)
1
a87
basepoint(x    y)
2310115d283e49377820195c8e67781b6f112a625b14b747fa4cc13d06eba0919
51277aeb91946f0cb83053a10f67c5a9ef00a4f0cf2466b3bedf4fdcd774b574
```

The following listing is a 384-bit curve using field prime $23 \cdot 2^{381} + 1$.

Listing 4.10   Test curve: Secure 384 bit

File: Curve_384_params.dat
```
prime
2e0000000000000000000000000000000000000000000000000000000000000000
⇒ 000000000000000000001
order
2e000000000000000000000000000000000000000000000000002275cc5f2f7fcc15352a2c993900
⇒ a851b3a75365a9ac54733
cofactor
1
curve(a4    a6)
1
310
basepoint(x    y)
23c0d9fcfaa3dc18b1eff7e89bf7678636580d17dd84a873b14b9c0e1680bbdc87647f3c3829
⇒ 02d2f58d2754b39bca874
28d7205f1be0a725d2aa7c3386f2e0b0ea7c558ca19f9770cdc72f91a1cbc262687810d4c5bd
⇒ 536818ccfa49aae2ed0cc
```

The following listing is a 512-bit curve using field prime $113 \cdot 2^{509} + 1$.

Listing 4.11   Test curve: Secure 512 bit

File: Curve_512_params.dat

```
prime
e2000000000000000000000000000000000000000000000000000000000000000000000000
➟ 00000000000000000000000000000000000000000000000000000001
order
e20000000000000000000000000000000000000000000000000000007788830d091d
➟ c57e3af7d7bbd15386ee9414602d88d1e6489cd056336922bbf4d
cofactor
1
curve(a4    a6)
1
41
basepoint(x    y)
518f204fe6846aeb6f58174d57a3372363c0d9fcfaa3dc18b1eff7e89bf7678636580d17dd84
➟ a873b14b9c0e1680bbdc87647f3c382902d2f58d2754b39bca875
c9fe7223aca476cde61f206be285898475f1dcbaefeda90057d3b8bae5146f3016ebf2139daa
➟ 73f39417193e8609a4229cd4c58389e4b9095fafcd68362b310fe
```

One of these files is read in at the top of the test routine as shown in listing 4.13. The command-line argument is one of 160, 256, 384, or 512. That parameter file is read in and then parsed into the correct arguments. The parsing process includes skipping text lines in the data file. The line-skipping subroutine is shown in the following listing. The index is maintained, so I track where each line is in the buffer.

Listing 4.12   Key exchange test code: Skip-line subroutine

```
int skipln(char *bfr, int strt, int skp)
{
  int i;                                    Number of lines to skip

  i = strt;
  while(skp)                                Index start
  {
    while(bfr[i] != '\n') i++;
    i++;
    skp--;
  }                       Index points to
  return i;   ⟵          start of next line
}
```

The prime value is the field over which the curve is computed. The order value is the order of the base point. All these curves have a cofactor of 1, so this is also the cardinality of the curve. The equation of the curve (coefficients a_4 and a_6) and the (x, y) coordinates of the base point are included. Once the values are converted and placed into the BASE_SYSTEM structure, the test is ready to begin.

Listing 4.13   Key exchange test code: Input curve parameters

```
int main(int argc, char *argv[])
{
  FILE *parm;
  mpz_t prm, sk, sok;
  long lvl;
  BASE_SYSTEM base;
  POINT Pk, Pok, Rk, Rok;
  char filename[256], *bufr, *ptr;
  int i, k;
  mpz_t myshare, theirshare, myrand, theirrand;

  if(argc < 2)
  {                                                    Verify input
    printf("Use: ./base_test <level>\n");              level exists.
    exit(-1);
  }
  lvl = atol(argv[1]);
  sprintf(filename, "Curve_%ld_params.dat", lvl);
  mpz_inits(prm, base.order, NULL);
  parm = fopen(filename, "r");
  if(!parm)
  {                                                    Get data file;
    printf("can't find file %s\n", filename);          else complains.
    exit(-2);
  }
  bufr = (char*)malloc(1024*4);
  i = 0;
  while(((!feof(parm)) && (i < 1024))
  {                                                    Read in
    bufr[i] = fgetc(parm);                             whole file
    i++;                                               to buffer.
  }
  fclose(parm);
```
Convert text to big numbers.
```
  i = skipln(bufr, 0, 1);
  gmp_sscanf(&bufr[i], "%Zx", prm);     Field prime
  gmp_printf("%Zd\n", prm);             initialized
  minit(prm);
  i = skipln(bufr, i, 2);
  gmp_sscanf(&bufr[i], "%Zx", base.order);     Base point
  gmp_printf("%Zd\n", base.order);             order and
  i = skipln(bufr, i, 2);                       cofactor initialized
  sscanf(&bufr[i], "%ld", &base.cofactor);
  i = skipln(bufr, i, 2);
  curve_init(&base.E);                                     Curve parameters
  gmp_sscanf(&bufr[i], "%Zx %Zx", base.E.a4, base.E.a6);   initialized
  gmp_printf("E: %Zx  %Zx\n", base.E.a4, base.E.a6);
  i = skipln(bufr, i, 3);
  point_init(&base.Base);                                          Base point
  gmp_sscanf(&bufr[i], "%Zx %Zx", base.Base.x, base.Base.y);       initialized
  point_printf("Base point: ", base.Base);
```

The next step is common to both Diffie-Helmann and MQV. The private key is created using a pass phrase. This code is shown in the following listing. I then create "the other side's" keys using random numbers.

Listing 4.14 Key exchange test code: Secret key generation

```
printf("Input pass phrase to generate secret key: ");
fflush(stdout);
i = 1024;                                          Read in
getline(&bufr, (size_t*)&i, stdin);                key phrase.
mpz_init(sk);
point_init(&Pk);
gen_key(sk, &Pk, bufr, base);  ← Convert phrase to public, private key.
gmp_printf("secret key: %Zx\n", sk);
point_printf("Public key: ", Pk);

mpz_init(sok);
point_init(&Pok);                                  Random data for "other side" key
sprintf(bufr,
"Secret Key Test For Other Side 157  164 218 149 124 108 253 26 40 ");

gen_key(sok, &Pok, bufr, base);  ← Convert random data to public, private key.
point_printf("Other side Public key: ", Pok);
```

The "o" in sok and Pok is for "other side."

4.3.2 *Diffie-Hellman test routines*

This section describes the test code to simulate Diffie-Hellman key exchange. With the secret and public keys generated for each side, we can now call the Diffie-Hellman routine to see that both sides get the same shared secret. The communications can't be done in this test, but we can ensure the math works.

Listing 4.15 shows how both sides calculate the same thing. "My side" uses the secret key created from the pass phrase and the "other" side's public key. "Their side" uses their randomly generated secret key and the "my side" public key. We then check to see whether the results match.

Listing 4.15 Key exchange test code: Diffie-Hellman

```
mpz_inits(myshare, theirshare, NULL);
diffie_hellman(myshare, sk, Pok, base.E);     Swap private and public keys
diffie_hellman(theirshare, sok, Pk, base.E);  for each side.
if(!mpz_cmp(myshare, theirshare))
  printf("Keys match.\n");
else
  printf("Keys DON'T match!\n");  ← Go find bugs!
gmp_printf("my keyshare:    %Zx\n", myshare);
gmp_printf("their keyshare: %Zx\n", theirshare);
```

Here's an example run with 256-bit security:

```
./base_test 256
⋮
Input pass phrase to generate secret key: this is another test
⋮
Keys match.
my keyshare:    df6363311da84770ea7779d9d2bf3991fc41548347041af34dcbb71b6abe
⮑ 72cf
their keyshare: df6363311da84770ea7779d9d2bf3991fc41548347041af34dcbb71b6abe
⮑ 72cf
```

4.3.3 MQV test routine

This section shows a simulation of the MQV key exchange code. Once we have static keys for a Diffie-Hellman-type exchange, we can easily generate ephemeral keys using a random number generator. This process is shown in the following listing.

Listing 4.16   Key exchange test code: MQV ephemeral keys

Generate a random secret and public keys for the MQV test.
```
    mpz_inits(myrand, theirrand, NULL);
    point_init(&Rk);                        Initialize
    point_init(&Rok);                       ram space.
    mqv_ephem(myrand, &Rk, base);       Create
    mqv_ephem(theirrand, &Rok, base);   random keys.
```

The last part of the MQV test is to compute each side's shared secret, as shown in listing 4.17. Each side only has to call the `mqv_share()` function once. But for this test, we want to see that both sides actually do get the same value, so the routine is called twice.

Listing 4.17   Key exchange test code: MQV full shared secret

Each side sends the other the public key and then computes the shared secret.
```
    mqv_share(myshare, sk, Pk, myrand, Rk, Pok, Rok, base);  ← "My side" key

    mqv_share(theirshare, sok, Pok, theirrand, Rok, Pk, Rk, base);  "Their side"
                                                                     key
    if(!mpz_cmp(myshare, theirshare))
      printf("MQV Keys match.\n");
    else
      printf("MQV Keys DON'T match!\n");  ← Go find bugs!
    gmp_printf("my keyshare:    %Zx\n", myshare);
    gmp_printf("their keyshare: %Zx\n", theirshare);
```

The output from the same 256-bit test is as follows:

```
MQV Keys match.
my keyshare:    9a2b4135e9e39f0daf8aa49a37d22ee551c96a3e6bf0f2c7e6056782d7a8
```

➡️ 166c
their keyshare: 9a2b4135e9e39f0daf8aa49a37d22ee551c96a3e6bf0f2c7e6056782d7a8
➡️ 166c

Answers to exercises

1 No. Clare's public key is $C = k_C G$, which can only be used to create two secret keys. One between Clare and Bob is $k_C B$, and the secret between Clare and Alice is $k_C A$.

2 Two. The value s_A in an integer modulo a prime. The value U_B has one point multiplication. The secret is found using $s_A U_B$, which is the second point multiplication.

Summary

- In elliptic curve key exchange, both sides compute the same point and use the x value for the shared secret.
- Diffie-Hellman uses one person's private key and another person's public key to create a shared secret key. The secret key is used with a standard single-key encryption algorithm.
- A hash function can be used to generate random bits from a text phrase. This creates a private key that does not require storage. The public key, private key pair is always the same for a given curve and base point.
- The Menezes-Qu-Vanstone (MQV) algorithm uses ephemeral private, public keys in addition to the users' static private key, public key pairs to create perfect forward secrecy.
- The NIST version of MQV includes an associate value function that outputs half an x value.
- MQV combines two private keys and two public keys that are multiplied to form a shared secret point. The x value is then used as the shared secret key.
- Once the ephemeral keys are created, they must be communicated between both sides. The actual calculations are quick.

Prime field elliptic curve digital signatures explained

5

In this chapter, I'll describe two algorithms used for digital signatures. A digital signature creates proof of authorship using mathematics. A person's private key is used along with a hash of a document to create a signature. The public key can then be used with the local hash of the same document to verify the signature. The connection between a person and their keys can be checked with key exchange methods or certificates in a database. Here we assume that a private key, public key pair only applies to one person, and their signature can be verified or rejected depending on whether they actually digitally signed a document.

A digital signature is usually attached to a digital document as part of the same file. The file header explains where the different parts of a document reside within the file. A way to find the public key for the signer should also be in the file. If the public key is attached to the file, you would still have to verify that the public key was real and not faked. This is where security becomes an independent issue from cryptography, and it is important to get it right in real-world applications.

Two methods of digital signature will be discussed in detail here:

- Schnorr signature
- NIST elliptic curve digital signature algorithm (ECDSA)

The Schnorr signature algorithm is short and concise. The ECDSA algorithm is a bit more involved. The Schnorr algorithm hashes the combination of a document with a point and verifies using that point. ECDSA goes through more math and outputs two values. Those values are used along with public points to do the verification. Schnorr requires more space to hold the data than ECDSA but takes a touch less time to compute. Each has a place depending on circumstances.

5.1 Schnorr digital signature

In this section, the Schnorr digital signature over elliptic curves is explained. The original version of the Schnorr digital signature scheme is over exponentials of numbers modulo a prime. By modifying it for use on elliptic curves, we can increase security and decrease the size of the primes. Fewer resources required implies a lower cost.

5.1.1 Schnorr elliptic curve math

This section describes the mathematics used to compute the Schnorr digital signature. Figure 5.1 shows the similarity between the Schnorr algorithm and the key exchange algorithms described in chapter 4. A (public key, private key) pair is generated over a secure curve. We'll take the private key to be s_p and the curve to be the same as equation 3.1 reproduced here

$$y^2 = x^3 + a_4 x + a_6$$

with base point B, which has prime order n. Then the public key is

$$P_p = s_p B$$

The capital P represents the public key, the lower case s represents the private key, and the subscript $_p$ represents the person to whom the key belongs.

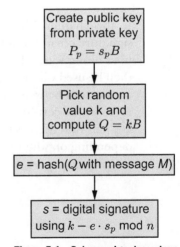

Figure 5.1 Schnorr signature steps

Create public key from private key
$P_p = s_p B$

Pick random value k and compute $Q = kB$

e = hash(Q with message M)

s = digital signature using $k - e \cdot s_p \bmod n$

The generation of a signature begins by choosing a random value k in the range of the order of the base point $\{1 \cdots n - 1\}$. For security, it's advisable to choose a new k for each signature. Once a signature is created, the value of k can be forgotten. Low Hamming weight (i.e., only a few bits set) for k is discouraged. For example, a value of k like 0x000A0008000050001 would be a poor choice, as would 0xFFFF5FFFA-FFFF7FFFE. If the number of bits set is about half the number of bits in the field size, it has maximal security.

A new public point is computed using

$$Q = kB$$

The document M is concatenated with the point Q and then hashed to a value that is the order of the base point. As shown in equation 5.1, we write this as

$$e = \text{hash}(Q.x \| Q.y \| M) \bmod n \tag{5.1}$$

The symbol $\|$ means to place the bit strings in sequence. Because it is a hash, the endianness does not matter so long as all implementations are consistent.

This value is combined with the random value k and the private key s_p using

$$s = k - e \cdot s_p \bmod n$$

The signature is then the point Q and the value s.

To verify that the document M actually was signed by public key P_p, the verifier has to compute e as in equation 5.1 and then, in equation 5.2, check that

$$Q \overset{?}{=} sB + eP_p \tag{5.2}$$

If it doesn't match, the signature is rejected.

To see why this works, put the expanded value of s into equation 5.2. Multiply through with B to get

$$kB - e \cdot s_p B + eP_p$$

Since $P_p = s_p B$, the last two terms cancel, and the result matches.

Exercise 5.1

In equation 5.2, how many times does the random value k appear? (Hint: twice in equation 5.1.)

5.1.2 *Schnorr sign subroutine*

The Schnorr digital signature subroutine is described in this section. Since digital signatures use multiple components, it makes sense to create a structure to hold both of them. The following listing shows the structure I used for Schnorr signatures.

Listing 5.1 Schnorr structure

```
typedef struct
{
  POINT Q;
  mpz_t s;
}SCHNORR;
```

The tricky part of the Schnorr routine is converting the x and y components into bytes. Leaving NULL bytes can lead to problems if different machines have different word sizes. Listing 5.2 shows how I solve this using the mpz_sizeinbase() with size 16, which counts nibbles. Dividing that by 2 gives the correct number of bytes for each component. In a way, it is kind of silly because I then multiply by 2 again to create space for each component. But this way, it is clear what is going on. The extra 2 bytes in the malloc call are to prevent accidents from happening.

Listing 5.2 Schnorr sign

```
void schnorr_sign(SCHNORR *sig, mpz_t sk, POINT Pk,
                  unsigned char *msg, long len, BASE_SYSTEM base)
{
  mpz_t k, e, tmp;
  unsigned char *cat;
  int xsz, i;

  mpz_inits(e, k, tmp, NULL);
  mrand(k);                                          │ Random number
  elptic_mul(&sig->Q, base.Base, k, base.E);         │ point for signature
  xsz = (mpz_sizeinbase(sig->Q.x, 16) + 1)/2;  ← Get number of bytes.
  cat = (unsigned char*)malloc(len + 2*xsz + 2);        │ Convert
  mpz_export(cat, NULL, -1, 1, 0, 0, sig->Q.x);         │ x and y
  mpz_export(&cat[xsz], NULL, -1, 1, 0, 0, sig->Q.y);   │ to strings.
  for(i=0; i<len; i++)
     cat[2*xsz + i] = msg[i];  ←── Add document to string buffer.
  hash(e, cat, len+2*xsz, base.order);          │
  mod_mul(tmp, sk, e, base.order);              │ s = k − e · s_k mod n
  mod_sub(sig->s, k, tmp, base.order);          │
  mpz_clears(e, k, tmp, NULL);
}
```

The function mpz_export() is used to convert a large integer into a string of bytes. The first argument is the buffer where the bytes are placed. The second argument is the output number of words, which we don't need, so this is simply NULL. The next two arguments are order and size. order = −1 means little endian, size = 1 means use byte size values. The next two zeros are not used because we are using bytes for output (these values deal with multibyte results). The last argument is the large integer input in GMP format.

Note the message is placed after the x and y components in the cat buffer. Once everything is in place, the hash() function is called, and the s component of the signature is computed.

5.1.3 *Schnorr verify subroutine*

The Schnorr digital verification subroutine is described in this section. In listing 5.3, we are going to assume the document and signature data are already separated. In addition, we are going to assume that the public key of the signer has been acquired securely. The verify routine is similar to the sign routine because the hash of the point Q with the message is the same process. The following listing shows the verify subroutine.

> **Listing 5.3 Schnorr verify**

```
int schnorr_verify(SCHNORR sig, POINT Pk, unsigned char *msg,
                   long len, BASE_SYSTEM base)
{
  mpz_t e;
  unsigned char *cat;
  int xsz, i;
  POINT U, V, Qck;

  mpz_init(e);
  xsz = (mpz_sizeinbase(sig.Q.x, 16) + 1)/2;      ← Get number of bytes.
  cat = (unsigned char*)malloc(len + 2*xsz + 2);      ┐ Convert
  mpz_export(cat, NULL, -1, 1, 0, 0, sig.Q.x);        │ x and y
  mpz_export(&cat[xsz], NULL, -1, 1, 0, 0, sig.Q.y);  ┘ to strings.
  for(i=0; i<len; i++)
     cat[2*xsz + i] = msg[i];   ◄── Add document to string buffer.
  hash(e, cat, len+2*xsz, base.order);
  point_init(&U);                 ↑
  point_init(&V);                 │ Compute hash.
  point_init(&Qck);
  elptic_mul(&U, base.Base, sig.s, base.E);      ┐ Q' = sB + ePk
  elptic_mul(&V, Pk, e, base.E);                 │
  elptic_sum(&Qck, U, V, base.E);                ┘
                        │ Verify computed Q matches
                        ↓ signature Q.
  if((!mpz_cmp(sig.Q.x, Qck.x)) && (!mpz_cmp(sig.Q.y, Qck.y)))
     i = 1;                  ┐ Save verify
  else                       │ result so we
     i = 0;                  │ can clear
  mpz_clear(e);              ┘ variables.
  point_clear(&U);
  point_clear(&V);
  point_clear(&Qck);
  return i;
}
```

The computation of e is clearly the same as the signature routine. Then I use three points to build the check. The first point is

$$U = sB$$

the second point is

$$V = eP_k$$

and the checkpoint is their sum

$$Q_{ck} = U + V$$

If both the x and y components match between the checkpoint Q_{ck} and input signature point Q, the signature is verified.

5.1.4   *Schnorr test example*

A simulated example of how to use the Schnorr digital signature and verify routines is described in this section. I added the Schnorr test code to the file with key exchange testing from chapter 4. To perform this test, I searched my drive for a text file that was reasonably small. I copied it over to my working directory as `sign_test.txt`. The following listing shows how I read in the sample.

Listing 5.4   Test message input

Now create a test
for a digital signature.

```
parm = fopen("sign_test.txt", "r");
if(!parm)
{
    printf("sign_test.txt not found??\n");     Always check
    exit(-7);                                   for errors.
}
k=0;
while((!feof(parm)) && (k < 4*1024))
{
    bufr[k] = fgetc(parm);                      Read document
    k++;                                        into RAM.
}
k -= 2;
```

Using the same public and private keys generated during the test shown in listing 4.14 and the curve parameters from listings 4.8 to 4.11, the Schnorr algorithm test is very simple as shown in the following listing. Subroutine `snr_init()` is given in listing 5.6.

Listing 5.5   Schnorr test

```
snr_init(&snr);
schnorr_sign(&snr, sk, Pk, bufr, k, base);  ← Schnorr signature document
```

```
if(schnorr_verify(snr, Pk, bufr, k, base))  ← Verify the signature.
  printf("Schnorr message verifies!\n");
else
  printf("Schnorr message does not match original signed.\n");  │ Go look
                                                                 │ for bugs!
```

When run with any of the curves, the output every time is `Schnorr message verifies!` The trick to signatures is making sure the message is the same every time. Even one bit wrong will cause the verify to fail. Packaging the message is a system-level problem.

Listing 5.6 Schnorr initialization

```
void snr_init(SCHNORR *sig)
{
    point_init(&sig->Q);    ← Initialize random value point.
    mpz_init(sig->s);       ← Initialize computed signature.
}
```

5.2   NIST elliptic curve digital signature algorithm

In this section, the NIST ECDSA is explained. It is similar to Schnorr in that a hash of the message is used. I'll follow the standard NIST (2023), which has a ton of details not included here. Figure 5.2 shows the steps involved in computing the signature.

The first step in computing the signature is to compute the hash of the message and convert that to a value modulo the order of the base point n. This is the hash function described in listing 4.1, so, for equation 5.3, we take

$$e = \text{hash}(M) \bmod n \qquad (5.3)$$

The second step is to pick a random number k (mod n) and compute the point

$$R = kB$$

The x component is the size of the field prime, so, in equation 5.4, we convert it to the order of the base point using

$$c = R.x \bmod n \qquad (5.4)$$

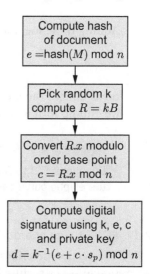

Figure 5.2   ECDSA signature steps

Assuming the signer's private key is s_p and their public key is $P_p = s_p B$, in equation 5.5, we finally compute

$$d = k^{-1}(e + c \cdot s_p) \bmod n \qquad (5.5)$$

The signature is then the pair of values (c, d).

To verify the signature, the hash of the document is done the same as in equation 5.3 to find the value e'. Then, as shown in equations 5.6 to 5.8, we compute

$$h = d^{-1} \bmod n \tag{5.6}$$

$$h_1 = e'h \bmod n \tag{5.7}$$

$$h_2 = ch \bmod n \tag{5.8}$$

From these values, in equation 5.9, we find the point

$$R' = h_1 B + h_2 P_p \tag{5.9}$$

and then check that

$$R'.x \overset{?}{=} c$$

So let's see how this works. Expanding h, we have

$$h = \frac{k}{(e + c \cdot s_p)}$$

The first term in R' is

$$h_1 B = e' \cdot hB = \frac{e' \cdot kB}{(e + c \cdot s_p)}$$

The second term is

$$h_2 P_p = c \cdot h \Gamma_p - \frac{c \cdot k \cdot s_p B}{(e + c \cdot s_p)}$$

Adding these together we have

$$R' = k \frac{e' + c \cdot s_p}{e + c \cdot s_p} B$$

So as long as the message has not been altered, $e' = e$, the fraction divides out, and we end up with $R' = R$, which implies $R'.x = c$.

> **Exercise 5.2**
>
> Equations 5.3 to 5.8 are all modulo n. Is n the field prime or the largest prime in the elliptic curve cardinality?

5.2.1 ECDSA sign subroutine

This section describes the code that implements ECDSA signatures. Like the Schnorr signature, a structure for the ECDSA signature is very useful. The structure is shown in listing 5.7 where the c value is from equation 5.4, and the d value is from equation 5.5.

Listing 5.7   ECDSA structure

```
typedef struct
{
    mpz_t c;
```

```
    mpz_t d;
}ECDSA;
```

Listing 5.8 shows the signing subroutine. The inputs are private and public keys, the message and its length, and system parameters (the `BASE_SYSTEM` structure, as shown in listing 4.2).

Listing 5.8   ECDSA signing subroutine

```
void ecdsa_sign(ECDSA *sig, mpz_t sk, POINT Pk,
                unsigned char *msg, long len, BASE_SYSTEM base)
{
  mpz_t k, e, tmp;
  POINT R;

  mpz_inits(e, k, tmp, NULL);
  hash(e, msg, len, base.order);
  mrand(k);
  point_init(&R);
  elptic_mul(&R, base.Base, k, base.E);
  mpz_mod(sig->c, R.x, base.order);
  mod_mul(tmp, sk, sig->c, base.order);
  mod_add(tmp, tmp, e, base.order);
  mod_div(sig->d, tmp, k, base.order);
  point_clear(&R);
  mpz_clears(e, k, tmp, NULL);
}
```

Annotations:
- `e = hash of document` — points to `hash(e, msg, len, base.order);`
- `Random value and matching point` — points to `mrand(k);` ... `elptic_mul(...)`
- $c = R.x \bmod n$ — points to `mpz_mod(sig->c, R.x, base.order);`
- $d = \dfrac{e + s_p c}{k}$ — points to the `mod_mul` / `mod_add` / `mod_div` block

Since the modulo arithmetic is done on the order of the base point, the `mod_*()` routines are used instead of the `m*()` routines. Because the `mod_div()` routine computes the inverse for us, there is no need to compute it separately. I just divide by $k \bmod n$.

5.2.2   *ECDSA verify subroutine*

The ECDSA verify routine is described in this section. The verification routine for ECDSA is a straightforward calculation of equations 5.6 through 5.9. Like Schnorr, this routine evaluates two points and then sums them to get the final point used to check the signature.

Listing 5.9   ECDSA verify subroutine

```
int ecdsa_verify(ECDSA sig, POINT Pk, unsigned char *msg, long len,
                 BASE_SYSTEM base)
{
  mpz_t h, h1, h2, e;
  POINT R, S, T;
  int rtn;

  mpz_inits(h, h1, h2, e, NULL);
  hash(e, msg, len, base.order);
```

Annotations:
- $e = $ **hash of message** — points to `hash(e, msg, len, base.order);`

```
mpz_invert(h, sig.d, base.order);  ⟵——— h = 1/d
mod_mul(h1, e, h, base.order);  ⟵ h₁ = eh
mod_mul(h2, sig.c, h, base.order);  ⟵ h₂ = ch
point_init(&T);
elptic_mul(&T, Pk, h2, base.E);
point_init(&S);
elptic_mul(&S, base.Base, h1, base.E);  R = h₁B + h₂Pₖ
point_init(&R);
elptic_sum(&R, T, S, base.E);
mpz_mod(h, R.x, base.order);  ⟵ Convert R.x mod n.
if(!mpz_cmp(h, sig.c))       Save verify
    rtn = 1;                 result so we
else                         can clear
    rtn = 0;                 variables.
point_clear(&R);
point_clear(&S);
point_clear(&T);
mpz_clears(h, h1, h2, e, NULL);
return rtn;
}
```

As with the Schnorr algorithm, the message must not change at all between signing and verifying. The main difference between ECDSA and Schnorr is that the latter uses a full point for comparison. With ECDSA, we must reduce the field element from a point to the order of the curve. The advantage of ECDSA is the size of the signature is two `mpz_t` elements, with Schnorr signature taking up three.

5.2.3   *ECDSA example code*

This section shows a simulated ECDSA sign and verify test routine. The test of the subroutines uses the same key generation as the previous tests and the same message text in the Schnorr example. Listings 4.8 to 4.11 have the base system data, which is selected as shown in listing 4.13. The following listing shows how to call the signing subroutine using these same arguments.

> **Listing 5.10   ECDSA signing example**

```
sig_init(&sig);
ecdsa_sign(&sig, sk, Pk, bufr, k, base);  ⟵ Sign message with private key.
```

Similarly, the verification is really simple, as shown in the following listing.

> **Listing 5.11   ECDSA verify example**

```
if(ecdsa_verify(sig, Pk, bufr, k, base))   Verify signature with message
                                           and public key.
    printf("message verifies!\n");
else
    printf("message does not match original signed.\n");  ⟵ Go look for bugs!
```

Running this test with every one of the example curves and some arbitrary pass phrase with the same test file used in the Schnorr example gives the same output `message verifies!`

Answers to exercises

1 Six times! The values $Q.x$ and $Q.y$ in equation 5.1 each count for one k appearance. s contains one direct value of k plus two from e. So there are five appearances of k on the left of equation 5.2 and one on the right for a total of six.

2 The value n is the largest prime in the elliptic curve cardinality. This is chosen as the order of the base point to maximize security.

Summary

- Schnorr digital signature combines a random value times a base point (called Q) with a document and computes the hash of the combination.
- With the Schnorr digital signature, the signer's private key is combined with the hash value and random value to create the other part of the signature.
- Verification of Schnorr uses the signer's public key with the signature to check for a match. Since this requires a hash of the point Q and document, even one bit difference will fail.
- NIST (2023) created a standard for the elliptic curve digital signature algorithm (ECDSA). ECDSA uses the hash of a message, a random value, and the signer's private key to create one value of the signature. The x component of the random value times the base point is the second value.
- To verify with ECDSA, several calculations are combined with the hash of the document and the signature. These values are multiplied by the base point and the signer's public key whose sum is then compared with a signature value. A match verifies and one bit error will fail.

Finding good cryptographic elliptic curves

This chapter covers

- Using PARI/gp command line
- PARI library programming
- A program to find the number of points on an elliptic curve
- What constitutes a good curve

In this chapter, I'll show you how to find good cryptographic curves using mathematicians' software tools. At the end of this chapter, I'll go over what "bad" and "good" mean for cryptography. The ability to find and use many different cryptographically secure curves increases security by forcing attackers to work hard to find breaks on every possible curve. The resulting curves are good for the applications in chapters 4 and 5.

Up to this point, we have assumed we know the cardinality of a curve (see section 4.1.1). Unfortunately, the mathematics of computing the number of points on an elliptic curve over finite fields is really deep. For those who want to dig into the details, I suggest starting with chapter VII in Blake et al. (1999). For this chapter, I am just going to use the mathematician's tool PARI/gp, which has the point-counting algorithms built in. In addition, the authors of PARI/gp have optimized their point-counting algorithms for efficiency.

Appendix A describes how to get hold of PARI/gp. For those who are skilled with Python, you can get SageMath, which has PARI as just one of the options available.

PARI/gp has many mathematical tools. We only care about a small but very important subset of those tools related to elliptic curve mathematics. I will describe the important mathematics and then explain how PARI/gp allows us to compute elliptic curve cardinalities.

6.1 PARI/gp for elliptic curves

In this section, I'll describe the mathematicians' tool PARI/gp. It is very useful for checking elliptic curve code. Before getting into the programming details, I am going to introduce the interactive use of the PARI/gp tool. The startup and how to set up elliptic curves over finite fields is described first. This is exceptionally useful for debugging code. You can find mistakes in code computations by duplicating programming steps using copy and paste entries from print_point() subroutines into PARI/gp.

The programming side of PARI using libpari will also be explained. This is what I use to find good curves. The method I used to eliminate poor curves will be explained, and then the actual code to accomplish the task of finding good curves follows.

6.1.1 Starting PARI/gp

In this section, I'll cover the startup of PARI/gp. The program gp is a mathematics calculator with elliptic curve functions, including finding the cardinality of curves and the order of points. When we first start gp, we get output that looks like this:

```
$ gp
Reading GPRC: /home/drmike/.gprc
GPRC Done.

    ⋮

PARI/GP is free software, covered by the GNU General Public License, and
comes WITHOUT ANY WARRANTY WHATSOEVER.

Type ? for help, \q to quit.
Type ?18 for how to get moral (and possibly technical) support.

PARIsizemax = 10000003072, primelimit = 500000
?
```

The line about "moral (and possibly technical) support" is very real. I have asked many stupid questions on the PARI mailing list and gotten a lot of very helpful answers. The ? is the gp prompt.

The file .gprc is used to set up the PARI environment, which is different from the default. In this case, the .gprc file I use is simply

```
PARIsizemax = 10000000000
read "PARI/funcs.gp";
```

The first line sets the heap to 10 GB, which on a 64 GB machine is reasonable. The second line reads in a predefined function that I find useful. That file is simply

```
numbits(x)={floor(log(x)/log(2))+1}
```

which tells me how many bits are in a value x. When looking at a 50-digit number, it is nicer to let PARI tell you how many bits it has.

6.1.2   *PARI/gp elliptic curves over finite fields*

In this section, I'll describe how PARI/gp works with finite field elliptic curves. There is one function that is particularly useful, which has finite field inputs and outputs its own ell structure.

PARI/gp has a function for creating elliptic curves using just a_4 and a_6. The function is ellinit() whose first argument is a single vector input [a_4, a_6]. The brackets [ ] are not optional because they tell gp that items contained within are components of a vector.

The second argument to ellinit() is the field. For the moment, this will be a prime number, which is the finite field we are using. This will be something more complicated when we dive into field extensions. The manual says, "The precise layout of the ell structure is left undefined and should never be used directly." They do define the first thirteen values as the common elliptic curve parameters

$$a_1, a_2, a_3, a_4, a_6, b_2, b_4, b_6, b_8, c_4, c_6, \Delta, j$$

which you can find described (in the same order) in section III.1 of Silverman (2009). If the output we see is [] (referred to as "null"), it means no curve can be constructed with the given inputs.

Since we are working with finite fields, there are several automatic values that PARI has access to when an ell structure is created. These are

- .no—The number of points on the curve
- .cyc—The cyclic structure of the curve
- .gen—The generators of the curve
- .group—The first three items as a vector [.no, .cyc, .gen]

As a simple example, let's look at a curve over the field $p = 1187$. I pick $a_4 = 1$ and $a_6 = 17$. gp gives the result:

```
? E=ellinit([1, 17], 1187)
%1 = [Mod(0, 1187), Mod(0, 1187), Mod(0, 1187), Mod(1, 1187), Mod(17, 1187),
     Mod(0, 1187), Mod(2, 1187), Mod(68, 1187), Mod(1186, 1187), Mod(1139,
     1187), Mod(743, 1187), Mod(910, 1187), Mod(95, 1187), Vecsmall([3]),
     [1187, [109, 236, [6, 0, 0, 0]]], [0, 0, 0, 0]]
```

I then request the entire group information:

```
? E.group
%2 = [1148, [1148], [[Mod(702, 1187), Mod(1007, 1187)]]]
```

This tells me that there are 1148 points on the curve, it is a simple cyclic curve (in chapter 15, we will see why this is "simple"), and it has a point which can generate all other points on the curve (702, 1007). The form Mod(702, 1187) means "702 modulo 1187," which is how PARI tracks a finite field number.

> **Exercise 6.1**
>
> How many points are on the curve $y^2 = x^3 + x + 97$ mod 95289871302753755165078 396311?

6.1.3 *Libpari with elliptic curves*

In this section, I'll show how to use PARI library subroutines with C programming. While it is possible to write scripts in PARI/gp, I find it easier to link directly with the PARI library, which is called libpari. The code initialization process is a touch different from the interactive command-line program.

To initialize libpari, we first specify the stack size and number of primes to precompute. In my code examples, I use

```
pari_init(1024*1024*1024, 5*1024*512);
```

which gives 1 GB of stack and 2.5 million primes.

Libpari uses the type GEN, which is a pointer to a set of longs. Internally, it knows what each GEN object is. If you give a routine the wrong kind of object, libpari will bail with an error. The debugging process is to first find the place where the error occurred and then attempt to figure out which argument was wrong.

The first 10 lines of listing 6.1 give an example of the C code initialization. Appendix A explains how to use PARIlib's Makefile for compiling your code.

6.2 *General ordinary curves*

In this section, I'll describe an algorithm to find the number of points on an elliptic curve to determine whether it is cryptographically useful. Equation 6.1 is the general equation for an ordinary elliptic curve over a large prime field:

$$E : y^2 = x^3 + a_4 x + a_6 \bmod p \tag{6.1}$$

Choosing a_4 and a_6 at random will give us a random curve. Many curves are isomorphic, which means they have the same number of points. For cryptographic purposes, we want the same points for each user, but we don't really care which curve we pick so long as the cardinality of the curve is a large prime.

The relationship between the field p and the cardinality $\#E$ is given by Hasse's theorem, shown in equation 6.2:

$$\#E = p + 1 - t \tag{6.2}$$

where the value of t is limited by equation 6.3

$$|t| \leq 2\sqrt{p} \tag{6.3}$$

(See chapter V in Silverman, 2009.) This is an important relationship between cardinality and the field prime. If we can find a negative t, which is odd, the cardinality might be a prime, which would be larger than the field. Since t has half as many bits as p, the cardinality is still the same bit size as p. The variable t is called the trace of Frobenius.

Figure 6.1 shows the generic algorithm for seeking good curves. The box $f = \#E$ represents PARI computing the cardinality. Then powers of 2 are removed one at a time until an odd number is found for f. The algorithm for accept or reject is shown in figure 6.2. An accepted curve is output; a rejected curve is ignored. Either way, the next curve is investigated by incrementing the a_6 value.

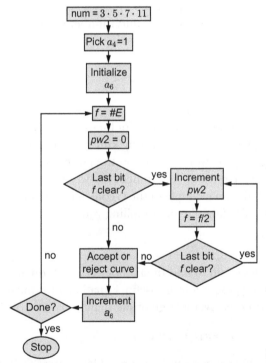

Figure 6.1   General curve-finding algorithm

My first requirement was to find curves with very small cofactors. So I created a number with the factors $3 \cdot 5 \cdot 7 \cdot 11$ (figure 6.1) and used the gcdii() function (figure 6.2) to test whether any of those primes were present in the cardinality.

If $\#E$ has too many primes, I want to ignore the curve. Figure 6.2 shows a flow chart of the logic. If the cardinality only has powers of 2, which I track with variable $pw2$, and a remaining prime, then I output it. If the cardinality is not prime and there are no small factors after removing 2^{pw2}, the number can be ignored because the factors are not good enough for a secure curve.

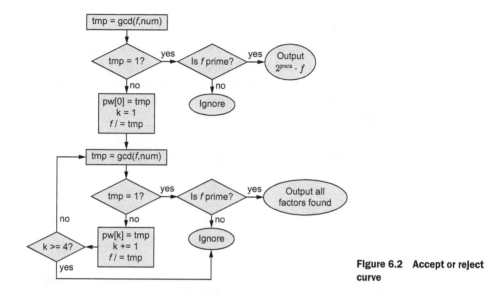

Figure 6.2 Accept or reject curve

Small factors are then removed one power at a time. The pw[] holds each set of removed factors. As long as the array length is less than four and we find a prime, then all factors are output. Otherwise, the number is ignored because it does not have a large enough prime factor to use. To create the elliptic curve parameters in listings 4.8 to 4.11, I modified one program into four separate versions so I could run them simultaneously on one desktop. The smaller primes gave a lot more results to choose from after an overnight run.

The primes used for the base field were taken from Riesel (2013). I used the table Primes of the Form: $h \cdot 2^n + 1$ and looked for field sizes close to 160, 256, 384, and 512 with as small an h as I could get. Table 6.1 shows the values chosen. The average density of good curves is about the same for every field prime. If you find a prime that is more useful for faster base field operations, you will most likely find just as many good curves as these choices provided.

Table 6.1 Primes for base field

field size	prime number
160	$43 \cdot 2^{158} + 1$
256	$43 \cdot 2^{252} + 1$
384	$23 \cdot 2^{381} + 1$
512	$113 \cdot 2^{509} + 1$

Exercise 6.2

In the curve of excercise 6.1, what is the value t from equation 6.2?

6.2.1 *Variables and initialization*

In this section, the initial code to find good curves is presented. Listing 6.1 shows the start of the program used to find 160 bit curves. The constant z is the first entry from table 6.1. The `ellinit()` library function in libpari requires a vector with five values. For general elliptic curves, this makes sense. For ordinary curves over large prime finite fields, only two values are required.

Listing 6.1 Finding curves: Initialize

```
int main()
{
  GEN y, E, f, z, a1, a3, a2, ell5, num, tmp;
  int k, pw2, pw[4];
  unsigned long a4coef, a6coef;
  PARI_sp av;

  PARI_init(1024*1024*1024, 5*1024*512);    │ Initialize PARI and finite field.
  z = gp_read_str("0xac000000000000000000000000000000000000001");
  y = ffgen(z, -1);    ← Create FFELT GEN object.
                             Hex value 43 · 2^158 + 1 ↑
  a1 = gen_0; │ constant 0
  a3 = gen_0; │ for unused
  a2 = gen_0; │ values
  ell5 = zerovec( 5);
  gel(ell5, 1) = a1;   │ Initialize
  gel(ell5, 2) = a2;   │ array to
  gel(ell5, 3) = a3;   │ integer values.
  a4coef = 1;      │ Inside loop
  a6coef = 0x01;   │ variables

  num = muluu(3, 5);    │ gcd constant
  num = mului(7, num);  │ num =
  num = mului(11, num); │ 3 · 5 · 7 · 11
```

The three variables `a1`, `a2`, and `a3` are assigned the constant value zero in GEN format. The other PARI constants available are 1 (`gen_1`) and 2 (`gen_2`). The `ell5` variable is set up to be a length 5 vector whose first three values are all zero. The names of the variables are there simply to remind me what those index positions stand for in the general elliptic curve equation.

Originally, I had changed the `a4coef` as part of the sweep of curves. But this was pointless because the curves were isomorphic to all the others found with $a_4 = 1$. The last part of the initialize is to create the constant with the four small primes $3 \cdot 5 \cdot 7 \cdot 11$.

6.2.2 Main loop

In this section, code for deciding to keep or reject a curve is described. The search for good curves requires calling the `ellinit()` function and then getting the cardinality of the curve. I then want to find the factors of the cardinality to determine whether there is a very large prime. The first factor to eliminate is powers of 2. Using the `bittst()` function, it is very simple to determine how many factors of 2 are in the cardinality. This is shown in listing 6.2.

The variable `av` marks the PARI stack. Every new variable in a loop increases the stack use. To remove temporary stack variables, the routine `gerepileall()` is called at the bottom of the loop. If you don't do this, the stack will overflow, and an attempted overnight run will only last an hour. More details can be found in the "User's Guide to PARI Library" (see appendix A).

Listing 6.2 Finding curves: Top of main loop

```
while(a6coef < 0xfffff)  ←── Arbitrary limit; reduce for larger primes.
{
  printf("%01x  %01x", a4coef, a6coef);   | Monitor
  fflush(stdout);                         | progress.
  av = avma;        ← Mark top of PARI stack.
  gel(ell5, 4) = stoi(a4coef);   | Convert integers
  gel(ell5, 5) = stoi(a6coef);   | to GEN
  E = ellinit(ell5, y, 0);       | and create curve.

  f = ellcard(E, NULL);  ← Compute cardinality of curve.
  k = bittest(f, 0);
  pw2 = 0;
  while(!k)
  {
                          | Track and
    pw2++;                | remove all
    f = gdivexact(f, gen_2);  | powers of 2.
    k = bittest(f, 0);
  }
```

The `stoi()` function converts a `long` to a PARI GEN. The variable `y` is already specified as a finite field using a prime, as shown in listing 6.1. The result from `ellcard()` is a PARI integer. The loop on `k` removes the powers of 2 if the last bit is a 0 in the cardinality value `f`.

The first seven lines of listing 6.3 show how `gcdii()` is used to test for only powers of 2. If the gcd(f, num) is 1 and f is a prime, then only powers of 2 can be factors of #E. The section of code following the `else` clause then goes on to remove the small factors to determine whether the cardinality is acceptable.

Listing 6.3 Finding curves: Small prime check

```
tmp = gcdii(f, num);
```

```
                                    | If gcd(f, num)==1,
   if(isint1(tmp))                  | then no small factors.
   {
      if(isprime(f))  ← If f is prime ...
         PARI_printf(" 2^%d * %Ps\n", pw2, f); | ... save powers of 2 and prime.
      else
         printf("\n");  | Otherwise, ignore this curve.
   }
   else ← gcd(f, num) != 1
   {
      pw[0] = itos(tmp);  ← Save first group small factors.
      k = 1;
      f = gdivexact(f, tmp);  ← Remove first group small factors.
      while((k < 4) && !isint1(tmp))  | Limit num³ max powers.
      {
         tmp = gcdii(f, num);  | If gcd(f, num)==1,
         if(isint1(tmp))       | then no small factors.
         {
            if(isprime(f))  ← If f is prime ...
            {
               printf(" 2^%d * %d ", pw2, pw[0]);  ← ... save powers of 2 and first group.
               k--;
               while(k)                          | Output:
               {                                 | remaining
                  printf(" * %d ", pw[k]);       | group
                  k--;                           | powers
               }
               PARI_printf(" * %Ps\n", f);  ← Large prime factor
            }
            else
               printf("\n");  | Otherwise, ignore this curve.
         }
         else ← gcd(f, num) != 1
         {
            pw[k] = itos(tmp);            | Save next group
            f = gdivexact(f, tmp);        | and remove
            k++;                          | from cardinality.
         }
      }
      if(k >= 4)
         printf("\n");  ← Hit limit so ignores curve
   }
   gerepileall( av, 1, &ell5);  ← Reduce stack size.
   a6coef++;    ← Go to next curve.
}
printf("all done\n");
```

The variable pw[] counts the powers of each factor discovered from the gcdii()
function. Suppose f has cofactor $3^2 \cdot 5^3$. When I take the gcd, only one power of 3
and 5 will be common. The variable pw[] is four deep because more powers than
four mean I should ignore this curve.

The line `f = gdivexact(f, tmp);` removes one set of small primes from the cardinality. When the `gcdii()` function goes to 1, there are no more small primes. At that point, I can call the function `isprime()` to determine whether the leftover value is a prime. If not, I can ignore this curve.

At the 160-bit level, an overnight run on a 4 GHz processor found over 1,000 curves with a large prime. Of those, over 100 were prime cardinality. At the 512-bit level, with the same timing of an overnight run, only eight worthwhile curves were found, with three having prime cardinality. Table 6.2 lists the cardinality of the largest prime found for each program in hexadecimal notation. All the parameters of each curve are in listings 4.8 to 4.11.

Table 6.2   Cardinality of best curves

160	0xac0000000000000000006543ba11adf8eb6345c77
256	0x2b00000000000000000000000000000002e7f521c85bba055a6e2161b956a47f69
384	0x2e0000000000000000000000000000000000000000000000002275cc5f2f7fcc15352a2c9939
	⇒ 00a851b3a75365a9ac54733
512	0xe20000000000000000000000000000000000000000000000000000000000000000000000007788830d
	⇒ 091dc57e3af7d7bbd15386ee9414602d88d1e6489cd056336922bbf4d

6.3   Bad curves

In this section, the difference between good and bad cryptographic curves is described. What a "good curve" is for cryptography will be a really "bad curve" for factoring large numbers. For cryptography, we require a large prime field for our points to float in. If there are many factors in the cardinality of the curve, there are many combinations of groups each point can belong to. So, the first aspect of a "good curve" for cryptography is that the cardinality has a large prime and small cofactor.

In chapter 13, I will get into the details of field extensions. A field extension takes a prime order field p to some power k, so the size of the field is p^k. The MOV attack on elliptic curve key sharing uses a field extension to map an elliptic curve to a small extension field, which can be manipulated more easily. The attack changes an elliptic curve discrete log problem into an exponential discrete log problem. The former is exponential in the size of the key; the latter is subexponential. For descriptions of this and other methods of solving for the private key from the public key and base point, see chapter V in Blake et al. (1999).

So, even if we have a large prime in the cardinality, having a low field extension would turn it into a "bad curve." Finding the actual value of the field extension is challenging, but all we really care about is that it should be large.

The average field extension on random curves is approximately $\sqrt{p}$. Since $\sqrt{p}$ has more than 80 bits for even the smallest security level, it's classified as "big" for a field extension. All the curves found using the previous program (listings 6.1 to 6.3) were found to have an extension greater than 256. They are immune to the MOV attack.

Other attacks on elliptic curves require a small cofactor. Since the curves chosen here have a cofactor of 1, those attacks can not be performed. Every point on the curve has the same order. While this means there are no shortcuts for computation, there are no handholds for an adversary to attack with.

There are other parameters involved than just the curve. The application environment also is a factor. Is speed really important? If so, then the field prime chosen might create a side channel attack vector. The security of your system depends on thinking about issues other than just cryptography. So, it might take a few overnight runs with many different field primes to find the best curve for your situation. Since you only have to do it once, the time is well worth the effort.

> **Exercise 6.3**
>
> The cardinality of the curve in excercise 6.1 is 97 bits, so it has a possible security level of 46 bits. Is this a good or bad cryptographic curve?

Answers to exercises

1. Using PARI/gp with `F=ellinit([1, 97], 952898713027537551650 78396311)`, type `F.group` to find:

   ```
   %2 = [952898713027532801177785972887, [952898713027532801177785972887]...
   ```

   The cardinality of the curve is thus 952898713027532801177785972887.

2. Rewriting equation 6.2 as $t = p + 1 - \#E$, PARI/gp gives

   ```
   ? 952898713027537551650 78396311 + 1 - 952898713027532801177785972887
   %10 = 475047292423425
   ```

3. This is a bad curve. Using the command `factor(952898713027532801177785972887)`, PARI/gp returns

   ```
   [         61 1]

   [    5151169 1]

   [ 9364883051 1]

   [32382378793 1]
   ```

Summary

- Ordinary elliptic curves over finite fields are defined by the equation

$$E : y^2 = x^3 + a_4 x + a_6 \bmod p$$

and $a_6 \neq 0$.
- The cardinality of an elliptic curve is

$$\#E = p + 1 - t$$

where $|t| < 2\sqrt{p}$ and t is called the trace of Frobenius.
- PARI/gp is both a math calculator and library with an API for computing cardinality and factors of elliptic curves.
- For this book, specific primes are chosen for several security levels. The form is $h \cdot 2^n + 1$.
- Libpari requires specific initialization. Requesting gigabytes helps with very large primes.
- Finding good curves for cryptography demands a small cofactor and one large prime for cardinality. For ordinary curves, demanding a cofactor of 1 is possible and highly recommended for best security.
- Bad curves for cryptography have too low an embedding degree or too many small cofactors. For random ordinary curves, both conditions are avoidable with careful searching.

Part 2

Interlude

In chapters 7 to 12, I'll go into the background subroutines required to implement elliptic curve pairings used in blockchain technology. It is essential to dig through these chapters to understand what is described in chapters 13 to 19.

The pairing of points on an elliptic curve requires the curve to have special properties. The majority of curves covered in part 1 do not have those properties. Our goal is to find pairing-friendly curves and use pairings to create cryptographic protocols. Rather than attempt a direct assault on the concepts of pairings, I'll first cover the mathematics of finite fields over polynomials, also called extension fields.

This mathematical interlude includes discussions on basic polynomials, multiplication of polynomials, taking polynomials to an exponential power, division of polynomials, and computing square roots. All these operations are done modulo a prime polynomial. There is a very real connection between prime numbers and prime polynomials.

An equivalent term for prime polynomial is *irreducible polynomial*. An irreducible polynomial has no other factors than itself and 1. That is why it is similar to a prime number. As we will see in detail during this part, factoring a polynomial depends on the field prime, which is the modulus for the polynomial coefficients.

Since this book describes the code to compute pairings, all the code to compute polynomial functions is listed in chapters 7 to 12. Each chapter builds on the subroutines of the previous chapters. The basic utilities for creating and printing polynomials are in chapter 7, along with how to add two polynomials. Then, chapter 8 discusses how to multiply using an irreducible polynomial as a modulus. The discussion is a bit detailed, but it's important to understand what happens under the hood.

Once we know how to multiply two polynomials, chapter 9 dives into how we can compute powers of a polynomial. Polynomials are cyclic just like prime field values. And one of the routines will show how polynomials are raised to the power of the field prime, which turns out to be a fundamental operation for other routines.

I'll describe Euclidean division modulo a prime polynomial in chapter 10. Following that is the greatest common divisor routine, and then inversion modulo a prime polynomial is explained.

To find irreducible polynomials requires the use of all the routines described in chapters 7 to 10. Using those routines, I'll then go into detail in chapter 11 of how to find irreducible polynomials, which can be used in all the previous chapters. Assuming the use of irreducible polynomials before being able to find them seems a bit circular, but essentially we will look for failure and discard polynomials that don't work.

Chapter 12 goes into the computation of square roots of polynomials modulo a prime polynomial. Polynomial square roots are not a lot different from taking square roots modulo a prime number. Determining whether a polynomial is a quadratic residue requires the use of something called the resultant of two polynomials. Because taking square roots of polynomials is required to find the y value of a point on the curve, the routines here are important for the implementation of elliptic curves over field extensions.

7
Description of finite field polynomial math

This chapter covers

- Essence of field extension is a polynomial
- Routines to create polynomials
- An addition routine for polynomials
- A debugging routine for polynomials

In this chapter, I'll show a simple structure for polynomials and how to add them together. The code developed here is used throughout the rest of the book. Understanding how pairings work on elliptic curves requires the use of field extensions. For an in-depth understanding of field extensions, take a look at chapter 1, section 4 of Lidl and Niederreiter (1997). These are polynomials with finite field coefficients. But they have all the properties of a finite field because there is a fixed number of elements, and they can be added, multiplied, and inverted. The following six chapters are short, so they cover just one aspect of an operation over a field extension. The code to execute the mathematics takes up more text than the mathematical description. Hopefully, it can be easily absorbed so that the code and math associated with elliptic curve pairing operations will then make more sense.

In this chapter, I will cover a polynomial structure, which is much simpler than those used in most mathematics packages. Typical use will be a fixed-sized polynomial, so a general construction is not necessary. A few utility subroutines will be described, along with the addition and subtraction routines.

7.1   Field extension

In this section, the general description of a field extension over a finite field is explained. This concept is essential for the rest of the book. A field extension means we extend a finite field by taking the prime defining the field to a power. So, a field of p elements can become an extension of degree k when we have p^k elements. As an example, suppose $p = 1187$ and $k = 3$. The base field has 1187 elements, and the field extension has $1187^3 = 1672446203$ elements.

Figure 7.1 expands figure 2.2 to show the idea behind a field extension. For a general field extension, any value is allowed for the leading coefficient (modulo the field prime). The polynomial from figure 7.1 is $x^2 - 2x + 4 \bmod 1187$. Counting backward from 0 gives negative values, but we can always change them to positive by adding p (in this case, 1187).

Figure 7.1   Finite field extension over prime numbers viewed as a clock ($p = 1187, k = 3$)

To keep track of each element in the extension field, we want an indexing method. To do that, we choose an arbitrary symbol like t or x and construct a polynomial of powers of that variable. The general form looks like equation 7.1:

$$a_{k-1}x^{k-1} + \cdots + a_1x + a_0 \tag{7.1}$$

In this form, each coefficient is taken modulo p. In our numerical example each coefficient $\{a_0, a_1, a_2\}$ has 1187 possible values, so the total number of indexes is 1187^3. We add two polynomials in a field extension by summing the coefficients of matching powers. Because the coefficients are modulo the field prime, each coefficient stays in the range of the prime, and there is no mixing between powers of the variable. The general form looks like

$$\begin{aligned} a_{k-1}x^{k-1} \cdots + a_1x + a_0 \\ + \quad b_{k-1}x^{k-1} \cdots + b_1x + b_0 \\ \hline c_{k-1}x^{k-1} \cdots + c_1x + c_0 \end{aligned}$$

Subtraction is identical. In fact, since everything is modulo a prime, we end up with positive results in software.

This introduction is missing a lot of important details. I will save these details for chapter 8, so we can concentrate on how to use polynomials in code.

Exercise 7.1

What is the sum of $37x^3 + 96x^2 + 7x + 3$ mod 127 and $14x^2 + 83x + 124$ mod 127?

7.2 Polynomial setup

In this section, polynomial support code is described. It is used in every subroutine for the rest of the book. To use polynomials, I create a simple structure as shown in listing 7.1. The value MAXDEGREE sets the maximum power of field extension I plan on dealing with. The structure gives all polynomials space for the same number of coefficients, even if they are not used. For small embedded systems, this is not efficient. The complexity involved with that efficiency would confuse the purpose of explaining how things work. A web search on "efficient representation of polynomials" will give ideas on sparse vectors and linked lists.

Listing 7.1 Polynomial structure

```
#define MAXDEGREE 32

typedef struct
{
  unsigned long deg;
  mpz_t coef[MAXDEGREE];
}POLY;
```

Because structure 7.1 is used in many places, it is placed in a header file poly.h. All the routines in the file poly.c are also listed as prototypes in the header file. These routines include initialization, clearing, addition, subtraction, and a few utilities, which will be explained here. The header also includes prototypes for the routines, which will be described in chapters 8 to 12. The first routine in file poly.c initializes a structure. This is shown in listing 7.2. The index to the coefficient array matches the power of the variable for the polynomial. So *.coef[4] is the coefficient to x^4.

Listing 7.2 Polynomial initialization

```
void poly_init(POLY *p)
{
  int i;

  for(i=0; i<MAXDEGREE; i++)    Create space for
    mpz_init(p->coef[i]);        every coefficient.
  p->deg = 0;    ← Constant term only
}
```

Creating a polynomial as a variable in a subroutine requires removing it before returning to avoid memory leaks. Listing 7.3 shows the routine that accomplishes this. I used the same syntax as GMP to be both consistent and lazy.

Listing 7.3   Polynomial clearing

```
void poly_clear(POLY *p)
{
  int i;

  for(i=0; i<MAXDEGREE; i++)        │ Remove every
    mpz_clear(p->coef[i]);          │ coefficient created.
}
```

7.3   Polynomial addition

In this section, I'll describe how two polynomials are added. Adding two polynomials is simple. But even simple things get complicated when they are not quite the same. If we have two polynomials of different degrees, the larger one will have coefficients which are copied to the result. So, the following listing first checks to see which input is larger. If they are equal, it picks the first input to define the degree.

Listing 7.4   Polynomial add

```
void poly_add(POLY *c, POLY a, POLY b)
{
  int i, dc;
  POLY rslt;

  poly_init(&rslt);
  if(a.deg > b.deg)
  {                                        │ a bigger than b;
    rslt.deg = a.deg;                      │ copy over higher
    for(dc=a.deg; dc>b.deg; dc--)          │ a coefficients.
      mpz_set(rslt.coef[dc], a.coef[dc]);
  }
  else if(b.deg > a.deg)
  {                                        │ b bigger than a;
    rslt.deg = b.deg;                      │ copy over higher
    for(dc=b.deg; dc>a.deg; dc--)          │ b coefficients.
      mpz_set(rslt.coef[dc], b.coef[dc]);
  }
  else
  {
      dc = a.deg;                          │ Same size;
      rslt.deg = a.deg;                    │ use a to define result.
  }
  while(dc >= 0)
  {
```

```
      madd(rslt.coef[dc], a.coef[dc], b.coef[dc]);   | Add common
      dc--;                                           | powers.
    }
    i = rslt.deg;
    while((i > 0) && (!mpz_cmp_ui(rslt.coef[i], 0)))
    {
      rslt.deg--;   | Remove
      i--;          | leading zeros.
    }
    for(i=0; i<=rslt.deg; i++)                         | Copy result
      mpz_set(c->coef[i], rslt.coef[i]);               | to designated
    c->deg = rslt.deg;                                 | storage.
    poly_clear(&rslt);
}
```

All the coefficients with common powers are then summed modulo the field prime. If higher-degree coefficients go to zero in this process, the degree of the resulting polynomial must be reduced. When I first tested this routine, that check was not included, and I found some interesting bugs down the line where a polynomial had multiple coefficients instead of one. This is labeled "Removes leading zeros" in listing 7.4.

The final step is to transfer the internal result to the specified place. At least I figured that one out ahead of time!

Once we have addition, we can do subtraction by negation of the second argument and calling addition, as shown in the following listing.

Listing 7.5   Polynomial subtract

```
void poly_sub(POLY *c, POLY a, POLY b)
{
  int i;
  POLY bneg;

  poly_init(&bneg);
  bneg.deg = b.deg;
  for(i=0; i<=b.deg; i++)
  {                                               | Negate each
    mpz_init_set(bneg.coef[i], b.coef[i]);        | coefficient
    mneg(bneg.coef[i], bneg.coef[i]);             | one at a time.
  }
  poly_add(c, a, bneg);    ← Then add to get the result.
  poly_clear(&bneg);
}
```

7.4 *Polynomial utilities*

In this section, useful low-level common routines are shown. They are used in many subroutines in the rest of the book. There are several routines that are useful for manipulating polynomials. These include copying, comparing, printing, and creating random polynomials. Duplication of a polynomial is common for routines that will manipulate inputs. The comparison routine can only check for equality. The concept of greater or lesser does not make sense when we are working modulo prime numbers in a cyclic field. Printing polynomials to the console is very useful for debugging and preserving work. Random polynomials are used for the square root algorithm and digital signatures, as we will see in chapters 12 and 18.

The utility for copying polynomials is shown in the following listing. The assumption is that the place being copied to has already been initialized.

Listing 7.6 Polynomial copy

```
void poly_copy(POLY *a, POLY b)
{
  int i;

  a->deg = b.deg;     ← First, copy degree . . .
  for(i=0; i<=b.deg; i++)                      . . . then each coefficient
    mpz_set(a->coef[i], b.coef[i]);   one at a time.
}
```

Comparing two polynomials is only useful to test if they are equal. The idea of "greater than" does not make a lot of sense because there are no negative numbers when we finish with the coefficients. The compare utility in the following listing returns 1 if the inputs are equal and 0 if not.

Listing 7.7 Polynomial compare

```
int poly_cmp(POLY a, POLY b)
{
  int i;

  if(a.deg != b.deg)  ← Different degree, then not equal
    return 0;
  for(i=a.deg; i>=0; i- -)              If any coefficient different,
    if(mpz_cmp(a.coef[i], b.coef[i]))   then not equal
      return 0;
  return 1;
}
```

The third utility is useful for debugging. I modified this routine several times either to make it look pretty or to be useful. This particular form is very useful for copying into PARI/gp. I found that comparing my calculation to PARI uncovered many problems.

By writing out each coefficient using the Mod() form along with the power of x it corresponds with, I can use the result directly as input to gp.

The following listing shows the core print routine. This is useful for debugging multiple items.

Listing 7.8 Polynomial print routine

```
void poly_print(POLY a)
{
  int i;
  mpz_t prm;

  mget(prm);    ← Modulus for PARI
  for(i=a.deg; i>0; i--)
  {
    if(mpz_cmp_ui(a.coef[i], 0))    │ Doesn't print if
      gmp_printf("Mod(%Zd, %Zd)*x^%d + ", a.coef[i], prm, i);   │ coefficient is zero
  }
  gmp_printf("Mod(%Zd, %Zd) ", a.coef[0], prm);    ← Doesn't print $x^0$
  printf("\n");
  mpz_clear(prm);
}
```

The next listing adds a string input so I can label the output and remind myself what I was trying to look at.

Listing 7.9 Polynomial print with string

```
void poly_printf(char *string, POLY a)
{
  printf("%s ", string);
  poly_print(a);
  printf("\n");    ← Add a blank line for visibility.
}
```

A final utility routine is the generation of random polynomials. This assumes an irreducible polynomial has been set, so the maximum degree is known. Then it creates random values for each coefficient. The following listing shows how easy this is to do.

Listing 7.10 Polynomial random value

```
void poly_rand(POLY *rnd)
{
  int i;

  rnd->deg = irrd.deg - 1;    ← Max degree possible
  for(i=0; i<irrd.deg; i++)    │ All coefficients
    mrand(rnd->coef[i]);    │ are random.
}
```

Answer to exercise

1 Modulo 127 we find:

$$37x^3 + 96x^2 + 7x + 3$$
$$14x^2 + 83x + 124$$
$$\overline{}$$
$$37x^3 + 110x^2 + 90x$$

Summary

- A degree k extension of a finite field p has p^k elements.
- Polynomial structure includes integer degree and a fixed number of coefficients.
- Adding two polynomials of different degrees results in the highest degree in the output.
- Care must be taken with output degree if the highest coefficient goes to zero.
- Random polynomials will be one degree less than the irreducible polynomial defining the field.

Multiplication of polynomials explained 8

In this chapter, we'll learn what irreducible polynomials are and how they depend on the underlying prime number modulus. The fundamental takeaway for this chapter is the multiplication table derived from an irreducible polynomial that defines an extension field. This table will allow us to compute extension field algorithms efficiently. The code for this chapter is the core of all the routines in the rest of the book.

As I said in chapter 7, I left out some details about finite field extensions. The first detail is that the arbitrary symbol x or t is not actually arbitrary. It is the solution to an irreducible polynomial equation. In this chapter, we dive into the detail of what makes a polynomial irreducible and how that is used like a prime number to create finite fields over polynomials.

The coefficients are reduced modulo a field prime, as shown in chapter 7, but the multiplication of two polynomials requires a modulus that is a polynomial. I will sometimes use the term *prime polynomial* instead of *irreducible polynomial*. The difference in terminology comes from the use of the polynomial as a modulus, where it is like a prime versus its use as a factor where it is irreducible.

8.1   Defining irreducible polynomials

In this section, I'll define what an irreducible polynomial is. Irreducible polynomials are fundamental to field extensions. They are also called prime polynomials because they act like prime numbers in a finite field. The concept is important for the rest of the book.

A reducible polynomial has multiple polynomial factors. In this section, I want to explain what is meant by an irreducible polynomial. With an example using different prime numbers, we'll see that the same equation can have different properties. The magic of field extensions is then shown by setting the irreducible polynomial equal to zero.

A general polynomial can have several factors. An irreducible polynomial has no reduction with smaller factors. An example of a factorable (or reducible) polynomial is

$$x^2 - 1 = (x+1)(x-1)$$

The polynomial $x^2 - 1$ has two factors. This formula is true no matter what the field prime is. Now let's take a look at a polynomial, which has different factors with different field primes. The formula

$$x^2 + 13x + 1 \bmod 1187$$

has no factors modulo 1187. But the same formula

$$x^2 + 13x + 1 \bmod 43$$

factors into

$$(x+25)(x+31) \bmod 43$$

The formula $x^2 + 13x + 1 \bmod 1187$ is irreducible but the same formula modulo 43 is reducible. So the choice of field prime also determines the choice of irreducible polynomial for creating a field extension.

In chapter 11, I will describe finding good irreducible polynomials for efficient programming. For now, I will assume we have an irreducible polynomial we can use with our chosen field prime so we can use it as a modulus.

The usefulness of an irreducible polynomial comes from setting it equal to zero. In the previous example, we have

$$x^2 + 13x + 1 = 0 \bmod 1187$$

so

$$x^2 = -13x - 1$$

Multiplying both sides by x, we have

$$x^3 = -13x^2 - x$$

Replacing x^2 with $-13x - 1$ gives

$$x^3 = -13(-13x - 1) - x = 168x + 13$$

multiply again by x to get

$$x^4 = 168x^2 + 13x = 168(-13x - 1) + 13x = -984x - 168 = 203x + 1019$$

where the last step replaces a negative number with its positive modulo equivalent by adding the prime 1187. So no matter what power we raise x to, we end up with $a \cdot x + b$ with a and b in the range $\{0 \ldots 1186\}$. The total number of field elements will be 1187^2.

Technically, x is a root of the irreducible polynomial. But since it is over a prime field, there is no integer value which satisfies the equation. The equation itself is the answer we want. The equation acts exactly like a prime number.

> **Exercise 8.1**
>
> $b = x^3 + x + 5 \bmod 131$ is irreducble. What is $x^5 \bmod b$?

8.2 Irreducible polynomial as modulus

In this section, I'll show how an irreducible polynomial becomes a modulus for all other polynomials. The general multiplication of polynomials will result in a highest power that is the sum of the highest powers of the factors. For an extension field of degree k, we only need $k - 1$ coefficients to create all p^k combinations, as shown in chapter 7. In this section, I show how we can use an irreducible polynomial as a modulus to maintain the p^k field size.

Assume we have a general irreducible polynomial we can write as equation 8.1:

$$t^n + a_{n-1}t^{n-1} + a_{n-2}t^{n-2} + \cdots + a_1 t + a_0 \tag{8.1}$$

This is called a monic polynomial because the leading coefficient is 1. To use this as a modulus, we would normally divide equation 8.1 into another polynomial to determine the remainder. The quotient would be thrown away, similar to how we find the remainder of a number modulo a prime.

There are easier ways to find a modular result, especially for multiplication. Setting equation 8.1 to zero gives equation 8.2:

$$t^n = -a_{n-1}t^{n-1} - a_{n-2}t^{n-2} - \cdots - a_1 t - a_0 \tag{8.2}$$

Taking the quotient of all powers of t less than n with the irreducible polynomial will not change the remainder. But once we hit n and get larger, we can use equation 8.2 to reduce the result back to a sum of powers less than n. If all our polynomials are reduced by the irreducible polynomial, they will all have maximum degree $n - 1$. Multiplying two polynomials that are already modulo a prime polynomial results in a polynomial with a maximum degree of $2n - 2$ before reduction.

To see this, take two polynomials $y_1 = a_k t^k + \cdots + a_0$ times $y_2 = b_k t^k + \cdots + b_0$. The largest possible term is $a_k b_k t^{2k}$. All the other terms will be of lower power in t. The process of multiplication only requires using a lookup table for all powers of t from 0 to $2n - 2$.

I am going to follow the brute-force method described in section 3.1.2 of Cohen (2000). As shown in equation 8.3, take the first arbitrary polynomial as

$$a = \sum_{i=0}^{r} a_i t^i \tag{8.3}$$

and, in equation 8.4, the second arbitrary polynomial as

$$b = \sum_{j=0}^{s} b_j t^j \tag{8.4}$$

The multiplication of equation 8.3 with equation 8.4 then gives equation 8.5

$$c = \sum_{k=0}^{r+s} c_k t^k \tag{8.5}$$

where, in equation 8.6, each coefficient c_k is given by

$$c_k = \sum_{i=0}^{k} a_i b_{k-i} \tag{8.6}$$

The trick with equation 8.6 is to take $a_i = 0$ when $i > r$ and $b_j = 0$ when $j > s$.

The computation of equation 8.5 results in powers of t up to t^{r+s}. But we want to reduce this modulo our irreducible polynomial. The process is diagrammed in figure 8.1. We first compute each coefficient c_k with equation 8.6. This is schematically drawn at the top of figure 8.1. Those values then multiply the corresponding row k of a precomputed table of powers t^k depicted as the box. All the columns are then summed with the result to find c modulo the irreducible polynomial (shown as d_k in figure 8.1).

8.3   *Building the matrix*

In this section, I'll show how the irreducible polynomial is used to construct a matrix of coefficients that helps with multiplication. The subroutines based on these ideas are fundamental to the rest of the book.

Figure 8.1 shows the general idea of our lookup table. In this section, I'll show how we compute each row, one at a time, using the previous row along with the nth row to find the full matrix.

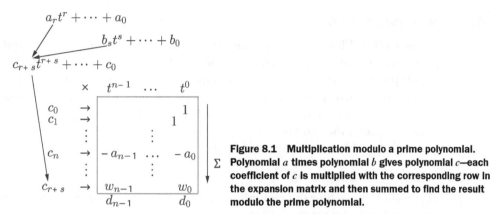

Figure 8.1 Multiplication modulo a prime polynomial. Polynomial a times polynomial b gives polynomial c—each coefficient of c is multiplied with the corresponding row in the expansion matrix and then summed to find the result modulo the prime polynomial.

The powers of t table is a matrix with each row being a power of t and each column a coefficient in the range of the field prime. Starting with row $t^0 = 1$ and multiplying each row by t, I create a matrix as shown in table 8.1. The first column lists the power of t. At row n, I have equation 8.2. Row $n + 1$ shows the algebra of multiplying equation 8.2 by t, which results in

$$t^{n+1} = -a_{n-1}t^n - a_{n-2}t^{n-1} \cdots - a_1 t^2 - a_0 t$$

Substitution of equation 8.2 in the first term gives the results in the table.

Table 8.1   Powers of t expanded modulo irreducible polynomial

			Coefficient index		
Power	$n-1$	$n-2$	$\cdots$	1	0
0	0	0	$\cdots$	0	1
1	0	0	$\cdots$	1	0
$\vdots$	$\vdots$	$\vdots$	$\cdots$	$\vdots$	$\vdots$
n	$-a_{n-1}$	$-a_{n-2}$	$\cdots$	$-a_1$	$-a_0$
$n+1$	$a_{n-1}^2 - a_{n-2}$	$a_{n-1}a_{n-2} - a_{n-3}$	$\cdots$	$a_{n-1}a_1 - a_0$	$a_{n-1}a_0$
$\vdots$	$\vdots$	$\vdots$	$\cdots$	$\vdots$	$\vdots$
$2n-2$	c_{n-1}	c_{n-2}	$\cdots$	c_1	c_0

Each subsequent row is then the same process. Multiplying the previous row by t shifts all the coefficients over, and the highest power coefficient is multiplied with row n. Then the two results are added together.

Exercise 8.2

Create the multiplication table for $x^4 + x^2 + 19 \bmod 131$.

8.4   Multiplication code

In this section, I'll describe the subroutines used to allow multiplication modulo a prime polynomial. As described in section 8.2, there are two main steps to perform a multiply. Since we usually pick an irreducible polynomial as a fixed parameter, the matrix of coefficients only has to be computed once. Once created, the table is used every time we multiply two polynomials modulo that prime polynomial. In this section, I'll show the code for creating the table of coefficients and then the routine that uses the table to complete a multiply.

8.4.1   Creating the multiplication table

This section shows how the multiplication table is created. The file `poly.c` contains the global variables `table` and `poly_degree` as shown here:

```
static mpz_t *table = NULL;    ◄─┐ Two-dimensional array
static long poly_degree;
```

The indexing into the array `table` will be row = power of t with variable `i` and column = coefficient index with variable `j`. I called the routine `poly_mulprep` because it prepares the multiplication table.

Listing 8.1 shows the initialization portion of the routine. The input is an irreducible polynomial. There is no check here that the input is a prime polynomial (remember that *prime* and *irreducible* mean the same thing for our situation with polynomials). I will show how to do that in later chapters. The input polynomial can be anything, so I will force it to be monic (meaning the leading coefficient is 1) using a normalization routine. I will explain normalization in section 8.5.

Listing 8.1   Multiply table initialization

```
void poly_mulprep(POLY f)
{
  int i, j, tst;
  mpz_t tmp;
  POLY fnrml;

  poly_init(&fnrml);
  poly_copy(&fnrml, f);
  poly_degree = f.deg;
  if(table)                          Multiple calls
    free(table);                     require clear before reuse.
  table = (mpz_t*)malloc(sizeof(mpz_t)*poly_degree*poly_degree*2);
  for(i=0; i<2*poly_degree; i++)   ◄─ 2n rows
    for(j=0; j<poly_degree; j++)   ◄─ n columns                    $2n^2$ coefficients
      mpz_init(table[poly_degree*i + j]);  ◄─┐
  mpz_init(tmp);                     Coefficient automatically zero
}
```

I first check to see whether the `table` was previously used and, if so, `free()` it. It is then set up to be a two-dimensional array of `mpz_t` values of size $2n^2$. Clearly, this is too big according to table 8.1 but not by too much.

The next step is easy: I fill in the first n rows of the matrix. The following listing shows that operation. Note that each diagonal element has a coefficient set to 1 with the same row and column index.

Listing 8.2   Multiply table low powers of *t*

```
/*  set lowest degree terms to x^j  */

  for(i=0; i<poly_degree; i++)
    mpz_set_ui(table[poly_degree*i + i], 1);  ← Diagonal coefficent = 1
```

The last step of the initial setup is to copy equation 8.2 to row n, as shown in the following listing. If the input polynomial is monic, the `poly_normal()` routine does nothing.

Listing 8.3   Multiply table row *n*

```
  poly_normal(&fnrml);  ← Force monic.
  for(j=0; j<poly_degree; j++)
  {
    mpz_neg(tmp, fnrml.coef[j]);                        Negative of each
    mpz_set(table[poly_degree*poly_degree + j], tmp);  coefficient in nth row
  }
```

The meat of the preparation is filling in the bottom half of the table. The entry at row n (=`poly_degree`) is used along with the previous table entry. The outer loop does each row, and the inner loop does each column of the matrix, as shown in the following listing.

Listing 8.4   Multiply table bottom half

```
  for(i=poly_degree+1; i<2*poly_degree; i++)  ← Start at row n+1.
  {
```
Add x^n entry to rotated coefficients.
```
    for(j=1; j<poly_degree; j++)         nth row           Highest coefficient
    {                                    this column       previous row

      mmul(tmp, table[poly_degree*poly_degree + j], table[i*poly_degree - 1]);
      madd(table[i*poly_degree + j], table[(i-1)*poly_degree + j - 1], tmp);
    }
    mmul(tmp, table[poly_degree*poly_degree], table[i*poly_degree - 1]);
    mpz_set(table[i*poly_degree], tmp);
  }                                                 $t^0$ coefficient
  mpz_clear(tmp);                                   special case
  poly_clear(&fnrml);
```

As seen in table 8.1, the last column of each row does not have the final term of all previous columns. That is why the `j = 0` term is done separately.

8.4.2 *Polynomial multiply*

This section shows how the multiplication table is used to compute the product of two polynomials modulo an irreducible polynomial.

Once the table has been created, computing the multiplication of two polynomials modulo the prime polynomial is a matter of bookkeeping. An easy way to ensure the rule of equation 8.6 is to create a list of coefficients with twice the maximum possible length and zero-out the coefficients beyond the size of the polynomial. Since initialization does this automatically, I create coefficient vector arrays, which are sized to be the sum of each input degree. The initialization is shown in the following listing.

Listing 8.5 Multiply initialization

```
void poly_mul(POLY *rslt, POLY a, POLY b)
{
  int i, j, m, n;                                     Space for maximum
  mpz_t coef[2*MAXDEGREE], acf[2*MAXDEGREE], bcf[2*MAXDEGREE];   possible degree
  mpz_t tmp;  Initialize space.

  m = a.deg;
  n = b.deg;                                          Actual space
  for(i=0; i<=n+m; i++)                               for maximum degree
    mpz_inits(coef[i], acf[i], bcf[i], NULL);
  for(i=0; i<=m; i++)             Copy over
    mpz_set(acf[i], a.coef[i]);  coefficients
  for(i=0; i<=n; i++)            for each
    mpz_set(bcf[i], b.coef[i]);  polynomial.
  mpz_init(tmp);
```

The next step is to compute the coefficients of equation 8.6, as shown in listing 8.6. The inner loop only goes from 0 to i, so we don't hit negative indexing. A lot of multiplies are zeros, so this is a point where more code can optimize fewer operations.

Listing 8.6 Multiply initial coefficients

```
for(i=0; i<=n+m; i++)  ← For each possible coefficient
{
  for(j=0; j<=i; j++)
  {
    mmul(tmp, acf[j], bcf[i - j]);   Compute
    madd(coef[i], coef[i], tmp);     equation 8.6.
  }
}
```

Once all the double-length coefficients are computed, I use the lookup table to reduce them to the size of $n - 1$. If the sum of the degrees of the two input polynomials is less than the degree of the prime polynomial, the result is simply transferred to the output. Otherwise, the result degree is set to $n - 1$ and each result coefficient less than n is copied to the matching output coefficient. The higher level coefficients are multiplied times the row in the mulprep table of each power above n, and this is added to the output. The code is shown in the following listing.

Listing 8.7   Multiply table reduction

Combine upper powers
with lower using table.

```
    if(n+m < poly_degree)
    {
      rslt->deg = n+m;                          Final degree
      for(i=0; i<=n+m; i++)                      less than
        mpz_set(rslt->coef[i], coef[i]);         prime polynomial
    }
    else
    {
      rslt->deg = poly_degree - 1;   ← Maximum possible degree
      for(i=0; i<poly_degree; i++)              Lower coefficients
        mpz_set(rslt->coef[i], coef[i]);        do not change.
      for(i=poly_degree; i<=n+m; i++)   ← For each degree n and above
      {
        for(j=0; j<poly_degree; j++)   ← For each coefficient
        {
          mmul(tmp, coef[i], table[i*poly_degree + j]);   Multiply row by coefficient
          madd(rslt->coef[j], rslt->coef[j], tmp);         and add to the result.
        }
      }
    }
```

The final step is to check that none of the highest-level coefficients went to zero. If they do, the degree of the polynomial result must be reduced. This chunk of code was discovered the hard way when really weird bugs showed up having high-degree polynomials with zero coefficients. The code is shown in the following listing.

Listing 8.8   Multiply check maximum degree

```
    while((mpz_cmp_ui(rslt->coef[rslt->deg], 0) <= 0) && (rslt->deg > 0))
      rslt->deg--;                           Most significant
    for(i=0; i<=n+m; i++)                     coefficient is zero?
      mpz_clears(coef[i], acf[i], bcf[i], NULL);
    mpz_clear(tmp);      Clean up stack                        And degree is still positive.
}
```

8.5   *Miscellaneous multiply routines*

This section describes routines that are rarely used in the rest of the book. The normalization routine is used in chapter 12. The debug routine is presented as an example of how to find problems in coding.

While the use of a monic polynomial to set up the irreducible polynomial means normalization is not required, the ability to normalize polynomials will come in handy later. I also want to include a debug routine that I found exceptionally useful. The multiply table has a specific form, which is easy to check when printed out. By using small numbers, I can verify that the code is behaving properly using a hand calculator or PARI/gp.

The normalization routine is shown in listing 8.9. The variable `tst` compares the indexed coefficient to 1. A result less than zero implies the indexed coefficient is zero, so the next coefficient is checked. When `tst == 0`, the indexed coefficient is 1, which implies the polynomial is already monic. When `tst > 0`, these two tests fail, the inverse of the indexed coefficient is computed, and the loop is terminated.

> **Listing 8.9   Normalization routine**

```
void poly_normal(POLY *a)
{
   int i, tst;
   mpz_t c;

   mpz_init(c);
   for(i=a->deg; i>=0; i--)
   {
      tst = mpz_cmp_ui(a->coef[i], 1);   ← Is leading coefficient == 1?
      if(tst < 0)
        continue;   ← Assumes coefficient must be zero
      if(!tst)      ← Leading coefficient = 1, so nothing to do
        return;
      minv(c, a->coef[i]);   │ Inverse leading coefficient;
      break;                 │ use on all other coefficients.
   }
   if(i < 0) return;      ← All zeros!
   while(i >= 0)
   {
      mmul(a->coef[i], a->coef[i], c);  ← Inverse times all coefficients
      i--;
   }
}
```

The inverse of the leading coefficient is then multiplied by all the coefficients. This forces the leading coefficient to 1 (this is not efficient, obviously) and adjusts all the other coefficients accordingly.

The final routine is a printing function to look at the table as it was generated. Since the table is a matrix of coefficients, all with the same degree and not in polynomial format, this is a special routine. The following listing shows the code. Once debugged, it was commented out using `#if`.

Listing 8.10 Debug table routine

```
#ifdef DEBUG
void poly_debug(int n)
{
  int i, j;

  for(i=0; i<2*n; i++)
  {
    for(j=n-1; j>=0; j--)
      gmp_printf("%Zd  ", table[i*n + j]);    Each row has
    printf("\n");                             all coefficients.
  }
}
#endif
```

Included in the repository is a program called `test_mod.c`, which includes a degree 4 polynomial. The initialization of the polynomial is shown in the following listing.

Listing 8.11 Test of polynomial routines

```
C.deg = 4;
mpz_set_ui(C.coef[4], 1);
mpz_set_ui(C.coef[3], 2);      The irreducible polynomial is
mpz_set_ui(C.coef[2], 1);      x⁴+2x³+x²+3x+5
mpz_set_ui(C.coef[1], 3);      mod 7.
mpz_set_ui(C.coef[0], 5);
poly_mulprep(C);
```

The irreducible polynomial is $x^4 + 2x^3 + x^2 + 3x + 5$ mod 7.

The debug routine outputs the table shown in listing 8.12. This is actually the same data marked off in the box of figure 8.1 and the columns to the right of "power" in table 8.1.

Listing 8.12 Mulprep debug output

```
 0   0   0   1
 0   0   1   0
 0   1   0   0
 1   0   0   0
-2  -1  -3  -5     | t⁴ row
 3   6   1   3
 0   5   1   6
 5   1   6   0
```

As you can see, the first four lines are the 1s on the diagonal, and then we have the negative of each coefficient on the t^4 row, followed by the shifted and added rows for the last three row entries. The middle row is negative because the modulus was not applied. In the last three rows, all calculations are done modulo 7, so they are always positive.

Answers to exercises

1 $x^3 = -x - 5$ so $x^4 = -x^2 - 5x$ and $x^5 = -x^3 - 5x^2$. Putting x^3 back in, we get $x^5 = -5x^2 + x + 5 = 126x^2 + x + 5$.

2 The first four rows are simple: $1 \rightarrow x \rightarrow x^2 \rightarrow x^3$. Row 5 is $x^4 = -x^2 - 19$, and row 6 is just a left shift $x^5 = -x^3 - 19x$. The last row requires the use of row 5 because $x^6 = -x^4 - 19x^2$. This becomes $x^6 = x^2 + 19 - 19x^2 = -18x^2 + 19$. So, the full table of coefficients is

	3	2	1	0
0	0	0	0	1
1	0	0	1	0
2	0	1	0	0
3	1	0	0	0
4	0	-1	0	-19
5	-1	0	-19	0
6	0	-18	0	19

Summary

- An irreducible polynomial over a finite field is defined as a polynomial having no other polynomial factors.
- The variable defining an irreducible polynomial is a root of the polynomial when set equal to zero.
- A matrix of coefficients with k columns and $2k$ rows allows the multiplication of any two polynomials modulo an irreducible polynomial. This lookup table is only computed once for an irreducible polynomial.
- A degree n polynomial multiplied by a degree m polynomial has intermediate result of degree $n + m$. The degrees higher than k are reduced by multiplying the coefficient at that power by all the coefficients in the corresponding row of the matrix and summed to the final result, which has, at most, k coefficients.
- A monic polynomial has a leading coefficient of 1. All irreducible polynomials used for field extensions are monic.
- Normalization of a polynomial inverts the leading coefficient and multiplies that with all coefficients leaving a monic polynomial.
- The term *prime polynomial* means the same as the term *irreducible polynomial* because working with a polynomial as a modulus is the same concept as working with a prime number as a modulus for integers.

Computing powers of polynomials

This chapter covers

- Exponentiation by expansion of an integer
- A square and multiply algorithm to compute powers of polynomials
- Examples for arbitrary powers of polynomials
- Examples for field prime powers of polynomials

In this chapter, we use the code from chapters 7 and 8 to compute exponentials of polynomials modulo a prime polynomial. These routines are important for computing elliptic curve point pairings that underlie the routines shown in chapters 18 and 19.

Now that we know how to multiply polynomials modulo a prime polynomial, we can compute powers of polynomials. We need this ability to find irreducible polynomials and to find pairing-friendly curves. In chapter 8, we found that powers of a variable modulo the irreducible polynomial are limited to one less than the degree of the irreducible polynomial.

Similar to how we used the double and add method to compute multiplication of a point on an elliptic curve, we are going to use the square and multiply method to compute powers of a polynomial modulo a prime polynomial. This is exponentially faster than the method used in chapter 8.

The next interesting step after computing a general power is to take x^p modulo the irreducible polynomial where p is the field prime. This will eventually connect back to the field extension when we compute x^{p^j}.

9.1   *Using square and multiply to rapidly compute powers*

In this section, I'll present an algorithm to rapidly compute high powers of polynomials modulo a prime polynomial. Generating large powers of x using the method in chapter 8, going one power at a time, is exceptionally time-consuming—especially if the power is a 160-bit number. We can more easily get there by expanding the exponent in powers of 2. Each power of 2 is a squaring operation. We write this as

$$x^k = x^{k_0 + 2(k_1 + 2(k_2 + \cdots + 2k_j)\cdots)}$$

where k_j is the most significant bit of k and k_0 is the least significant bit. I'll give an example after the algorithm description.

Figure 9.1 shows the full x^k power algorithm. The inputs are polynomial x and power k. The result is $r = x^k$ modulo the irreducible polynomial.

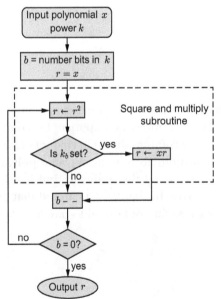

Figure 9.1   Polynomial square and multiply algorithm, which will be used in chapter 12 to compute square roots

The most significant bit is always set, so we start with $x^1 = x^{k_j}$ and then square to get x^{2k_j}. Multiplying by $x^{k_{j-1}}$ gives $x^{2k_j + k_{j-1}}$. If bit k_{j-1} is 0, then that is simply multiplying by 1, which means we skip that step.

Proceeding this way through the entire integer k requires j squarings and Hamming weight multiplies (minus 1). Even if the variable x is a polynomial in t, the same process applies. Each step is done modulo the irreducible polynomial using the multiply routine from chapter 8.

In chapter 13 and beyond, I will use a tiny example to illustrate some of the elliptic curve pairing properties. The irreducible polynomial in that example is $x^2 + x + 3$ mod 43. Let's see what the square and multiply routine gives when we take x^5 modulo $x^2 + x + 3$.

The exponent is 5, which in binary is 101. With the most significant bit always being set ($=1$), we start with x. We then square this to get x^2. Now we have to replace x^2 with $-x - 3$. The bit in the exponent is clear ($=0$), so we do not multiply by x this round.

$-x - 3$ squared is the same as $(x + 3)^2 = x^2 + 6x + 9 = -x - 3 + 6x + 9 = 5x + 6$. The last bit is set, so we multiply by x to get $5x^2 + 6x = 5(-x - 3) + 6x = x - 15 = x + 28$. Thus, we have x^5 modulo $x^2 + x + 3$ is $x + 28$ (whose coefficients are modulo 43). The lookup table makes this process far more efficient, especially when we get to very large coefficients.

> **Exercise 9.1**
>
> Using the irreducible polynomial $c = x^4 + x^2 + 19$ mod 131 and the table found from exercise 8.2, find x^{17} mod c. (Hint: Be careful when squaring.)

9.2 *Polynomial powers code for general exponents*

In this section, I'll implement the code for computing powers of polynomials. As shown in figure 9.1, there is a single-stage square and multiply subroutine within dotted lines. This will be useful in a later routine for field prime exponents. In this section, I'll explain how to compute powers of polynomials modulo an irreducible polynomial with an arbitrary exponent.

I break up the power routine into two simple subroutines:

- Single-stage square and multiply
- General polynomial power function

Listing 9.1 shows the inner squaring routine. This takes an input called `flag`, which is the next bit in the integer power. If the flag is clear, the output is simply x^2. If the flag is set, the input a is used to compute ax^2 for the result.

Listing 9.1   Square and multiply

```
void poly_sqm(POLY *x2, POLY x, POLY a, int flag)
{
    POLY tmp;
```

```
    poly_init(&tmp);
    poly_mul(&tmp, x, x);    ← Compute x².
    if(flag)
        poly_mul(x2, tmp, a);    ← The output is ax² with flag set.
    else
        poly_copy(x2, tmp);    ← The output is x² with flag clear.
    poly_clear(&tmp);
}
```

The routine `poly_mul()` assumes the irreducible polynomial table has already been initialized. So the operations in listing 9.1 are automatically done modulo the chosen prime polynomial.

The next routine implements the full exponentiation process. The input polynomial g is taken to the power k. Listing 9.2 shows how the variable `bitcnt` acquires the number of bits in the exponent. As with the double and add routine, this is decremented by two for the same reason: the most significant bit is already taken care of, and the base of counting is 1.

Listing 9.2   Polynomial exponentiation

```
void poly_pow(POLY *h, POLY g, mpz_t k)
{
    int bitcnt, bit;
    POLY a;

    poly_init(&a);
    poly_copy(&a, g);    ← Start with g¹.
    bitcnt = mpz_sizeinbase(k, 2) - 2;    ← Number of bits left to do
    while(bitcnt >= 0)
    {
        bit = mpz_tstbit(k, bitcnt);    ⎤ Square at this position
        poly_sqm(&a, a, g, bit);        ⎟ and multiply if
        bitcnt--;                        ⎦ bit set.
    }
    poly_copy(h, a);    ← Allow operation in place.
    poly_clear(&a);
}
```

For each bit in the field prime, the routine calls the square and multiply routine with the result and initial input, overwriting the result. The end of the loop happens when `bitcount == 0`, and the last bit determines whether there is a final multiply.

9.3   *Explicit polynomial example*

In this section, I'll give an example of what to expect from powers of polynomials modulo a prime polynomial. The whole point of cryptographic security is to work with very large numbers. However, to see what is going on, it is a lot easier to work with very small numbers. The number 43 is a nice small prime, and the irreducible polynomial $x^2 + x + 3$ mod 43 has $43^2 = 1849$ elements. In this section, I'll use this irreducible polynomial to examine what happens when values are taken to a power modulo $x^2 + x + 3$. This tiny example is used in many places throughout the book. Listing 9.3 shows a simple test program to exercise routine `poly_pow()`. The random number selection is always the same because the state of the program is the same every time, but for this, it doesn't matter.

Listing 9.3   Example program for `poly_pow()`

```c
#include "poly.h"

#define PRIME 43

int main(int argc, char *argv[])
{
  POLY r, tst, pow;
  mpz_t n, pk2;
  int ck;

  if(argc < 2)                              When I forget how to use
  {                                         program
    printf("Use: ./poly_exp_test <exponent>\n");
    exit(-1);
  }
  mpz_init_set_ui(n, PRIME);
  minit(n);                                 Set up field prime.
  mpz_init_set_str(pk2, argv[1], 10);
  gmp_printf("pk2= %Zd\n", pk2);
  poly_init(&r);
  r.deg = 2;                                Irreducible
  mpz_set_ui(r.coef[0], 3);                 polynomial
  mpz_set_ui(r.coef[1], 1);                 x^2 + x + 3
  mpz_set_ui(r.coef[2], 1);
  poly_mulprep(r);        ← Set up polynomial multiply table.
  poly_printf("r = ", r);
  poly_init(&tst);
  poly_init(&pow);
  tst.deg = 1;
  mrand(tst.coef[1]);      Random
  mrand(tst.coef[0]);      coefficients
  poly_pow(&pow, tst, pk2);
  poly_printf("taking ", tst);             Use PARI/gp
  printf("to power %s\n", argv[1]);        to check code.
  poly_printf("gives ", pow);
}
```

Given the input power 25, the output is

```
pk2= 25
r = Mod(1, 43)*x^2 + Mod(1, 43)*x^1 + Mod(3, 43)

taking Mod(11, 43)*x^1 + Mod(3, 43)
```

```
to power 25
gives Mod(3, 43)*x^1 + Mod(26, 43)
```

Now let's see what happens when the input power is 1848:

```
pk2= 1848
r = Mod(1, 43)*x^2 + Mod(1, 43)*x^1 + Mod(3, 43)

taking Mod(11, 43)*x^1 + Mod(3, 43)

to power 1848
gives Mod(1, 43)
```

The result is 1! This is exactly what we expect from Fermat's Little Theorem $a^{p^2-1} = 1$. In this case, the total number of elements is $43^2 = 1849$, so $p^2 - 1 = 1848$. In a field extension, we operate with powers of the field prime.

9.4   *Powers of field prime*

In this section, I'll give a routine to compute polynomials to powers of the field prime. This is used in chapter 11 to find irreducible polynomials. Taking a polynomial to powers of the field prime means we have multiple levels of exponents. The formula is

$$x^{p^j} = x^{\overbrace{p \cdot p \cdots p}^{j}}$$

This is a very useful function all by itself, as shown in listing 9.4. The only difference between the general form in listing 9.2 and the special form in the following listing is there is no exponent for input because the field prime is the exponent.

Listing 9.4   Polynomial to field prime power

```
void poly_xp(POLY *xp, POLY x)
{
  int i, bitcnt, bit;
  mpz_t prm;
  mget(prm);          ←┘ Power is field prime.
  bitcnt = mpz_sizeinbase(prm, 2) - 2;  ← Number of bits left to do
  poly_copy(xp, x);   ← Start with x¹.
  while(bitcnt >= 0)
  {
    bit = mpz_tstbit(prm, bitcnt);   │ Square and
    poly_sqm(xp, *xp, x, bit);       │ multiply each
    bitcnt--;                        │ bit position.
  }
  mpz_clear(prm);
}
```

By sending the previous output back into the routine again, we obtain a way to compute

$$(x^{p^m})^p = x^{p^{m+1}}$$

This will be useful in later routines where we are looking for irreducible polynomials.

There is one more useful routine shown in listing 9.5. This takes a polynomial to the power of $(p-1)/2$. This is a miscellaneous routine that will be useful when hunting down elliptic curves for pairings. Since the field prime is always odd, $p-1$ is always even, so the call to `mpz_divexact()` always works.

> **Listing 9.5 Polynomial to half field prime power**

```
void gpow_p2(POLY *h, POLY g)
{
  mpz_t prm;

  mget(prm);
  mpz_sub_ui(prm, prm, 1);          Compute
  mpz_divexact_ui(prm, prm, 2);     (p − 1)/2.
  poly_pow(h, g, prm);         ◄──┐
  mpz_clear(prm);                  │
}                                  Return g^((p−1)/2).
```

Answer to exercise

1 17 in binary is 10001. Starting with x^1, we square to get x^2. The second bit (from the left) is clear, so we just square again to get $x^4 = -x^2 - 19$. The third bit is also clear so there is no multiply by x. Now life gets interesting because we square again to get $x^8 = x^4 + 38x^2 + 99$. Substitution for x^4 leaves $37x^2 + 80$. We square again to find $x^{16} = 59x^4 + 25x^2 + 112$. Multiplying x^4 by 59 amounts to subtraction of $59x^2 + 73$ from $25x^2 + 112$. The result is $-34x^2 + 39$. The last bit is set so we multiply by x to get the final result: $x^{17} = -34x^3 + 39x = 97x^3 + 39x$ mod 131.

Summary

- The square and multiply algorithm computes powers of x modulo a prime polynomial. The variable x can also be a polynomial, and the same algorithm applies. The square and multiply algorithm is exponentially faster than a straightforward multiplication algorithm.
- Exponentiation uses the square and multiply routine for every bit in a power. Every bit forces a squaring operation; only set bits force a multiply operation.
- Fermat's Little Theorem applies to field extensions. For prime polynomial f of degree k

$$x^{p^k - 1} \cong 1 \bmod f$$

  This is used to find square roots and irreducible polynomials.
- Computing x^{p^i} is an important subroutine for finding irreducible polynomials.

Description of polynomial division using Euclid's algorithm

This chapter covers

- Quotient and remainder from Euclid's algorithm
- Greatest common divisor of polynomials
- Inversion modulo an irreducible polynomial

In this chapter, I'll cover polynomial division, which is required to compute the point addition algorithm for points on a field extension elliptic curve. To compute elliptic curve formulas over finite fields consisting of polynomials, we started in chapters 7 to 9 working with polynomials performing addition and multiplication. In this chapter, we are going to dive into division so we can compute slopes of lines in an extension field. Working with an irreducible polynomial is similar to working with a prime number in terms of fields. Inversion modulo an irreducible polynomial is similar to inversion modulo a prime number. I'll also cover Euclid's division algorithm applied to polynomials. Using that algorithm, I'll then look at the greatest common divisor function. The greatest common divisor (gcd) of polynomials will be used to help us find irreducible polynomials in chapter 11.

The last algorithm of this chapter covers inversion modulo a prime polynomial. Inversion is really the extended Euclidean algorithm, but we don't need the quotient portion. I then show that division of two polynomials modulo an irreducible polynomial is inversion followed by multiplication.

10.1 Euclid's algorithm and gcd

In this section, I'll describe Euclid's algorithm applied to polynomials. This implementation of Euclid's algorithm gives a quotient and remainder for a general division application. To find slopes on an elliptic curve over an extension field requires an inverse modulo an irreducible polynomial. In computing inverses modulo a prime polynomial, the denominator is an irreducible polynomial, so there will always be a remainder. For the gcd function, only the remainder will be useful. The gcd function will be used to find irreducible polynomials. I give an example of Euclid's division algorithm using very simple polynomials so each step can be seen. The basic idea behind division using Euclid's algorithm is to find the quotient q and remainder r from the division of a/b. I'm going to use the method 3.1.1 in Cohen (2000). In the following description, $lc()$ means leading coefficient, and $deg()$ means degree of.

Figure 10.1 describes Euclid's algorithm for polynomials. The remainder is set to the numerator (a), and the degree of the remainder is compared with the degree of the denominator (b). If the remainder is a lower degree than b, the routine is done because the remainder is what is left after division. The process then goes one coefficient at a time, which is similar to how division of polynomials is done by hand. After computing the division of the leading coefficients, the correct index position of the quotient is set, and the remainder is reduced by s times the denominator b.

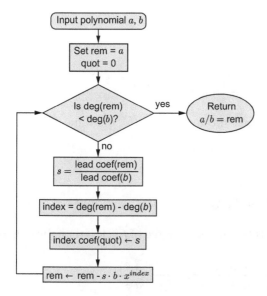

Figure 10.1   Polynomial Euclid's algorithm, which is the guts of inversion in elliptic curve pairing algorithms.

In more mathematical detail, we start by initializing the remainder and quotient, as in equation 10.1:

$$r \longleftarrow a, q \longleftarrow 0 \tag{10.1}$$

Then loop while $deg(r) >= deg(b)$, as shown in equation 10.2:

$$s \longleftarrow \frac{lc(r)}{lc(b)}$$
$$q[deg(r) - deg(b)] \longleftarrow s \tag{10.2}$$
$$r \longleftarrow r - s \cdot b \cdot x^{deg(r) - deg(b)}$$

Line 10.1 initializes the remainder to the numerator and the quotient to zero. The first two lines in equation 10.2 compute the leading coefficient of the quotient for the leading degree in the quotient result. The last line in equation 10.2 reduces the degree of r. This loop continues until the degree of r is less than the degree of b.

The second line in equation 10.2 places the value of s in the variable q at index $deg(r) - deg(b)$. This makes sense because the leading coefficient of r is at index $deg(r)$, and the leading coefficient of b is at index $deg(b)$, so the result of their division must be at the difference of the degrees.

As a concrete example of Euclid's algorithm, let's look at input polynomials

$$a = x^3 + 2x^2 + 3x + 1$$

and

$$b = 5x^3 + x + 6$$

with all coefficients modulo 7. Initialize

$$r = a = x^3 + 2x^2 + 3x + 1$$

and

$$q = 0$$

Then we have the value of s is

$$s = \frac{1}{5} \bmod 7 = 3$$

(because $5 \times 3 = 15 = 1 \bmod 7$). Since the $deg(r) = deg(b)$, the value of q is

$$q = s = 3$$

We then compute

$$r \leftarrow r - s \cdot b = x^3 + 2x^2 + 3x + 1 - 3(5x^3 + x + 6) = 2x^2 + 4$$

At this point, the algorithm halts because the degree of r is less than the degree of b. This example of

$$\frac{x^3 + 2x^2 + 3x + 1}{5x^3 + x + 6} = 3 + \frac{2x^2 + 4}{5x^3 + x + 6}$$

is from the program `test_mod.c` used to test the subroutines.

> **Exercise 10.1**
>
> Find the quotient and remainder from $\frac{13x^7+14x^3+19x+6}{x^5-x^2+17}$ mod 43.

The gcd is useful for finding factors of polynomials. Using Euclid's division algorithm, finding the gcd between two polynomials is very easy. I modified the routine 3.2.1 of Cohen (2000) to include the following initialization, shown in equation 10.3:

$$\text{if } a = 0 \text{ return } b \qquad (10.3)$$

$$\text{if } b = 0 \text{ return } a$$

$$a_w \longleftarrow \text{highest degree polynomial } (a, b)$$

$$b_w \longleftarrow \text{smallest degree polynomial } (a, b)$$

If one of the arguments is zero, the gcd of both arguments is the other argument. If both arguments are zero, the routine returns zero by definition. The reason for this is that everything divides zero. That is,

$$\frac{0}{b} = 0$$

My first reaction to this was a headache. But really it's "obvious" because 0 is smaller than every possible number, and any number not 0 can divide 0, so the greatest divisor is the nonzero number.

As shown in equation 10.4, the main loop of the gcd routine is then

$$\text{while } deg(b_w) > 0$$

$$r \longleftarrow a_w / b_w$$

$$a_w \longleftarrow b_w \qquad (10.4)$$

$$b_w \longleftarrow r$$

The first line in equation 10.4 is the remainder from Euclidean division. The assumption is that a_w has a larger degree than b_w; otherwise, the remainder degree is negative, which would terminate the loop on the first step. The following two steps keep the reduction process going.

As an example, let's find $\gcd(x^2 - x + 4, x^2 + 12x + 1)$ mod 17. Since both polynomials have the same degree, take $a_w = x^2 - x + 4$ and $b_w = x^2 + 12x + 1$. From equation 10.4 we have

$$r = \frac{x^2 - x + 4}{x^2 + 12x + 1} = -13x + 3$$

and the values for a_w and b_w become

$$a_w = x^2 + 12x + 1$$

and

$$b_w = -13x + 3$$

The next iteration gives

$$r = 0$$
$$a_w = -13x + 3 = x + 5$$
$$b_w = 0$$

The original factors are $(x+5)(x-6)$ and $(x+5)(x+7)$ so we see the algorithm got it right.

> **Exercise 10.2**
>
> What is the gcd of $(x+14)(x^2+22x+8)$ mod 23 and $(x+4)(x+19)(x^2+22x+8)$ mod 23?

10.2 *Inversion and division of polynomials*

In this section, I'll describe Euclid's extended algorithm applied to polynomials. These algorithms are used to compute point addition on field extension elliptic curves. As shown in chapter 3, the formulas for adding points over an elliptic curve require inversion modulo a field prime. The same formula applies to extension fields. There are more complex algorithms involved with pairings of points on extension field elliptic curves, which also use inversion and division of polynomials modulo a prime polynomial.

Inversion modulo an irreducible polynomial uses the same steps as the extended Euclidean algorithm. In this section, I go over these steps and then use a very simple example to show how each step appears for a real computation. Elliptic curve algorithms use division, so I also describe how a division subroutine is created from the inversion routine.

Inversion of polynomials is done with respect to a given irreducible polynomial. To compute a polynomial inverse, I use most of the extended Euclidean algorithm described in section 3.2 of von zur Gathen and Gerhard (1999) along with the same variable names. In equation 10.5, the initialization step is

$$v \longleftarrow irrd$$
$$u \longleftarrow b$$
$$r \longleftarrow 0$$
$$w \longleftarrow 0 \tag{10.5}$$
$$q \longleftarrow 0$$
$$t \longleftarrow 0$$
$$y_0 \longleftarrow lc(b)$$

where *irrd* is the irreducible polynomial of the field, y_0 means coefficient of t^0 in polynomial y (the constant coefficient), and $lc(b)$ means leading coefficient of input polynomial b.

In equation 10.6, we then perform the loop:

$$(q, r) = v/u$$
$$\rho = 1/lc(r)$$
$$r \longleftarrow \text{normal}(r)$$
$$t \longleftarrow \rho(w - qy)$$
$$w \longleftarrow y \tag{10.6}$$
$$y \longleftarrow t$$
$$v \longleftarrow u$$
$$u \longleftarrow r$$
$$\text{until } r = 1$$

This loop uses both the quotient and remainder from Euclid's algorithm. The third line uses the `poly_normal()` routine from chapter 8. At the termination of the loop, we will have $r = 1$. At that point, the variable t is the inverse. The reason this works is that the extended Euclidean algorithm maintains $t \cdot b = r$. On each step, t is increased, and r is decreased until $r = 1$, which is the $\gcd(irrd, b)$. Then we have

$$t \cdot b = 1 \bmod irrd$$

Thus t is the inverse of b modulo the irreducible polynomial.

When doing general polynomial equations modulo an irreducible polynomial, the formula will include division. This is easy to write as a formula but not so easy to execute directly. As shown in equation 10.7, a simple subroutine is all it takes to convert

$$\frac{a}{b} = a \cdot \frac{1}{b} \tag{10.7}$$

It just makes life easier to have division modulo a prime polynomial as a single call.

For an example, I will use the irreducible polynomial

$$x^2 + x + 3 \bmod 43$$

to find the inverse of

$$x + 17$$

Following the initialization step in equation 10.5, we have

$$v = x^2 + x + 3$$
$$u = x + 17$$
$$r = w = q = t = 0$$
$$y = 1$$

The steps in 10.6 give us

- Compute quotient q and remainder r from

$$(q, r) = v/u = x - 16, 17$$

- Compute ρ from $\rho = 1/lc(r)$

$$\rho = 1/17 = 38$$

- Compute r from

$$r = \text{normal}(17) = 1$$

- Compute $t = \rho(w - qv)$

$$t = 38(0 - (x - 16)1) = -38x + 6$$

- Transfer w, y, v, and u

$$w = 1$$
$$y = -38x + 6$$
$$v = x + 17$$
$$u = 1$$

Since $r = 1$, the loop ends with t as our answer. Adding 43 to the leading coefficient in t to make it positive, we find

$$\frac{1}{x + 17} = 5x + 6 \bmod x^2 + x + 3$$

10.3   *Euclid's algorithm code*

In this section, the subroutine to compute Euclid's algorithm for polynomials is described. Euclid's algorithm is a low-level division routine required to create a polynomial inversion routine. There are a few subroutines where we require both the quotient and remainder of a division. The subroutine to accomplish this is shown in the following listing.

Listing 10.1   Polynomial Euclid algorithm

```
void poly_euclid(POLY *q, POLY *r, POLY a, POLY b)
{
  int i, j;
  mpz_t s;
  POLY tmp;
  int k;

  poly_copy(r, a);             | r = a
  q->deg = 0;                  | q = 0
  mpz_set_ui(q->coef[0], 0);
  if(b.deg > a.deg) return;    ← if b > a then all done
```

**Perform division of
each coefficient.**

```
    mpz_init(s);
    poly_init(&tmp);                    Quotient
    q->deg = a.deg - b.deg;   ←─┘degree        Degree of r
    while((r->deg >= b.deg) && r->deg)  ←─┘> b and not zero
    {
        j = r->deg - b.deg;  ← Index of coefficient
        mdiv(s, r->coef[r->deg], b.coef[b.deg]);  ← s = lc(r)/lc(b)
        mpz_set(q->coef[j], s);
        for(i=0; i<=b.deg; i++)                    Compute
            mmul(tmp.coef[i + j], s, b.coef[i]);   s · b.
        tmp.deg = r->deg;
        poly_sub(r, *r, tmp);  ← Reduce r by s · b.
    }
    mpz_clear(s);
    poly_clear(&tmp);
}
```

The initialization assumes q may have a previous value, so I force q to zero. If the degree of a is less than the degree of b, then the remainder is a as it should be. The degree of the quotient is the difference in degrees of numerator and denominator. The loop then executes the formulas described in equation 10.2. When the degree of r is less than the degree of b, the loop terminates. The extra check for degree of r not being zero comes from an edge case when b is a degree zero polynomial (a constant).

10.4 Gcd code

This section shows the code to compute the greatest common divisor between two polynomials. The gcd algorithm uses the remainder from Euclidean division to find the common factors between two polynomials. When there are no common factors, we have found an irreducible polynomial. The initial checks take up more lines of code than the main loop. The following listing shows how equation 10.3 is implemented. The subscript w indicates "working" so the working value of a_w is always the larger degree polynomial.

Listing 10.2   Gcd initialization

```
void poly_gcd(POLY *d, POLY a, POLY b)
{
    POLY aw, bw, q, r;

    poly_init(&aw);  ← Set aw = 0.
    if(poly_cmp(a, aw))
    {
        poly_copy(d, b);       Input a = 0
        poly_clear(&aw);       output d = b
        return;
    }
```

```
poly_init(&bw);   ← Set bw = 0.
if(poly_cmp(b, bw))
{
  poly_copy(d, a);
  poly_clear(&aw);      | Input b = 0 and
  poly_clear(&bw);      | output d = a
  return;
}
if(a.deg >= b.deg)
{
  poly_copy(&aw, a);    | a > b
  poly_copy(&bw, b);    | good order
}
else
{
  poly_copy(&aw, b);    | b > a
  poly_copy(&bw, a);    | swap order
}
```

The following listing shows the main loop and termination of the gcd routine after initializing the quotient and remainder variables.

Listing 10.3 Gcd main loop

```
poly_init(&q);
poly_init(&r);            | Loop until
while(bw.deg > 0)   ←     | bw == 0.

{                              | Quotient and remainder
  poly_euclid(&q, &r, aw, bw);  ← | from aw / bw
  poly_copy(&aw, bw);   ← aw = bw
  poly_copy(&bw, r);    ← bw = r
}
if(!mpz_cmp_ui(bw.coef[0], 0))   | If bw == 0
  poly_copy(d, aw);              | aw, holds result . . .
else                          | . . . otherwise
  poly_copy(d, bw);           | bw is the result.
poly_clear(&r);
poly_clear(&q);
poly_clear(&bw);
poly_clear(&aw);
}
```

The loop continues until the degree of b_w goes to zero. At that point, the value of b_w coefficient to t^0 is checked to see whether it is zero. If it is, then all of a_w is the gcd result. Otherwise, the result is b_w, which will be 1 if there are no common factors, or it could be a constant value.

10.5 Inversion modulo a prime polynomial

This section describes the code that computes the inverse of a polynomial. To compute the slope between two points on a field extension curve, we need a denominator of the sum of the y values of the two points (equation 3.2). As with a field prime, we first compute the inverse modulo the prime polynomial.

The inversion routine uses both the quotient and remainder from Euclid's algorithm. The initialization follows equation 10.5, and the main loop follows equation 10.6. The variable t is the answer we seek, and all the other variables keep track of previous quotients and remainders to allow the reduction process to proceed.

Listing 10.4 shows the initialization process for inversion. Every variable in equation 10.5 is created and automatically set to zero. The nonzero variables are each set to their initial condition. Note that the value of one is a polynomial of degree 0 with the coefficient of t^0 set to 1.

Listing 10.4   Inversion initialization

```
void poly_invert(POLY *a, POLY b)
{
  mpz_t rho;
  POLY r, u, q, one, t, w, tmp, y, v;
  int done, i;

  mpz_init(rho);       ← ρ = 0
  poly_init(&v);
  poly_copy(&v, irrd);    | v = Irrd
  poly_init(&r);       ← r = 0
  poly_init(&u);
  poly_copy(&u, b);      | u = b
  poly_normal(&u);
  poly_init(&w);       ← w = 0
  poly_init(&q);       ← q = 0
  poly_init(&one);
  mpz_set_ui(one.coef[0], 1);   | one = 1 · t⁰
  poly_init(&t);       ← t = 0
  poly_init(&y);
  minv(y.coef[0], b.coef[b.deg]);  | y = 1/lc(b) · t⁰
```

In listing 10.5, the variable done is used to check whether the remainder goes to 1. The inverse of the leading coefficient of r is kept as a separate value in rho, and then r is normalized using routine 8.9. To compute the fourth line in equation 10.6, the variable tmp holds $q \cdot y$, so it can be subtracted from w. Every coefficient in t is then multiplied by rho. The rest of the loop is copying new values to old ones and then checking to see whether the loop is finished.

Listing 10.5   Inversion main loop

```
  poly_init(&tmp);
```

```
    done = 0;              Finished when
    while(!done)           r == 1
    {                                      Quotient and remainder
      poly_euclid(&q, &r, v, u);       ◄─┘ from v /u
      minv(rho, r.coef[r.deg]);    ◄─ ρ = 1/lc(r)
      poly_normal(&r);    ◄─ r *= ρ
      poly_mul(&tmp, q, y);       t = w - q · y
      poly_sub(&t, w, tmp);
      for(i=0; i<=t.deg; i++)
        mmul(t.coef[i], t.coef[i], rho);    t *= ρ
      poly_copy(&w, y);       w = y
      poly_copy(&y, t);       y = t
      poly_copy(&v, u);       v = u
      poly_copy(&u, r);       u = r
      done = poly_cmp(r, one);    ◄─ Is r == 1?
    }
    poly_copy(a, t);    ◄─ Output t as the result.
    mpz_clear(rho);
    poly_clear(&r);
    poly_clear(&u);
    poly_clear(&q);              Clean up stack.
    poly_clear(&one);
    poly_clear(&t);
    poly_clear(&w);
    poly_clear(&tmp);
    poly_clear(&y);
    poly_clear(&v);
}
```

There are a lot of variables in this routine, so the end is simply saving the final result to the expected output location and clearing out all the variables to prevent memory leaks.

10.6 *Division modulo a prime polynomial*

In this section, the inversion code is extended to act as division of two polynomials. The last routine in this chapter is very simple. The division routine is shown in listing 10.6. The variable q holds the inverse of input c. The input b is multiplied by q, and we are done. This is exactly the same process as the mod_div() and mdiv() routines from chapter 2. The main difference here is the lack of a check for division by zero. Eventually, mod_div() will be called in poly_euclid(), and that error will be exposed. The program will halt, and the long process of debugging will begin.

Listing 10.6   Division modulo irreducible polynomial

```
void poly_div(POLY *a, POLY b, POLY c)
{
  POLY q;
```

```
    int i;

    poly_init(&q);
    poly_invert(&q, c);
    poly_mul(a, b, q);
    poly_clear(&q);
}
```
$$\mathbf{a} = \frac{1}{c} \cdot b$$

Answers to exercises

1 Initialize with rem $= 13x^7 + 14x^3 + 19x + 6$ and quot $= 0$.
Then $s = 13$, index $= 2$, and quot $= 13x^2$. Then compute $s \cdot b \cdot x^2 = 13x^7 - 13x^4 + 6$.
Subtracting from rem gives rem $= 13x^4 + 14x^3 + 19x$.
The final result is quotient $= 13x^2$, and the remainder $= 13x^4 + 14x^3 + 19x$ mod 43.

2 $x^2 + 22x + 8$. When multiplied out, it would be $\gcd(x^3 + 13x^2 + 4x + 12, x^4 + 22x^3 + 2x^2 + 16x + 11)$. This becomes tedious without a computer.

Summary

- Euclid's division algorithm applies to polynomials over a finite field as well as to integers.
- The greatest common divisor (gcd) function between two polynomials returns the other argument if one input is zero.
- The gcd of two polynomials uses the remainder from Euclidean division.
- The gcd code is used to find irreducible polynomials.
- Inversion modulo a prime polynomial uses the extended Euclidean algorithm to solve the equation:
$$A \cdot t \cong 1 \bmod f$$
  The polynomial $t = 1/A$.
- Division of polynomials is interpreted as inversion then multiplication.
- All the routines in this chapter are essential for computing pairing algorithms in part 3.

Creating irreducible polynomials

Computing pairings of points on elliptic curves over field extensions requires an irreducible polynomial. The irreducible polynomial defines the specific values of the field extension. In this chapter, the details of how to create an irreducible polynomial are described.

In chapter 8, I defined an irreducible polynomial over a finite field as a polynomial with coefficients taken modulo a prime number, which has no other factors. A field extension of degree k will have a defining irreducible polynomial of degree k. There are a great many irreducible polynomials one can choose to define a field extension. The simplest polynomial with the highest probability of existence is the trinomial (a three-term polynomial) for any field prime. I'll first describe the theory for finding irreducible trinomials and then explain the code for finding irreducible trinomials.

11.1 Basic theory of irreducible polynomials

In this section, I'll cover the theory behind the construction of irreducible polynomials. It's actually more like discovering because the process involves trial and error. I'll discuss a few theorems that we can take advantage of and then explain an algorithm that will find irreducible polynomials we can use.

I have found Lidl and Niederreiter (1997) to be very useful for understanding finite fields over polynomials and finite field extensions. Von zur Gathen and Gerhard (1999) is very useful for algorithms associated with field extensions and polynomials. Both of these books prove the statement: the product of all monic irreducible polynomials whose degrees divide n is $x^{q^n} - x$. That is a very powerful thing to know and is pretty mind-bending. *All* the possible irreducible polynomials of degree n (and n's factors) are contained in that tiny formula.

Theorem 3.84 in Lidl and Niederreiter (1997) says, "For a prime n, the trinomial $x^n + x + a$ will be irreducible under certain conditions." Rather than compute those conditions, I'll use Ben-Or's algorithm explained in section 14.9 of von zur Gathen and Gerhard (1999) to test for irreducible polynomials.

For security purposes, I chose prime field extensions for values of n. Alternatives for efficiency using small factors for n are described as towers in Koblitz and Menezes (2005). An example would be $n = 15$, where you can have a polynomial of three terms be coefficients for a polynomial with five terms, as shown in equation 11.1:

$$(s_{52}t^2 + s_{51}t + s_{50})x^5 + (s_{42}t^2 + s_{41}t + s_{40})x^4 + \cdots \quad (11.1)$$

Over a finite field $q = p^n$, Ben-Or's algorithm is shown in figure 11.1. This uses the previous statement that all monic irreducible polynomials whose degree divides i are contained in $x^{q^i} - x$. We search for polynomials of degree 1 to $n/2$, which could be factors in a chosen polynomial.

As an example of how the algorithm works, take the irreducible polynomial from chapter 8: $f = x^2 + 13x + 1 \bmod 1187$. We first set $i = 1$ and compute the $\gcd(x^{1187} - x, f)$. PARI/gp gives the constant 849, which can be normalized to 1. Since $n = 2$, we are actually done. But to double-check, I used PARI/gp to find $\gcd(x^{1187^2} - x, f)$. The result was f, which is to be expected since $x^2 + 13x + 1$ must be one of the factors of $x^{1187^2} - x$ by the theorems mentioned at the start of this section.

Ben-Or's algorithm starts by choosing a random polynomial. The idea here is that irreducible polynomials are uniformly distributed over all possible coefficients. The power index is initialized with $i = 1$. The main step is to check whether there are any common factors between polynomial f and $x^{q^i} - x$. If there are, then f has factors, so it can not be irreducible. We only need to search i up to $n/2$ because any factor larger was found by its smaller companion. By combining the theorem for prime degree with Ben-Or's algorithm, the random choice can be replaced with a counter on the coefficient to the constant term (x^0) of polynomial f.

According to theorem 3.86 in Lidl and Niederreiter (1997), the density of irreducible polynomials goes as q/n where $q = p^n$ is a field extension, and n is the degree of

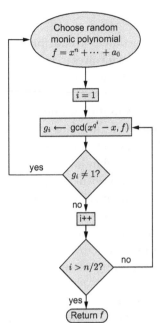

Figure 11.1   Ben-Or's algorithm for finding irreducible polynomials using trial and error

the irreducible polynomial we seek. For our case, p is over 160 bits, and n is 4 to 6 bits. We expect to find an irreducible polynomial very quickly!

Exercise 11.1

Find the first irreducible trinomial for $x^7 + x + b$ mod 29. (Hint: Use PARI/gp to factor: `Mod(1, 29)*x^7 + Mod(1, 29)*x + Mod(b, 29)`.)

11.2 Code for finding irreducible polynomials

In this section, I'll describe one way to deal with using and finding irreducible polynomials. I'll first introduce storage and methods for setting and retrieving values. Then I'll dive into the execution of Ben-Or's algorithm to find an irreducible trinomial.

Because a field extension requires a fixed irreducible polynomial as a reference, I create two variables as globals in the `poly.c` file. The variable `irrd` has been seen before. The variable `ptok` is $q = p^k$ in Ben-Or's algorithm. The following listing shows these variables.

Listing 11.1   Irreducible static variables

```
                          Irreducible basis polynomial
                          (degree k)
static POLY irrd;
static mpz_t ptok;        p^k
```

Listing 11.2 shows how the irreducible polynomial is set into the variables in listing 11.1. The input polynomial i is placed into the static variable irrd. The degree of polynomial i is used to compute $q = p^k$.

Listing 11.2   Irreducible set function

```
void poly_irrd_set(POLY i)
{
  poly_init(&irrd);        | Polynomial irrd
  poly_copy(&irrd, i);     | initialized
  mget(ptok);        ← get p
  mpz_pow_ui(ptok, ptok, i.deg); | Save field size p^k.
}
```

The following listing shows two simple routines that return either the irreducible polynomial or the value of q.

Listing 11.3   Irreducible get functions

```
void poly_irrd_get(POLY *i)
{
  poly_copy(i, irrd);   ← Return irreducible polynomial.
}

void poly_q_get(mpz_t pk)
{
  mpz_init(pk);
  mpz_set(pk, ptok);   ← Copy extension field cardinality.
}
```

Listing 11.4 shows the start of the routine that finds an irreducible polynomial of a specified degree. If the requested degree is larger than the maximum-sized polynomials allowed, the routine returns 0, which means it did not find an irreducible polynomial. The calling program should trap the error at that point because none of the mathematics will work without one.

Listing 11.4   Irreducible polynomial startup

```
int poly_irreducible(POLY *f, long n)
{
  POLY q, r, x, xp[MAXDEGREE/2], xpm1;
  mpz_t j, prime;
  long i, mlimt, done;

  if(n > MAXDEGREE)     | Safety check
    return 0;           | change MAXDEGREE to fix
```

Listing 11.5 shows the variable initialization. The polynomial r is the trial polynomial. If this passes Ben-Or's test, it is returned as the result. It starts out as $x^n + x + 2$. The array of polynomials xp[] holds the powers of x^{p^i} modulo r. The variable xpm1 holds $x^{p^i} - x$ for each i through the loop.

Listing 11.5   Irreducible polynomial variable initialization

```
poly_init(&r);
r.deg = n;                          Test polynomial.
mpz_set_ui(r.coef[n], 1);           r = x^n + x
mpz_set_ui(r.coef[1], 1);
poly_init(&x);                      Variable x
x.deg = 1;                          is 1 · x^1.
mpz_set_ui(x.coef[1], 1);
poly_init(&q);      ← gcd result
poly_init(&xpm1);   ← x^{p^m} - x
mlimt = n/2;                        Space for
for(i=0; i<mlimt; i++)             x^{p^m}
  poly_init(&xp[i]);               for all m < n/2
mget(prime);
mpz_init_set_ui(j, 2);   ← Start at a_0 = 2.
```

Listing 11.6 is the main rejection loop. For initial testing, the value of prime is small, so I check that the variable j, which is the coefficient of x^0, does not exceed the prime value. For large primes, this would take the age of the universe, so it is pointless.

Listing 11.6   Irreducible polynomial rejection loop

```
done = 0;
while((mpz_cmp(j, prime) < 0) && !done)   ← For small primes, check j < p.
{
  mpz_set(r.coef[0], j);   ← Convert counter to coefficient.
  mpz_add_ui(j, j, 1);     ← Increment counter
  poly_mulprep(r);         ← Create multiplication table.
  i = 0;
  q.deg = 0;                          Keep going while
  while((i<mlimt) && !q.deg)          gcd result is 1.
  {
    if(!i)
      poly_xp(&xp[0], x);             Index i
    else                              is 1 less than
      poly_xp(&xp[i], xp[i-1]);       exponent power.
    poly_sub(&xpm1, xp[i], x);        q = gcd(x^{p^i} - x, r)
    poly_gcd(&q, xpm1, r);
    i++;
  }
  if(q.deg)    ← Has factors, so not irreducible
    continue;
```

Once the polynomial r is set, it is used to create the multiplication matrix described in chapter 8. The variable i is used as an index for the array of powers of x modulo r.

But as we see in Ben-Or's algorithm, the first power is 1. So the index is off by 1 for each power, which means $xp[i] = x^{p^{i+1}}$.

The inner while loop checks for $q.deg$ being zero. If it is not, then r has a factor in $x^{p^{i+1}} - x$, so it can not be irreducible. If the inner loop bails out with $q.deg > 0$, the next j value will be tested.

If i is incremented to mlimit and $q.deg$ has remained zero for every test, then we have found an irreducible polynomial. The following listing shows the end of the routine.

Listing 11.7   Irreducible polynomial finish

```
                    If we get this far,
                    it is irreducible.

  done = 1;                │ Finished with loop
  poly_copy(f, r);         │ and output result
}
poly_clear(&r);
poly_clear(&x);
poly_clear(&q);
for(i=0; i<mlimt; i++)
  poly_clear(&xp[i]);                Clean up stack.
poly_clear(&xpm1);
mpz_clears(j, prime, NULL);
if(done)
  return 1;
return 0;     ← Will never be executed!
}
```

The main task is cleaning up all the variables. The expectation is that done will always be set, and the last line of code will never be executed. While Lidl and Niederreiter (1997) omits the proof, theorem 3.86 of that text ensures us that trinomials used in the previous routine will be irreducible with high probability.

Answer to exercise

1 $b = 7$ is the first irreducible trinomial. PARI/gp gives

```
factor(Mod(1,29)*x^7+Mod(1,29)*x+Mod(7,29))
%29 =
[Mod(1, 29)*x^7 + Mod(1, 29)*x + Mod(7, 29) 1]
```

Summary

- Trinomials are the simplest polynomials with a high probability of being irreducible over a finite field. Trinomials reduce the amount of work required in computing polynomial products and remainders.
- A k degree polynomial f is irreducible when

$$\gcd(x^{p^i} - x, f) = 1$$

for all $1 \leq i \leq k/2$.
- We can find irreducible trinomials incrementing the constant term a_0 until one passes Ben-Or's algorithm. Mathematicians have proven the density of irreducible polynomials is high, so this is guaranteed to work in only a few steps.

Taking square roots
of polynomials

12

This chapter covers

- Polynomial pseudo-division
- Resultant function of two polynomials
- Quadratic residue for a polynomial
- Square root of a polynomial modulo a prime polynomial

In this chapter, we'll dive into the details of computing square roots modulo a prime polynomial so we can find solutions to the elliptic curve equation. At the end of chapter 2, I showed you how to compute square roots over a prime number field. The same process is used over a field created by an irreducible polynomial.

The equation of an elliptic curve has the form $y^2 = f(x)$. The example given in chapter 3 is $y^2 = x^3 - 5x + 5$, where $f(x) = x^3 - 5x + 5$. To find the y coordinate requires taking a square root. When the field we are using is an extension of a prime field, the coordinates are polynomials.

Computing square roots modulo an irreducible polynomial is similar to computing square roots modulo a prime number. The main difference is that we are looking for two identical polynomial factors. This is similar to factoring a polynomial.

In the article by Doliskani and Schost (2011), there are descriptions of algorithms for exceptionally high polynomial degrees. They show that the algorithm of Tonelli-Shanks is perfectly adequate for our purposes since our embedding degrees are small. This is fortunate because we already know how to perform the Tonelli-Shanks algorithm with prime numbers.

The methods proposed in Doliskani and Schost (2011) include using a function called a resultant of two polynomials. A resultant of two polynomials is zero if they have a common factor. We will use the resultant of a polynomial with the irreducible polynomial of the field extension to determine whether a polynomial is a quadratic residue. As we saw in chapter 2, knowing whether something is a quadratic residue tells us we can, in fact, compute a square root. To compute a resultant, I will follow algorithm 3.3.7 in Cohen (2000).

The computation of the resultant uses, in turn, an algorithm called pseudo-division. So, in the following description of how to compute a square root, I'll describe how the resultant computes a quadratic residue and how pseudo-division helps compute the resultant.

After the theory is described, routines to compute pseudo-division, resultant, quadratic residue, and the square root itself will be listed.

12.1   *Mathematics for square root modulo a prime polynomial*

In this section, I'll cover the algorithms used to find a square root over a field extension so we can ensure a point is on an elliptic curve. Factoring polynomials is a complicated process. Factoring polynomials modulo an irreducible polynomial over a prime field can get fairly deep. Fortunately, we don't need most of that machinery to search for a square root. From the formula for an elliptic curve ($y^2 = x^3 + a_4 x + a_6$), we only need the square root of a polynomial modulo the prime polynomial to find the y coordinate. Similar to how a square root was done in chapter 2 modulo a prime number, we first want to know whether we can even take a square root by determining whether the polynomial is a quadratic residue.

Figure 12.1 shows the same algorithm as described in chapter 2 with primes replaced by polynomials. Instead of checking the last two bits of field prime p, we check the last two bits of p^k. If both are not set, we perform the Tonelli-Shanks algorithm.

The most significant change is the bolded box in figure 12.1, which requires finding a polynomial quadratic nonresidue. Solving this problem took a roundabout path, which involved learning about factoring high-degree polynomials.

Doliskani and Schost (2011) is a general factorization process for finite field elements modulo an irreducible polynomial f. In section 3.2, the authors first state that testing whether an element a has a t-th root is the same as testing whether $a^{(q-1)/t} = 1$ where $q = p^n$. They go on to say, "In the particular case when t divides $p - 1$, we can actually do better: we have $a^{(q-1)/t} = \text{res}(f, a)^{(p-1)/t}$, where $\text{res}(\cdot, \cdot)$ is

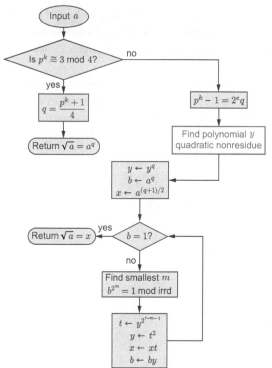

Figure 12.1 Polynomial square root algorithm for finding y value of point on elliptic curve

the resultant function." For us, what that means is finding out whether a polynomial a is a quadratic residue or not requires checking

$$\text{res}(f, a)^{(p-1)/2} \stackrel{?}{=} 1$$

If the result is 1, we can take a square root; otherwise, we cannot. Figure 12.2 lays out the quadratic residue algorithm as it will be written in code.

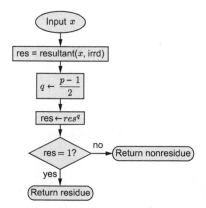

Figure 12.2 Polynomial quadratic residue algorithm to determine whether a polynomial has a square root

A resultant of two polynomials is a single value modulo the field prime. Section 3.3.2 of Cohen (2000) describes a couple of equivalent definitions. One is a determinant of the coefficients of both polynomials f and a. Another is the product of the difference in every root of both polynomials. The resultant algorithm 3.3.7 in Cohen uses neither of those definitions. Cohen proves his algorithm gives the correct answer, and that algorithm is what I use.

The resultant algorithm is shown in figure 12.3. If either input polynomial is zero, the resultant is zero. The next thing we see in the algorithm of computing the resultant is $a \leftarrow \mathrm{cont}(A)$, which is the content of a polynomial. The content of a polynomial is found by taking the greatest common divisor (gcd) of all the coefficients. For monic polynomials, this is always 1.

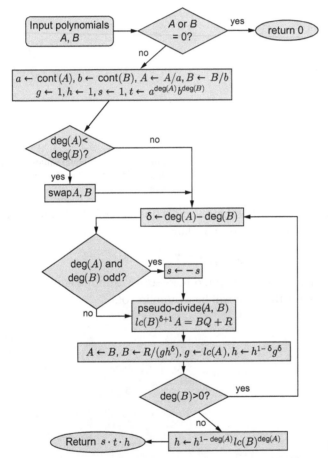

Figure 12.3   Resultant algorithm

As an example look at

$$a = 4x^4 + 24x^3 + 12x^2 + 4x + 32$$

The $\mathrm{cont}(a) = 4$. The first step in finding a resultant is removing the content of each polynomial by dividing each coefficient by the common factor.

Along with removing the content of each polynomial, the result variables are initialized. The higher degree polynomial is forced to be A. If both polynomials have odd degree, the sign variable s is set to -1.

The main loop starts by setting δ to the power that would come from dividing A/B. If both polynomials have odd degree, the sign of s is toggled. The quotient and remainder from pseudo-division are then computed. The reduction step modifies A, B, g, and h. The loop terminates when $\deg(B)$ goes to zero.

A degree zero B means it is a constant, so the $lc(B)$ in the last step is the only coefficient of B. The final output is the product of sign, initial content values, and variable h.

It is pretty amazing this algorithm computes the determinant of a matrix created by the coefficients of two polynomials. It definitely works to determine quadratic residues.

An important step within the resultant algorithm is pseudo-division. This works with the leading coefficients (symbolized by $lc(\cdot)$) of the divisor polynomial. Given two polynomials A and B with $lc(B) = d$, then

$$d^{\deg(A)-\deg(B)+1}A = BQ + R$$

where Q is the quotient and R the remainder with $\deg(R) < \deg(B)$.

Figure 12.4 shows the pseudo-division algorithm taken from Cohen's (2000) algorithm 3.1.2. The first step initializes the quotient Q and remainder R as well as the starting exponent e and leading coefficient d. The reason the second step checks whether the algorithm is done is in case $\deg(A) < \deg(B)$, at which point there is nothing more to do.

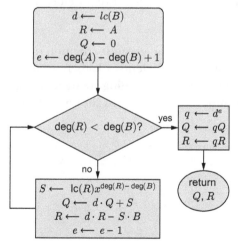

Figure 12.4   Pseudo-division algorithm

The compute step puts the leading coefficient of R into the coefficient of temporary variable S, which would be the leading coefficient of a division of R/B. The variable S is then used to modify Q and R, and the exponent is decremented.

There is a lot of similarity between the algorithm in figure 12.4 and equation 10.2. There is no actual division computation, so calling this pseudo-division makes sense.

Exercise 12.1

In the computation of polynomial square roots, the resultant has a similar task to what function in the calculation of square roots modulo a prime number?

12.2 Code for square roots modulo a prime polynomial

In this section, the code for computing square roots of polynomials is described. We need these routines to find random points on field extension curves. Those points are needed to compute the pairing calculations of chapters 18 and 19.

There are five subroutines involved in computing a square root modulo an irreducible polynomial. These routines are

- Content of a polynomial
- Pseudo-division of polynomials
- Resultant of two polynomials
- Quadratic residue of a polynomial
- Computing the square root of a polynomial

The simplest are content and checking whether a polynomial is a quadratic residue. The more complicated routines are pseudo-division, resultant, and taking the square root. The order of calling is content, pseudo-division, resultant, residue check, and, finally, square root. The following sections are in order of requirement.

12.2.1 Content routine

Computing the content of a polynomial finds the greatest common divisor of all the coefficients. If the gcd between any two coefficients is 1, there is no reason to check the remaining coefficients. So I start with the leading coefficient, hoping the polynomial is monic and that the routine can exit early, as shown in the following listing.

Listing 12.1   Content of a polynomial

```
void poly_cont(mpz_t cont, POLY A)
{
  int i;
  mpz_t rslt;

  mpz_init_set(rslt, A.coef[A.deg]);    ← set result to lc(A)
  for(i=A.deg-1; i>=0; i--)    | From the leading coefficient
  {                            | down to the lowest
    mpz_gcd(rslt, rslt, A.coef[i]);
```

```
   if(!mpz_cmp_ui(rslt, 1))          When the gcd of the result
      break;                         with coefficient
                                     == 1, then done
   }
   mpz_set(cont, rslt);    ← Copy result to return value.
   mpz_clear(rslt);
}
```

The comparison `mpz_cmp(rslt, 1)` will give 0 when the variable `rslt` is 1. If there is a common factor, `rslt` will contain it on every `mpz_gcd()` call. So the returned value is the common factor that defines the content.

12.2.2 *Pseudo-division routine*

The pseudo-division routine has three phases. The initialization is easy, the main loop is messy, and the cleanup is the last phase. The following listing shows the initialization phase.

Listing 12.2   Pseudo-division initialize

```
void poly_pseudo_div(POLY *Q, POLY *R, POLY A, POLY B)
{
   long e, i, k;
   mpz_t d;
   POLY S, T;

   poly_init(&S);          Set S = 0
   poly_init(&T);          T = 0 and
   poly_copy(R, A);        R = A.
   Q->deg = 0;
   mpz_set_ui(Q->coef[0], 0);     Set Q = 0.
   e = A.deg - B.deg + 1;            Set e to degree difference
   mpz_init_set(d, B.coef[B.deg]);  and d to lc(B).
```

The return values are quotient Q and remainder R. As with the division routine, I assume variable Q might be something random, and so I force it to zero. Variables e and d are set according to the first block in figure 12.4.

The main loop is shown in listing 12.3. The loop continues while the $\deg(R) \geq \deg(B)$. The variable T holds $S \cdot B$, which is really just a shift of B by the $\deg(S)$ multiplied by the leading coefficient of R. Since only one coefficient of S is set, that coefficient is cleared at the end of the loop.

Listing 12.3   Pseudo-division main loop

```
   while(R->deg >= B.deg)  ← While remainder greater than divisor
   {
      S.deg = R->deg - B.deg;     ← Degree of S if division happened
      mpz_set(S.coef[S.deg], R->coef[R->deg]);  ← lc(S) = lc(R)
      for(i=0; i<=Q->deg; i++)            Scale Q
         mmul(Q->coef[i], Q->coef[i], d); by d.
```

```
poly_add(Q, *Q, S);     ← Q ← Q + S
for(i=0; i<=R->deg; i++)            | Scale R
   mmul(R->coef[i], R->coef[i], d);  | by d.
k = S.deg;
for(i=0; i<=B.deg; i++)                         |
   mmul(T.coef[i + k], B.coef[i], S.coef[k]);  | T = B · S
T.deg = B.deg + k;                              |
poly_sub(R, *R, T);   ← Reduce R by T.
e--;                   | Decrement exponent
mpz_set_ui(S.coef[k], 0);  | clear S to 0.
}
```

The change of variable from `s.deg` to `k` was simply to make the multiply indexing easier to read.

When the loop finishes, we have a remainder, which is smaller than the denominator. The following listing shows the cleanup phase.

Listing 12.4   Pseudo-division cleanup

```
if(e >= 1)  ← Only change Q and R for e > 0.
{
  mpowi(d, d, e);    ← d ← d^e
  for(i=0; i<=Q->deg; i++)            | Scale Q
     mmul(Q->coef[i], Q->coef[i], d);  | by d.
  for(i=0; i<=R->deg; i++)            | Scale R
     mmul(R->coef[i], R->coef[i], d);  | by d.
}
mpz_clear(d);      | Clean
poly_clear(&S);    | up
poly_clear(&T);    | stack.
}
```

If variable e is zero, then $d^e = 1$ and there is no change to the quotient or remainder. Otherwise, the value of d^e is multiplied with every coefficient of both quotient and remainder. The internal variables are cleared out to prevent memory leaks, and the routine is done.

12.2.3 *Resultant subroutine*

In this section, I'll describe the code that computes the resultant of two polynomials. The resultant subroutine breaks up into four phases. The description in figure 12.3 has a main loop, which I'll show as one phase. The first phase determines whether either input is zero, and then the routine just returns zero, as shown in the following listing.

Listing 12.5   Resultant zero check

```
void poly_resltnt(mpz_t rsltnt, POLY A, POLY B)
```

```
{
  POLY Aa, Bb, Q, R;
  mpz_t g, h, ta, tb, a, b;
  long dlta, s, i;
  if(!A.deg && !A.coef[0])        If either A or B is zero,
  {                               resultant is zero.
    mpz_set_ui(rsltnt, 0);
    return;                       Both degree
  }                               and coefficient
  if(!B.deg && !B.coef[0])        must be zero
  {                               to exit.
    mpz_set_ui(rsltnt, 0);
    return;
  }
```

The initialization portion uses variables `ta` and `tb` to hold the value of $\text{cont}(A)^{\deg(B)}$ and $\text{cont}(B)^{\deg(A)}$, respectively. The variables `Aa` and `Bb` hold $A/\text{cont}(A)$ and $B/\text{cont}(B)$. The remaining variables are the same as in figure 12.3.

Listing 12.6   Resultant initialization

```
mpz_inits(g, h, ta, tb, a, b, NULL);   Initialize local variables.
poly_cont(a, A);       Get content
poly_cont(b, B);       of input polynomials.
poly_init(&Aa);
if(mpz_cmp_ui(a, 1))     ← content != 1
{
  Aa.deg = A.deg;
  for(i=0; i<=A.deg; i++)                Aa← A/a
    mdiv(Aa.coef[i], A.coef[i], a);
  mpowi(ta, a, B.deg);     ← ta← a^deg(B)
}
else
{
  poly_copy(&Aa, A);       If content == 1,
  mpz_set_ui(ta, 1);       just copy A to Aa.
}
poly_init(&Bb);
if(mpz_cmp_ui(b, 1))     ← content != 1
{
  Bb.deg = B.deg;
  for(i=0; i<=B.deg; i++)                Bb← B/b
    mdiv(Bb.coef[i], B.coef[i], b);
  mpowi(tb, b, A.deg);     ← tb← b^deg(A)
}
else
{
  poly_copy(&Bb, B);       If content == 1,
  mpz_set_ui(tb, 1);       just copy B to Bb.
}
mpz_set_ui(g, 1);
```

```
mpz_set_ui(h, 1);          Initialize
poly_init(&Q);             g, h, and s.
s = 1;
if(A.deg < B.deg)      ← Make A larger than B.
{
  poly_copy(&Q, Aa);        Swap A, B
  poly_copy(&Aa, Bb);       to ensure
  poly_copy(&Bb, Q);        A > B.
}
poly_init(&R);
```

The main loop from figure 12.3 is shown in the following listing. The loop continues as long as deg(B) is not zero.

Listing 12.7   Resultant main loop

```
while(Bb.deg > 0)   ← Terminate when B turns into constant.
{
  dlta = Aa.deg - Bb.deg;      ← dlta is degree after division.
  if((Aa.deg & 1) && (Bb.deg & 1))   Both polynomials are odd,
    s = -s;                          so change sign.
  poly_pseudo_div(&Q, &R, Aa, Bb);   ← Quotient and remainder from pseudo-division
  poly_copy(&Aa, Bb);
  mpowi(a, h, dlta);
  mmul(b, a, g);
  Bb.deg = R.deg;                    A ←B
  for(i=0; i<=R.deg; i++)            B ← R/(gh^δ)
    mdiv(Bb.coef[i], R.coef[i], b);

  mpz_set(g, Aa.coef[Aa.deg]);   Save new h, g values.
  i = 1 - dlta;
  mpowi(a, h, i);                    g← lc(A)
  mpowi(b, g, dlta);                 h← h^{1-δ}g^δ
  mmul(h, a, b);
}
```

On exit from the main loop, the last line in figure 12.3 becomes listing 12.8. This is a straightforward computation.

Listing 12.8   Resultant final output

**Finished;
compute final resultant.**

```
i = 1 - Aa.deg;
mpowi(a, h, i);
mpowi(b, Bb.coef[0], Aa.deg);   h← h^{1-deg(A)} lc(B)^{deg(A)}
mmul(h, a, b);
mmul(rsltnt, h, ta);
mmul(rsltnt, rsltnt, tb);
if(s < 0)                       output = s·h·t
  mneg(rsltnt, rsltnt);
poly_clear(&Aa);
```

```
    poly_clear(&Bb);
    poly_clear(&Q);          Clean up stack.
    poly_clear(&R);
    mpz_clears(g, h, ta, tb, a, b, NULL);
}
```

Rather than create the variable t as in the algorithm, I just left `ta` and `tb` as separate values. The final value is always a positive number modulo the field prime.

12.2.4 Quadratic residue

In this section, I'll give the code, which determines whether a polynomial has a square root. Now that we have the resultant function, we can find out whether a polynomial is a quadratic residue. If so, we can take a square root. The following listing shows how to compute a polynomial quadratic residue.

> **Listing 12.9   Quadratic residue routine**

```
int poly_sqr(POLY x)
{
  mpz_t res, p, q;
  int k;
                                    Compute resultant
  mpz_inits(res, q, NULL);          between the input
  poly_resltnt(res, x, irrd);    ◄─ and prime polynomial.
  mget(p);
  mpz_sub_ui(q, p, 1);
  mpz_div_ui(q, q, 2);           │ (p − 1)/2
  mpz_powm(res, res, q, p);      ◄── res(x, f)^{(p−1)/2}
  k = mpz_cmp_ui(res, 1);        ◄──┐ k is 0
  mpz_clears(res, p, q, NULL);      │ If res
  if(!k)                            │ is 1.
    return 1;
  return 0;
}
```

The trick here is that we have to save the result so we can clear temporary variables off the stack and internal heap of GMP. The compare function returns zero on an exact match, and ± 1 otherwise. If $res(x, f)^{(p-1)/2}$ equals 1 the polynomial x is a quadratic residue.

12.2.5 Polynomial square root routine

In this section, the code to implement square roots of a polynomial is described. This is used to find points on field extension elliptic curves. The assumption I make for the square root routine is that the check for quadratic residue happens first. This is normally the case for embedding because checking for a square root takes less effort than computing the square root and finding out there isn't one.

As with square roots modulo a prime, if the value of $p^k \cong 3 \bmod 4$, then we can power our way to a square root, as shown in the following listing.

Listing 12.10   Polynomial square root $p^k = 3$ mod 4

```
void poly_sqrt(POLY *sqt, POLY a)
{
  long r, i, ck, m, m2;
  mpz_t pk, q;
  POLY x, b, y, one, bpw, t;
```

See if $p^k = 3$ mod 4.

```
  poly_q_get(pk);
  mpz_init(q);
  if(mpz_tstbit(pk, 0) && mpz_tstbit(pk, 1))
  {
    poly_init(&y);
    mpz_add_ui(q, pk, 1);
    mpz_divexact_ui(q, q, 4);
    poly_pow(&y, a, q);
    poly_copy(sqt, y);
    poly_clear(&y);
    mpz_clears(q, pk, NULL);
    return;
  }
```

Last two bits set in p^k use easy method.

$q = \dfrac{p^k + 1}{4}$

Allow in place square root = a^q.

As with the description of Tonelli-Shanks in chapter 2, there is an initialization section as shown in listing 12.11. The main difference is that most of the variables are now polynomials instead of numbers. The coefficients of the polynomials are modulo the same field prime.

Listing 12.11   Polynomial square root initialize

$p^k = 1$ mod 4, so do Tonelli-Shanks.

```
mpz_sub_ui(q, pk, 1);
r = 0;
while(!mpz_tstbit(q, 0))
{
  mpz_divexact_ui(q, q, 2);
  r++;
}
poly_init(&y);
ck = 1;
while(ck)
{
  poly_rand(&y);
  ck = poly_sqr(y);
}
poly_pow(&y, y, q);
poly_init(&b);
poly_pow(&b, a, q);
poly_init(&x);
mpz_add_ui(pk, q, 1);
mpz_divexact_ui(pk, pk, 2);
poly_pow(&x, a, pk);
```

Find $p^k - 1 = 2^r q$.

Choose random nonresidue polynomial.

$y \leftarrow y^q$

$b = a^q$

$x = a^{(q+1)/2}$

```
poly_init(&one);
one.deg = 0;                          Polynomial constant one
mpz_set_ui(one.coef[0], 1);
poly_init(&bpw);
poly_init(&t);
```

The initialization is slightly different here than in the field prime code. The formula in equation 2.5 is a value for x and b. Multiplying b out, we have

$$b = ax^2 = a(a^{(q-1)/2})^2 = a^q$$

The final value for x is then

$$x = a(a^{(q-1)/2}) = a^{(q+1)/2}$$

While the code looks different, it is actually doing the same job.

The main loop is also similar, but instead of checking whether a value is 1, I check whether a polynomial is 1. While, technically, it is the same thing, the structures being worked with are different. The following listing shows the main loop.

Listing 12.12   Polynomial square root main loop

```
while(!poly_cmp(b, one))   ← Done when b equals 1
{
    m = 0;
    while(!poly_cmp(bpw, one))
    {
        m++;                            Find smallest m
        m2 = 1 « m;                     such that $b^{2^m}$
        mpz_set_ui(pk, m2);             equals 1
        poly_pow(&bpw, b, pk);  ←── modulo prime polynomial.
        if(m == r)
        {
            printf("square root failed\n");
            return;                                     Should never happen
        }
    }
    mpz_set_ui(bpw.coef[0], 0);   ← Clear test polynomial.
    i = r - m - 1;
    m2 = 1 « i;                         $t = y^{2^{r-m-1}}$
    mpz_set_ui(pk, m2);
    poly_pow(&t, y, pk);  ←
    poly_mul(&y, t, t);   ←  $y \leftarrow t^2$
    r = m;
    poly_mul(&x, x, t);      $x \leftarrow x\,t$
    poly_mul(&b, b, y);      $b \leftarrow b\,y$
}
```

The test for m == r should never succeed if the polynomial is a quadratic residue. When the loop is finished, the value for the square root is copied to the desired result storage location, and all variables are cleaned out from the stack, as shown in the following listing.

Listing 12.13   Polynomial square root cleanup

```
poly_copy(sqt, x);    ← Copy result to output.
poly_clear(&x);
poly_clear(&b);
poly_clear(&y);
poly_clear(&one);
poly_clear(&bpw);               Clean up stack.
poly_clear(&t);
mpz_clears(pk, q, NULL);
}
```

With the code complete for taking a square root of a polynomial modulo an irreducible polynomial, we can now embed random polynomial x values on an elliptic curve defined over the same irreducible polynomial. Visualizing x and y axes, which are finite field polynomials of dimension k with an elliptic curve running through the space, is challenging. The best we can do is revisit the curve from chapter 3 and pretend we know what is going on because the equations are the same. As pointed out in chapter 3, finite field elliptic curves have a one-to-one correspondence with curves over the complex plane. The symmetry we see in figure 12.5 applies to elliptic curves over field extensions. Using images like figure 12.5, we can see how picking some random x polynomial would give rise to two points on an elliptic curve.

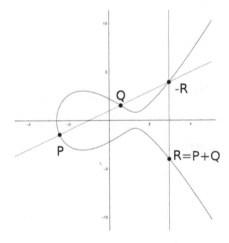

Figure 12.5   Elliptic curve $y^2 = x^3 - 5x + 5$

Answer to exercise

1 The resultant is similar to the Legendre symbol. Both functions determine whether it is possible to compute a square root.

Summary

- The resultant of two polynomials is a single value modulo the field prime of the coefficients. The resultant is used to determine whether a polynomial has a square root.

- A polynomial A modulo a prime polynomial f has a square root when

$$resultant(A, f)^{(p-1)/2} = 1$$

The polynomial A is called a quadratic residue when this is true. When true, we have a point on a field extension elliptic curve.

- The content of a polynomial is the gcd of all its coefficients. Removing the content of a polynomial is an essential step in computing a square root.

- The resultant is computed using pseudo-division and a reduction step. The resultant is used to determine whether a polynomial has a square root.

- A polynomial A mod f, which is a quadratic residue over an extension field that is congruent to 3 mod 4, has a square root computed using

$$A^{(p^k+1)/4}$$

Otherwise, the Tonelli-Shanks algorithm is used. This is the same process used in chapter 2 and has the same purpose: to find a point on an elliptic curve.

Part 3

Pairings

Chapters 13 to 19 use the subroutines from chapters 2 through 12 to develop the code required to compute elliptic curve pairings of points on field extensions. The code to compute pairings used in blockchain technology is the goal of this last part.

Now that we have the background of elliptic curves over field extensions under our belts, we can begin to tackle the pairing of points on field extension curves. Knowing how to compute pairings will allow us to verify aggregated signatures from multiple people, so only one test is performed to determine the validity of a signature. It will also give us the ability to compute zero-knowledge proofs using state-of-the-art protocols.

The pairing of two points of order n on an elliptic curve is a form of multiplication. The result of the operation is just a field element. The field element has the special property of being an nth root of unity. So if r is the result of a pairing, $r^n = 1$. That is what makes elliptic curve pairing such a useful one-way trap door function. Given r and one of the points in the pairing, you cannot find the other point.

Chapter 13 covers elliptic curve subroutines over finite field extensions using the polynomial routines already described. It is very similar to chapter 3 in terms of the routines because we have the same job to do. The (x, y) values are now polynomials with coefficients modulo the prime field, and these polynomials are modulo an irreducible polynomial. In a sense, we have just "leveled up" to a new field, which is called a field extension.

Chapter 14 goes into the details of how low embedding degree curves can be constructed. For the curves in part 1, we desire a very high embedding degree, so the MOV attack can not be used. We still require a degree high enough that the MOV attack will fail but not so high that we can not use the curve. While there are many algorithms to choose from, I will describe two that are useful for prime number embedding degrees.

The general mathematics of pairings are described in chapter 15. I'll explain the algorithms used to compute pairings and develop the code as a set of subroutines for the following two chapters. The use of a reference point as a third point in the calculation is explained here.

In chapter 16, I'll explain the Weil pairing. Weil pairings use the subroutines from chapter 15 symmetrically. The Weil pairing requires both points to have the same order. One of the properties of the Weil pairing is that if the input points have the same base, the result will be 1. For some algorithms, this can be a problem because 1 = 1 will result even when the inputs are not correct.

Chapter 17 covers the Tate pairing. Tate pairings use the routines from chapter 15 in an asymmetric manner. The input points do not require the same order but must have a related prime in their order for the pairing to work. For some algorithms, the asymmetry of the Tate pairing allows two points with the same base to give an nth root of unity result.

Chapters 18 and 19 go into the use of pairings. Both of these uses of pairings are exceptionally useful in blockchain technology for multiple node signatures and proof of activity without revealing ownership. Extensions of the BLS signature are covered in chapter 18. Multiple signers of a single document can create an aggregate signature. This signature is easily verified using pairings. Chapter 19 explains zk-SNARKS, which are zero-knowledge proofs. The fundamental idea of zero knowledge is the ability to prove data is real without exposing the data.

Finite field extension
curves described

In this chapter, I'll dive into elliptic curves over finite field extensions. These curves are required to compute pairings. The cryptographic protocols enabled by pairings of points over elliptic curves have a lot of advantages. But before we can compute pairings, we first need a point addition algorithm over a field extension of an elliptic curve.

Elliptic curve subroutines using polynomials are the subject of this chapter. I'll first cover some of the rules required to create a field extension and then assume we already have found a useful curve. In chapter 14, I'll go into how that actually happens. As with chapter 3, I will cover routines that manipulate point and curve structures, embed polynomials on a curve, create random points, add points, and multiply points. While most places replace an `m*` routine with a `poly*` routine, there are a few differences because polynomials are more complicated than numbers.

To help visualize the ideas here and in the next few chapters, I will use a very tiny curve as an illustration. This curve was definitely cherry-picked to contain as many useful examples as possible.

13.1 *Field extension properties*

Recall from chapter 2 that a finite field has elements that can be added, multiplied, and inverted. In this section, I will expand that same concept using irreducible polynomials in place of prime numbers. This is another reason an irreducible polynomial is synonymous with a prime polynomial.

In chapter 8, I showed how irreducible polynomials act as a modulus for polynomial multiplication and, in chapter 10, how irreducible polynomials act as the modulus for inversion. Since we also have addition, it seems pretty clear that an irreducible polynomial creates a finite field. In this section, we are going to make use of an irreducible polynomial to create an extension field of a precise size. With the polynomial routines of part 2 as a base, creating elliptic curve routines similar to chapter 3 is then easy.

Theorem 1.87 of Lidl and Niederreiter (1997) states that an irreducible polynomial f creates a field extension with the root of f as the defining element. Setting $f(t) = 0$ defines those roots. We did that in chapter 8 to create the polynomial multiplication table. Everything we did in part 2 allows us to do mathematics over a field extension.

Figure 13.1 is a conceptual illustration of a field extension. A prime field p is extended to a k dimensional vector space. Each dimension acts like the prime field p, but there are k of these fields. A polynomial is used to keep track of where we are in each dimension.

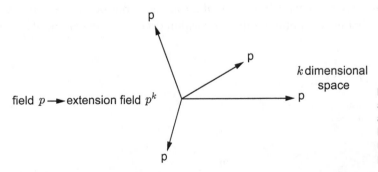

Figure 13.1 Expanding a prime base field p to an extension field p^k. Extension fields are required to compute pairings.

An elliptic curve can be defined over any finite field. However, we can not just pick any irreducible polynomial for a field extension of degree k. Extending a curve from a number field p to a field extension p^k has special rules.

Suppose we have a specific elliptic curve over a prime finite field p with cardinality $\#E$ as in equation 6.2 ($\#E = p + 1 - t$). Let's assume there is a large prime r as a factor of $\#E$. For pairings to work, the extension field p^k must also have a factor of r in the extension curve cardinality ($\#E_k$). The smallest value of k for which there is a factor of r in $\#E_k$ is called the embedding degree.

From Freeman et al. (2006), the rule is written as shown in equation 13.1:

$$p^k \cong 1 \bmod r \tag{13.1}$$

Equation 6.2 is true for extension curves but is rewritten as equation 13.2:

$$\#E_k = p^k + 1 - t_k \tag{13.2}$$

Homework problem 5.13 in Silverman (2009) gives a recurrence relation for t_k. Starting with $t_0 = 2$ and $t_1 = p + 1 - \#E$ (equation 6.2), there is equation 13.3:

$$t_{n+2} = t_1 t_{n+1} - p t_n \tag{13.3}$$

which takes the prime p and trace of Frobenius of the curve t_1 to find the cardinality of the field extension $\#E_k$.

According to Freeman et al. (2006), the average embedding degree for arbitrary curves over a prime field p with points of order r is on the order of r. A prime r with 160 bits means the number of coefficients is around 2^{160}, and each coefficient is 160 bits. Even imagining the level of computational impossibility is difficult.

Curves over a finite field p are called group 1 curves or G_1. Curves over a field extension p^k are called group 2 curves or G_2. The same coefficients in equation 3.1 ($y^2 = x^3 + a_4 x + a_6$) on a G_1 curve are used to create the points on a G_2 curve. The coefficients a_4 and a_6 are still modulo the same field prime but turn into coefficients of t^0 modulo an irreducible polynomial. So the x and y values become polynomials for the G_2 curve.

After listing all the polynomial elliptic curve code, I will give a really tiny example so the G_1 and G_2 points can be listed. This will make the meaning more visible.

Exercise 13.1

Suppose we have an elliptic curve over a field prime of 41. There is a "large prime factor" in the cardinality of 29. What is the embedding degree?

13.2   *Elliptic curve routines*

This section repeats the code from chapter 3 but changes it to work with polynomials in a field extension. The routines that implement elliptic curves over a field extension are similar to the routines of chapter 3. In addition to operating modulo a field prime, they also operate modulo an irreducible polynomial. Similar to chapter 3, I set up a structure for points and curves but using polynomials. Initializing and clearing these structures is used in all the following routines:

- `poly_test_point()`
- `poly_fofx()`
- `FF_bump()`
- `poly_elptic_embed()`
- `poly_point_rand()`
- `poly_elptic_sum()`
- `poly_elptic_mul()`

Code for copying points, as well as printing points and curves for field extensions, will then be shown. A routine to test for the point at infinity (`poly_test_point()`) followed by a routine to compute the right-hand side of equation 3.1 ($x^3 + a_4x + a_6$) (`poly_fofx()`) over a field extension is presented.

For embedding a point, a special routine is created to increment a polynomial (`FF_bump()`). It is overly complicated, so it will work with the tiny example curve. With that special routine, the embedding code itself is then presented (`poly_elptic_embed()`). Creating a random point on a field extension then calls the embedding routine (`poly_point_rand()`). The routines to compute addition (`poly_elptic_sum()`) and multiplication (`poly_elptic_mul()`) of finite field extension points are at the end of this section.

13.2.1   *Polynomial curve setup*

This section defines structures used with field extension points and curves. These will be used in all the remaining subroutines in this book. I'll start off with a header that defines a point and curve structure using polynomials as shown in the following listing. I put this in a file called `poly_eliptic.h` (and I still can't spell!).

> **Listing 13.1   Polynomial elliptic curve structures**

```
#include "poly.h"

typedef struct
{
    POLY    x;          Polynomials for
    POLY    y;          x and y values
}POLY_POINT;

typedef struct
{
```

```
   POLY  a4;        | Polynomials for
   POLY  a6;        | curve parameters
} POLY_CURVE;
```

As with structures for group 1 curves, the structures in listing 13.1 require initialization and clearing. These routines are shown in the following listing.

Listing 13.2 Polynomial elliptic curve structure manipulation

```
void poly_point_init(POLY_POINT *P)
{
  int i;

  P->x.deg = 0;                              | Zero out
  P->y.deg = 0;                              | both x and y
  for(i=0; i<MAXDEGREE; i++)    ◄──────┘ components.
    mpz_inits(P->x.coef[i], P->y.coef[i], NULL);
}

void poly_point_clear(POLY_POINT *P)
{
  int i;

  for(i=0; i<MAXDEGREE; i++)                | Remove all components
    mpz_clears(P->x.coef[i], P->y.coef[i], NULL);  ◄─┘ from the GMP heap.
}

void poly_curve_init(POLY_CURVE *E)
{
  int i;

  E->a4.deg = 0;
  E->a6.deg = 0;
  for(i=0; i<MAXDEGREE; i++)                | Put polynomials a₄
    mpz_inits(E->a4.coef[i], E->a6.coef[i], NULL);  ◄─┘ and a₆ on the stack.
}

void poly_curve_clear(POLY_CURVE *E)
{
  int i;

  for(i=0; i<MAXDEGREE; i++)                | Remove a₄ and
    mpz_clears(E->a4.coef[i], E->a6.coef[i], NULL);  ◄─┘ a₆ from the stack.
}
```

The polynomial code is not space-efficient. It is just a lot easier to see what is going on by simply allowing the possibility of a maximum degree polynomial.

13.2.2 *Polynomial curve utilities*

In this section, a few basic routines are described for manipulating polynomial points. Utility routines are shown in the following listing. Copying a point and printing points, which are polynomials, are simple `poly*` calls for the x and y components.

Listing 13.3   Polynomial elliptic curve utility functions

```
void poly_point_copy(POLY_POINT *R, POLY_POINT P)
{
  int i;

  poly_copy(&R->x, P.x);        │ Copy x component.
  poly_copy(&R->y, P.y);        │ Copy y component.
}

void poly_point_printf(char *str, POLY_POINT P)
{
    printf("%s ", str);
    printf("x: ");                │ Output x and y
    poly_print(P.x);             │ components on
    poly_printf("y: ", P.y);     │ separate lines.
}

void poly_curve_printf(char *str, POLY_CURVE E)
{
    printf("%s ", str);
    poly_printf("a4: ", E.a4);   │ Output a4 and a6
    poly_printf("a6: ", E.a6);   │ components on
}                                │ separate lines.
```

As with prime field curves, the point at infinity is the same test over polynomial curves. The following listing shows the routine for this test.

Listing 13.4   Polynomial elliptic curve test point at infinity

```
int poly_test_point(POLY_POINT P)
{
  int i;

  if(P.x.deg || P.y.deg)   ← Neither polynomial constant, then not 0
    return 0;
  if(!mpz_cmp_ui(P.x.coef[0], 0) && !mpz_cmp_ui(P.y.coef[0], 0))
    return 1;              ┌ Both x and y zero for
  return 0;                │ point at infinity
}
```

This is pretty easy to bail on: if either the x or y is actually a polynomial, it can't be zero. If both x and y are constants, then I can check whether both are zero.

13.2.3 *Polynomial curve point embedding*

In this section, the code for embedding a polynomial onto a field extension curve is explained. There are several subroutines used to embed polynomial points on a curve. The fofx() routine is the same as before, but there is a new routine to increment an x value. The following listing shows the polynomial version of fofx(), which is the right-hand side of equation 3.1 ($x^3 + a_4 x + a_6$).

| **Listing 13.5   Polynomial elliptic curve right-hand side** |

```
void poly_fofx(POLY *f, POLY x, POLY_CURVE E)
{
  POLY t1, t2;

  poly_init(&t1);
  poly_init(&t2);
  poly_mul(&t1, x, x);           t1 = x³
  poly_mul(&t1, t1, x);
  poly_mul(&t2, E.a4, x);     ← t2 = xa₄
  poly_add(f, t1, t2);
  poly_add(f, *f, E.a6);         f = x³ + xa₄ + a₆
  poly_clear(&t1);
  poly_clear(&t2);
}
```

$t1 = x^3$

$t2 = xa_4$

$f = x^3 + xa_4 + a_6$

Listing 13.6 shows the new routine to increment an x value. The problem I found is that the coefficients will just cycle because they are modulo a prime. When a coefficient rolls over, I want to then increment the next coefficient. This goes all the way up the chain to the maximum possible degree. The only time this really happens is for very small prime fields.

| **Listing 13.6   Polynomial elliptic curve finite field increment** |

```
void FF_bump(POLY *x)
{
  int i;
  mpz_t one;
  POLY ird;

  mpz_init_set_ui(one, 1);          Create constant 1.
  poly_init(&ird);
  poly_irrd_get(&ird);              Get Irreducible polynomial.
  i = 0;
  while(i < ird.deg)
  {
    madd(x->coef[i], x->coef[i], one);   ← Increment iᵗʰ coefficient.
    if(mpz_cmp_ui(x->coef[i], 0))         No rollover,
      return;                             then all done
    i++;
    if((i > x->deg) && (x->deg < ird.deg))   Next coefficient
      x->deg++;                              and Increase
  }                                          degree of x.
  mpz_clear(one);
  poly_clear(&ird);
}
```

To know the limit of how far I can increment, the irreducible polynomial is retrieved. The input polynomial is assumed to be of a small enough degree that its size can be increased. If a coefficient at index i rolls over, then i is incremented. If index i is larger than the input degree, then the degree of x is also incremented but only if the degree is less than the prime polynomial.

To embed a polynomial x on a curve, I first compute the right-hand side of equation 3.1 using function `poly_fofx()` as shown in listing 13.5. I then check to see whether this is a quadratic residue using `poly_sqr()` (listing 12.9). The variable x is incremented using `FF_bump()` from listing 13.6 until a quadratic residue is found. This first part of the embedding routine is shown in the following listing.

Listing 13.7 Polynomial elliptic curve embedding

```
void poly_elptic_embed(POLY_POINT *P1, POLY_POINT *P2, POLY x, POLY_CURVE E)
{
  POLY f;
  int done, i;
  mpz_t tmp;

  poly_init(&f);
  poly_copy(&P1->x, x);     ← Work with copy of input.
  done = 0;
  while(!done)
  {
    poly_fofx(&f, P1->x, E);    Look for f(x),
    if(poly_sqr(f) > 0)         which is quadratic residue.
      done = 1;
    else
      FF_bump(&(P1->x));     ← It was not, so try the next value.
  }
  poly_copy(&(P2->x), P1->x);   ← Two y values at same x
  poly_sqrt(&(P1->y), f);                              y₁ = √f
  for(i=0; i<=P1->y.deg; i++)                          y₂ = −y₁
    mneg(P2->y.coef[i], P1->y.coef[i]);   ←
  P2->y.deg = P1->y.deg;
  done = mpz_cmp(P2->y.coef[P2->y.deg], P1->y.coef[P1->y.deg]);
  if(done < 0)
  {                                              The smallest leading
    mpz_init(tmp);                               y coefficient
    for(i=0; i<=P1->y.deg; i++)                  becomes y₁.
    {
      mpz_set(tmp, P1->y.coef[i]);
      mpz_set(P1->y.coef[i], P2->y.coef[i]);
      mpz_set(P2->y.coef[i], tmp);
    }
    mpz_clear(tmp);
  }
  poly_clear(&f);
}
```

The second part of the routine is not required. The idea is to set the first point with the "smaller" *y* value, which is determined by the leading coefficient. This really is arbitrary since a smaller positive value means a larger negative one over a prime field. Doing this helps keep track of things while debugging.

13.2.4 *Polynomial curve random point*

In this section, I'll show how a random polynomial is converted into a point. This will be used in chapter 18 for several protocols. Choosing random points is straightforward once we have an embedding routine. Listing 13.8 shows the routine. Since there are two points to choose from, the last bit from the lowest coefficient of the returned random polynomial is used to determine which of the two is actually used.

> **Listing 13.8 Polynomial elliptic curve random point**

```
void poly_point_rand(POLY_POINT *P, POLY_CURVE E)
{
  POLY r;
  POLY_POINT mP;

  poly_init(&r);
  poly_rand(&r);      ← Create random polynomial modulo prime polynomial.
  poly_point_init(&mP);  ← Dummy point
  if(mpz_tstbit(r.coef[0], 0))
    poly_elptic_embed(P, &mP, r, E);
  else
    poly_elptic_embed(&mP, P, r, E);
  poly_clear(&r);
  poly_point_clear(&mP);
}
```

Last bit set
return first point;
otherwise,
second point.

13.2.5 *Polynomial elliptic curve addition*

In this section, I'll show how point addition is computed on a field extension curve. Adding two points over a field extension curve uses the same equations 3.2 to 3.4 with each value becoming a polynomial modulo the irreducible polynomial. The equations are as shown in equation 13.4:

$$
\begin{aligned}
\lambda &= \frac{x_1^2 + x_1 x_2 + x_2^2 + a_4}{y_1 + y_2} \\
x_3 &= \lambda^2 - x_1 - x_2 \\
y_3 &= \lambda(x_1 - x_3) - y_1
\end{aligned}
\tag{13.4}
$$

Compared with the routines from chapter 3, the code expands a bit because each polynomial variable has to be initialized and removed from the stack separately.

The following listing shows the head of the point addition routine. The first thing is to check whether either input point is the point at infinity and, if so, to return the other point.

Listing 13.9   Polynomial elliptic curve addition zero check

```
void poly_elptic_sum(POLY_POINT *R, POLY_POINT P, POLY_POINT Q, POLY_CURVE E)
{
  POLY lmbda, ltp, lbt, t1, t2, t3;
  POLY_POINT rslt;                    See whether either input
                                      is a point at infinity.
  if(poly_test_point(P))
  {
    poly_point_copy(R, Q);            First point at infinity
    return;                           return second point.
  }
  if(poly_test_point(Q))
  {
    poly_point_copy(R, P);            Second point at infinity
    return;                           return first point.
  }
```

There is still a check whether the slope λ is infinite to determine whether the result really is the point at infinity or if a different form for λ should be used. This portion is shown in the following listing. If $y_1 + y_2$ is zero, we need to check whether $x_1 - x_2$ is zero. Only under those two conditions being true do we return the point at infinity, and then, of course, clean up the stack.

Listing 13.10   Polynomial elliptic curve addition slope calculation

```
  poly_init(&t1);
  poly_init(&t2);
  poly_init(&t3);
  poly_init(&ltp);                    Initialize all
  poly_init(&lbt);                    temporary variables.
  poly_init(&lmbda);
  poly_mul(&t1, P.x, P.x);            Compute lambda
  poly_mul(&t2, P.x, Q.x);            using general form.
  poly_mul(&t3, Q.x, Q.x);
  poly_add(&ltp, t1, t2);             Numerator =
  poly_add(&ltp, ltp, t3);            $x_1^2 + x_1 x_2 + x_2^2 + a_4$
  poly_add(&ltp, ltp, E.a4);
  poly_add(&lbt, P.y, Q.y);          ← Denominator = $y_1 + y_2$

  if(!lbt.deg && !mpz_cmp_ui(lbt.coef[0], 0))
  {                                                    If ($y_1 = -y_2$),
    poly_sub(&lbt, Q.x, P.x);                          denominator is zero.
    if(!lbt.deg && !mpz_cmp_ui(lbt.coef[0], 0))  ← Really P == -Q?
    {
      R->x.deg = 0;              ↑ $x_1 == x_2$
      mpz_set_ui(R->x.coef[0], 0);
      R->y.deg = 0;                      Return point at
      mpz_set_ui(R->y.coef[0], 0);       infinity.
      poly_clear(&t1);
```

```
      poly_clear(&t2);
      poly_clear(&t3);          Clean up
      poly_clear(&ltp);         stack.
      poly_clear(&lbt);
      poly_clear(&lmbda);
      return;
   }
   poly_sub(&ltp, Q.y, P.y);
}
```

The last chunk of the routine computes equation 13.4 for x_3 and y_3 and then cleans up the temporary variables, as shown in the following listing.

Listing 13.11 Polynomial elliptic curve addition result point

```
                    Finally, compute
                    resulting point.

   poly_div(&lmbda, ltp, lbt);   ← λ = correct version
   poly_point_init(&rslt);
   poly_mul(&t1, lmbda, lmbda);
   poly_add(&t2, P.x, Q.x);             x₃ = λ² - (x₁ + x₂)
   poly_sub(&rslt.x, t1, t2);
   poly_sub(&t1, P.x, rslt.x);
   poly_mul(&t2, t1, lmbda);            y₃ = (x₁ - x₃)λ - y₁
   poly_sub(&rslt.y, t2, P.y);
   poly_point_copy(R, rslt);    ← Copy to output.

   poly_clear(&t1);
   poly_clear(&t2);
   poly_clear(&t3);
   poly_clear(&ltp);
   poly_clear(&lbt);            Clean up stack.
   poly_clear(&lmbda);
   poly_point_clear(&rslt);
}
```

$$x_3 = \lambda^2 - (x_1 + x_2)$$

$$y_3 = (x_1 - x_3)\lambda - y_1$$

13.2.6 *Polynomial elliptic curve point multiplication*

In this section, code to compute point multiplication over field extension curves is shown in listing 13.12. The last routine in the chapter does look the same as its counterpart in chapter 3. The only differences are the calls to polynomial routines instead of modular math routines. The double and add method still applies, and a local result is copied to the destination at the end.

Listing 13.12 Polynomial elliptic curve multiplication

```
void poly_elptic_mul(POLY_POINT *Q, POLY_POINT P, mpz_t k, POLY_CURVE E)
{
  int bit, j;
  POLY_POINT R;
```

```
poly_point_init(&R);          │ Allow in-place
poly_point_copy(&R, P);      ←─┘ operation.
j = mpz_sizeinbase(k, 2) - 2;   ← Number of bits to go
while(j >= 0)
{
  poly_elptic_sum(&R, R, R, E);   ← Double at every bit position.
  bit = mpz_tstbit(k, j);        │ If this bit is set,
  if(bit)                        │ add in original
    poly_elptic_sum(&R, R, P, E);│ point.
  j--;
}
poly_point_copy(Q, R);    │ Copy to output and
poly_point_clear(&R);     │ cleans up stack.
}
```

13.3 *Tiny example*

In this section, example code for a curve with small field prime value is shown. In the next few chapters, I will cover how to find the cardinality of a field extension as well as how to find the order of a point on a curve over a finite field. I chose the following example using a field prime $p = 43$ with a specific curve that had cardinality of 55 with an embedding degree of 2. This was a very rare curve. This example will be used in chapters 15 and 16 on pairings, so there are a few subroutines used in the following listings, which will be covered later. The program name is `weil_6_bit_pairing.c`. Figure 13.2 shows the procedure followed in the tiny example. The field prime determines what irreducible trinomial will work for the tiny extension field. Both the field prime and irreducible polynomial determine the order of the elliptic curve. The "large prime" for the tiny example base curve is 11. The group structure of the extension field is 11×165. The pairing examples appear in chapter 15.

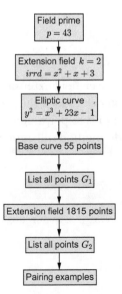

Figure 13.2   Tiny example overall description

13.3.1 *Tiny example variables*

This section describes the initialization code for the tiny example. The start of the tiny example lists the includes for points and curves of both G_1 and G_2 types. It also creates space for all the variables on the stack; many will be used in later chapters. The following listing is the start of the program.

> **Listing 13.13   Tiny example startup**

```
#include "poly_eliptic.h"
#include "eliptic.h"
#include "pairing.h"

#define M 43

int main(int argc, char *argv[])
{
  FILE *pnts;
  POLY_CURVE Ex;        ← extension
  CURVE E;              ← base
  POLY_POINT Px1, Px2, Qx, Tx;   ← extension
  POINT P1, P2;              ← base
  mpz_t prm, x, ordr, factors[8], tor;
  POLY irrd, xtnd, t1, t2, t3, t4;
  int i, j, k, m, which, skip;

  mpz_init_set_ui(prm, M);     │ Initialize
  minit(prm);                  │ field prime.
  poly_init(&irrd);
  if(poly_irreducible(&irrd, 2))    │ Find irreducible polynomial.
    poly_printf("Found irreducible polynomial:\n", irrd);
  else
    printf("no irreducible polynomial found...\n");
  poly_irrd_set(irrd);      │ Set up prime polynomial
  poly_mulprep(irrd);       │ and multiplication table.
```

POINTs P1, P2 and POLY_POINTs Px1, Px2 along with CURVE E and POLY_CURVE Ex will be used to find all the points on the base curve and the field extension curve. The prime field is initialized to 43 using the variable prm, and then an irreducible polynomial is found. If that failed, the program should really just exit. So far, in all my tests, poly_irreducible() never fails to find an irreducible polynomial. Once the irreducible polynomial is found, the multiplication table is created for all the polynomial multiplication routines.

Since none of this is random, the output is always the same:

```
Found irreducible polynomial:
Mod(1, 43)*x^2 + Mod(1, 43)*x^1 + Mod(3, 43)
```

which is $x^2 + x + 3$. This means all polynomials will be degree 1 (or zero) for the x and y values.

13.3.2 *Tiny example base curve*

This section describes the base curve of the tiny example in detail. Computing the points on the G_1 group comes from the curve I found using a PARI search. The curve is

$$y^2 = x^3 + 23x + 42 \bmod 43$$

This curve is plotted in figure 3.6. This curve was chosen because it has a very small number of points and a field extension that is also very small. A duplicate of figure 3.6 is shown in figure 13.3.

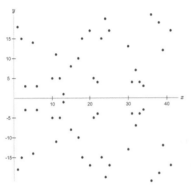

Figure 13.3   All points on tiny elliptic curve $y^2 = x^3 + 23x - 1$ **mod 43**

The initialization for that curve is shown in the following:

```
pnts = fopen("all_points_prm_43.dat", "w");   ← Save points to file.
curve_init(&E);                  Initialize
mpz_set_ui(E.a4, 23);            curve to
mpz_set_ui(E.a6, 42);            y² = x³ + 23x + 42.
```

A file to hold all the points is also created.

The search for points is in listing 13.14. I start with two counters. Variable i is used to keep track of the x value. Since `eliptic_embed()` increments x until it finds a value on the curve, I have to update i at the end of the loop to match the new x value.

Listing 13.14   Tiny example base points

```
i = 1;       Variable I becomes x;
j = 0;       variable J is point index.
while(i<M-1)
{
  mpz_set_ui(x, i);
  elptic_embed(&P1, &P2, x, E);     Find next
                                    available x value.
  get_order(ordr, P1, E, factors, 3);   ← Find order of point.
  gmp_fprintf(pnts, "%2d: (%Zd, %Zd) order: %Zd\n", j, P1.x, P1.y, ordr);
  j++;
  gmp_fprintf(pnts, "%2d: (%Zd, %Zd)\n", j, P2.x, P2.y);     Save both
                                                             points to disk.
  j++;
```

```
    while(mpz_cmp_ui(P1.x, i) >= 0) i++;  ← Increment I until 1 past x.
}
fprintf(pnts, "\n");
```

The variable j counts each point. The two points are printed to the file along with the order of the points. The subroutine `get_order()` is a simple brute-force operation, which I'll explain in chapter 16.

The reason I use variable `i` instead of `P1.x` directly is because the `while` loop requires an integer. Sample output from the file looks like this:

```
0:  (1, 18) order: 5
1:  (1, 25)
2:  (2, 15) order: 55
3:  (2, 28)
4:  (3, 3) order: 11
5:  (3, 40)
6:  (5, 14) order: 55
7:  (5, 29)
8:  (6, 3) order: 55
9:  (6, 40)
10: (10, 5) order: 55
11: (10, 38)
12: (11, 11) order: 11
13: (11, 32)
14: (12, 5) order: 55
15: (12, 38)
16: (13, 1) order: 55
17: (13, 42)
```

There are 54 points in G_1 listed in the file. The order is 55 because the point at infinity is included in the size of the group. This is true of each group. There are 4 points of order 5, 10 points of order 11, and 40 points of order 55 in the list. All the points of order 55 eventually become points of order 5 or 11. That is one reason to always choose a base point of prime order. For these examples, I will choose points of order 11 because they are prime order and will not mix with other points of other orders.

13.3.3 *Tiny example field extension curve*

This section describes the field extension points for the tiny example. The field extension curve uses the same coefficients as the base curve, but they are polynomials. Here is the code that sets up the curve for the group 2 points:

```
poly_curve_init(&Ex);
mpz_set_ui(Ex.a4.coef[0], 23);
mpz_set_ui(Ex.a6.coef[0], 42);
```

We see from listing 13.2 that the degree of the coefficients is set to zero during initialization. So, these values are polynomial constants.

As a first step, let's see how many points we expect on the field extension curve. From equation 13.3, we have $t_0 = 2$, $t_1 = -11$, so

$$t_2 = t_1 \times t_1 - 43 \times t_0 = -11 \times (-11) - 43 \times 2 = 35$$

This gives us (from equation 13.2)

$$\#E_2 = 43^2 + 1 - 35 = 1815$$

From listing 13.7, two points are returned from the `poly_embed()` routine. The input x value is now a polynomial, which I call xtnd. Here is the initialization:

```
poly_point_init(&Px1);
poly_point_init(&Px2);
poly_init(&xtnd);     ← start at x = 0
j = 0;
```

The variable j is again tracking the number of points. As we just computed, the cardinality of the curve is 1815. The j counter limit is one less than that because the point at infinity is part of the cardinality, but not on the curve. The variable j is incremented after each point found is saved to the file.

Listing 13.15 has one line that embeds the next x on the extension curve. As shown in section 13.2.3, this skips past gaps as in figure 13.3, but in two dimensions. The next line finds the order of the point. Routine `poly_get_order()` is described in chapter 16. The next block of lines prints the points in a nice readable format. The output is specific to this tiny example and not general. The last two lines update the xtnd variable to one past the x value of the point saved using routine `FF_bump()` described in listing 13.6.

Listing 13.15 Tiny example field extension points

```
while(j < 1814)   ← Known number of points
{
  poly_elptic_embed(&Px1, &Px2, xtnd, Ex);   ← Embed next value of x onto curve.
  poly_get_order(ordr, Px1, Ex, factors, 8);   ← Find order of point.
  gmp_fprintf(pnts, "%2d: x = ", j);   ← Save index to file.
  if(Px1.x.deg)
    gmp_fprintf(pnts, "%Zd*x + ", Px1.x.coef[1]);
  gmp_fprintf(pnts, "%Zd  y = ", Px1.x.coef[0]);    | Save x and y
  if(Px1.y.deg)                                      | values to file.
    gmp_fprintf(pnts, "%Zd*x + ", Px1.y.coef[1]);   |
  gmp_fprintf(pnts, "%Zd  order: %Zd | %ld\n", Px1.y.coef[0], ordr, g1g2(Px1));
  j++;
  gmp_fprintf(pnts, "%2d: x = ", j);
  if(Px2.x.deg)
    gmp_fprintf(pnts, "%Zd*x + ", Px2.x.coef[1]);   | Repeat
  gmp_fprintf(pnts, "%Zd  y = ", Px2.x.coef[0]);    | for
  if(Px2.y.deg)                                      | second
    gmp_fprintf(pnts, "%Zd*x + ", Px2.y.coef[1]);   | point.
```

```
    gmp_fprintf(pnts, "%Zd | %ld\n", Px2.y.coef[0], g1g2(Px2));
    j++;
    poly_copy(&xtnd, Px1.x);
    FF_bump(&xtnd);          ← Increment polynomial x.
  }
  fclose(pnts);
```

The routine g1g2() looks at the degree of the x and y polynomials. If both are zero, it returns 1; if degree of x is 1 and y is zero, it returns 2; if x degree is 0 and y is 1, it returns 3; and if both degrees are 1, it returns 4. This was more for curiosity than useful.

The output from this search for points has many G_1 points to start with:

```
 0: x = 0   y = 4*x + 2   order: 11 | 3
 1: x = 0   y = 39*x + 41 | 3
 2: x = 1   y = 18   order: 5 | 1
 3: x = 1   y = 25 | 1
 4: x = 2   y = 15   order: 55 | 1
 5: x = 2   y = 28 | 1
 6: x = 3   y = 3   order: 11 | 1
 7: x = 3   y = 40 | 1
 8: x = 4   y = 10*x + 5   order: 33 | 3
 9: x = 4   y = 33*x + 38 | 3
10: x = 5   y = 14   order: 55 | 1
11: x = 5   y = 29 | 1
12: x = 6   y = 3   order: 55 | 1
13: x = 6   y = 40 | 1
14: x = 7   y = 6*x + 3   order: 33 | 3
15: x = 7   y = 37*x + 40 | 3
```

But, in addition, there are many G_2 points as well. Every constant x value (i.e., degree zero value) has a point on the curve. When x becomes a degree 1 polynomial, then gaps begin to appear:

```
276: x = 6*x + 3    y = 2*x + 16   order: 11 | 4
277: x = 6*x + 3    y = 41*x + 27 | 4
278: x = 6*x + 6    y = 19*x + 21  order: 165 | 4
279: x = 6*x + 6    y = 24*x + 22 | 4
280: x = 6*x + 8    y = 16*x + 32  order: 55 | 4
281: x = 6*x + 8    y = 27*x + 11 | 4
282: x = 6*x + 10   y = 20*x + 40  order: 55 | 4
283: x = 6*x + 10   y = 23*x + 3 | 4
284: x = 6*x + 12   y = 17*x + 19  order: 165 | 4
285: x = 6*x + 12   y = 26*x + 24 | 4
286: x = 6*x + 14   y = 6*x + 39  order: 165 | 4
287: x = 6*x + 14   y = 37*x + 4 | 4
288: x = 6*x + 17   y = 2*x + 38  order: 165 | 4
289: x = 6*x + 17   y = 41*x + 5 | 4
```

The purpose of this example is to show that a field extension of a curve has all the points of the base field plus a lot more. This becomes very useful as we get into pairing calculations.

Unfortunately, attempting to graph this tiny example on paper is challenging. There are two dimensions for the x value and two dimensions for the y value, so the graph sits on a four-dimensional plane. Field extensions for cryptographic purposes require 11 to 31 dimensions. Using graphs like figure 13.3 for the base curve or graphs like figure 13.4 (both copied from chapter 3) allows us to imagine what is happening with the mathematics. The formulas are the same, so this abstract connection is perfectly valid.

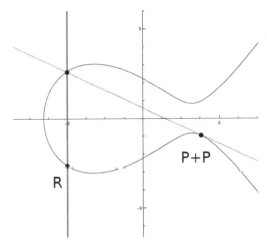

Figure 13.4   General shape of an elliptic curve to help with field extension abstraction

Answer to exercise

1 Embedding degree = 4 because $41^4 = 1 \bmod 29$.

Summary

- An elliptic curve over a finite field has cardinality $\#E = h \cdot r$ with r a large prime. That curve has field extension k when

$$p^k \cong 1 \bmod r$$

For elliptic curve pairings, we want k to be small.
- The cardinality of a field extension curve is

$$\#E_k = p^k + 1 - t_k$$

with t_k found from the recurrence relation

$$t_{n+2} = t_1 t_{n+1} - p t_n$$

This is used to find cofactors of field extension curves.

- Points on a field prime curve are labeled G_1. Points on an extension curve are labeled G_2. A field extension curve has the same coefficients as a field prime curve, but they are constructed as zero-degree polynomials.

- Testing for a polynomial point at infinity uses the degree of the polynomials as well as the lowest coefficient to determine whether both x and y are zero. This is used to determine the order of a point on a field extension curve.

- Embedding a polynomial point on a polynomial curve requires a "bump" routine that increments the next coefficient. It is only used for small test cases since large coefficients will never roll over.

- The polynomial random point function embeds a random polynomial on a polynomial curve. This is used to find reference points for pairing calculations.

- Polynomial elliptic curve addition uses the same formulas as field prime elliptic curve point addition. It just calls polynomial functions to process the math. These routines are used in aggregated signature and zero-knowledge algorithms.

- Polynomial elliptic curve multiplication is also the same as field prime elliptic curve multiplication. The double and add formula is exactly identical. These routines are used in aggregated signature and zero-knowledge algorithms.

- A tiny example shows how G_1 and G_2 points are on the same curve. A field extension has both G_1 and G_2 points. A prime field curve can only see G_1 points.

Finding low embedding degree elliptic curves

This chapter covers

- Algorithms for finding low embedding degree field extensions
- The *j*-invariant and Hilbert class polynomials
- The method of complex multiplication, used to find elliptic curves
- Routines to find secure curves with low embedding degree

In this chapter, I'll explain the reasons for choosing a specific size of extension field to create a secure pairing-friendly curve. The optimal size depends on the security level desired—too small and it might be broken; too large and it may not be efficient for practical use. I then discuss algorithms that can find curves of a low embedding degree. This involves searching for primes using mathematical functions. The parameters found during this process will allow us to use another mathematical function to find curves that have the prime number of points found for pairings.

The method used to find the curves of interest is called complex multiplication. One of the parameters from the search process will tell us which function we use to find the curve coefficients. The factoring of that function is the last step in theory before diving into code.

14.1 Security of field extensions for elliptic curve pairing

In this section, I'll cover the security requirements of pairings over elliptic curve field extensions. Knowing the security level you want drives the field sizes and embedding degrees. Finding the private key from the public key and base point is called the elliptic curve discrete log problem. For curves over a prime field, the difficulty comes from the size of the prime and goes as the square root of the order of the base point. So, an equivalent symmetric key is half the size of an elliptic curve key. The elliptic curve is still an exponential security level.

In the article by Diem (2011), the author argues that elliptic curve field extensions require the same exponential effort as the base curve. Cryptography mathematicians assume that field extensions can be attacked with algorithms similar to factoring. These are subexponential, so the number of bits required for security grows more rapidly. This assumption becomes a problem for pairing applications because both the base curve and the field extension must be secure at the same level.

Table 14.1 is taken directly from Freeman et al. (2006). The first column is the number of bits for a symmetric key system such as AES. The second column is the number of bits required for an equivalent security level for key exchange using elliptic curves over a prime field, as in chapter 3. The third column is the number of bits required for the same level of security for an elliptic curve over a field extension, as in chapter 13. The last column is the embedding degree required to go from the field in column two to the extension field in column three. It is derived by dividing column 3 by column 2.

Table 14.1 Elliptic curve field sizes for pairings

Security level	Subgroup size	Extension field	Embedding degree
80	160	960–1280	6–8
112	224	2200–3600	10–16
128	256	3000–5000	12–20
192	384	8000–10000	20–26
256	512	14000–18000	28–36

What is not shown in table 14.1 is the size of the prime field. The Subgroup Size column indicates the number of bits in a large prime factor within the cardinality, usually called r. The ratio of the number of bits in the field prime (p) to the number of bits in the subgroup size is called ρ. In formula form,

$$\rho = \frac{log_2(p)}{log_2(r)}$$

One of the early descriptions of pairing-friendly curves, which has gained wide use, is called BLS curves (Barreto et al., 2003). These curves have a ρ value near 1.5 while the curves from Freeman et al. (2006) are less than 1.1 for embedding degrees above 19. For security levels above 128 bits, this is quite a large savings in resources and thus a lower cost for the same level of security.

In the preface and about this book, I describe how one of the primary goals of this book is to ensure the best level of security rather than high speed or efficiency. I choose embedding degrees of prime value for that reason. The choice of embedding degree is then 7, 11, 13, 17, 19, 23, 29, or 31 for the security levels shown in table 14.1. Freeman et al. (2006) gives many algorithms for any embedding degree, but I will use only two of them applicable to these primes.

The methods of Freeman et al. (2006) determine a field prime and a large prime order for a given embedding degree, along with the cardinality of the base curve. They then call on the method of complex multiplication (CM) to find a curve that fits the parameters. It is at this point that the mathematical rabbit hole gets very, very deep (see chapter II in Silverman, 1994).

In the following sections, I describe the mathematics at a functional level. Two formulas from Freeman et al. (2006) each apply to some of the primes in table 14.1. Then I give a very simplified description of how the CM method works. References for deeper understanding include Blake et al. (2000), Cohen (2000), and Silverman (1994).

As part of the trip down the rabbit hole, we are going to run across two terms that you may have run across before. The first is the *discriminant* of a quadratic equation. This discriminant really is similar to what you ran across in high school solving quadratic equations. In equation 14.1, the quadratic equation is

$$Dy^2 = 4q - t^2 \tag{14.1}$$

where q is the field prime, t is the trace of Frobenius, y is being solved for, and D is the discriminant. For details on where this formula comes from, see Freeman et al. (2006).

The second term is called the *j-invariant*. This is the last value in the list from chapter 6 of PARI's elliptic curve parameters. Elliptic curves that have the same *j*-invariant are isomorphic, which means they have the same number of points. We can find curve coefficients a_4 and a_6 once we know the value of a *j*-invariant.

The method of complex multiplication is a search process seeking prime values of q and r with known values of D. Using q and D, we can find the roots of a polynomial, which will give us the *j*-invariant of an elliptic curve with those values of q, r, and t. As part of the trip down the rabbit hole, keep track of the relationships $\#E = q + 1 - t = h \cdot r$.

Exercise 14.1

Define the meaning of the variables $\#E$, q, t, h, and r in the previous sentence.

14.2 Low embedding degree

In this section, I'll describe how low embedding degree field extensions are found. In chapter 13, I pointed out that the typical embedding degree for average curves with large prime r as a factor in the cardinality normally has an embedding degree the same size as r. This is many orders of magnitude too large for pairing, where we only need an embedding degree in the 6-bit range. Mathematicians have spent a lot of time and effort developing methods to solve this problem. Here, I'll discuss just two of the many methods that have been developed.

Figure 14.1 shows the algorithm that will be described for finding pairing-friendly curves. Choosing from the list of primes determines which set of formulas we pick from Freeman et al. (2006). A sweep over the inputs to those functions will eventually find a prime value of r. If q is not also prime, the sweep continues. The dashed line is a dividing point in my software implementation. Above the line is a sweep program; below the line is the curve-finding program.

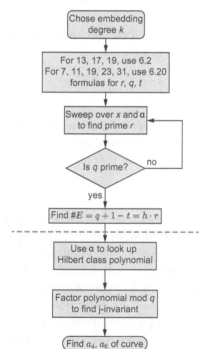

Figure 14.1 Pairing-friendly curves algorithm. Above the dashed line is one program that searches for good parameters. Below the dashed line is a program that finds one curve for one set of parameters.

The curve-finding program uses the α value and q to factor a polynomial. Those factors are the j-invariant for the curve we seek. Once the j-invariant values are known, the curve parameters a_4 and a_6 can be computed.

Freeman et al. (2006) goes through many other methods, listing a table for each embedding degree value and which algorithm gives the lowest value of ρ. I am actually going to combine two construction algorithms with theorem 6.19 from Freeman et al. for a simplified description of the algorithms.

The algorithms to find curves with low embedding degree use functions for a large prime factor common to both G_1 and G_2 called $r(x)$, the trace of Frobenius $t(x)$, and the field prime $q(x)$ for a specific embedding degree k (first column of table 14.2). Theorem 6.19 in Freeman et al. (2006) says we can replace x^2 in all these functions by $z = \alpha x^2$ where α is a square-free value. It turns out this value is the discriminant in equation 14.1. For the two algorithms of interest here, there are specific values of α that will create useful curves.

Table 14.2　Low embedding algorithms

Construction	6.2	6.20
k	13, 17, 29	7, 11, 19, 23, 31
$r(z)$	$z^{k-1} - z^{k-2} + \cdots - z + 1$	$z^{k-1} - z^{k-2} + \cdots - z + 1$
$t(z)$	$1 - z$	$1 + z^{(k+1)/2}$
$q(z)$	$(z^{k+2} + 2z^{k+1} + z^k + z^2 - 2z + 1)/4$	$(z^{k+1} + z^k + 4z^{(k+1)/2} + z + 1)/4$

The first line of table 14.2 shows the k values allowed for the embedding degree formulas that I will use. The allowed values for α in $z = \alpha x^2$ are

$$\alpha = 7, 11, 15, 19, 23 + a \times 20 \text{ for } a \in \{0, 1, \cdots, 7\}$$

and x is any value.

These formulas require a great deal of testing. Sweeps in both α and x are required to determine whether both $r(z)$ and $q(z)$ are primes because most are not. Once a triplet of (r, t, q) is found, the next step is to find a curve that fits that triplet.

14.3　*Complex multiplication*

In this section, I'll show how to find a curve that meets the low embedding degree parameters. After choosing security parameters, these methods give a curve that satisfies those parameters. This is the place where the theory of elliptic curves gets really deep. It is fun to dive into the details of the mathematics, but it is not essential to creating pairing-friendly curves. Next, I'll lay down the rules of mathematics used to solve the problem without explaining where those rules come from.

Taking the value of the discriminant, we look up a formula whose roots are the j-invariant. Once we know a j-invariant value, we can write down the equation of the curve as in equation 14.2

$$y^2 = x^3 + 3cx + 2c \tag{14.2}$$

where, as shown in equation 14.3,

$$c = \frac{j}{1728 - j} \tag{14.3}$$

See section VIII.2 of Blake et al. (1999) for more details.

The j-invariant can be computed from roots of the Hilbert-Class polynomial modulo the prime q. Rather than attempt to explain what that means, we are going to just use PARI to give us the polynomials for each of the previously listed α values. The connection between the complex plane, the j-invariant modular function, and integer results is mind-bending, and I urge you to read as much as you can deal with. For example, the largest α in the list is 163. In section 7.2.3 of Cohen (2000), the author shows that $e^{\pi\sqrt{163}}$ is almost an integer within 12 decimal places.

Appendix B lists the code that prints out the Hilbert polynomials along with the output file itself. Since the roots of these polynomials find a j-invariant and the previous formulas give curves based on the j-invariant value, we should be done, right? No, we have one more problem called the twist curve. This comes from the value of t in table 14.2 having the possibility of being positive or negative in the cardinality equation 6.2 ($\#E = p + 1 - t$).

For polynomials with several roots, we can keep trying curves until we find the one with cardinality factors we desire. For Hilbert polynomials with one root, we only have a 50% chance of getting the correct curve. When we don't get the right curve, we use the method described in section VIII.2 of Blake et al. (1999), which picks a quadratic nonresidue f and changes equation 14.2 to equation 14.4:

$$y^2 = x^3 + 3cf^2x + 2cf^3 \tag{14.4}$$

The method of determining the correct curve is to choose a random point on the curve and then multiply by the desired cardinality. If we get the point at infinity, it is the curve we want. The twist curve will not result in the point at infinity.

14.4 Factoring a Hilbert class polynomial

In this section, I'll explain what a Hilbert class polynomial looks like and how it can be factored. Each factor gives a j-invariant that can be used to find the curve that has the prime field and large prime factor used to compute pairings. This completes the method of complex multiplication as shown below the dashed line in figure 14.1.

The Hilbert class polynomial has unique factors in the form of equation 14.5:

$$H(x) = \prod_i (x - j_i) \tag{14.5}$$

where j_i is unique for each i. While the formula looks the same for every discriminant, the results are different for each modulus. The method to solve for the factors comes from algorithm 1.6.1 in Cohen (2000), which is diagrammed in figure 14.2. The flow chart is actually part of a recursive algorithm with input $P(x)$ coming from one of the two possible outputs at the end of the algorithm.

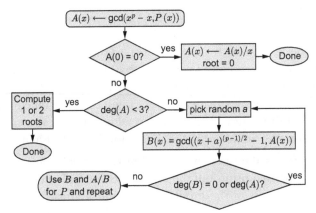

Figure 14.2   Roots mod p of P(x)

Our input is actually a polynomial of the form

$$P(x) = a_n x^n + a_{n-1} x^{n-1} + \cdots a_1 x + a_0$$

The process of factoring breaks this down into two factors, each of which can be processed again to find smaller factors. At some point, we get down to degree 1 or degree 2 polynomials, which we can directly solve for the roots.

The first step in figure 14.2 computes the greatest common divisor (gcd) by first defining $h(x) = x^p \bmod P(x)$ and then computing $\gcd(h(x) - x, P(x))$. The same process occurs in the computation of $B(x)$. If $A(0) = 0$, then there is a root equal to zero, and a new $A(x)$ is found by division with x. Done means finished with that root, and we can proceed to check any others.

If the degree of $A(x)$ is less than 3, we can directly compute one or two roots. If the degree is 1, then we have equation 14.6:

$$x = -\frac{a_0}{a_1} \tag{14.6}$$

If the degree is 2, then we can use the quadratic solution using the method described in algorithm 1.6.1 from Cohen (2000), as shown in equation 14.7:

$$\begin{aligned} d &\leftarrow a_1^2 - 4a_0 a_2 \\ e &\leftarrow \sqrt{d} \\ x_1 &= \frac{-a_1 + e}{2a_2} \\ x_2 &= \frac{-a_1 - e}{2a_2} \end{aligned} \tag{14.7}$$

For the degree of $A(x)$ larger than 2, the algorithm picks a random value a and computes $h(x) = (x + a)^{(p-1)/2} \bmod A(x)$ to find $B(x) = \gcd(h(x) - 1, A(x))$. If the $\deg(B)$ is zero or the same as $\deg(A)$, we try a different random a. If the value for $\deg(B)$ is acceptable, we use $B(x)$ and $A(x)/B(x)$ for the next round.

The actual implementation pushes each polynomial $B(x)$ and $A(x)/B(x)$ on a stack and adds roots to an array. The initial degree of the Hilbert class polynomial determines the number of roots. Every time we hit a done portion, we have popped a polynomial off the stack and found roots. In this way, all roots are found, and the process for finding curves can begin.

14.5 Code for finding pairing-friendly curves

In this section, I'll present two programs that help find pairing-friendly curves:

- The first program inputs the embedding degree and number of bits in r and sweeps over α and x searching for prime q and prime r.
- The second program takes the first program's output α, q, and t as input to find a curve by solving for the roots of the correct Hilbert class polynomial.

14.5.1 Pairing sweep

In this section, I'll get into the details of sweeping over many possible inputs to equations $r(z)$, $t(z)$, and $q(z)$ from table 14.2. After describing the subroutines for those functions, the main program will explain how the inputs are chosen to perform the sweep. Figure 14.3 shows the flow chart for the main program. Remember that $z = \alpha x^2$. The sweep changes α independently from x.

The sweep over α and x in formulas shown in table 14.2 leads to a maximum size in r of x^{2k-2}. The program input asks for maximum bit size because that is how we think about security. Calling the input lg2r, I take the maximum sweep over x to be $2^{\lg 2r/(2k-2)}$. This is a little too big because it does not account for α, but it is close enough to be reasonable.

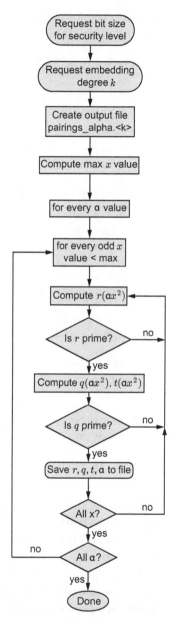

Figure 14.3 Program that sweeps over α to find pairing-friendly curves

The opening of program pairing_sweep_alpha.c brings in the modulo and polynomial function headers along with math.h. I then put in several subroutines to compute $r(z)$, $q(z)$, and $t(z)$. The following listing shows the top of the program along with the routine that computes $r(z)$.

Listing 14.1   Pairing sweep $r(z)$ routine

```
#include "modulo.h"
#include "poly.h"
#include <math.h>                              ← Input α and x
                                                as separate values,
void phi4k(mpz_t r, long k, mpz_t alpha, mpz_t x)  ← k is embedding degree.
{
  int i;
  mpz_t z[36], ck;   ← Max embedding degree assumed < 36

  mpz_init_set_ui(ck, 1);
  mpz_init(z[0]);                         z[0] = αx²
  mpz_mul(z[0], x, x);
  mpz_mul(z[0], alpha, z[0]);
  mpz_sub(ck, ck, z[0]);     ← Start at 1 − z.
  for(i=1; i<k-1; i++)
  {
    mpz_init(z[i]);
    mpz_mul(z[i], z[i - 1], z[0]);    z[i] = zⁱ⁻¹
    if(i & 1)
      mpz_add(ck, ck, z[i]);
    else                     Alternate sign
      mpz_sub(ck, ck, z[i]); between terms.
  }
  mpz_set(r, ck);   ← Output result
  mpz_clear(ck);
  for(i=0; i<k-1; i++)      Clean up stack.
    mpz_clear(z[i]);
}
```

The name of the routine comes from the cyclotomic polynomial that defines r. The inputs include the embedding degree k, the discriminant α, and the value of x. I found that even x values never result in a prime, so the calling loops include only odd x values.

The purpose of subroutine phi4k() is to compute the formula $r(x)$ in table 14.2. The routine starts by computing $z = \alpha x^2$ and then begins with $1 - z$. The array z[] holds each power of z, so it is easy to add or subtract the correct power and then compute the next power on each loop. The index zero holds z^1, so the loop ends at $k - 2$, which is z^{k-1}. As seen in the $r(z)$ line of table 14.2, that is the correct final power.

The $q(z)$ routines are similar to each other, but as seen in table 14.2, they are different enough to require their own routines. Listing 14.2 shows the code for algorithm 6.20, and listing 14.3 has the code for algorithm 6.2. These routines are

just straight calculations of the formulas. The exponents are slightly different in each
routine. It's interesting that the structure of the formulas is quite similar otherwise.

Listing 14.2 Pairing sweep $q(z)$ algorithm 6.20

```
void qofz_20(mpz_t q, long k, mpz_t alpha, mpz_t x)   ◄┘ Input α and x
{                                                          as separate values,
  long k1, k2;                                             k is embedding degree.
  mpz_t  t1, t2, t3, t4, z;

  mpz_inits(z, t1, t2, t3, t4, NULL);
  k1 = k + 1;         | Offset to
  k2 = k1/2;          | embedding degree.
  mpz_mul(z, x, x);
  mpz_mul(z, z, alpha);      | z = αx²
  mpz_pow_ui(t1, z, k1);     | z^(k+1)
  mpz_pow_ui(t2, z, k);      | z^k
  mpz_pow_ui(t3, z, k2);
  mpz_mul_ui(t3, t3, 4);     | 4z^((k+1)/2)
  mpz_add_ui(t4, z, 1);
  mpz_add(t1, t1, t2);
  mpz_add(t1, t1, t3);       | (1 + z + 4z^((k+1)/2) + z^k + z^(k+1))/4
  mpz_add(t1, t1, t4);
  mpz_fdiv_q_ui(q, t1, 4);
  mpz_clears(z, t1, t2, t3, t4, NULL);
}
```

Where the annotations correspond to:

$$z = \alpha x^2$$
$$z^{k+1}$$
$$z^k$$
$$4z^{(k+1)/2}$$
$$\frac{1 + z + 4z^{(k+1)/2} + z^k + z^{k+1}}{4}$$

Listing 14.3 Pairing sweep $q(z)$ algorithm 6.2

```
void qofz_2(mpz_t q, long k, mpz_t alpha, mpz_t x)   ◄┘ Input α and x
{                                                         as separate values,
  long k1, k2;                                            k is embedding degree.
      mpz_t  t1, t2, t3, t4, z;

  mpz_inits(z, t1, t2, t3, t4, NULL);
  k1 = k + 1;         | Offset to
  k2 = k + 2;         | embedding degree.
  mpz_mul(z, x, x);
  mpz_mul(z, z, alpha);      | z = αx²
  mpz_pow_ui(t1, z, k2);     | z^(k+2)
  mpz_pow_ui(t2, z, k1);
  mpz_mul_ui(t2, t2, 2);     | 2z^(k+1)
  mpz_pow_ui(t3, z, k);      | z^k
  mpz_sub_ui(t4, z, 1);
  mpz_mul(t4, t4, t4);       | (z − 1)²
  mpz_add(t1, t1, t2);
```

Where the annotations correspond to:

$$z = \alpha x^2$$
$$z^{k+2}$$
$$2z^{k+1}$$
$$z^k$$
$$(z - 1)^2$$

```
  mpz_add(t1, t1, t3);
  mpz_add(t1, t1, t4);
  mpz_fdiv_q_ui(q, t1, 4);
  mpz_clears(z, t1, t2, t3, t4, NULL);
}
```

$$\frac{z^{k+2} + 2z^{k+1} + z^k + (z-1)^2}{4}$$

Listing 14.4 shows the code for $t(z)$ algorithm 6.20 and listing 14.5 shows $t(z)$ for algorithm 6.2. These are very simple. As with the other routines, α and x are inputs.

Listing 14.4   Pairing sweep $t(z)$ algorithm 6.20

Input α and **x** as separate values, **k** is embedding degree.

```
void tofz_20(mpz_t t, long k, mpz_t alpha, mpz_t x)
{
  mpz_t z, t1;
  long k1;

  mpz_inits(z, t1, NULL);
  mpz_mul(z, x, x);
  mpz_mul(z, z, alpha);        z = αx²
  k1 = (k + 1)/2;
  mpz_pow_ui(t1, z, k1);
  mpz_add_ui(t, t1, 1);        t = 1 + z^{(k+1)/2}
  mpz_clears(z, t1, NULL);
}
```

Listing 14.5   Pairing sweep $t(z)$ algorithm 6.2

Input α and **x** as separate values, **k** is embedding degree.

```
void tofz_2(mpz_t t, long k, mpz_t alpha, mpz_t x)
{
  mpz_t z, one;

  mpz_init(z);
  mpz_mul(z, x, x);
  mpz_mul(z, z, alpha);        z = αx²
  mpz_init_set_ui(one, 1);
  mpz_sub(t, one, z);          t = 1 - z
  mpz_clears(z, one, NULL);
}
```

Listing 14.6 is the beginning of the main routine for sweeping a specific embedding degree. The variables atab[] and ktab[] are arrays for the α and k values in table 14.2. The array algt[] tells which algorithm to use (6.2 or 6.20) for each value in the ktab[] array.

The program expects one input. This is the largest number of bits in r desired. The sweep will find many values smaller than this, so overestimating by 5 or 6 bits is useful.

Listing 14.6   Pairing sweep main

```
int main(int argc, char *argv[])
{
  FILE *pair;
  mpz_t r, alpha, x, q, t;
  long k, u, lg2r, alphabase, rpm, qpm, rsz, qsz;      α table
  long max, atab[5] = 7, 11, 15, 19, 23;               starting values
  double rho;
  int j, m, nmrpm, a, kdex;              Prime embedding degrees
  int ktab[9] = 5, 7, 11, 13, 17, 19, 23, 29, 31;
  int algt[9] = 1, 0,  0,  1,  1,  0,  0,  1,  0; // 1 == 6.2  0 == 6.20
  double xsz, asz;
  char filename[128];       Flag for which
                            algorithm to use
  if(argc < 2)                                   Expect number of
  {                                              security bits for input.
    printf("Use: ./pairing_sweep_alpha  <log2(r) max range>\n");
    exit(-1);
  }
  lg2r = atol(argv[1]);
  if(lg2r < 3)
  {                                          Small to play
    printf("need more bits to work with\n");   is ok but not
    exit(-2);                                    too small!
  }
  printf("choose embedding degree k from 5, 7, 11, 13, 17, 19, 23, 29, 31: ");
  fflush(stdout);
  scanf("%ld", &k);
  for(kdex=0; kdex<9; kdex++)
    if(k == ktab[kdex])         Request embedding degree
      break;                    and check whether in table.
  if(kdex > 8)
  {
    printf("k must be from list.\n");
    exit(-1);                     Ignore input
  }                              if not found.
  sprintf(filename, "pairings_alpha.%02ld", k);   Create file
  pair = fopen(filename, "w");                     for found parameters.
  nmrpm = 0;
  mpz_inits(r, alpha, x, q, t, NULL);
  max = exp2(lg2r/2/(k - 1));     ← Compute largest x.
```

The program asks for an embedding degree after listing the acceptable options. After scanning the `ktab[]` array for a match, it will exit the program on an incorrect input. For an acceptable choice, a new file is created to hold the prime values r, q, and all other parameters for the chosen embedding degree.

The variable `nmrpm` is a count of the number of r prime values found. The GMP variables are named according to their use from the formulas.

Listing 14.7 shows the full sweep. The outer loop adds the multiple $20a$ to α. The variable m steps through the atab[] array. Between these two loops, all possible values of α available from the Hilbert class polynomial list are attempted.

Listing 14.7   Pairing sweep loop

```
for(a=0; a<8; a++)
{
  for(m=0; m<5; m++)
  {
    alphabase = atab[m] + a*20;      ← Integer version of α
    printf("processing alpha = %ld\n", alphabase);        Long, slow process;
                                                          let user know
    mpz_set_ui(alpha, alphabase);                         program running.
    for(j=1; j<max; j+=2)        Only odd
    {                            values of x
      mpz_set_ui(x, j);          are useful.
      phi4k(r, k, alpha, x);     ← Both algorithms use same r(x).
      rsz = mpz_sizeinbase(r, 2);      Is returned
      if(rsz > lg2r)                   r value
        break;                         an acceptable size?
      rpm = mpz_probab_prime_p(r, 25);    ← Is r value prime?
      if(rpm)          Yes, so
      {                increment number
        nmrpm++;       r primes found.
        if(algt[kdex])
        {
          qofz_2(q, k, alpha, x);
          tofz_2(t, k, alpha, x);
        }
        else                     Use correct
        {                        algorithm for
          qofz_20(q, k, alpha, x);   this embedding degree.
          tofz_20(t, k, alpha, x);
        }
        qsz = mpz_sizeinbase(q, 2);  ← Number of bits in q
        qpm = mpz_probab_prime_p(q, 25);
        if(qpm)                                  Is q prime?
        {
          gmp_fprintf(pair, "k= %ld alpha = %Zd  x = %Zd\n", k, alpha, x);
          gmp_fprintf(pair, "r = %Zd numbits: %ld\n", r, rsz);
          gmp_fprintf(pair, "q = %Zd  numbits: %ld\n", q, qsz);
          fprintf(pair, "rho = %lf\n", (double)qsz/(double)rsz);
          gmp_fprintf(pair, "t = %Zd\n\n", t);
        }
      }                     Save all parameters
    }                       including ρ
  }                         to file.
}
fclose(pair);
```

```
   mpz_clears(r, alpha, x, q, t, NULL);
   printf("found %d r primes\n", nmrpm);
}
```

The variable j is converted to the x value used in all the formulas. Only odd values are useful, so the loop increment is 2. Since both algorithms use the same formula for $r(x)$, this is computed first. If the size of r exceeds the requested limit, the j loop is terminated.

The routine `mpz_probab_prime()` checks to see whether r is prime. The GMP manual says values between 15 and 50 are reasonable for the second argument, so I chose 25. Higher values take longer, and lower values run the risk of being wrong since the algorithm is probabilistic.

If r is a prime, then q and t are computed using the correct subroutines for this choice of embedding degree. The value of q is also checked to ensure it is, in fact, a prime. There is no output if q is not prime.

Once good values for r and q are found, all the values are saved to the file. Here is an example of embedding degree 13. From table 14.1, the subgroup size of 224 can use embedding degree 13. But when used as input, the only value found is much too small. When an input size of 260 is requested, then one value is found as shown here:

```
$ ./pairing_sweep_alpha 260
choose embedding degree k from 5, 7, 11, 13, 17, 19, 23, 29, 31: 13
processing alpha = 7
processing alpha = 11
processing alpha = 15
  :
  :
processing alpha = 151
processing alpha = 155
processing alpha = 159
processing alpha = 163
found 182 r primes
```

Of the 182 r values that were prime, only three had corresponding prime q values. Listing 14.8 is the output from this particular run. Low embedding degrees have higher ρ values—in this case, $\rho = 280/226 = 1.2$. For higher security levels, the value of ρ drops below 1.1.

Listing 14.8 Output pairing_sweep.13

```
k= 13 alpha = 35   x = 1
r = 3285353271721733941 numbits: 62
q = 38320360561362304687789   numbits: 76
rho = 1.225806
t = -34

k= 13 alpha = 39   x = 3
r = 3486983164606836942954707537101 numbits: 102
```

```
q = 380205022584152061630276872755726824401  numbits: 125
rho = 1.225490
t = -350

k= 13 alpha = 55  x = 91
r = 796791580025037971227974698155761712215242287642831604395780426558821
    numbits: 226
q = 188201910506566789076013521962076573175506406392106419771149765094125925
    5989359586529  numbits: 280
rho = 1.238938
t = -455454
```

14.5.2 *Finding the curve*

In this section, the code to find a curve using one set of parameters from the sweep program is described. The prime q values in listing 14.8 are the modulus used for finding the roots of the Hilbert class polynomials listed in appendix B. Each curve will have different roots even though the equation is the same for the same α value. The get_curve.c program described in this section takes the α, q, and t values from the pairing_sweep.* file as inputs. It scans the Hilbert_Polynomials.list file for the correct polynomial and then proceeds to find all the factors modulo q. Once we have those factors, we can compute the coefficients for pairing-friendly curves.

Since each root is a j-invariant, the values for a_4 and a_6 can be computed using equation 14.3. The cardinality is computed using equation 6.2 ($\#E = p + 1 - t$) with the input t value. Multiplying a random point on the curve by the cardinality should give the point at infinity. If not, I keep trying roots until one is found that works. If none work, then the twist of the first curve attempted is computed. This is again tested with a random point, and if that fails, the program gives up. The program has never failed to find a curve (so far).

If the degree of the Hilbert class polynomial is 1, the root is just the negative of the zeroth degree coefficient because the Hilbert polynomial is monic. If the degree is 2, we can use the quadratic formula of equation 14.7 modulo q to find the two roots. For higher degrees, we need to break the polynomial down into smaller chunks and peel off 1- and 2-degree factors at a time, as shown in figure 14.2.

The program get_curve.c starts with a subroutine for computing the quadratic roots modulo q as shown in the following listing.

> **Listing 14.9   Finding curve quadratic roots subroutine**

```
#include "poly.h"
#include "eliptic.h"
#include <string.h>

void tworoots(mpz_t j1, mpz_t j2, POLY hc)    ⟵  Input polynomial hc;
{                                                 outputs roots j₁, j₂.
  mpz_t d, e, f;
```

```
if(hc.deg != 2)    ← Just bail out if not degree 2.
  return;
if(mpz_cmp_ui(hc.coef[2], 1))
{
  mdiv(hc.coef[1], hc.coef[1], hc.coef[2]);
  mdiv(hc.coef[0], hc.coef[0], hc.coef[2]);    Force monic.
}
mpz_inits(d, e, NULL);
mmul(d, hc.coef[1], hc.coef[1]);
mpz_init_set_ui(f, 4);
mmul(e, hc.coef[0], f);                        d = a² − 4b
msub(d, d, e);
msqrt(e, d);                    ← e = √d
mpz_neg(j1, hc.coef[1]);
mpz_neg(j2, hc.coef[1]);
madd(j1, j1, e);
msub(j2, j2, e);                j₁ = (−a + e)/2
mpz_set_ui(f, 2);
mdiv(j1, j1, f);                j₂ = (−a − e)/2
mdiv(j2, j2, f);
mpz_clears(d, e, f, NULL);
}
```

If the input polynomial is not degree 2, the routine immediately bails out. The polynomial is then normalized. With the input polynomial being

$$x^2 + ax + b = 0$$

the subroutine then computes equations 14.7. Note that in equation 14.7, there is division by a_2. By forcing the equation to be monic $a_2 = 1$, that is ignored in the code.

The main() routine of the get_curve.c program is in listing 14.10. This checks for proper input and looks for the Hilbert_Polynomials.list file. If not found, the program exits. After opening the file, it reads all of Hilbert_Polynomials.list into memory for easy random access.

Listing 14.10   Finding curve initialize.

```
int main(int argc, char *argv[])
{
  FILE *hilb;
  POLY hc, stack[16], x1, hofx, Aofx, Bofx, rem;
  int i, j, k, alpha, xs, xe, sign, stckp, done;
  mpz_t root[16], p, c, a4[16], a6[16], tp, b, j0;
  mpz_t two, tri, t, crde;
  char *hcdat;
  POINT R, P0;
  CURVE E;

  if(argc < 4)    ←——— Check input values are all on the command line.
  {
```

```
printf("Use: ./get_curve <discriminant> <prime> <t>\n");
printf("  values from output of pairings_alpha.k\n");
exit(-1);
}
```

> Read in
> Hilbert class polynomials.

```
hilb = fopen("Hilbert_Polynomials.list", "r");
if(!hilb)
{
  printf("can't find file Hilbert_Polynomials.list\n");
  exit(-2);
}
hcdat = (char*)malloc(6*1024);
k = 0;
while(!feof(hilb))
{
  hcdat[k] = fgetc(hilb);
  k++;
}
fclose(hilb);
k -= 2;
```

> Ensure Hilbert
> polynomials file is there.

> Read in
> entire file
> to small
> buffer.

The following listing shows the scan for the discriminant. If the input value is not one of the values used in creating the Hilbert polynomial list, the program issues an error and exits.

Listing 14.11   Finding curve check discriminant

See whether discriminant in list.

```
alpha = atol(argv[1]);
if(alpha < 0)
  alpha *= -1;        ← Technically, discriminant is negative.
i = 0;                ← Buffer index
j = 0;                ← α value from file
while((j < alpha) && (i < k))
{
  sscanf(&hcdat[i], "%d", &j);
  j *= -1;
  if(j == alpha)
    break;            ← Found correct polynomial
  while(hcdat[i] != '\n')
    i++;
  i++;
}
if(j != alpha)
{
  printf("invalid discriminant %d\n", alpha);
  exit(-3);
}
```

> Use positive
> values to make
> search and limit
> easier.

> Skip to
> end of line.

> Exit if
> not found.

The discriminant values are actually negative. The output value from program pairing_sweep_alpha.c is positive, so I chose to make the comparison with the assumption that the input is positive. If the input is actually negative, I make it positive so the compare works. Obviously, there are many different ways to do this.

The beginning of each line in the Hilbert_Polynomials.list file holds the α value. Scanning for the newline character and then skipping over the newline put the index at the start of the next entry. If the index goes past the end of the buffer, no match is found, and the program issues an error and stops.

Listing 14.12 starts by checking whether inputs q and t are integers. If not, the program exits. If they are, the field prime modulus is initialized. The Hilbert class polynomial is then converted from text to internal representation. The polynomial is monic so the first x has no coefficient in the text file. If there is a ^ after the first x entry, the degree of the Hilbert polynomial is set. If not, the degree is set to 1.

The variable j then keeps track of the remaining coefficients. The first thing to look for is a + or - sign. After that, the end of the coefficient is found with the asterisk, which is changed to a zero. The GMP conversion routine then places the coefficient in the right place with a binary format. The sign is applied, and the final result is reduced modulo the field prime.

Listing 14.12   Finding curve set parameters

```
if(mpz_init_set_str(p, argv[2], 10) < 0)        │Set up mod q operations.
{
  printf("invalid prime string\n");              Make sure
  exit(-4);                                       prime modulus
}                                                 is an integer.
minit(p);                      ← Initialize base field prime.

if(mpz_init_set_str(t, argv[3], 10) < 0)        │Input factor t = p + 1 - #E
{                                                Make sure
  printf("invalid t string\n");                  Frobenius trace
  exit(-5);                                       is an integer.
}
Read in Hilbert polynomial.
poly_init(&hc);
xs = i;                        ← xs is the coefficient start index.
while(hcdat[xs] != 'x') xs++;
if(hcdat[xs + 1] == '^')                        │No first coefficient,
{                                                so check for
  xs += 2;                                       degree of
  sscanf(&hcdat[xs], "%ld", &hc.deg);            polynomial.
}
else
  hc.deg = 1;        ← Special case degree 1
mpz_set_ui(hc.coef[hc.deg], 1);  ← Monic polynomial
```

```
j = hc.deg - 1;                           For all remaining
while(j >= 0)              ←┘              coefficients
{
  while((hcdat[xs] != '+') && (hcdat[xs] != '-'))
    xs++;
  if(hcdat[xs] == '-')
    sign = -1;                            Look for sign.
  else
    sign = 1;
  xs++;
  xe = xs+1;
  while((hcdat[xe] != '*') && (hcdat[xe] != '\n'))    * marks end
    xe++;                                             of coefficient
  hcdat[xe] = 0;                          Convert text
  mpz_set_str(hc.coef[j], &hcdat[xs], 10);  to binary.
  if(sign < 0)                            Apply sign
    mpz_neg(hc.coef[j], hc.coef[j]);      and ensures modulo field prime.
  mpz_mod(hc.coef[j], hc.coef[j], p);
  j--;        ←┐ Continue with next coefficient.
}
```

If the polynomial degree is 1 or 2, we can directly solve for the *j*-invariant, as shown in the following listing. Degree 1 is trivial, and degree 2 calls the subroutine tworoots() from listing 14.9.

Listing 14.13 Finding curve low degree Hilbert polynomial

```
/*  for order 1 and 2, output result directly  */
  stckp = 0;          ← Stack pointer for polynomials
  if(hc.deg < 3)      ←┐
  {                    Degree 1 or 2
                       no stack
    if(hc.deg == 1)
    {
      mpz_init_set(root[0], hc.coef[0]);    Degree 1 root
      mpz_neg(root[0], root[0]);            from only coefficient
    }
    else
    {
      mpz_inits(root[0], root[1], NULL);    Degree 2
      tworoots(root[0], root[1], hc);       subroutine gets both roots.
    }
  }
```

For Hilbert class polynomials of degree larger than 2, the section of code shown in listing 14.14 is executed. The polynomial multiplication table is prepared using the Hilbert class polynomial hc(x). The polynomial x^p mod hc(x) is computed, and then x is subtracted to give $h(x) = x^p - x$ mod hc(x). The polynomial $A(x)$ is then computed as the $\gcd(h(x), hc(x))$. If the result is a constant, something is wrong, and the program exits.

To create the flow of figure 14.2, the variable $B(x)$ is initialized along with a fixed-size stack of polynomials. $A(x)$ is then pushed on the stack.

Listing 14.14 Finding curve high degree initialize

```
else                         │ Enter this when
{                            │ Hilbert polynomial > 3.

    │ Find h(x) = x^p mod hc(x).
    poly_mulprep(hc);     ← Sets up polynomial power table
    poly_init(&x1);
    x1.deg = 1;                  │ Polynomial x1 = x^1
    mpz_set_ui(x1.coef[1], 1);   │
    poly_init(&hofx);
    poly_xp(&hofx, x1);          │ hofx = (x^p mod hc(x)) - x
    poly_sub(&hofx, hofx, x1);

    │ A(x) = gcd(x^p - x, hc(x))

    poly_init(&Aofx);
    poly_gcd(&Aofx, hc, hofx);   │ A(x) = gcd(hofx, hc(x))
    if(!Aofx.deg)
    {
        printf("no roots found for this combination:\n");
        poly_print(hc);                     │ Extreme badness;
        gmp_printf("prime: %Zd\n", p);      │ should never happen.
        exit(-5);
    }
    poly_init(&Bofx);    │ Initialize stack
    poly_init(&rem);     │ polynomials.

    │ Push first A(x) on stack.
    for(i=0; i<16; i++)              │ Create all
        poly_init(&stack[i]);        │ possible stack entries.
    poly_copy(&stack[stckp], Aofx);   ← Pushes first A(x) on stack

    │ Initialize all roots to zero.
    for(i=0; i<hc.deg; i++)     │ Initialize all
        mpz_init(root[i]);      │ possible roots.
    j = 0;              ← Root index counter
    stckp++;            ← One item on stack
}
```

The meat of the root finding routine is shown in listing 14.15. This implements the algorithm shown in figure 14.2. By pushing and popping polynomials off a stack, it is easy to break down each factor until the degree is 1 or 2 and a direct root can be added to the list.

Listing 14.15 Finding curve high degree root

```
while(stckp)     ← Continue until all factors removed from stack.
{
  stckp--;   ← Pop next A(x) off stack.
  poly_copy(&Aofx, stack[stckp]);
  done = 0;
  while(!done)
  {
    if(!Aofx.coef[0])              ← Is A(0) = 0?
    {
      j++;   ←——| Array value is zero already.
      for(i=1; i<=Aofx.deg; i++)
        mpz_set(Aofx.coef[i - 1], Aofx.coef[i]);
      Aofx.deg--;
      if(!Aofx.deg)
        done = 1;     ← Go to next item on stack.
    }
    if(Aofx.deg == 1)
    {
      if(!mpz_cmp_ui(Aofx.coef[1], 1))
        mpz_set(root[j], Aofx.coef[0]);   ←——| Monic single root
      else
        mdiv(root[j], Aofx.coef[0], Aofx.coef[1]);  ←——| Normal single root
      mneg(root[j], root[j]);
      j++;
      done = 1;       ← Go to next item on stack.
    }
    else if(Aofx.deg == 2)
    {
      tworoots(root[j+1], root[j], Aofx);   ← Degree 2; get roots directly.
      j += 2;
      done = 1;       ← Go to next item on stack.
    }
    if(!done)
    {
      Bofx.deg = 0;
      poly_mulprep(Aofx);      ← Set up multiplication table.
      while(!Bofx.deg || (Bofx.deg == Aofx.deg))
      {
        mrand(x1.coef[0]);
        gpow_p2(&hofx, x1);
        mpz_sub_ui(hofx.coef[0], hofx.coef[0], 1);
        poly_gcd(&Bofx, hofx, Aofx);
      }
      poly_copy(&stack[stckp], Bofx);
      stckp++;
      poly_euclid(&stack[stckp], &rem, Aofx, Bofx);
      stckp++;
      done = 1;
    }
  }
}
```

Annotations (right margin):

If last coefficient is zero, divide by x.

For random a, compute $(x+a)^{(p-1)/2} - 1 \bmod A(x)$ until deg(B) < deg(A).

Push $B(x)$ on stack.

Push $A(x)/B(x)$ on stack.

```
    if(stckp > 15) exit(0);   ← Max degree is 10, so this should never happen.
}
```

As long as there are polynomials on the stack, the loop continues to pull one off. The variable done flags when roots have been added to the list, and no more polynomials will be added to the stack. A root of zero will continue processing unless $A(x)$ actually is zero. If $A(x)$ has one or two roots, they are added to the list, and the next item on the stack will be processed.

If the done flag is not set, the polynomial multiplication table is prepared with $A(x)$. A random value a is placed in the constant coefficient of x1 to create $(x+a)$. The value $(x+a)^{(p-1)/2} \bmod A(x)$ is then computed using the gpow_p2() routine. The value $B(x) = \gcd((x+a)^{(p-1)/2} - 1, A(x))$ is then found. This is repeated until $B(x)$ has a degree smaller than $A(x)$. Then the polynomials $B(x)$ and the quotient from $A(x)/B(x)$ are both pushed on the stack for further processing.

Once all the roots are found, they are printed out as shown in the following listing.

Listing 14.16   Finding curve output roots

```
for(i=0; i<hc.deg; i++)                    Output all
    gmp_printf("%d:  %Zd\n", i, root[i]);  found roots.
```

Each root in the array is a j-invariant, which can be used in equation 14.3. The values of a_4 and a_6 are then easy to compute from equation 14.2. I create an array of these for each root as shown in listing 14.17. The constants 1728, 2, and 3 are created outside the loop. Inside the loop, each a_4 and a_6 coefficient is then added to the appropriate array and printed out.

Listing 14.17   Finding the curve a_4, a_6 coefficient array

```
mpz_inits(c, tp, b, j0, two, tri, NULL);
mpz_set_ui(j0, 1728);    Set up
mpz_set_ui(two, 2);      constants
mpz_set_ui(tri, 3);      1728, 2, and 3.
for(i=0; i<hc.deg; i++)    Compute a4 and a6
{                          for each root.
  mpz_inits(a4[i], a6[i], NULL);
  mpz_set(tp, root[i]);
  msub(b, j0, tp);         Compute c =
  mdiv(c, tp, b);          j/(1728 – j).
  mmul(a4[i], c, tri);     Place a4, a6
  mmul(a6[i], c, two);     into respective arrays.
  gmp_printf("%d: a4= %Zd  a6= %Zd\n", i, a4[i], a6[i]);
}
```

The next code segment determines which of the roots gives the correct curve and which gives the twist curve. Listing 14.18 starts by computing the curve cardinality from the input value of t. A curve for every table entry of a_4 and a_6 is created, and a random point on that curve is created. If the order of the curve times the random point gives the point at infinity, we have the right curve. Otherwise, we have the twist.

Listing 14.18   Finding curve twist or correct for each coefficient

Compute #E * random point
on each curve.
If we get point at infinity,
this is the curve we want.

```
mpz_init_set(crde, p);          Compute cardinality
mpz_add_ui(crde, crde, 1);      #E = p + 1 - t
mpz_sub(crde, crde, t);         from input.
gmp_printf("#E = %Zd\n", crde);
point_init(&R);                 Initialize random point
curve_init(&E);                 curve and
point_init(&P0);                test variables.
done = 0;
for(i=0; i<hc.deg; i++)
{
  mpz_set(E.a4, a4[i]);         Pick random
  mpz_set(E.a6, a6[i]);         point on
  point_rand(&R, E);            curve.
  elptic_mul(&P0, R, crde, E);  Does multiply by cardinality
  if(test_point(P0))            give point at infinity?
  {
    printf("curve %d is right curve!\n", i);
    done = 1;    ← If yes, then no need for twist calculation
  }
  else
    printf("curve %d is not right curve.\n", i);
}
```

If any of the roots give a correct result from a test for the point at infinity, then the program is finished except for cleaning up the stack. If the done flag is not set after checking every possible curve, then the coefficients for a twist curve are computed using the first root. This is shown in the following listing.

Listing 14.19   Finding curve compute twist coefficients

```
if(!done)           If no curve is right,
{                   compute twist of
  k = 1;            first one and try again.
  while(k >= 0)
  {
    mrand(c);       Find random
    k = msqr(c);    quadratic
  }                 nonresidue.
  mmul(b, c, c);            Twist a4
  mmul(E.a4, a4[0], b);     is c²a4.
```

```
        mmul(b, b, c);                    Twist a₆
        mmul(E.a6, a6[0], b);             Is c³a₆.
        point_rand(&R, E);
        elptic_mul(&P0, R, crde, E);      Does multiply by cardinality
        if(test_point(P0))                give point at Infinity?
        {
            gmp_printf("a4 = %Zd  a6 = %Zd\n", E.a4, E.a6);
            printf("twist is right curve!\n");
        }                                 Output result.
        else
            printf("twist is not right curve.\n");
    }
    mpz_clears(c, tp, b, j0, two, tri, NULL);
    mpz_clear(p);
    poly_clear(&x1);
    poly_clear(&Aofx);
    poly_clear(&Bofx);
    poly_clear(&hofx);
    for(i=0; i<=hc.deg; i++)              Clean
        mpz_clears(root[i], a4[i], a6[i], NULL);   up
    point_clear(&R);                      stack.
    curve_clear(&E);
}
```

A random value is chosen that is a quadratic nonresidue. This might take a few tries. Then new coefficients are computed using equation 14.4. The check for the point at infinity after multiplication by the curve cardinality is then checked again. Since all the roots are the same, if this fails, something is wrong, and there is no point in trying anything else.

After compiling and linking get_curve, we can use the output from the last entry of listing 14.8 as inputs. The result is shown in the following listing.

Listing 14.20   Output get_curve

```
$ ./get_curve 55 188201910506566789076013521962076573175506406392106419771 1
⇒ 49765094125925598935958652 9 -455454
0:  10381915282303069242307852620219465127238184424874008859342944209378072 5
⇒ 1730662541635
1:  13022856817500785369356331748826651558297374880378122862677642619268285 0
⇒ 308011676860
2:  15764889262604729629727458602668587233154646245967454969042871692601051 5
⇒ 6499548298462
3:  10191291874655480406231759994644597118878713119542007839576372854919232 5
⇒ 3427359971476
0: a4= 32318475827870701680078028964256768757999682178174509959153869168539 3
⇒ 193067046598812   a6= 147013590889624993837394367284222279556707257135206
⇒ 198202024228417768299370937456894
1: a4= 25320959040576559533780203168999975941443251105648298577934899990599
⇒ 822998245456275   a6= 142348579698095565739862482852651047179767154335114 1
```

⮕ 664192955033954572719325070028536
2: a4= 8005674394900595681820152381025154940992784222991313970476155348 79362
⮕ 470629762792943   a6= 17883910297038183059614336384821874839028949908 13463
⮕ 729839408790547081151079414919648
3: a4= 16308266543764100486309965655700707504322981196732736802398501658 7349
⮕ 315940968015165   a6= 13634011803355392637488232507851818711988625839255 94
⮕ 377156988445019072381286885067796
#E = 18820191050656678907601352196207657317550640639210641977114976509 412592
⮕ 55989360041984
curve 0 is right curve!
curve 1 is right curve!
curve 2 is not right curve.
curve 3 is not right curve.

From appendix B, we see that the Hilbert class polynomial for discriminant 55 is 4th order. The four roots are output first, followed by the curve coefficients for each root. The cardinality is printed next, followed by the random point check. In this case, the first two curves are the curve we want.

It does not matter which coefficient set we chose here. While the points on the two curves will be different, the total number of points on each curve is identical. By definition, they are isomorphic.

At this point, we have found a base curve, which has an extension to a degree 13 polynomial. Using the find irreducible polynomial routine `poly_irreducible()` and that routine's output in `poly_mulprep()`, we are ready to work on a field extension curve. All the routines from chapter 13 allow us to work on the field extension curve.

Answer to exercise

1   #E is the cardinality of an elliptic curve, q is the field prime the curve is defined over, t is the trace of Frobenius, h is the small cofactor of the cardinality, and r is the large prime factor that determines the security of the elliptic curve.

Summary

- The ratio of the number of bits in the field prime to the number of bits in the largest prime factor determines the efficiency of a field extension. The algorithms chosen get this ratio as close to 1 as possible.
- Low embedding degree algorithms for all possible degrees are available. To maximize security, only prime embedding degrees are described here.
- Curves with the same j-invariant are isomorphic. The correct curve (or its twist) will always be found by using the j-invariant to compute the curve coefficients.
- The method of complex multiplication (CM) uses the j-invariant to find the curve equation. We still have to test for the twist curve, but it is straightforward to change the coefficients to get the curve we want.
- The discriminant used to find a field prime and large prime order defines the Hilbert class polynomial used to find the j-invariant. While this is an active area

of research to obtain exceptionally large discriminants, smaller values have not been found to be insecure.

- Factoring a k degree Hilbert class polynomial is a recursive process that finds k roots. Each root gives one j-invariant.
- The algorithms for low embedding degree have a low probability of success. Many values must be tested to find acceptable parameters.
- Direct calculation with the j-invariant can find the twist of the desired curve. It is necessary to verify the point at infinity is reached when a random point is multiplied by the curve cardinality. This proves we have the correct curve.

15

General rules of elliptic curve pairing explained

This chapter covers

- An introduction to elliptic curve point pairing
- A geometric description of the pairing function
- The essential rules of pairing mathematics
- Routines to compute common pairing functions

This chapter presents the point-pairing mathematics over field extension elliptic curves. I'll explain the general mathematical rules of pairings at a high level. The rules are mostly symbolic manipulation, so the meanings will be explained before we get into details.

With the background mathematics under our belts, we can now begin to look at the mathematics of pairing points on an elliptic curve. Pairing points gives us a one-way trap door function that is efficient and secure. It also gives us efficient ways to compute algorithms that would be horribly complicated otherwise. Point pairing is a very deep subject, and I will do my best to ignore most of it. The fundamental reason for ignoring this depth is that the underlying mathematics works, and fully understanding why it works is not critical to writing functional code.

The two fundamental subroutines used in the following chapters are the guts of computing elliptic curve pairings. In this chapter, I'll give a geometric hand-waving argument that completely ignores the actual mathematical underpinnings of these routines. While the theory is extremely interesting, it is not necessary to understand everything to use the algorithms. To gain a deeper understanding of the theory, I recommend reading sections III.8 and XI.9 in Silverman (2009).

15.1 Mathematical rules of elliptic curve pairings

In this section, I'll explain an elliptic curve group structure required for pairings to work mathematically. The result of a pairing operation is not a point. I describe what the result actually is and use vectors on the complex plane to get the idea across.

The group structure of an elliptic curve over a finite field is either cyclic or the product of two cyclic groups. In fact, we can always say it is the product of two cyclic groups if one of the groups has the size of one element. It is just more convenient to think of a base curve having only one cyclic group.

From section III.3 in Blake et al. (1999), we find that the structure of an elliptic curve over a finite field is written as equation 15.1:

$$E_{F_q} \cong \frac{Z}{d_1 Z} \times \frac{Z}{d_2 Z} \qquad (15.1)$$

where d_1 divides d_2. The meaning of the symbol $\frac{Z}{d_j Z}$ is "all integers divided by d_j times all integers." This boils down to integers modulo d_j. For cryptographic purposes, we look for groups where d_1 is a large prime. Since d_1 is a factor of d_2, the order of the curve is at least d_1^2, and there are no points of order d_1^2 because the two groups are separate.

For base curves, the field q is a prime number, and for almost all cases, $d_1 = 1$. That means there is just one cyclic group. When I described the group sizes in chapter 2, this is what I was referring to. In chapter 3, I showed the doughnut with two vectors, which is repeated here in figure 15.1. The two vectors represent the two independent groups d_1 and d_2. We now look for curves over a field extension with two separate groups so we can create elliptic curve pairings.

Figure 15.1   Elliptic curve over the complex plane

Figure 15.2 shows a circle to represent a cyclic group. For pairings to work, a double cyclic structure is required. Pairings will not work if there is only one cyclic group. The phrase "single cycle" means $d_1 = 1$; the group structure is not complex enough to allow pairings to work.

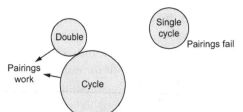

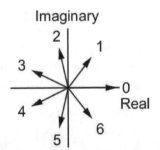

Figure 15.2   **Elliptic curve group structure for pairings to work**

There must be a large prime that is squared in the order of the curve, and each factor must be part of the two groups described by equation 15.1. I am pretty sure this is what makes pairings so difficult to comprehend. It is not just that the rules are complicated. Finding curves with the correct group structure is challenging on top of the complexity.

Given two points P and Q on an elliptic curve of order m, the pairing of those points is written as

$$e_m(P, Q) = \mu_m$$

The form $e_m(\cdot, \cdot)$ is the pairing function, and the symbol μ_m is an mth root of unity. As an example from complex numbers, an mth root of unity is

$$\mu_m = e^{2i\pi n/m}$$

where m and n are integers and $i = \sqrt{-1}$. Taking μ_m to the mth power gives

$$\mu_m^m = e^{2i\pi n} = 1$$

Figure 15.3 shows what μ_7 looks like on the complex plane. Each number in the figure is the value of n in $e^{2i\pi n/m}$. All the angles are $2\pi/7 \cdot n$, which clearly gets us back to 2π when $n = 7$. The same idea applies to pairings of points over elliptic curves.

For pairings, μ_m is a member of the field extension p^k that defines the points P and Q. That means there are elements of order m in the extension field and points of order m on the elliptic curve.

Note that the way we compute the order of a point is mP, but the way we compute the order of a field element is μ_m^m (i.e., μ_m to the mth power). In the order of a point, we get the identity element, which is the point at infinity, and in the order of an mth root of unity, we get the identity element 1. The process of pairing points takes us from multiplication of points (which is addition) to powers of elements (which is multiplication).

Figure 15.3 n^{th} **root of unity for $n = 7$ using complex numbers. Multiply any of these vectors by 7, and the result is 1.**

This is an important form of magic, so let's look at some of the rules. The rules I cover here include bilinearity and nondegeneracy. Different pairings will have additional capabilities. These two rules are fundamental to all pairing operations.

Exercise 15.1

Show that $32x + 34 \bmod 43$ is an 11th root of 1 modulo $p = x^2 + x + 3 \bmod 43$.
(Hint: Use PARI/gp.)

15.1.1 Elliptic curve point pairing rule of bilinearity

In this section, the mathematical rule of bilinearity is described. It is fundamental to how pairings work. The primary rule of importance for pairings is bilinearity, which means it has the same results on the right and left sides of the pairing. Take three points of order m as R, S, and T. Then, in equation 15.2, the rule is

$$e_m(R + S, T) = e_m(R, T)e_m(S, T)$$
$$e_m(R, S + T) = e_m(R, S)e_m(R, T) \tag{15.2}$$

That is, the pairing of the sum of two points is the multiplication of the pairings of those points. The rule converts addition of points to multiplication of pairings.

To expand on this rule, we can take a multiplication of a point with some integer n and pair it with another point. The result will be the power of the pairing of the two points. That is

$$e_m(nS, T) = e_m(S, T)^n$$

Similarly, by linearity we have

$$e_m(S, nT) = e_m(S, T)^n$$

If we take integers a and b multiplied with points S and T, then the same rule as equation 15.2 becomes equation 15.3:

$$e_m(aS, bT) = e_m(S, T)^{ab} \tag{15.3}$$

Another important and useful relationship is shown in equation 15.4:

$$e_m(-S, T) = e_m(S, -T) = e_m(S, T)^{-1} \tag{15.4}$$

Equation 15.4 is consistent with equations 15.2 and 15.3. It will allow us to create some interesting protocols.

This ability to combine points from an additive domain into a multiplicative domain is what makes pairings such a powerful tool for cryptographic algorithms. The result is no longer a point on the curve; it is a field element in p^k. Given the number of possible combinations of points that lead to a field element, the use of pairings as a one-way trap door function has a lot of appeal.

Exercise 15.2

Show that $e_m(aR + bS, cT) = [e_m(R, T)^a e_m(S, T)^b]^c$.

15.1.2 *Nondegeneracy rule with the point at infinity*

This section describes how nondegeneracy works. This rule prevents division by zero. The point at infinity is not actually on an elliptic curve. It is required to be the identity element on an elliptic curve for the arithmetic to work. Point pairing operations may hit the point at infinity as an input, so a special rule of nondegeneracy is included to ensure pairings work under all possible conditions.

If one of the points of a pairing is the point at infinity, the rule of nondegeneracy states we get 1 for an answer. The reason for this rule is to prevent division by zero. We can write this rule as equation 15.5:

$$e_m(S, \mathbf{0}) = e_m(\mathbf{0}, S) = 1 \tag{15.5}$$

This is true for any point S of order m on the curve. For example, if we take point Q as the point at infinity and attempt to compute a pairing with T and $-T$, one of those results is the same as the inverse of the other. That is

$$e_m(\mathbf{0}, T) = e_m(\mathbf{0}, -T) = e_m(\mathbf{0}, T)^{-1} = 1$$

The main advantage of this rule is that it forces our code to behave nicely. The algorithms presented in the next section take this rule into account as a special case.

15.2 *Algorithms for pairing*

In this section, I'll introduce two algorithms that are used to compute pairings. For the first algorithm, I will use a geometric image to give an idea of how it works. The real mathematics is much deeper, but you don't need to know it all to use the algorithm correctly. The second is called Miller's algorithm, which is named after the mathematician who developed it.

The first algorithm is actually a function used in Miller's algorithm. Miller's algorithm is a function used in the pairings to be presented in chapters 16 and 17. The details of both algorithms can be found in section XI.8 in Silverman (2009). In the mathematical literature, both of these functions have different symbols, so I will follow Silverman and call the first function $h_{P,Q}(R)$ and the second function $f_P(R)$.

15.2.1 *Function $h_{P,Q}(R)$*

This section explains the core function of elliptic curve pairing operations. The first algorithm is the heart of point pairing. It does not really have a name, so the symbol $h_{P,Q}(R)$ is the best reference. I'll show how two points are paired using a third point as a reference. In the symbol, P and Q are the points being paired, while R is the reference.

Figure 15.4 is an attempt to depict the relationships between three points P, Q, and $R = (x, y)$. This is on the same curve shown in chapter 3 with

$$y^2 = x^3 - 5x + 5$$

The sum of points P and Q results in the point $P+Q$. The line between P and Q intersects the curve at x coordinate x_{P+Q} shown with a dashed vertical line in the figure.

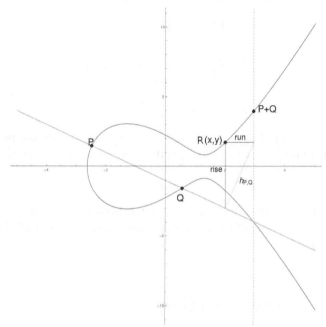

Figure 15.4 $h_{P,Q}(R)$ function diagram: the line between points P and Q defines rise and run to reference point R.

Taking an arbitrary point $R = (x, y)$ on the curve that is not related to P or Q and not the point at infinity, we can define the distance from that point to the x coordinate of $P+Q$ as the "run." This is labeled in figure 15.4.

The vertical distance from the line intersecting P and Q to the point R is called the "rise," which is also labeled in figure 15.4. The function $h_{P,Q}$ is defined as the rise over the run:

$$h_{P,Q}(R) = \frac{\text{rise}}{\text{run}}$$

The horizontal distance defining the run is easy to see as $x - x_{P+Q}$. The vertical distance is easy to derive. We know that the slope of the line between P and Q is λ, which we found in chapter 3. Let's take the line intersecting P and Q as $y' = \lambda x' + v$. The distance labeled rise in figure 15.4 is then $y - \lambda x - v$.

Combining the rise $= y - \lambda x - v$ with the run $= x - x_{P+Q}$ gives us

$$h_{P,Q} = \frac{y - \lambda x - v}{x - x_{P+Q}}$$

From chapter 3 equation 3.3, we have

$$x_{P+Q} = \lambda^2 - x_P - x_Q$$

Since the point P is on the line, we can take

$$v = y_P - \lambda x_P$$

Plugging these two formulas into the formula for $h_{P,Q}$ gives equation 15.6:

$$h_{P,Q}(R) = \frac{y - y_P - \lambda(x - x_P)}{x + x_P + x_Q - \lambda^2} \tag{15.6}$$

In the special case when $P = -Q$, the slope of the line between them is infinity. In equation 15.7, the function $h_{P,Q}(R)$ is then defined to be

$$h_{P,Q}(R) = x - x_P \qquad \lambda = \infty \tag{15.7}$$

As seen in figure 15.4, this is just the "run" between the vertical line and the point R.

The final special case is when either P or Q is the point at infinity. Then we have equation 15.8:

$$h_{P,Q}(R) = 1 \qquad P = \mathbf{0} \text{ or } Q = \mathbf{0} \tag{15.8}$$

The software subroutines will first check whether either input is the point at infinity, then check whether the slope is infinite, and then compute equation 15.6 if those tests are not applicable.

Exercise 15.3

Is there any problem with the $h_{P,Q}(R)$ when P and Q are the same point?

15.2.2 Miller's algorithm

In this section, I'll cover Miller's algorithm as a sequence of steps using a flow chart. The inputs to Miller's algorithm are two points on the curve, with one of them being the reference point mentioned in the $h_{P,Q}(R)$ algorithm.

Miller's algorithm looks like the multiplication of a point by m, the order of the point. The double and add algorithm is followed for every bit in m as shown in figure 15.5. The output of the algorithm is written as $f_P(R)$ with the subscript point being one of the points in the pairing and the point R being a reference point. In chapters 16 and 17, we see how Miller's algorithm is used.

The function $h_{T,T}(R)$ means the slope λ is a tangent, and we use equation 3.2 to compute the slope. Equation 15.9 repeats the equation here

$$\lambda = \frac{x_1^2 + x_1 x_2 + x_2^2 + a_4}{y_1 + y_2} \tag{15.9}$$

with $x_1 = x_2 = x_T$ and $y_1 = y_2 = y_T$. For the addition step, we use equation 15.9 with $x_1 = x_T$ and $x_2 = x_P$. Similarly, $y_1 = y_T$ and $y_2 = y_P$.

Miller's algorithm takes two points as input and returns a field element. All the equations are computed on a field extension of a curve. The value of every variable is a polynomial modulo the prime polynomial that defines the field extension. So the

equations look simple, but all the subroutines of the previous chapters are required
to make them work.

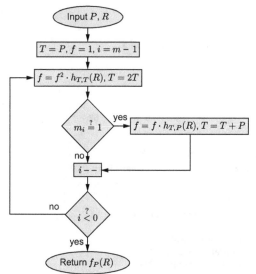

Figure 15.5   Miller's algorithm flow chart

15.3 *Subroutine* $h_{P,Q}$

In this section, I'll describe code that implements the $h_{P,Q}(R)$ function. I'll first deal
with the exceptional inputs that might cause problems and then describe the main
algorithm that does the calculations.

The pairing subroutines are in file `pairing.c`. In this chapter, I'll describe the
primary routines used for computing pairings. In chapters 16 and 17, I'll explain
both the pairing computation itself along with some of the utility functions.

This section covers the routine that computes the equations 15.6 to 15.8. The
routine `hpq()` is shown in listing 15.1. The inputs are three points and the elliptic
curve the points are on. The output is a single polynomial value.

The first check on entry is for either input being the point at infinity. If either
point does test positive as the point at infinity, the output of `hpq()` is set to 1. The
function returns without creating any internal variables.

Listing 15.1   Computing $h_{P,Q}$ infinite slope check

```
void hpq(POLY *h, POLY_POINT P, POLY_POINT Q, POLY_POINT R, POLY_CURVE E)
{
```

```
POLY t, lmbda, b, tx, t1;

if((poly_test_point(P)) || poly_test_point(Q))    ← Is either point 0?
{
  h->deg = 0;
  mpz_set_ui(h->coef[0], 1);           Yes; return value of 1.
  return;
}
poly_init(&t);
poly_init(&b);
poly_add(&b, P.y, Q.y);
if(!b.deg && !mpz_cmp_ui(b.coef[0], 0))   ← Is yP + yQ = 0?
{
  poly_sub(&b, P.x, Q.x);           ← Is xP − xQ = 0?
  if(!b.deg && !mpz_cmp_ui(b.coef[0], 0))   ← Really P == −Q?
  {
    poly_sub(h, R.x, P.x);
    poly_clear(&t);                The slope is infinite; return xR − xQ.
    poly_clear(&b);
    return;                        y sum was zero;
  }                                x difference is not,
  poly_sub(&t, P.y, Q.y);          so slope is computable.
}
```

The variables t and b are for top and bottom of the slope λ calculation. If the two y inputs sum to zero, then a check that the x coordinates are not the same is used to determine if the slope is infinite. If the two x coordinates are the same, then we return the value specified in equation 15.7. If the two x coordinates are different, then we can compute the slope as the difference in y coordinates divided by the difference in x coordinates.

The conditions that make the first if statement true are rare, so most cases enter the else section as shown in listing 15.2. This computes the t and b variables directly from the numerator and denominator of equation 15.9. On exit from the else section, both t and b are set and λ is found by their division.

Listing 15.2   Computing $h_{P,Q}$ slope

```
else            ← Not a special case;
{                 compute lambda (slope between P and Q)
                  using secure form.
  poly_init(&t1);
  poly_init(&tx);
  poly_mul(&t, P.x, P.x);
  poly_mul(&t1, P.x, Q.x);
  poly_mul(&tx, Q.x, Q.x);          xP² +
  poly_add(&t, t, t1);             xPxQ +
  poly_add(&t, t, tx);             xQ² +
  poly_add(&t, t, E.a4);           a4
  poly_add(&b, Q.y, P.y);    ← yQ + yP
```

```
}
poly_init(&lmbda);
poly_div(&lmbda, t, b);   ← The slope is top/bottom.
```

Listing 15.3 shows the calculation of equation 15.6. The variables t and b are reused for the numerator and denominator. Once the value of $h_{P,Q}$ is placed in the designated output location, the stack is cleaned up, and the routine is finished.

Listing 15.3   Computing $h_{P,Q}$

```
poly_sub(&t, R.y, P.y);
poly_sub(&tx, R.x, P.x);    numerator =
poly_mul(&tx, tx, lmbda);   y_R − y_P − λ(x_R − x_P)
poly_sub(&t, t, tx);
poly_mul(&tx, lmbda, lmbda);
poly_sub(&b, R.x, tx);      Denominator =
poly_add(&b, b, P.x);       x_R + x_P + x_Q − λ²
poly_add(&b, b, Q.x);
poly_div(h, t, b);          Finally, compute h.
poly_clear(&t);
poly_clear(&b);
poly_clear(&tx);            Clean
poly_clear(&t1);            up
poly_clear(&lmbda);         stack.
}
```

numerator = $y_R - y_P - \lambda(x_R - x_P)$

Denominator = $x_R + x_P + x_Q - \lambda^2$

15.4 Miller's algorithm code

This section presents the code that computes point pairings at the lowest level. The subroutine in listing 15.4 will be called by routines in chapters 16 and 17. The code to compute the algorithm shown in figure 15.5 is very similar to the routines described for point multiplication in chapters 3 and 13. The fundamental difference is that now there are three points involved as well as a field element to keep track of.

Listing 15.4   Miller's algorithm routine

```
void miller(POLY *f, POLY_POINT P, POLY_POINT R, mpz_t m, POLY_CURVE E)
{
  POLY_POINT T;
  POLY h;
  long mask;

  mask = mpz_sizeinbase(m, 2) - 2;   ← 1 less than number of bits
  poly_point_init(&T);
  poly_point_copy(&T, P);
  f->deg = 0;                        Initialize f = 1
  mpz_set_ui(f->coef[0], 1);         and T = P.
  poly_init(&h);
  while(mask>=0)   ← For every bit in m
```

Initialize $f = 1$ and $T = P$.

```
{
    hpq(&h, T, T, R, E);
    poly_mul(f, *f, *f);       | f ← f² · h_T,T
    poly_mul(f, *f, h);
    poly_elptic_sum(&T, T, T, E);   ← T ← 2T
    if(mpz_tstbit(m, mask))    ← Is this bit set?
    {
        hpq(&h, T, P, R, E);   | f ← f · h_T,P
        poly_mul(f, *f, h);
        poly_elptic_sum(&T, T, P, E);   ← T ← T+P
    }
    mask--;    ← Go to next bit.
}
poly_point_clear(&T);      | Clean up stack.
poly_clear(&h);
}
```

The point T keeps track of the multiplication of input point P by the order of the point (which is m). The $h_{P,Q}$ function uses T and R in the doubling step and all three points T, P, and R in the addition step.

At both the doubling step, which happens for every bit, and the addition step, which happens for every set bit, the value of f is modified by the appropriate formula, as shown in figure 15.5.

Since there is no chance of overwriting an input point, the output $f_P(R)$ is computed at each step directly. The variable f is assumed initialized before the call, and whatever it was before is lost.

The `miller()` routine is fundamental to pairing calculations. In the next two chapters, we will use it to compute related but quite different pairings.

Answers to exercises

1 Create the irreducible polynomial p using the `Mod()` command:

```
? p = Mod(1,43)*x^2+Mod(1,43)*x+Mod(3,43)
%59 = Mod(1, 43)*x^2 + Mod(1, 43)*x + Mod(3, 43)
```

Then make $32x + 34$ a polynomial modulo p:

```
? a = Mod(Mod(32,43)*x+Mod(34,43),p)
= Mod(Mod(32, 43)*x + Mod(34, 43), Mod(1, 43)*x^2 + Mod(1, 43)*x + Mod(3,
43))
```

Finally take a to the 11th power:

```
? a^11
%61 = Mod(Mod(1, 43), Mod(1, 43)*x^2 + Mod(1, 43)*x + Mod(3, 43))
```

The result is 1, which shows that $32x + 34$ modulo $x^2 + x + 3$ is an 11th root of unity.

2 From the point addition rule, we have $e_m(aR + bS, cT) = e_m(aR, cT)e_m(bS, cT)$. From the rule of equation 15.3, this becomes $e_m(R, T)^{ac}e_m(S, T)^{bc}$. Factoring out c from the exponent gives the result $[e_m(R, T)^a e_m(S, T)^b]^c$.

3 No. This is similar to point doubling, where the slope is tangent to the elliptic curve. Since λ is finite, equation 15.6 still applies.

4 No. i and m are integers, and m_i is a bit. T and P are points that are pairs of polynomials and f (which is equal to $f_P(R)$) is a polynomial modulo a prime polynomial.

Summary

- To incorporate elliptic curve pairing algorithms, curves that allow pairings must have a dual group structure of the form

$$E_{F_q} \cong \frac{Z}{d_1 Z} \times \frac{Z}{d_2 Z}$$

Purely cyclic curves described in chapter 3 will not work.

- The pairing of points on an elliptic curve results in a field element that is a root of unity. If the order of the points is m, then the polynomial result of pairing is an mth root of unity. This gives us a one-way trap door function for cryptographic use.

- The pairing function $e_m(R, T)$ is bilinear. The general form to show this is

$$e_m(aS, bT) = e_m(S, T)^{ab}$$

This gives us a way to convert point addition over an elliptic curve to multiplication over a finite field, which is used in algorithms shown in chapters 18 and 19.

- The pairing function is nondegenerate, which means it never blows up. If one of the input points is the point at infinity, the value of the function is 1. This is essential to ensure algorithms work under any condition.

- The function $h_{P,Q}(R)$ can be viewed geometrically as a relation between the line adding P plus Q and a reference point R. $h_{P,Q}(R)$ is the core of Miller's algorithm.

- Miller's algorithm computes the function $f_P(R)$. The input is a point of order m and a reference point. The output is a field element based on multiplying the input point by m and using the $h_{P,Q}$ function for doubling and adding. Miller's algorithm is the function used in chapters 16 and 17 to compute different kinds of pairings.

Weil pairing defined 16

In this chapter, I'll describe Weil pairings. These will be used with the example application shown in chapter 18. In chapter 15, I covered the fundamental functions that compute all pairings. I will now explain the Weil pairing, which has properties that make it unique. For some cryptographic protocols, these properties make the Weil pairing more useful, and for other protocols, the Weil pairing does not work. All the protocols explained in chapters 18 and 19 use different base points for the pairing algorithms, so the Weil pairing could work in principle. If you run across algorithms that have the same base point for both pairing input points, the Weil pairing will not work; use the Tate pairing from chapter 17 instead.

The formula that computes the Weil pairing uses the Miller $f_P(R)$ function from chapter 15. After showing the properties of the Weil pairing, I'll describe formulas in gory detail so you can get a feel for why certain calculations should give specific results. This enables us to debug our code because the math has to work.

There are several utility routines included in this chapter along with the Weil subroutine. After describing these routines, I use the tiny example from chapter 13 to show how specific inputs from G_1 and G_2 points give useful and failing results. The purpose of the example is to show how the Weil pairing works, not to explain any particular protocol.

As a reminder, G_1 are points on a base curve, and G_2 are points on a field extension curve. The subroutines are written with the assumption that all points are on the field extension G_2.

16.1 Weil pairing formula

In this section, I'll describe the Weil pairing formula. In 1940, A. Weil introduced the concept of pairing points of order n as a general concept to solve a problem unrelated to elliptic curves. The method was then applied to elliptic curves as a way to uncover the secret key. Today, we have algorithms that take advantage of the rules Weil developed. Here, I'll go over the formulas that compute the Weil pairing and describe the rules that result from those computations.

There are several definitions of the Weil pairing. I am going to use the version in section XI.8 of Silverman (2009). The definition uses three points. Two points are being paired, and the third point is a reference point. The reference point must not be in the same subgroup as the points being paired. Figure 16.1 is a duplicate of figure 15.4.

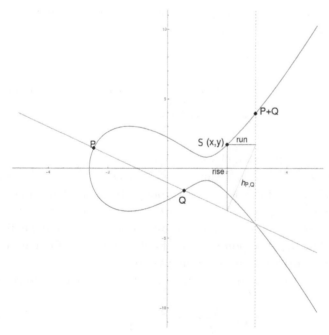

Figure 16.1 Relations between points P, Q being paired and reference point S

We take two points of prime order m, call them P and Q. The third point is S, which is not in the same subgroup of P and Q. That is, it has order different from m. As pointed out in chapters 2 and 13, elliptic curves over finite fields have groups of points with the number of points in each group related to the factors making up the cardinality of the curve. For the point S, it is OK for m to be one of many factors in the order of S. Typically, most random points on a field extension will have that property simply because the size of the group m is small compared to the extension field curve cardinality.

Using the function $f_P(R)$ from section 15.2.2, the Weil pairing is defined as equation 16.1:

$$e_m(P, Q) = \frac{\dfrac{f_p(Q + S)}{f_p(S)}}{\dfrac{f_Q(P - S)}{f_Q(-S)}} \tag{16.1}$$

Equation 16.1 is written as a fraction of two fractions to show the relationship to the reference point S and the two input points. The first argument of the pairing is the input parameter to f on the top fraction, and the second argument of the pairing is the input parameter to f on the bottom fraction. This symmetry leads to a new rule for the Weil pairing that is not available with other pairing definitions.

The Weil pairing has a property called alternating. If both input points are the same, we have equation 16.2:

$$e_m(T, T) = 1 \tag{16.2}$$

An additional part of this alternating property is that swapping the arguments inverts the result, as shown in equation 16.3. That is,

$$e_m(P, Q) = e_m(Q, P)^{-1} \tag{16.3}$$

Equation 16.3 seems obvious from equation 16.1. But equation 16.2 implies that

$$\frac{f_T(-S)}{f_T(S)} = \frac{f_T(T + S)}{f_T(T - S)}$$

While these values are equal, they don't have to be equal to 1. A hand-waving argument why this should be true (other than the mathematicians have proved it) is that we only care about the distance from the reference point to the vertical line attached to the sum of the two points in figure 16.1. The choice of a positive or negative point for the reference point does not matter. Clearly, it actually does matter, or the definition would be different. The negative points are in the denominator of equation 16.1. The math works, so we work with the equations as defined.

Let's rewrite equation 16.1 in a more computational-friendly manner as equation 16.4:

$$e_m(P, Q) = \frac{f_Q(-S)}{f_P(S)} \frac{f_P(Q + S)}{f_Q(P - S)} \tag{16.4}$$

and examine the rule

$$e_m(P, -Q) = e_m(P, Q)^{-1} = e_m(Q, P)$$

The expansion of this using equation 16.4 is equation 16.5:

$$\frac{f_{-Q}(-S)}{f_P(S)} \frac{f_P(S - Q)}{f_{-Q}(P - S)} = \frac{f_P(S)}{f_Q(-S)} \frac{f_Q(P - S)}{f_P(Q + S)} = \frac{f_P(-S)}{f_Q(S)} \frac{f_Q(P + S)}{f_P(Q - S)} \qquad (16.5)$$

A quick glance at this equation is rather head-scratching. In the first term, we have $f_{-Q}(-S)$ and $f_{-Q}(P - S)$, which do not appear in either of the other two terms. In the second term, we have $f_P(Q + S)$ in the denominator with $f_Q(P + S)$ in the numerator of the third term. According to the rules of pairings, all these formulas are, in fact, identical. We can use equations like equation 16.5 to ensure our code is correct. Computing the three different Weil pairings around an inverse should all give the same answer. If they don't all give the same result, we know we have a bug to find.

> ### Exercise 16.1
>
> The Diffie-Hellman protocol uses two public keys created from different private keys and the same base point. Why would the Weil pairing of those two public keys be useless? (Hint: Review the pairing rule in equation 15.3.)

16.2 Pairing subroutines

This section provides the code to implement the Weil pairing of points on field extension elliptic curves. The Weil pairing subroutine is simple with just four calls to the Miller algorithm from section 15.4. In addition to showing that listing, I also add the routines mentioned in chapter 13. Utilities include computing the cardinality recurrence equation 13.3 and finding the order of a point for both base and extension fields.

The Weil pairing calculation is shown in listing 16.1. There are three points derived from the input points shown in equation 16.1. These are the points $Q + S$, $-S$, and $P - S$. The first is computed directly from the input points. The value for $-S$ is created by first copying over the x component into the initialized point mS and then subtracting the y component of S from the zeroed-out y component of mS. Adding this value to the point P gives the final point we need.

After computing the four Miller functions, the top two are divided, followed by the bottom two. The final answer is the division of these two intermediate results. The last operation is cleaning up the stack.

Listing 16.1 Weil pairing routine

```
void weil(POLY *w, POLY_POINT P, POLY_POINT Q, POLY_POINT S, mpz_t m,
        POLY_CURVE E)
{
  POLY_POINT QpS, mS, PmS;
  POLY t1, t2, t3, t4, w1, w2;
```

```
    poly_point_init(&QpS);
    poly_elptic_sum(&QpS, Q, S, E);        Create Q + S point.
    poly_point_init(&mS);
    poly_copy(&mS.x, S.x);
    poly_point_init(&PmS);                 Create −S point.
    poly_sub(&mS.y, PmS.y, S.y);
    poly_elptic_sum(&PmS, P, mS, E);       ← Create P − S point.
    poly_init(&t1);
    miller(&t1, P, QpS, m, E);   ← Compute fₚ(Q +S).
    poly_init(&t2);
    miller(&t2, P, S, m, E);     ← Compute fₚ(S).
    poly_init(&t3);
    miller(&t3, Q, PmS, m, E);   ← Compute f_Q(P − S).
    poly_init(&t4);
    miller(&t4, Q, mS, m, E);    ← Compute f_Q(−S).
    poly_init(&w1);
    poly_div(&w1, t1, t2);        Well pairing =
    poly_init(&w2);               fₚ(Q +S) /fₚ(S)
    poly_div(&w2, t3, t4);        over
    poly_div(w, w1, w2);          f_Q(P − S) /f_Q(−S)

    poly_clear(&w1);
    poly_clear(&w2);
    poly_clear(&t1);
    poly_clear(&t2);
    poly_clear(&t3);
    poly_clear(&t4);              Clean up stack.
    poly_point_clear(&QpS);
    poly_point_clear(&PmS);
    poly_point_clear(&mS);
}
```

The equation for cardinality of a curve over a field extension is given in chapter 13, along with the recurrence relation in equations 13.2 and 13.3. Copied here as equation 16.6, they are

$$\#E_k = p^k + 1 - t_k$$
$$t_{n+2} = t_1 t_{n+1} - p t_n$$

(16.6)

The routine to compute this is shown in listing 16.2. The inputs to this routine are the trace of Frobenius and the embedding degree. It is assumed that the field prime has already been set.

Because the input variable is t, I used the array v[] to keep track of the t_n in equation 16.6. Since we start at zero and go to k, there are $k + 1$ elements in the v[] array. After space is allocated, the array elements are initialized to zero, and then the first two are set to the correct values to start the recurrence.

Listing 16.2   Field extension cardinality

```
void cardinality(mpz_t crd, mpz_t t, long k)
{
    mpz_t *v, t1, t2, p, pk;
```

```
int i;

v = (mpz_t *)malloc(sizeof(mpz_t)*(k+1));          Allocate space
for(i=0; i<=k; i++)                                 for k + 1
   mpz_init(v[i]);                                   variables.
mpz_set_ui(v[0], 2);                                The first two values are
mpz_set(v[1], t);                                    2 and t.
mpz_inits(t1, t2, NULL);
mget(p);                                           ←  Recover field prime.
for(i=2; i<=k; i++)                                ←  First two values are already set.
{
   mpz_mul(t1, t, v[i - 1]);                        Recurrence is
   mpz_mul(t2, p, v[i - 2]);                        t_{n+2} = t_1 t_{n+1} − p t_n.
   mpz_sub(v[i], t1, t2);
}
poly_q_get(pk);                                     Get p^k from
mpz_set(crd, pk);                                   global static storage.
mpz_add_ui(crd, crd, 1);                            Compute
mpz_sub(crd, crd, v[k]);                            #E_k = p^k + 1 − t_k.
for(i=0; i<=k; i++)
   mpz_clear(v[i]);
mpz_clears(t1, t2, p, pk, NULL);                    Clean up stack.
}
```

With the field prime collected from the modulo.c static global, the recurrence relation is computed in the loop. The value of p^k is taken from global storage in file poly.c, and equation 16.6 is computed for the cardinality.

16.3 Example code with tiny curves

In this section, an example with printable points that implements the Weil pairing is shown. In chapter 13, I introduced a tiny field prime and extension curve. I want to show what happens with several of the points from that example when used with the Weil pairing. First I'll describe the routines used in chapter 13 that checked the order of a point. Then I'll look at the remainder of the program introduced in chapter 13 to examine Weil pairings.

Two utility routines were used in the example code from chapter 13. These look for the order of a point. The assumption is that we have already found all the possible factors. These routines won't work on really large extension fields. In fact, it is the difficulty of factoring these very large numbers that helps with their security. Figure 16.2 is a flow chart for the routine which finds the order of a point. The inputs include the point, curve, and list of factors that make up the order of the curve as well as the number of factors. If all the factors are correct, no error should ever occur.

Listing 16.3 takes a point and a curve as input. It also expects an array of integers that are all the possible factors the point could have. The length of that array is the final input value. The routine brute force tests multiplication of each factor with the point until one of the multiplies hits the point at infinity. If none of the factors is correct, the routine halts the program with an error that some factor is missing.

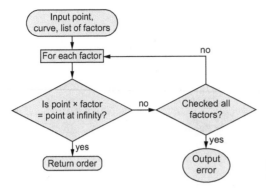

Figure 16.2   Subroutine to find the order of a point with known factors

Listing 16.3   Order of point on base curve

```
int get_order(mpz_t order, POINT P, CURVE E, mpz_t *factors, int n)
{
  int i;
  POINT R;                                           Array of factors
                                                     and number of factors

  point_init(&R);
  for(i=0; i<n; i++)
  {
    elptic_mul(&R, P, factors[i], E);    When a factor
    if(test_point(R))                    gives point at infinity,
      break;                             we have point order.
  }
  if(i<n)
    mpz_set(order, factors[i]);          ← Set output order.
  else
  {
    printf("missing order in base!!\n");          Catastrophic error;
    exit(-3);                                      kill program.
  }
  point_clear(&R);
  return i;                    ← Return index of factor as well.
}
```

Listing 16.4 shows the same process for polynomial field extension points and curves. As we'll see in the example code, the factor list is the same array as in listing 16.3, but the list is longer.

Listing 16.4   Order of point on field extension

```
int poly_get_order(mpz_t order, POLY_POINT P, POLY_CURVE E,
                   mpz_t *factors, int n)
{
  int i;                              Array of factors
  POLY_POINT R;                       and number of factors
```

```
poly_point_init(&R);
for(i=0; i<n; i++)
{
  poly_elptic_mul(&R, P, factors[i], E);   | When a factor
  if(poly_test_point(R))                    | gives point at infinity,
    break;                                  | we have point order.
}
if(i<n)
  mpz_set(order, factors[i]);        ← Set output order.
else
{
  printf("missing order in xtended!!\n");   | Catastrophic error;
  exit(-4);                                 | kill program.
}
poly_point_clear(&R);
return i;                      ← Return index of factor as well.
}
```

In listing 13.3, I showed the start of a test program. The object of showing the code was to list the points for a tiny example. In the printout, I showed the order of each point using the routines in listings 16.3 and 16.4. The input variable factors[] is set up as shown in the following listing.

Listing 16.5 Factors setup for tiny example

```
for(i=0; i<8; i++)           | Initialize each element
  mpz_init(factors[i]);    ◄─┘ in the array.
mpz_set_ui(factors[0], 5);
mpz_set_ui(factors[1], 11);    | First three numbers
mpz_set_ui(factors[2], 55);    | are for base curve.
mpz_set_ui(factors[3], 3);
mpz_set_ui(factors[4], 33);    | The last set
mpz_set_ui(factors[5], 15);    | includes all
mpz_set_ui(factors[6], 165);   | remaining possibilities.
mpz_set_ui(factors[7], 1815);  ← No points of this order!
```

The order of the G_1 curve is 55, which has factors 5 and 11. So the first three entries are used to define all the possible orders for the base curve. The extension curve has 1,815 points with factors 3, 5, and 11^2. Notice that there is no group of order 121 points. As described in chapter 15, the structure of the field extension curve is

$$E_{F_q} \cong \frac{Z}{d_1 Z} \times \frac{Z}{d_2 Z}$$

with $d_1 = 11$ and $d_2 = 165$ for the tiny example. The two groups are independent, so there are no points of order 121.

The tiny example base curve all by itself will not work with the Weil pairing. It does not have a squared prime value that splits between two groups. The tiny example extension curve does have a squared prime value. So we can use all the points of order 11 on the curve as inputs to the Weil pairing routine.

In the listings of chapter 13, I explained how the points were generated. In listing 16.6, I show how they are saved in a table. I also indexed the order of each point along with the group "type," which again does not mean anything. It was useful for picking out G_1 and G_2 points.

Listing 16.6   Tiny example point saving

```
while(j < 1814)
{
  poly_elptic_embed(&Px1, &Px2, xtnd, Ex);      ← Embed next point on curve.
  poly_get_order(ordr, Px1, Ex, factors, 8);    ← Find the order of the point.
  :
  :
  poly_point_init(&table[j]);         | Put first point
  poly_point_copy(&table[j], Px1);    | into table.
  grp[2*j] = g1g2(Px1);
  grp[2*j + 1] = mpz_get_ui(ordr);    ← Convert GMP value to integer.
  j++;
```

The vertical dots in listing 16.6 are the print statements in listing 13.13. With every point placed in `table[]` and every order placed in `grp[]`, it is now possible to see how the Weil pairing works.

The main usefulness of the `g1g2()` routine is to pick out base points versus extension field points. Values of 1 are all on the base curve, and values of 2, 3, and 4 are on the extension curve. Points of order 11 were chosen because that is a "large prime" in the base curve and because the structure of the extension field curve is [11 x 165].

To test the Weil pairing, I chose four points. Three of the points are order 11, and the fourth point is order 55. The fourth point is used as the reference point, and the other three points are combined to test equation 15.2.

The entire test program and all the output are in the code repository, found at https://github.com/drmike8888/Elliptic-curve-pairings. The points for both the base and extension fields are found in directory Chapter13 while the Weil pairing output can be found under directory Chapter16. Some of the output is just debugging data.

Here I want to point out some of the test results because failure shows up. If you run across these kinds of problems while testing your programs, this might be a useful clue on what to fix.

For the G_1 x G_1 test, three points are on the base curve. The chosen points were $P = (3, 40)$, $Q = (11, 11)$, and $T = (23, 24)$. The reference point was chosen to be $S = (x, 22x + 32)$. All these numbers are modulo 43, the value of the field prime. The irreducible polynomial for the extension field is $x^2 + x + 3$.

The Weil pairing of the points $e_m(P, Q)$ and $e_m(P, T)$ were both 1. From equation 16.2, these act like the same point. The powering equation 15.3 says

$$e_m(aS, bT) = e_m(S, T)^{ab}$$

so the points are directly related to each other by some factor with $Q = aP$ and $T = bP$. Because the numbers are small, we could figure out what the multiplier is. The idea behind the exercise is G_1 x G_1 fails to be useful.

For the G_1 x G_2 test, I left P as the same point and chose $Q = (x + 4, 15x + 18)$ and $T = (3x + 1, 41x + 32)$. The reference point S was also left to be the same. This time, in equation 16.7, the pairings came out to be

$$e_m(P, Q) = 36x + 25$$
$$e_m(P, T) = 11x + 2 \tag{16.7}$$

The point $T + Q = (24x + 36, 6x + 36)$ and the Weil pairing of P with $T + Q$ came out as

$$e_m(P, T + Q) = 37x + 23$$

Multiplication of $e_m(P, Q)$ with $e_m(P, T)$ gives

$$e_m(P, Q)e_m(P, T) = 37x + 23$$

which is what we expect from the rules of pairings.

Remember that all these operations are done modulo the irreducible polynomial that defines the field extension. Taking these last two results to the 11th power because the order of the points being used is 11, the expected result of 1 is output. That is, two points of order 11 fed into the Weil pairing algorithm result in an 11th root of unity.

In the test for a G_2 x G_2 example, I changed the value of P to $(x + 39, 39x + 4)$. The value for Q was $(3x + 1, 2x + 11)$, T was chosen to be $(3x + 16, 41x + 11)$, and S was left as $(x, 22x + 32)$. In equation 16.8, the results came out to be

$$e_m(P, Q) = 34x + 19$$
$$e_m(P, T) = 11x + 2$$
$$e_m(P, Q)e_m(P, T) = 32x + 34$$
$$e_m(P, Q + T) = 32x + 34 \tag{16.8}$$
$$e_m(P, Q + T)^{11} = 1$$

I did not do a G_2 x G_1 test. We expect that it would work, and we know from equation 16.3 that using the same values from the G_1 x G_2 test, we should get the inverse result. For the Weil pairing, the order of the arguments matters. The G_1 x G_1 test shows the nondegeneracy property, but otherwise it is not useful.

Answer to exercise

1 With base point T and two private keys a and b, the Weil pairing of the two public keys is

$$e_m(aT, bT) = e_m(T, T)^{ab} = 1^{ab} = 1$$

The Weil pairing of two directly related points is always 1.

Summary

- The Weil pairing is computed using four calls to Miller's algorithm. Two points of the same order m are paired, and a third reference point of different order is an input to the operation. The input values are field extension points, and the output is a field extension value that is an mth root of unity.
- A Weil pairing of a point with itself gives a result of 1. Most other pairings do not have this property. Algorithms with multiple base points work well with Weil pairing.
- A Weil pairing will compute an inverse result if the input points are exchanged. That is,

$$e_m(P, Q) = e_m(Q, P)^{-1}$$

This is a very useful way to test that the code is working correctly.

- The cardinality of an extension curve is easy to compute. It may be exceptionally difficult to factor. For very large field primes, this inability to completely factor the cardinality increases the security of pairing-friendly curves.

Tate pairing defined

This chapter covers

- A mathematical description of Tate pairing
- An implementation of Tate pairing
- A test with a tiny example to see how Tate pairings work

In this chapter, the Tate pairing is described. This will be used with the example in chapter 19. The Tate pairing has the properties of bilinearity and nondegeneracy but not the alternating property that the Weil pairing of chapter 16 possesses. I will first go over the mathematical description of the Tate pairing. In chapter 16, pairing test code utility routines were described, so this chapter will just show how the Tate pairing is computed with one listing. The tiny example introduced in chapter 13 will again be used to show how the number of points available for the Tate pairing is enlarged over the Weil pairing. Explaining the math with words is great, but seeing an example should help to get an intuitive feel for what the mathematics actually mean. Using the same tiny example, we will explore the Tate pairing in detail.

17.1 *Tate pairing mathematics*

In this section, the mathematics of the Tate pairing is explained. Similar to the general pairing description of a curve having two cyclic groups, the Tate pairing is described in section XI.9 in Silverman (2009) with the mathematical statement shown in equation 17.1:

$$\tau : E[m] \times \frac{E}{mE} \longrightarrow \mu_m \tag{17.1}$$

The symbol τ is the Tate pairing operation. To distinguish it from the Weil pairing, I'll use $\tau(\cdot, \cdot)$ for the Tate pairing of two points. The symbol $E[m]$ means all the points of order m on the curve E. The symbol μ_m is again the mth root of unity. That leaves the symbol $\frac{E}{mE}$, which, to be honest, threw me for a loop the first time I ran across it. It's actually pretty simple. It means the points on curve E with all the points m times every point on E removed. The reason this confused me is that the points of order m go to the point at infinity. Those points are *not* removed. Points that have an order with a factor of m are also not removed. The points that are not the point at infinity after multiplication by m are removed, so we are left with points of order m and all points that have m as one of the factors of their order. Figure 17.1 shows a concrete example taken from the tiny field extension curve. Each circle represents all the points with the order given by the number in the circle. When points of order 55 and 33 are multiplied by 11, the result is a point of order 5 and 3, respectively. Points of order 11 go to infinity, so that circle is empty. Points of order 5 and 3 are removed from the possible points in a Tate pairing, but the points of order 55 and 33 can be used. That is really cool.

The Tate pairing calculation formula is found in section 5.1 of Menezes (2005). In terms of Miller's formula $f_p(R)$, in equation 17.2, it is

$$\tau(P, Q) = \left(\frac{f_P(Q + S)}{f_P(S)} \right)^{(p^k - 1)/m} \tag{17.2}$$

where m is the order of the points we are interested in. Equation 13.1 ($p^k \cong 1 \bmod m$) says that m divides $p^k - 1$. That means the exponent in equation 17.2 is an integer. For high-security situations, it is a very large integer, as seen in table 14.1. For a 256-bit security level, that exponent is over 15,000 bits. So while the Weil pairing requires four calls to the Miller function, the Tate pairing requires two calls to the Miller function plus a final power operation. I have seen arguments in the literature that one is faster than the other, but the reality is it depends on the case.

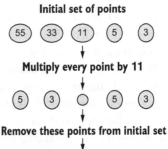

Initial set of points

Multiply every point by 11

Remove these points from initial set

Quotient set of points

Figure 17.1   Example of quotient set $\frac{E}{mE}$ **for $m = 11$. The first row shows all possible point orders, the second row shows the resulting orders of points after multiplying all points by 11, and the third row shows the first row minus the second row.**

If the two points of input are the same, we do not get 1 as an answer. This is different from the Weil pairing. In addition, if we swap the inputs, we do not get an inverse; we get a completely different result. Most protocols that use the Tate pairing are very specific about which points go into each slot, especially if there is a requirement to use a G_1 x G_2 pairing.

> ### Exercise 17.1
>
> An elliptic curve with field prime 41 and large prime $m = 29$ has embedding degree 4. What is the exponent value for a Tate pairing of this field extension curve?

17.2 The Tate pairing subroutine described

In this section, the code to compute the Tate pairing of points on an elliptic curve over a field extension is described. The execution of equation 17.2 is straightforward. The use of the Tate subroutine is illustrated in figure 17.2, and the code is shown in listing 17.1. As with the Weil pairing, the first two points are being paired, and the third point is the reference for the Miller calculation. Unlike the Weil pairing, the second point only requires that it have the factor m in the order of the point. The first point must be of order m. I verified this with brute-force testing, as we'll see in a bit.

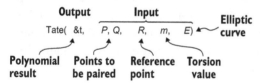

Figure 17.2 Tate pairing subroutine calling parameters

Listing 17.1 Tate pairing routine

```
void tate(POLY *t, POLY_POINT P, POLY_POINT Q, POLY_POINT S, mpz_t m,
          POLY_CURVE E)
{
  POLY_POINT QpS;
  POLY t1, t2;
  mpz_t pw;

  poly_point_init(&QpS);
  poly_init(&t1);
  poly_init(&t2);
  poly_elptic_sum(&QpS, Q, S, E);    | Create point
                                     | Q+S.
  miller(&t1, P, QpS, m, E);    ← Numerator = fp(Q+S)
  miller(&t2, P, S, m, E);      ← Denominator = fp(S)
  poly_div(t, t1, t2);    ← fp(Q+s)/fp(S)
  poly_q_get(pw);
  mpz_sub_ui(pw, pw, 1);    | Compute power (p^k - 1)/m.
  mpz_divexact(pw, pw, m);  |
```

```
    poly_pow(t, *t, pw);      ← Full result
    poly_point_clear(&QpS);
    poly_clear(&t1);                    Clean
    poly_clear(&t2);                    up
    mpz_clear(pw);                      stack.
}
```

The reference point S cannot be related to either input point. One suggestion I found in the literature was to choose a point S with x component equal to zero. Unfortunately, that might be a point of order m, so that choice would not work in every case.

Listing 17.1 follows equation 17.2 directly. The point $Q + S$ is found, and then the Miller algorithm is computed for that point. The Miller algorithm is computed for the point S, and then the two results are divided. The value $(p^k - 1)/m$ is computed. This is used as the power to the result from division of Miller functions, and the final result is placed in the requested location. Now that we have all the machinery of modulo polynomial operations available, it looks easy.

17.3 *Testing the Tate pairing using a tiny example*

In this section, a printable point code example of the Tate pairing is explained. The Weil tiny example program discussed in chapter 16 was copied and modified to use the Tate pairing. The program is in the repository under directory Chapter17 as is the output. Saving the points to a file was removed. But the table of points was kept, so any point could be tested. Listing 17.2 shows the essential setup copied from the Weil tiny example into the Tate tiny example. The group size is 11 and the extension curve has the same coefficients.

Listing 17.2 Tate tiny setup

```
    mpz_init_set_ui(prm, M);
    minit(prm);                         Set up field prime to 43.
    poly_init(&irrd);
       :
    poly_irrd_set(irrd);                Set up Irreducible polynomial
    poly_mulprep(irrd);                 and multiplication table.
       :
    mpz_set_ui(factors[2], 11);        ← m = 11 Is prime group order.
       :
    mpz_init_set(tor, factors[2]);
       :
    poly_curve_init(&Ex);
    mpz_set_ui(Ex.a4.coef[0], 23);      Same curve
    mpz_set_ui(Ex.a6.coef[0], 42);      for tiny example
       :
```

Rather than pick specific points to test the algorithm, I decided to use the built-in random number generator of gcc initialized with the nanosecond clock as a seed. The setup for this is shown in the following listing.

Listing 17.3 Tate random setup

```
#include <time.h>              Use internal
       :                       clock to change
  struct timespec ts;          rand seed.
       :

  clock_gettime(CLOCK_MONOTONIC_RAW, &ts);   Use nanoseconds
  srand(ts.tv_nsec);                         to stir things up.
```

Since the order of the point matters for the algorithm, I set up an array with each index into the list of points separated by order. The first step was to determine how many points were in each order. I modified listing 13.15 to increment a counter with the same index as the factor found from the `poly_get_order()` routine. This is shown in listing 17.4. There are two points for every embedded value, so the counter is bumped by two each time.

Listing 17.4 Tate order counting

```
  k = poly_get_order(xtndordr[j], xtndpnt[j], Ex, factors, 7);
  numxtdpnts[k] += 2;          Increment correct order.
    :

    :
  for(i=0; i<7; i++)           Output number of points
  {                            in each order.
    gmp_printf("order %Zd has %d points\n", factors[i], numxtdpnts[i]);
    pdex[i] = 0;
  }
```

The following listing shows the output from listing 17.4.

Listing 17.5 Tate orders found

```
order 3 has 2 points
order 5 has 4 points
order 11 has 120 points
order 15 has 8 points
order 33 has 240 points
order 55 has 480 points
order 165 has 960 points
```

The largest order has 960 points, and there are seven different orders, so the index list is seven groups of 1,000 index values. Table 17.1 is a schematic layout of the point list array. The point list array holds an index into the list of points created by brute-force embedding, not the (x, y) values for each point.

Table 17.1   Point array for Tate pairing test

Order	3	5	11	15	33	55	165
	P_3^1	P_5^1	P_{11}^1	P_{15}^1	P_{33}^1	P_{55}^1	P_{165}^1
	P_3^2	P_5^2	P_{11}^2	P_{15}^2	P_{33}^2	P_{55}^2	P_{165}^2
Points		P_5^3	P_{11}^3	P_{15}^3	P_{33}^3	P_{55}^3	P_{165}^3
		P_5^4	P_{11}^4	P_{15}^4	P_{33}^4	P_{55}^4	P_{165}^4
		$\vdots$	$\vdots$	$\vdots$	$\vdots$	$\vdots$	$\vdots$

The creation of the `point_list[]` array was by brute force, as shown in listing 17.6. Every point and every possible order was checked. This allowed me to take the points found from the embedding order and create the array as shown in table 17.1.

Listing 17.6   Tate `point_list[]` array creation

```
point_list = (int*)malloc(sizeof(int)*7*1000);      ← One column for each factor;
for(j=0; j<XTEND; j++)                                 one entry for each point
{
                            |
                            | Loop over each point.
  for(i=0; i<7; i++)
    {                       | Loop over each factor.
      if(!mpz_cmp_ul(factors[i], grp[?*j + 11))    ← Look for which column this
        {                                             point belongs.
          k = i*1000 + pdex[i];      | 2D index into point_list
          point_list[k] = j;         | saves this point's place
          pdex[i]++;                 ← Each column has an index counter.
        }
    }
}
```

A random point was selected from a particular column as shown in listing 17.7. The input to the routine includes the `grp[]` array, which holds the order and group type, a pointer to one of the columns in the `point_list[]` array, the length of that array, and 0 for a G_1 or 1 for a G_2 point. If there is no G_1 point for a selected order, it is an infinite loop that never exits. I realized this mistake a few times. The purpose of this test is education, so I learned a lot!

Listing 17.7   Tate random selection

```
int rndselect(long *grp, int *point_list, int nmpnt, int type)
{                                  ↑                     ↑       ↑ G1=0, G2=1
  int j, k, r;                     |                     | Number of points to pick from
                                   | Pointer to column with correct order
  r = -1;
  while(r < 0)
    {                              | Pseudo random modulo length of array
      k = rand() % nmpnt;    ←
      j = point_list[k];     ← Index of point in grp[] table
```

```
    if(!type && (grp[2*j] == 1))
       r = j;
    else if(type && (grp[2*j] > 1))
       r = j;
  }
  return j;
}
```
`Choose Index`
`If correct group.`

`← Repeat forever if no match!`

For the tests of orders 11x11 and 11x55, the point S was found using the criteria that it be in $G2$ and have order 3. Since there are only two points of order 3, there is not much choice. For tests with orders 11x33, I changed S to be order 5 in G_1. I left S as order 5 in G_1 for 11x165 tests as well.

I also tried reversing the orders using 33x11, 55x11, 165x11, and 55x55. As shown in equation 17.3, every single one of these failed to compute a correct pairing such that

$$\tau(P, Q+T) = \tau(P, Q)\tau(P, T) \tag{17.3}$$

On occasion, one of these backward tests would give a matching result, but running the random selection 20 times showed these were accidents of luck.

Listing 17.8 shows one of the test programs performed where the second group is order 165, which is only possible for a G_2 group. The two tests are orders 11x165 with G_1 x G_2, and G_2 x G_2. The point S was reset to order 5 at the beginning of this test.

Listing 17.8   Tate 11x165 test

```
k = rndselect(grp, &point_list[1000], numxtdpnts[1], 0);
poly_point_copy(&S, xtndpnt[k]);
poly_point_printf("order 5 S:\n", S);
printf("===========================================\n");
printf("Tate G1 x G2* (order 11x165)\n\n");
k = rndselect(grp, &point_list[2000], numxtdpnts[2], 0);
poly_point_copy(&P, xtndpnt[k]);
poly_point_printf("P:\n", P);
k = rndselect(grp, &point_list[6000], numxtdpnts[6], 1);
poly_point_copy(&Q, xtndpnt[k]);
poly_point_printf("Q:\n", Q);
k = rndselect(grp, &point_list[6000], numxtdpnts[6], 1);
poly_point_copy(&T, xtndpnt[k]);
poly_point_printf("T:\n", T);
tate(&t1, P, Q, S, tor, Ex);
poly_printf("tate(P, Q): ", t1);
tate(&t2, P, T, S, tor, Ex);
poly_printf("tate(P, T): ", t2);
poly_mul(&t3, t1, t2);
poly_printf("(P, Q)*(P, T): ", t3);
poly_elptic_sum(&TpQ, T, Q, Ex);
tate(&t4, P, TpQ, S, tor, Ex);
poly_printf("(P, T+Q): ", t4);
```

`Set S to order 5, G₁.`

`Set P to order 11, G₁.`

`Set Q to order 165, G₂.`

`Set T to order 165, G₂.`

`← Compute $\tau(P, Q)$.`

`← Compute $\tau(P, T)$.`

`← Product $\tau(P, Q)\tau(P, T)$`

`← Compute $Q + T$.`

`← Compute $\tau(P, Q+T)$.`

`Compare output.`

```
printf("================================================\n");
printf("Tate G2 x G2* (order 11x165)\n\n");
k = rndselect(grp, &point_list[2000], numxtdpnts[2], 1);
poly_point_copy(&P, xtndpnt[k]);                              Set P to
poly_point_printf(" P:\n" P);                                 order 11, G₂.
k = rndselect(grp, &point_list[6000], numxtdpnts[6], 1);
poly_point_copy(&Q, xtndpnt[k]);                              Set Q to
poly_point_printf(" Q:\n", Q);                                order 165, G₂.
k = rndselect(grp, &point_list[6000], numxtdpnts[6], 1);
poly_point_copy(&T, xtndpnt[k]);                              Set T to
poly_point_printf(" T:\n", T);                                order 165, G₂.
tate(&t1, P, Q, S, tor, Ex);        ← Compute τ(P,Q).
poly_printf("tate(P, Q): ", t1);
tate(&t2, P, T, S, tor, Ex);        ← Compute τ(P,T).
poly_printf("tate(P, T): ", t2);
poly_mul(&t3, t1, t2);              ← Product τ(P,Q)τ(P,T)
poly_printf(" (P, Q)*(P, T): ", t3);  ←────────────────┐
poly_elptic_sum(&TpQ, T, Q, Ex);   ← Compute Q+T.       │ Compare
tate(&t4, P, TpQ, S, tor, Ex);     ← Compute τ(P,Q+T).  │ output.
poly_printf(" (P, T+Q): ", t4);         ←───────────────┘
```

I ran this test many times and was happy to see equation 17.3 matched every time. Table 17.2 shows the summary of two of these runs. Each run has a G_1 x G_2 column with point P being the G_1 value and points Q and T being order 165 in G_2. The second column of each run has P being order 11 in G_2. There are enough random points that we see no duplicates. Each point entry is an x, y pair and all values are modulo 43.

Table 17.2   Tate pairing tiny test random points 11x165

	Run 1		Run 2	
	G_1 x G_2	G_2 x G_2	G_1 x G_2	G_2 x G_2
S	39, 12		39, 31	
P	30, 30	$13x+17, 10x+21$	24, 20	$19x+12, 37x+30$
Q	$27x+35, 2x+16$	$7x+36, 18x+5$	$13x+21, 10x+1$	$23x+35, 42x+35$
T	$15x+32, 5x+4$	$25x+25, 42x+29$	$40x+35, 18x+38$	$33x, 41x+8$
$\tau(P,Q)$	$6x+29$	$12x+17$	$31x+5$	$7x+32$
$\tau(P,T)$	$36x+25$	$11x+2$	$31x+5$	$9x+28$
$\tau(P,Q)\tau(P,T)$	$32x+34$	$36x+25$	$37x+23$	$34x+19$
$\tau(P,T+Q)$	$32x+34$	$36x+25$	$37x+23$	$34x+19$

At the bottom of the table, we see that the multiply of Tate pairings equals the Tate pairing of the sum of points. We also see duplicate values for pairings. This makes sense because there are only 11 possible values for pairing results. They must be 11th roots of unity, and only 11 of the $43^2 = 1849$ values have this property.

Answer to exercise

1 From equation 17.2, we get

$$\frac{41^4 - 1}{29} = 97440$$

Summary

- The Tate pairing is a bilinear pairing between two points on an elliptic curve defined over a finite field.
- The Tate pairing works with points that have a factor m of large prime order for the second point. The first point must only be of large prime order m. Mathematically, this is written as

$$E[m] \times \frac{E}{mE} \longrightarrow \mu_m$$

- The Tate pairing uses two calls to the Miller algorithm followed by being taken to the power of $(p^k - 1)/m$. The formula is

$$\tau(P, Q) = \left(\frac{f_P(Q + S)}{f_P(S)} \right)^{(p^k - 1)/m}$$

Exploring BLS multi-signatures

This chapter covers

- Aggregate signature of multiple users
- Subgroups using membership keys
- Pairing mathematics for verification

In this chapter, I'll dive into an advanced signature system that takes advantage of elliptic curve pairings. The method is an extension of BLS signatures that use pairings to accomplish the same digital signature task described in chapter 5. The advantage of this method is the ability to combine multiple signatures into one verification step.

Chapters 18 and 19 include a lot of mathematical variables. To help keep track of them, you will find a list of all the variables used throughout the entire book in appendix C.

18.1 Introduction to multi-signatures

The initials BLS show up in two places within the pairing literature. In chapter 14, I mentioned BLS curves, associated with the authors Barreto, Lynn, and Scott. BLS signatures are associated with the authors Boneh, Lynn, and Shacham. Lynn is the same in both, but everyone else is different. The theory of digital signatures using pairings presented in this chapter follows the BLS signature scheme. It is an extension from BLS short signature to multiple signers.

I'll explain Boneh et al. (2018), which has Boneh as an author in common with the BLS signatures' original article. The two ideas presented here from that paper are called multi-signatures with key aggregation and accountable subgroup multi-signatures. Multi-signatures with key aggregation combine all the public keys from every person signing a document, so the verification process only has to do two calculations to verify everyone who has claimed to sign a document actually did. This is much faster than checking each person's signature separately.

Figure 18.1 shows a schematic of the idea behind accountable subgroup multi-signatures. A subgroup of users sign the same message. The individual signatures are combined to create a signature, which requires only three pairing calculations to verify. The setup is a bit longer than a complete group signature because everyone has to compute a row in a matrix, combining everyone else's public key with their private key. The typical use case is blockchain, so a new row only needs to be computed when an additional node is added to a system of servers.

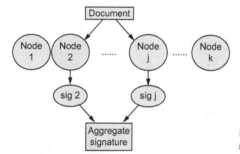

Figure 18.1 Subgroup signature basic schematic showing how only a few nodes sign the document

In both cases, the order of the keys in the aggregation matters because a hash is taken of the public key data. The protocols also assume each user has a specific index into the list of keys. This can be accomplished in many ways in the real world. I will just follow the math in Boneh et al. (2018) and use an index to reference each person (or machine) who can sign a document.

After each theory section, I will show the code that implements the math. As we will see, there are several types of hash outputs that use the same underlying Kangaroo Twelve algorithm we used before in chapter 4.

Finally, an example test system will be presented using an extended field with $k = 11$ over a 261-bit field prime for 110-bit security level. The public key communications are completely absent, but a simulated file is created, so the keys are always in the correct order.

18.2 Multi-signatures with key aggregation

In this section, I'll describe the concept of multiple signatures for one document being combined so only one computation is required to check all the signatures are valid. When multiple people (or nodes) sign a document, each signature is unique. To reduce the computation time of checking each individual signature, the aggregation of all the signatures into one value to create a multi-signature is highly desirable. In addition, combining all the keys into one value reduces the verification time tremendously. Here, I'll describe a system that aggregates keys and signatures to create a multi-signature algorithm.

The starting point for multi-signatures is the parameters for fields and curves. This includes a large prime factor r with groups in G_1, G_2 (defined in section 13.1) and μ_r (defined in section 15.1). They assume a pairing function e and generators g_1 in G_1 and g_2 in G_2. To make this happen in the real world, we require a field prime p with embedding degree k such that r is a factor in both G_1 and G_2. From chapter 14, we know how to do this.

Figure 18.2 is a duplicate of figure 1.6. Now that we have all the mathematical and programming background, the details of this process can be described.

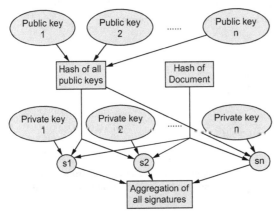

Figure 18.2   Aggregated digital signature signing detailed schematic

The multi-signatures algorithm uses two hash functions:

- *The hash of the document*—Hashes to a point in G_1
- *The hash of public keys*—Hashes to a value modulo r

The private key is taken modulo r, and the public key is a point on G_2. All the public keys are combined using the hash to modulo r, so they can all be multiplied over G_2 to create a single point. Each person must sign the same document with their private key and then send that to a combiner who creates a single G_1 point. The signature is verified using the combined signature, combined public keys, and hash of the original document.

18.2.1 *The hash functions used in key aggregation algorithms*

In this section, two hash functions that use the same subroutine to form two different results are described. These are used in both signature applications described in this chapter.

The two hash functions are labeled H_0 and H_1 in Boneh et al. (2018). A quick schematic is shown in figure 18.3. In the algorithm, H_0 takes a message M as input and outputs a point on G_1. The function H_1 takes a concatenation of the public keys (similar to what we did with the Schnorr algorithm in chapter 5) and outputs a value modulo r.

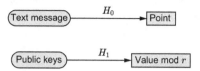

Figure 18.3   Hash functions used with aggregation

As pointed out in chapter 4, the number of bytes returned by the hash function should be extended by the number of bits required for security. Now that we have two hash functions, I separated that calculation out to its own subroutine. Since H_0 embeds a value on the curve, the input to the embedding routine should be modulo the field prime.

Figure 18.4 shows the algorithm for converting an arbitrary message M into a point on the base curve. The conversion of $t \bmod p$ to value h requires t to have the number of bits in p plus the number of bits for security. If p is 256 bits for 128-bit security, the size of t should be at least 384 bits. This was mentioned in chapter 4 from Faz-Hernandez et al. (2021).

Unlike the curves in chapter 6, which did not have cofactors, embedding degree curves will always have them. We try to find a ρ value that is close to 1, so the cofactors are small. The last multiply by the cofactor ensures we have a point of order r for the output of the H_0 algorithm.

The H_1 routine uses the same hash function as H_0, except the input is different data and the output is an integer modulo the large prime factor of the curve. This is shown in figure 18.5. The difference between the number of bytes delivered by the `KangarooTwelve()` function will depend on ρ, the ratio of the field prime size to the large prime torsion factor r defining the pairing operation. In figure 18.4, the number of bytes in t depends on the size of p. In figure 18.5, the number of bytes in t depends on r. For good security, we need to pay attention to these details.

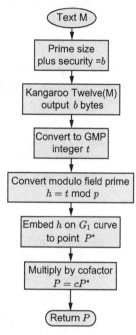

Figure 18.4   Hash $H_0(M)$ to base curve: converts a text message into a point on the curve using a hash function.

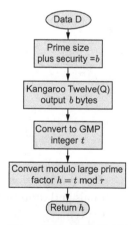

Figure 18.5   Hash $H_1(Q)$ to large prime factor in base curve: hashes the concatenation of public keys to a single value.

Exercise 18.1

A secure elliptic curve over a prime field $p = 273$ bits has a large prime factor $r = 259$ bits and embedding degree = 31. How many bits should the hash function calls return for H_0 and H_1 assuming 128-bit security?

18.2.2 Key aggregation algorithm for multi-signatures

This section describes the mathematics used to combine multiple signatures. Private keys are sized to be over r, and public keys are polynomial values on the extension curve. A point of order r is taken as the generator of all public keys and is designated g_2. To aggregate multiple keys, in equation 18.1 we let each user be designated by an index i, and label each person's private key as ψ_i and public key as P_i with the relationship:

$$P_i = \psi_i g_2 \tag{18.1}$$

The methods used to keep each person's private key secret on their systems can take on many implementations. I like using a hash of an input pass phrase, so the private key is never stored. But that has human problems of forgetfulness. For our purposes, we assume only one person has access to their private key.

Similarly, the public keys can be distributed in many ways. The assumption here is they are in a specific order, and everyone using key aggregation has access to everyone else's public keys in the same order. How that order is created does not matter, but keeping the order the same for all users does matter.

The key aggregation method creates a value a_j for each user j using their public key twice in a hash, as shown in figure 18.6.

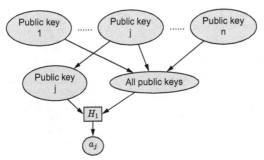

Figure 18.6   Schematic of key aggregation method

The computation involves taking all the public keys in order as x, y pairs of polynomials and then converting them to a long string of bytes. With n users, that can be written as

$$\{P_1, P_2, \cdots, P_n\}$$

In equation 18.2, the value of a_j is taken to be

$$a_j = H_1(P_j, \{P_1, P_2, \cdots, P_n\}) \tag{18.2}$$

In other words, user j's public key is put in front of everyone's public keys, including theirs, and the whole thing is hashed to a value modulo r. Since the public keys are on G_2, the input to H_1 could be a few kilobytes.

The idea here is to create a value that locks all the keys together in a way that identifies each individual user. This is why the order of all the keys matters. Everyone can create the array of a_j values for all the users in the public key list.

The aggregation of all the public keys is turned into a G_2 point using equation 18.3:

$$A = \sum_{i=1}^{n} a_i P_i \tag{18.3}$$

The purpose of locking everything up this way is to prevent tampering with the public keys. The attacker first has to solve the hash problem of substitution for a fake public key P_j^* to find a_j^*, which can then be used to create A^*. To be secure, both the hash size and extension field size must be large enough for this to be practically impossible.

> **Exercise 18.2**
>
> How many times does person i's public key show up in the ith term of A in equation 18.3?

18.2.3 *Digital multi-signature mathematics and verification algorithm*

This section shows how pairings are used to verify aggregated signatures. The multi-signature algorithm requires everyone to sign the same message. This implies a communications path because every private key is held in a separate location. Once everyone has signed the message, the signatures are then combined into a final value. The combined signatures are on G_1 as is the hash of the message. The keys are on G_2 and so is the g_2 generator. Boneh et al. (2018) show how pairings verify the signature but do not specify the pairing to use. Since all the public keys and signatures are required to be multiples of g_2, I chose to verify using Weil pairings.

To compute a signature, everyone uses the H_0 hash function with the message as input. The output is a point on G_1. In equation 18.4, the signature for each person i is then

$$s_i = a_i \psi_i H_0(m) \tag{18.4}$$

From equation 18.2, we see that this is actually combining H_1 and H_0 along with the private key. Since the large prime factor of the curve is r, we see that H_1 should be of this order. If it is larger or smaller, it leaves a hole that could be exploited by an attacker as described by the Internet Engineering Task Force argument in chapter 4.

The communication of all the signatures then goes to a combiner. This communication could be done in multiple ways. As shown in equation 18.5, whoever gets the job has to compute the point:

$$\sigma = \sum_{i=1}^{n} s_i \tag{18.5}$$

The aggregate signature is then the pair (σ, A). Of course, the list of public keys that go into A is really part of this signature as well.

Using a Weil pairing, the verification of the aggregate signature is done with equation 18.6:

$$e(\sigma, g_2) \stackrel{?}{=} e(H_0(m), A) \tag{18.6}$$

To see how this works, we plug equation 18.4 into equation 18.5 to get equation 18.7:

$$\sigma = \sum_{i=1}^{n} a_i \psi_i H_0(m) \tag{18.7}$$

Next plug equation 18.1 into 18.3 to get equation 18.8:

$$A = \sum_{i=1}^{n} a_i \psi_i g_2 \tag{18.8}$$

Finally, put equations 18.7 and 18.8 into 18.6 to get equation 18.9:

$$e\left(\sum_{i=1}^{n} a_i \psi_i H_0(m), g_2\right) \stackrel{?}{=} e\left(H_0(m), \sum_{i=1}^{n} a_i \psi_i g_2\right) \tag{18.9}$$

Notice that $H_0(m)$ is common to every term of the sum in the first pairing, and g_2 is common to every term of the sum in the second pairing. The sums are integers modulo p. Using the rules of pairing math described in chapter 15, we can rewrite equation 18.9 as equation 18.10:

$$e\left(H_0(m), g_2\right)^{\sum_{i=1}^{n} a_i \psi_i} \stackrel{?}{=} e\left(H_0(m), g_2\right)^{\sum_{i=1}^{n} a_i \psi_i} \tag{18.10}$$

which shows that both sides are, in fact, the same as long as all the public keys are hashed in the same order and all the messages are the same. If any one message is not the same, $H_0(m')$ will not factor out from the sum, and the two sides will not match.

> **Exercise 18.3**
>
> Define the variables g_2, ψ_i and m in equation 18.9.

18.3   *Multi-signatures code description*

This section explains the structure used to hold field extension information for multiple signature applications. A pairing-based system has three levels of parameters that relate to security. The lowest level is the field prime, which will be larger than the torsion value by the factor ρ. The base curve and extension curve will have coefficients determined by solving the low embedding degree formulas of chapter 14. These public parameters must be decided before any keys are generated.

All the parameters for the aggregate signature system are easily passed around the code using a single struct. The structure shown in the following listing has been defined for just this purpose.

Listing 18.1   Signature system structure

```
typedef struct
{
  mpz_t prime;        │ Field prime modulus
  CURVE E;
  mpz_t cardE;        │ G₁ base curve
  mpz_t tor;          │ and large torsion prime
  mpz_t cobse;
  POINT G1;           │ Base point for G₁
  POLY irrd;          │ Irreducible polynomial modulus
  mpz_t cardEx;       │ G₂ extension curve
  mpz_t coxtd;        │ parameters
  POLY_POINT G2;      │ Base point for G₂
  POLY_CURVE Ex;
} SIG_SYSTEM;
```

The G_1 and G_2 curves must have the same coefficients, or pairings will not work. The field prime defines the coefficients of the irreducible polynomial. One should have the value `cardE` equal to `tor * cobse`. The extension curve should have two factors of `tor`, so the expectation is that `cardEx` is equal to $\text{tor}^2 * \text{coxtd}$.

The base points `G1` and `G2` must be of order `tor`. As all this is public information and tied to the fundamentals of how everything works, a little time spent ensuring all the values have high security is worthwhile.

The code presented here to generate multi-signatures can not include the communications between users or nodes in a system. I will show the following:

- How to create public keys from a block of data
- The hash functions H_0 and H_1
- How to compute the a_i values and A point
- How to compute the individual signatures
- How to compute the aggregate signature

Everywhere a calculation on the curve happens, the structure in listing 18.1 will be an input.

18.3.1 Key generation code explained

In this section, code to generate private and public keys over field extension elliptic curves is described. Once a private key has been created, computing the public key is trivial. My favorite method of creating a private key is through the use of a hash of a pass phrase. However, in the following tests, I'm going to pull random numbers from a site called `rand.org` just to make life simple. Tests don't have to worry about security. For real security, ensure your users have a consistent way to create a private key that is physically difficult for an adversary to determine.

The key generation subroutine is shown in listing 18.2. The length of the data string `ptr` should be related to the size of the field prime or the large prime factor of the curve (`tor` in the `SIG_SYSTEM` structure). Once the data string is converted into an integer, the public key is generated by an elliptic curve multiplied over the field extension curve.

Listing 18.2   Key generation for pairing signatures

```
void keygen(mpz_t sk, POLY_POINT *PK, POLY_POINT G2, POLY_CURVE Ex,
            unsigned char *ptr, int len)
{
  mpz_import(sk, len, -1, 1, 0, 0, ptr);    Convert input bits
                                            to an integer.
  poly_elptic_mul(PK, G2, sk, Ex);          Create public key
}                                           from that integer.
```

18.3.2 *Hash functions code description*

In this section, I'll explain the two hash functions H_0 and H_1 used in the aggregate multi-signature algorithm. Both of them require smashing data down to a size, which will be taken modulo a large prime. As we saw in chapter 4, this means we should add a security level of bits to our hash output to ensure the final modulus has low probability of having a hole that could be exploited by an adversary.

Since H_0 is modulo the field prime and H_1 is modulo the torsion factor, this large prime is an input to a subroutine that computes the required number of bytes to recover from the variable length hash function. This is shown in the following listing.

Listing 18.3   Number bytes for secure hash

```
long secbyte(mpz_t p)
{
  int m, k, b;

  m = mpz_sizeinbase(p, 2);      Get number of
                                 bits in prime.
  if(m < 208)
    k = 80;                      Use only four
  else if(m < 320)               security sizes.
    k = 128;
  else if(m < 448)
    k = 192;
  else
    k = 256;
  b = m + k + 7;        Force odd result to
  b >>= 3;             round up byte number.
  return b;
}
```

The routine is simply checking whether the number of bits is within a set of limits to determine the number of extra bits to add. If any of the last three bits are set, adding 7 will round the number of bytes up by 1.

The H_1 hash function is shown in listing 18.4. In addition to the data to be hashed, the large prime factor for the base point is also an input. The output is an integer modulo this large prime factor.

Listing 18.4   Hash function H_1

```
void hash1(mpz_t hsh, unsigned char *dat, long len, mpz_t r)
{
  unsigned char *outp, *dst;
  mpz_t zero;
  long b;

  dst = (char*)malloc(24);
  sprintf(dst, "Hash_1 pring&sig");      Create domain separation tag.

  b = secbyte(r);                        Find security level;
                                         add to bit size of prime.
  outp = (unsigned char*)malloc(b + 2);  Compute secure size
  KangarooTwelve(dat, len, outp, b, dst, 16);   hash of input + dst.

  mpz_import(hsh, b, -1, 1, 0, 0, outp);  Convert hash bytes
                                          into an integer.
  mpz_init(zero);
  mod_add(hsh, hsh, zero, r);            Force to be mod r.
  mpz_clear(zero);
  free(outp);
  free(dst);
}
```

The domain separation tag is taken from the words *pairing* and *signature*. The extensible hash version of `KangarooTwelve()` gives the specified number of bytes computed from listing 18.3. The output of `KangarooTwelve()` is converted into an integer and then converted modulo the torsion factor r by adding zero. The stack is cleaned up, and the routine is finished.

The hash function H_0 returns a point on the base curve. This is shown in listing 18.5. In this routine, the domain separation tag is also based on the words *signature* and *pairing* but in a different order. Similar to the H_1 routine, the output of the hash is converted modulo the field prime by adding zero.

Listing 18.5   Hash function H_0

```
void hash0(POINT *H, SIG_SYSTEM sig, unsigned char *dat, long len)
{
  unsigned char *outp, *dst;
  mpz_t hsh, zero, prm;
  POINT mP;
  long b;

  dst = (char*)malloc(24);
  sprintf(dst, "signat H_0 parng");      Create domain separation tag.
```

```
    mget (prm) ;
    b = secbyte(prm);                        Find security level;
    outp = (unsigned char*)malloc(b+2);      add to bit size of prime.

                                             Compute secure size
    KangarooTwelve(dat, len, outp, b, dst, 16);   hash of input + dst.

    mpz_inits(hsh, zero, NULL);              Convert hash bytes
    mpz_import(hsh, b , -1, 1, 0, 0, outp);  into an integer.
    madd(hsh, hsh, zero);                    Force to be mod p.
    point_init(&mP);
    elptic_embed(H, &mP, hsh, sig.E);        Embed hashed value on curve
    elptic_mul(H, *H, sig.cobse, sig.E);     and force to torsion order.
    mpz_clears(hsh, zero, prm, NULL);
    point_clear(&mP);
    free(outp);
    free(dst);
}
```

To get the hashed result onto the curve, I then use the `elptic_embed()` routine. The order of this point most likely will be the largest possible on the curve. We can reduce this to an order we require by multiplying the embedded point by the cofactor of the curve.

The odds of the resulting point being the point at infinity is 1 over the torsion value r. For r on the order of 160 bits (80-bit security level), this is mind-numbingly microscopic. If you are building secure systems for nuclear weapons, you probably want to check H is not the point at infinity; otherwise, the odds are in your favor that it is of order r.

18.3.3 *Computing the public key hash* a_j

This section explains the code that computes the hashing parameter a_j. This is used in both signature algorithms described in this chapter. Equation 18.2 computes a hash value using function H_1 of all the public keys. I want to thank Dr. Drijvers for explaining how to do this. The fundamental part is converting the polynomial data into a string of bytes. The memory layout is shown in figure 18.7, with each public key having an x and y polynomial value. The storage of the polynomials includes a lot of null (or zero) elements. For consistent results from the hash, only the nonzero bytes are copied into the buffer for hashing. I have two subroutines for computing the a_j of equation 18.2. The first copies the polynomial point data into a string buffer, and the second computes all the a_j as a vector. A third routine, which is the sum over a_j, that computes equation 18.3 is then presented.

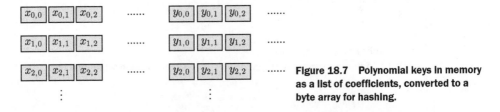

Figure 18.7   Polynomial keys in memory as a list of coefficients, converted to a byte array for hashing.

Listing 18.6 is the routine `point2text()` that converts a polynomial point value into bytes. The inputs include the degree of the polynomial, the number of bytes in each coefficient, and the point to be converted. The output is assumed to be a safe place to copy data into. The export routine is called with little endian order. Each coefficient is placed in memory based on the `msz` parameter. I learned the hard way that the `mpz_export()` routine is lazy in that it does not write leading zeros. To eliminate what seemed like a very strange bug, I just had to make sure all the bytes were clear before `mpz_export()` was called.

Listing 18.6   Polynomial point to bytes

```
void point2text(unsigned char *ptr, POLY_POINT P, long msz, long deg)
{
  long j;

  for(j=0; j<2*deg*msz; j++)        ← Ensure all bytes are zero.
    ptr[j] = 0;                       Convert x and y integer
  for(j=0; j<deg; j++)                values to byte data.
    mpz_export(&ptr[msz*j], NULL, -1, 1, 0, 0, P.x.coef[j]);
  for(j=0; j<deg; j++)
    mpz_export(&ptr[msz*(deg + j)], NULL, -1, 1, 0, 0, P.y.coef[j]);
}
```

The routine to compute each a_j of equation 18.2 is shown in listing 18.7. The input is the array of public keys and the number of them, along with the signature system parameters. Since each coefficient in the polynomials making up a point is taken modulo the field prime, this is the value used to determine the number of bytes to set aside in the text buffer. The total size of the text buffer is the size of each coefficient times the number of coefficients times two polynomials for each point times the number of public keys in the list. The number of public keys is all the keys plus 1 for each duplicate key shown in equation 18.2 as P_j.

Listing 18.7   Computing a_j

```
void aj_hash(mpz_t *ajhsh, SIG_SYSTEM sig, POLY_POINT *PK,
             long numkey)
{
  long i, j, k, m, bfsz;
  unsigned char *srcbfr;

  m = (mpz_sizeinbase(sig.prime, 16) + 1)/2;   | Round up number of bytes.
  bfsz = m*sig.irrd.deg*2*(numkey + 1);        | Degree*2*bytes*
  srcbfr = (unsigned char*)malloc(bfsz);       | number of keys
  for(i=0; i<numkey; i++)
    point2text(&srcbfr[m*(sig.irrd.deg*2*(i + 1))], PK[i], m, sig.irrd.deg);

  for(i=0; i<numkey; i++)          ↑ Each key into
  {                                 | the buffer sequentially
```

```
   mpz_init(ajhsh[i]);                           Repeat each key at
   point2text(srcbfr, PK[i], m, sig.irrd.deg);   start of buffer for
   hash1(ajhsh[i], srcbfr, bfsz, sig.tor);       a_j combination.
 }
 free(srcbfr);
}
```

Each public key is converted to text using the routine in listing 18.6 in the same order as the input array of public keys. Once these keys are placed in the text buffer, they remain constant for the a_j calculation. The first entry is changed in the for() loop to duplicate each public key once and then compute the hash of the buffer using the H_1 algorithm.

This is one of the few routines where I chose to initialize the GMP structure inside the routine. Part of the reason is that the a_j is persistent for many algorithms.

Equation 18.3 is a sum of every a_j times its public key P_j. This point is used throughout the aggregate and subgroup signature verification schemes. The following listing shows how the calculation can be accomplished.

Listing 18.8   All public keys summed

```
void aj_sum(POLY_POINT *APK, SIG_SYSTEM sig, POLY_POINT *PK,
            mpz_t *ajhsh, long nmkey)
{
  int i;
  POLY_POINT Tmp;

  APK->x.deg = 0;
  mpz_set_ui(APK->x.coef[0], 0);        Clear initial
  APK->y.deg = 0;                       point value
  mpz_set_ui(APK->y.coef[0], 0);        to zero.
  poly_point_init(&Tmp);
  for(i=0; i<nmkey; i++)
  {
    poly_elptic_mul(&Tmp, PK[i], ajhsh[i], sig.Ex);   Compute a_i P_i ...
    poly_elptic_sum(APK, *APK, Tmp, sig.Ex);          ... and sum with all others.
  }
  poly_point_clear(&Tmp);
}
```

The inputs are again the list of all public keys, the number of keys, the signature system parameters, and the vector of a_j values output from listing 18.7. After setting the result value to the point at infinity, the loop over all keys computes the point $a_j P_j$ and adds it to the result point. The variable name APK comes from its definition in Boneh et al. (2018). This is a public portion of every signature.

18.3.4 *Multi-signature and verification subroutines*

This section describes the first algorithm for multiple signatures and how to verify them. As shown in equation 18.4 ($s_i = a_i \psi_i H_0(m)$), each node signs a message using its private key. Every node then sends its individual signature to a combiner who computes equation 18.5 ($\sigma = \sum_{i=1}^{n} s_i$). The signature is verified using a hash of the message, the combined public keys, and aggregated sum of signatures. Routines to accomplish these tasks along with some helper routines for functionality are presented next.

To compute equation 18.4, I use listing 18.9. The inputs are the message and its length, the signer's private key and associated a_j value, and the signature system parameters. The output is the signature point. If any one person has a different message than that being signed by everyone else, the aggregate signature will fail to verify.

Listing 18.9   Individual signature algorithm

```
void sign(POINT *S, SIG_SYSTEM sig, mpz_t sk, mpz_t aj,
          unsigned char *msg, long msgln)
{
  mpz_t xpnt;
  POINT H0;

  point_init(&H0);
  hash0(&H0, sig, msg, msgln);    ← Convert message to point via hash.
  mpz_init(xpnt);
  mpz_mul(xpnt, aj, sk);          | Multiply point by
  elptic_mul(S, H0, xpnt, sig.E); | ψ_i a_j for signature.
  mpz_clear(xpnt);
  point_clear(&H0);
}
```

The assumption here is that each of these signatures is performed on a different node. Either a central server for everyone is a combiner, or some node is selected out of all the nodes to be the combiner for a message signature. Whoever accumulates all the signatures creates the aggregate signature using the following listing.

Listing 18.10   Aggregate signature routine

```
void agregat_sig(POINT *Sigma, SIG_SYSTEM sig, POINT *S, long nmsig)
{
  int i;

  point_copy(Sigma, S[0]);
  if(nmsig == 1) return;     | If only one message, we are done.
  for(i=1; i<nmsig; i++)                     | Add remaining
    elptic_sum(Sigma, *Sigma, S[i], sig.E);  | signatures to total.
}
```

Since each individual signature is a point on the base curve, the aggregate signature is the sum of all the points. The first point in the list is copied to the result, and then the remaining points (if there are any) are added in. Figure 18.8 gives an idea of how this would work in reality.

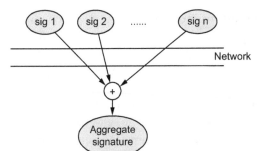

Figure 18.8   Individual nodes create a signature of the document, and then a single node sums all signatures into composite point.

To verify a message signature by multiple nodes, we use equation 18.6 ($e(\sigma, g_2) \overset{?}{=} e(H_0(m), A)$). The signature system parameter g_2 is public, as is the list of each node's public keys. It is up to the system designer to attach A, which is the "all public keys sum" $A = \sum_{i=1}^{n} a_i P_i$ (equation 18.3), to a signature or just list the nodes involved so A can be recomputed. The calculation of $H_0(m)$ should be done every time a verification is required to make sure message m did not change.

However the data is packaged, listing 18.11 shows how a signature is verified. The operation tog2() is a subroutine that is shown in listing 18.12. The weil() calculation requires all points to be polynomials. As we saw in chapter 15, G_1 points are on the G_2 curve. They are just constants with a degree of zero for the polynomial. The $H_0(m)$ point is also transferred to G_2.

Listing 18.11   Multi-signature verification

```
int multisig_verify(SIG_SYSTEM sig, POINT Sigma, POLY_POINT APK,
                    unsigned char *msg, long msgln)
{
  POLY_POINT S2, H20, R;
  POINT H0;
  POLY w1, w2;
  int eql;

  poly_point_init(&S2);         | Move input G₁
  tog2(&S2, Sigma);             | to polynomial G₂.

  point_init(&H0);                | Compute hash of
  hash0(&H0, sig, msg, msgln);    | message to a G₁ point.
  poly_point_init(&H20);
  poly_point_init(&R);
  tog2(&H20, H0);                 | Move point to G₂.
  poly_init(&w1);
  poly_init(&w2);
  poly_point_rand(&R, sig.Ex);     | Create arbitrary reference point.
  weil(&w1, S2, sig.G2, R, sig.tor, sig.Ex);  | Compute e(S, G₂).
  poly_printf("e(sigma, g2): ", w1);
  weil(&w2, H20, APK, R, sig.tor, sig.Ex);      | Compute e(hash, A).
  poly_printf("e(H0, apk): ", w2);
```

```
eql = poly_cmp(w1, w2);          | Return 1 If equal, 0 If different.
poly_clear(&w1);
poly_clear(&w2);
poly_point_clear(&H20);          | Clean
poly_point_clear(&S2);           | up
poly_point_clear(&R);            | stack.
point_clear(&H0);
return eql;
}
```

A random point is created for the reference. The odds of this point being related to any of the points being paired are astronomically small. For systems requiring extreme reliability, the choice of reference point as a fixed value might be worth some effort.

The signature is paired with the G_2 base point, and the message hash point is paired with the sum of all public keys. If the Weil pairings match, the routine will return 1.

The tog2() routine in listing 18.12 assumes the destination is already initialized. The polynomial degree is zero, and the (x, y) values are moved to the constant coefficient. The point does not change; only the representation of it does.

Listing 18.12   Change point from G_1 to G_2

```
void tog2(POLY_POINT *G2, POINT G1)
{
  G2->x.deg = 0;                      | Constant coefficient
  mpz_set(G2->x.coef[0], G1.x);
  G2->y.deg = 0;
  mpz_set(G2->y.coef[0], G1.y);      | Value turns Into polynomial
}
```

18.4 *Accountable subgroup multi-signatures*

This section describes a second algorithm for multiple signatures. The term *subgroup* in "accountable subgroup multi-signatures" means only a few of the n possible people agree to sign a message. Using Fraktur font for P, let the entire list of public keys be as shown in equation 18.11:

$$\mathfrak{P} = \{P_1, P_2, \cdots, P_n\} \tag{18.11}$$

In equation 18.12, we write a subset of all the keys using the subset or equal symbol

$$S \subseteq \mathfrak{P} \tag{18.12}$$

which reads "S is a subset of or equal to the set P."

The subgroup algorithm uses three hash functions: H_0, H_1, and H_2. The first two are identical to the H_0 and H_1 previously described. The third one is identical to H_0 in that it outputs a point on G_1, but it has different inputs. In the real world, we can separate H_0 from H_2 using the domain separation tag (dst) and leave the rest of the code identical.

The primary addition to the subgroup algorithm from the aggregation algorithm is the matrix of membership keys. The matrix is defined in equation 18.13 as

$$\mu = \begin{matrix} a_1\psi_1 H_2(A, 1) & a_2\psi_2 H_2(A, 1) & \cdots & a_n\psi_n H_2(A, 1) \\ a_1\psi_1 H_2(A, 2) & a_2\psi_2 H_2(A, 2) & \cdots & a_n\psi_n H_2(A, 2) \\ \vdots & \vdots & \ddots & \vdots \\ a_1\psi_1 H_2(A, n) & a_2\psi_2 H_2(A, n) & \cdots & a_n\psi_n H_2(A, n) \end{matrix} \tag{18.13}$$

The value of A comes from equation 18.3, which in turn comes from equation 18.2, which itself is based on $\mathfrak{P}$. This is shown in figure 18.9 to help visualize how the math is connected.

$$\boxed{P_i \,(18.1)} \longrightarrow \boxed{a_j \,(18.2)} \longrightarrow \boxed{A \,(18.3)}$$ **Figure 18.9 Equations creating value A**

Mathematically, everyone uses their private key to compute a column of the matrix, as shown in equation 18.14:

$$\mu_{i,j} = a_j\psi_j H_2(A, i) \text{ for all } i \neq j. \tag{18.14}$$

and sends this to all other nodes. The only term not transmitted is the $\mu_{i,i}$ matrix element on the diagonal. It would be silly to transmit it to yourself anyway.

Once the matrix is distributed, everyone sums across a row, which includes their own $\mu_{i,i}$ element to get their membership key defined by equation 18.15:

$$M_i = \sum_{j=1}^{n} \mu_{i,j} \tag{18.15}$$

Now that the setup is complete, a subset S of nodes can sign a message m using equation 18.16:

$$s_i = M_i + \psi_i H_0(A, m) \tag{18.16}$$

These signatures are sent to a combiner. In equation 18.17, the combining node computes two sums of points:

$$P_S = \sum_{j \in S} P_j \qquad \sigma_S = \sum_{j \in S} s_j \tag{18.17}$$

These two components are the signature. The list of nodes that signed (S) are an obviously important component as well.

The verification of the subset signature is computed using equation 18.18:

$$e(H_0(A, m), P_S) \cdot e\left(\sum_{j \in S} H_2(A, j), A\right) \stackrel{?}{=} e(\sigma_S, g_2) \tag{18.18}$$

All the values on the left side are public. It is assumed the signers that make up the list S are known, so the public key sum in the second paring on the left side can be computed by anyone. Any change in either the message or the public keys will invalidate the pairings, and the signature will not verify.

So let's expand equation 18.18 to see how this works. Let's start with the right side by putting equation 18.17 in for σ_S in equation 18.19:

$$e(\sigma_S, g_2) = e\left(\sum_{j \in S} s_j, g_2\right) \tag{18.19}$$

We now put equation 18.16 in for s_j in equation 18.20:

$$e(\sigma_S, g_2) = e\left(\sum_{j \in S} \left(M_j + \psi_j H_0(A, m)\right), g_2\right) \tag{18.20}$$

We can rewrite this as the addition of two sums as in equation 18.21:

$$e(\sigma_S, g_2) = e\left(\sum_{j \in S} M_j + \sum_{j \in S} \psi_j H_0(A, m), g_2\right) \tag{18.21}$$

From the rules of pairings, we know that the pairing of a sum of points is the multiplication of the pairings of those points (see chapter 15). We can now convert equation 18.21 into equation 18.22:

$$e(\sigma_S, g_2) = e\left(\sum_{j \in S} M_j, g_2\right) \cdot e\left(\sum_{j \in S} \psi_j H_0(A, m), g_2\right) \tag{18.22}$$

Equation 18.18 has two pairings on the left. Equation 18.22 also has two pairings. Let's start with the second pairing on the right side of equation 18.22. The factor $H_0(A, m)$ is common to every term in the sum, so we can factor it out. This gives equation 18.23:

$$e\left(\sum_{j \in S} \psi_j H_0(A, m), g_2\right) = e\left(H_0(A, m), g_2\right)^{\sum_{j \in S} \psi_j} \tag{18.23}$$

Putting equation $P_S = \sum_{j \in S} P_j$ from equation 18.17 into the left term of equation 18.18 gives equation 18.24:

$$e(H_0(A, m), P_S) = e(H_0(A, m), \sum_{j \in S} P_j) \tag{18.24}$$

which in turn expands to equation 18.25:

$$e(H_0(A, m), P_S) = e(H_0(A, m), \sum_{j \in S} \psi_j g_2) \tag{18.25}$$

Since g_2 is common to all the terms in the sum of the second point on the right side, we see that this term does, in fact, match equation 18.23.

As shown in equation 18.26, the same process will show that the expansion of M_j in equation 18.22 using equations 18.13 and 18.15 will give the other term on the left in equation 18.18:

$$e\left(\sum_{j \in S} H_2(A, j), A\right) = e\left(\sum_{j \in S} M_j, g_2\right) \qquad (18.26)$$

The expansion of A with the sum of $\psi_i a_i$ and the expansion of M_j with the same terms that cause $H_2(A, j)$ to factor out give the desired equality.

Expanding the system of nodes by adding a new public key to the list in equation 18.11 requires adding a new column and row to the matrix in equation 18.13. This would break all previous signatures if old membership keys are not kept. This system of subgroup signatures is realistically practical as long as the list of public keys of all the nodes and historical membership keys are kept track of.

Exercise 18.4

Expand equation 18.26 using equations 18.3, 18.15, and 18.14 to show both sides are equal.

18.5 *Description of the subgroup multi-signatures code*

This section describes the routines that can compute the subgroup multi-signature algorithm. To implement the subgroup multi-signature algorithm, we use the sum of all keys (A) from listing 18.8 to create the hash values of the membership matrix μ (equation 18.13). Each node uses its private key (ψ_i) and public values of (a_j) (the output of listing 18.7) to create a column of the μ matrix. Each element is then sent to all other nodes.

From a practical standpoint, N nodes will generate $(N-1)^2$ data transfers for this part of the setup. If N is greater than 10, it might make sense to create a central server that collects the matrix and then sends the row data to each node once everyone has transmitted their column. While each transmission is larger, there are only $2N$ transmissions total—something to think about when actually implementing this system.

An additional requirement for the subgroup signature is the list of nodes that make up the subgroup. The ordering of the subgroup is not important. The ordering of the full set of all keys is important because the sum of all keys includes the hash of all the public keys in a specific order.

The routines to compute an individual signature and their combination to create subgroup aggregate signatures are given in this section. The idea of a central server to act as both setup and combiner may be something else to think about for practical implementation.

Listing 18.13 creates a column in the μ matrix. The inputs are the sum of all keys A, the signature system parameters, the node's a_j, and private key (sk) along with the number of keys. The full column is computed because the diagonal element will be needed when the membership key is computed.

Listing 18.13 Calculation of μ column vector

```
void mu_column(POINT *muvec, POLY_POINT APK, SIG_SYSTEM sig,
               mpz_t aj, mpz_t sk, long nmkey)
{
  long i, j, bfsz, m;
  mpz_t apsi;
  unsigned char *hshbfr;

  mpz_init(apsi);
  mod_mul(apsi, sk, aj, sig.tor);        Compute a_jψ_j.
  m = (mpz_sizeinbase(sig.prime, 16) + 1)/2;   Round up number of bytes.
  bfsz = m*sig.irrd.deg*2 + sizeof(long);    Space for long
  hshbfr = (unsigned char*)malloc(bfsz + 8);  plus 2 polynomials
  point2text(hshbfr, APK, m, sig.irrd.deg);   Put A into buffer as string.
  for(i=0; i<nmkey; i++)
  {
    *(long*)(&hshbfr[m*sig.irrd.deg*2]) = i;   Put key number into buffer.
    hash2(&muvec[i], sig, hshbfr, bfsz);     Hash down to point
    elptic_mul(&muvec[i], muvec[i], apsi, sig.E);  and multiply by a_jψ_j.
  }
  free(hshbfr);
  mpz_clear(apsi);
}
```

The product of private key ψ_j and public key hash a_j is computed modulo the torsion value from system parameters. The sum of all keys A is placed in a hash buffer that has room for an index. The loop then performs the hash $H_2(A, i)$ and places each point in the result vector. Each result is multiplied by the $a_j\psi_j$ value in place.

Once the column is computed, it is up to each node to send the results to every other node or a central node, depending on implementation. After all nodes collect their own row of data, they can then compute their membership key using equation 18.15 ($M_i = \sum_{j=1}^{n} \mu_{i,j}$). This routine is shown in the following listing.

Listing 18.14 Membership key calculation

```
void membership_key(POINT *Memkey, POINT *Murow, long numkey, CURVE E)
{
  long j;
  POINT Tmp;
                       Initialize automatically
  point_init(&Tmp);    point at infinity.
  for(j=0; j<numkey; j++)
    elptic_sum(&Tmp, Tmp, Murow[j], E);   Sum all points in vector.
  point_copy(Memkey, Tmp);   Copy result to specified location.
```

```
  point_clear(&Tmp);
}
```

From equation 18.16 ($s_i = M_i + \psi_i H_0(A, m)$), we see that a signature uses both the private key and the membership key along with a hash of the sum of all keys and the message. In addition, the signature system parameters are also an input, as shown in the following listing. The individual node's signature point is the output.

Listing 18.15 **Subgroup signature individual node**

```
void subgrp_sign(POINT *S, POLY_POINT APK, SIG_SYSTEM sig,
                 POINT Mk, mpz_t sk, unsigned char *msg, long msgln)
{
  long j, m, bfsz;
  unsigned char *apkmsg;
  POINT H0;

  m = (mpz_sizeinbase(sig.prime, 16) + 1)/2;     | Round up number of bytes.
  bfsz = m*sig.irrd.deg*2 + msgln;               | Degree*2*bytes
  apkmsg = (unsigned char*)malloc(bfsz + 8);     |+ message length
  point2text(apkmsg, APK, m, sig.irrd.deg);      | Convert A to string.
  for(j=0; j<msgln; j++)
    apkmsg[m*2*sig.irrd.deg + j] = msg[j];       | Put message in buffer with A.
  point_init(&H0);
  hash0(&H0, sig, apkmsg, bfsz);                  | Hash to a point on G_1.
  elptic_mul(S, H0, sk, sig.E);                   | Multiply by ψ_i.
  elptic_sum(S, *S, Mk, sig.E);                   | Add in membership key M_i.
  point_clear(&H0);
  free(apkmsg);
}
```

After all the members of the subgroup sign the message, one of them—or, again, a central server—combines all the signatures into a single point as in equation 18.17 ($\sigma_S = \sum_{j \in S} s_j$). In addition, they create the sum of all the public keys of the members who signed the message. In both sums, we require a list of nodes who signed the message. Since the sum of all keys A requires a specific order, the input list will be taken as an array of integers containing the index of public keys from the ordered list of all public keys.

Listing 18.16 shows the subroutine that performs the aggregation of the public keys and signatures for the subgroup of nodes that signed the message. The `list[]` array is used as an index into the public keys. Note that the order of the signatures does not need to be the same as the order of public keys in the list because the output is just the sum of all of them. Note also that the public key sum is on the field extension curve, and signature aggregation is on the base curve.

Listing 18.16   Subgroup signature aggregation routine

```
void subgrp_combine(POLY_POINT *PK, POINT *Ssum, SIG_SYSTEM sig,
POINT *Svec, POLY_POINT *Pubky, long *list, long nmlst)
{
  long i, j;

  mpz_set_ui(Ssum->x, 0);          | Ensure output value
  mpz_set_ui(Ssum->y, 0);          | starts with point at infinity.
  PK->x.deg = 0;
  mpz_set_ui(PK->x.coef[0], 0);    | Same with G2 point
  PK->y.deg = 0;
  mpz_set_ui(PK->y.coef[0], 0);
  for(i=0; i<nmlst; i++)
  {                                | Get the public key index
    j = list[i];              <——  | for this signature.
    elptic_sum(Ssum, *Ssum, Svec[i], sig.E);    | Add a digital signature to G1 point.
    poly_elptic_sum(PK, *PK, Pubky[j], sig.Ex); | Add a public key for this signature.
  }
}
```

When the time comes to verify a subgroup signature, we see from equation 18.18 $(e(H_0(A, m), P_S) \cdot e\left(\sum_{j \in S} H_2(A, j), A\right) \stackrel{?}{=} e(\sigma_S, g_2))$ that we require two hash values using the sum of all keys with the message or each index from the list of nodes as well as three pairing calculations. Listing 18.17 takes the signature system parameters, the sum of all keys, the message, the list of nodes that signed the message, the aggregate sum of keys, and the sum of signatures that constitute the signature as inputs. It returns 1 if the signature verifies, and 0 if it does not.

The first term I deal with is the hash of the message with the sum of all public keys. The Weil pairing of this hash with the sum of nodes' public keys participating in the signature is then computed. This Weil pairing is saved in variable w1.

Listing 18.17   Subgroup signature verification code

```
int subgrp_verify(SIG_SYSTEM sig, POLY_POINT APK, unsigned char *msg,
      long msgln, long *list, long nmlst, POLY_POINT PK, POINT Ssum)
{
  POLY w1, w2, w3, ck;
  POINT *H2, Hsum, H0;
  POLY_POINT H02, R;
  long i, j, bfsz, m;
  unsigned char *bufr;
  int eql;

  m = (mpz_sizeinbase(sig.prime, 16) + 1)/2;   | Round up number of bytes.
  bfsz = m*sig.irrd.deg*2 + msgln;             | Degree*2*bytes
  bufr = (unsigned char*)malloc(bfsz + sizeof(long)); | + message length
  point2text(bufr, APK, m, sig.irrd.deg);      | Convert A to a string.
  for(j=0; j<msgln; j++)
```

```
    bufr[m*2*sig.irrd.deg + j] = msg[j];
```
| Put message in buffer with A.

```
point_init(&H0);
hash0(&H0, sig, bufr, bfsz);
```
| Hash to a point on G_1.
```
poly_point_init(&H02);
tog2(&H02, H0);
```
| Move to polynomial on G_2.
```
poly_point_init(&R);
poly_point_rand(&R, sig.Ex);
```
| Create random point for reference.
```
poly_init(&w1);
weil(&w1, H02, PK, R, sig.tor, sig.Ex);
```
| Compute $e(\text{hash}, P_S)$.
```
poly_printf("e(H0(A, m), PK)= ", w1);

H2 = (POINT*)malloc(sizeof(POINT)*nmlst);
```
Allocate space for
number of points in list.
```
bfsz = m*sig.irrd.deg*2 + sizeof(long);
```
| Reset size to
| 2 polynomials + 1 long.
```
for(i=0; i<nmlst; i++)
{
  j = list[i];
```
| A is already in buffer.
```
  point_init(&H2[i]);
  *(long*)(&bufr[m*2*sig.irrd.deg]) = j;
```
| Put in key index number . . .
```
  hash2(&H2[i], sig, bufr, bfsz);
}
```
| . . . and hash to G_1 point.

```
point_init(&Hsum);
```
| Start with point at infinity.
```
for(i=0; i<nmlst; i++)
  elptic_sum(&Hsum, Hsum, H2[i], sig.E);
```
| Sum all hashed points.

```
tog2(&H02, Hsum);
```
| Move from G_1 to polynomial G_2.
```
poly_init(&w2);
weil(&w2, H02, APK, R, sig.tor, sig.Ex);
```
| Compute $e(\sum\text{hash points}, A)$.
```
poly_printf("e(H2(APK, j), APK) = ", w2);

tog2(&H02, Ssum);
```
| Move signatures from G_1 to G_2.
```
poly_init(&w3);
weil(&w3, H02, sig.G2, R, sig.tor, sig.Ex);
```
| Compute $e(\sigma_S, g_2)$.

```
poly_printf("e(s, g_2): ", w3);
poly_init(&ck);
poly_mul(&ck, w1, w2);
```
| Multiply first two pairings.
```
eql = poly_cmp(ck, w3);
```
| Return comparison
| with 3rd pairing.
```
poly_clear(&w1);
poly_clear(&w2);
poly_clear(&w3);
poly_clear(&ck);
for(i=0; i<nmlst; i++)
  point_clear(&H2[i]);
```
| Clean up stack.
```
point_clear(&Hsum);
point_clear(&H0);
free(bufr);
poly_point_clear(&H02);
poly_point_clear(&R);
return eql;
}
```

The next term is the hash of all public keys along with the index values of the nodes participating in the signature. This is going to be an important detail at the system level, with each index belonging to the correct public key. As long as you are consistent, the math will work.

Once the hash of each member node is computed, the sum of all those hashes is created as the G_1 input to a Weil pairing. The G_2 input is the sum of all keys. This Weil pairing is saved as variable w2.

The last Weil pairing is computed using the aggregate sum of signatures with the G_2 base point for the signature system parameters. The polynomial value of $w_1 \cdot w_2$ is then compared to w_3. This is the returned result after the stack is cleaned up.

18.6 Aggregate BLS signatures example program

This section describes a simulated multiple-signatures program that tests both algorithms explained in this chapter. Testing the subroutines presented in this chapter requires many public and private keys, which would normally be distributed around the internet. Rather than attempt a system-level approach, my goal is to ensure the mathematics has been correctly formulated in software. To accomplish that, I want to create a file of private and public keys that can be used in multiple tests.

Preliminary to creating the keys, we need to choose the curves and field extension the keys work over. That data will also be written to a file for use with multiple test programs. In this section, I'll first discuss the choice of curve test parameters, utility routines to read and write binary point data, and a program to save generated test parameters to files. After that, a test program to read in those files and execute the subroutines from this chapter will be presented.

18.6.1 Initial test parameters

This section explains the choice of test parameters used to run the simulation program. To test the subroutines in this chapter and chapter 19, I chose the fundamental system parameters using the `pairing_sweep_alpha` program from chapter 14 with embedding degree 11 and 220 bits for the large prime torsion factor r. These parameters are used to create base points in both G_1 and G_2.

Listing 18.18 shows the output from the `pairing_sweep_alpha` program I used for the signature system parameters. These numbers were then fed into the `get_curve` program from chapter 14 to find the coefficients for the curve. The value of alpha in listing 18.18 factors to alpha = $156643 = 31^2 \times 163$, so the alpha input to `get_curve` is 163 (or −163 for perfectionists). The following listing shows the curve coefficients as well.

> **Listing 18.18 Embedding degree 11 curve data**

```
k= 11 alpha = 156643   x = 5
r = 848222711223348251273816343240321778327803280959919975351835864551
numbits: 220
```

```
q = 3252011917820513804209601668228184687614933135935522716335534348924920411135269  numbits: 261
rho = 1.186364
t = 36066666535150504729620771010373535156260

a4 = 21763362284570451751871760036927205986040444146723611751167933456546798
44960925

a6 = 18709802207603359833355804345129603526578715673761331415778323312674575
76039896
```

Listing 18.19 shows the utility routines to read and write points for both G_1 and G_2 curves as well as polynomials. The data is written and read in binary format. For all routines, the input includes a standard FILE pointer.

Listing 18.19   Point file input/output routines

```
void point_write(POINT *P, FILE *f)
{
  mpz_out_raw(f, P->x);       Write x, y value to a file.
  mpz_out_raw(f, P->y);
}

void point_read(POINT *P, FILE *f)
{
  mpz_inp_raw(P->x, f);
  mpz_inp_raw(P->y, f);         Read x, y value from a file.
}

void poly_write(POLY *p, FILE *f)
{
  int i, k;              Only save degree and
                         number coefficients.
  k = p->deg;       ←
  fwrite(&k, sizeof(long), 1, f);
  for(i=0; i<=k; i++)
    mpz_out_raw(f, p->coef[i]);
}

void poly_read(POLY *p, FILE *f)
{
  int i, k;

  fread(&k, sizeof(long), 1, f);    Recover degree . . .
  p->deg = k;                       . . . and read in that many
  for(i=0; i<=k; i++)               coefficients.
    mpz_inp_raw(p->coef[i], f);
}

void poly_point_write(POLY_POINT *P, FILE *f)
{
  poly_write(&P->x, f);       Write x, y polynomials to a file.
  poly_write(&P->y, f);
}
```

```
void poly_point_read(POLY_POINT *P, FILE *f)
{
  poly_read(&P->x, f);          Read in x, y polynomials
  poly_read(&P->y, f);          from a file.
}
```

18.6.2 Multi-signatures simulated key generation test program

This section describes a program used to create files for use in testing the multiple-signatures algorithms. The values from listing 18.18 were copied into the program `signatures_11_keygen.c`. The program variables, along with the initialization of the parameters, are shown in listing 18.20. The value of t from output 18.18 is used to compute the cardinality of the base curve and field extension curve. The cofactors are computed by dividing out the torsion value r, which is the large prime factor for system security.

We know from chapter 15 that the extension curve cardinality is of the form $d_1 \times d_2$ where d_1 is a factor of d_2. From all the examples I have seen, the base curve cardinality is d_1. I don't know how to prove that, so I just divide out the factor r twice from the extension curve and call the remaining value the cofactor. There may be common factors in d_1 included that are not required. This does not hurt when embedding random points on the field extension curve; it just wastes time.

Listing 18.20   Multi-signatures test program setup

```
#include "signature.h"
#include <string.h>

#define EMBED_DEGREE 11              Embedding degree set here.

int main(int argc, char *argv[])
{
  FILE *rnd, *key;
  POLY_CURVE Ex;
  CURVE E;
  POLY_POINT G2, Tst2, PK;
  POINT G1, Tst1;
  POLY irrd;
  mpz_t prm, t, cardE, cardEx, tor;
  mpz_t cobse, coxtd, sk;
  int i, j, k;
  unsigned char *rndat;                 Value q is base prime.

  mpz_init_set_str(prm,
    "3252011917820513804209601668228184687614933135935522716335534348924920
    411135269", 10);
  minit(prm);
  curve_init(&E);                       Curve coefficients a4 and a6
  mpz_set_str(E.a4,
    "217633622845704517518717600369272059860404441467236117511679334565467 9
```

```
⮕ 844960925 ", 10);
  mpz_set_str(E.a6,
⮕ "1870980220760335983335580434512960352657871567376133141577832331267457
⮕ 576039896 ", 10);

  poly_init(&irrd);
  if(poly_irreducible(&irrd, EMBED_DEGREE))
    poly_printf("Found irreducible polynomial:\n", irrd);
  else
    printf("no irreducible polynomial found...\n");
  poly_irrd_set(irrd);                    Find irreducible polynomial
  poly_mulprep(irrd);                     and set up multiplication table.
  poly_curve_init(&Ex);
  mpz_set(Ex.a4.coef[0], E.a4);           Copy base curve to
  mpz_set(Ex.a6.coef[0], E.a6);           field extension curve.
  mpz_init_set_str(tor,
⮕ "848222711223348251273816343240321778327803280959919975351835864551 ", 10);
```

Set torsion value r.

```
  mpz_init_set_str(t, "3606666653515050472962077101037353515626 ", 10);
  mpz_inits(cardE, cardEx, cobse, coxtd, NULL);
  mpz_add_ui(cardE, prm, 1);         |$p+1$
  mpz_sub(cardE, cardE, t);          |$-t$
  gmp_printf("base has %Zd points\n", cardE);

  mpz_div(cobse, cardE, tor);        |Cofactor = $\#E/r$
```

Compute base curve. $\#E = p + 1 - t$

```
  cardinality(cardEx, t, EMBED_DEGREE);   |Compute #E on extension curve.
  gmp_printf("extension has %Zd points\n", cardEx);
  mpz_div(coxtd, cardEx, tor);       |Remove $r^2$ for
  mpz_div(coxtd, coxtd, tor);        |extension cofactor.
```

The random base points are created as shown in listing 18.21. The listing also shows how the system parameters are then written to disk as binary data.

Listing 18.21   Multi-signatures test system parameters file creation

```
  point_init(&G1);
  point_rand(&G1, E);                  |Pick random point times
  elptic_mul(&G1, G1, cobse, E);       |cofactor to ensure torsion order.
  point_printf("G1 generator: ", G1);

  poly_point_init(&G2);
  poly_point_rand(&G2, Ex);
  poly_elptic_mul(&G2, G2, coxtd, Ex);   |Same thing for extension curve
  poly_point_printf("G2 generator:\n", G2);
```

Save system parameters to disk.

```
  key = fopen("curve_11_parameters.bin ", "w");
  mpz_out_raw(key, prm);
  mpz_out_raw(key, E.a4);
  mpz_out_raw(key, E.a6);
```

```
mpz_out_raw(key, cardE);          Binary output function
mpz_out_raw(key, tor);            saves base prime,
mpz_out_raw(key, cobse);          G₁ curve, and torsion r
point_write(G1, key);             along with fixed base point.
poly_write(&irrd, key);           Save irreducible polynomial.
mpz_out_raw(key, cardEx);         Extension curve cardinality
mpz_out_raw(key, coxtd);          and cofactor
poly_point_write(&G2, key);    ← Output extension curve base point.
fclose(key);
```

In addition, the first program uses random data collected from https://www.random.org/ to create 20 private and public keys. These are written to a separate file for testing the aggregate signature routine. The second program imports the key data and signature system parameters along with random data as a message to test the multi-signature and subgroup signature subroutines.

To generate a set of simulated nodes with private and public keys, I downloaded random bytes from random.org to create private keys. The file was text byte data read in, as shown in listing 18.22. There are many ways to do this simulation; choosing randomness off the internet is a fun way. The data are all bytes in the range 0 to 255. The gcc compiler stopped complaining when I used hhd as the input type. This means "half, half, signed," which equals a signed byte. I could have also used %hhu for a "half, half, unsigned" byte.

Listing 18.22   Multi-signatures random data input

```
rnd = fopen("random.data", "r");
if(!rnd)
{
  printf("can't find file random.data\n");    Open data file
  exit(-1);                                    or bail out if not there.
}
rndat = (unsigned char*)malloc(2048);
i = 0;
while(!feof(rnd))
{
  fscanf(rnd, "%hhd", &rndat[i]);              Convert text to binary
  i++;                                         and stuff it into buffer.
}
fclose(rnd);
```

The random data was used to create private keys using the keygen() subroutine from listing 18.2. Each private and public key was then written to disk in binary format as shown in listing 18.23. The filename references the embedding degree (11) and extension skpk comes from "secret key public key."

Listing 18.23   Multi-signatures simulated keys for multiple nodes

```
key = fopen("key_data_11.skpk", "w");          Create file with special name.
poly_point_init(&PK);
mpz_init(sk);
k = 20;                                          Large enough example
fwrite(&k, sizeof(int), 1, key);                 to prove things work
for(i=0; i<k; i++)
{                                                Use a different random number
  keygen(sk, &PK, G2, Ex, &rndat[i*32], 32);     for each key pair.
  mpz_out_raw(key, sk);                           Save private key as single value.
  poly_point_write(&PK, key);                    Save public key
}                                                as polynomial point.
fclose(key);
```

18.6.3 *Multi-signatures signing and verifying simulation*

This section explains the test program that uses both multiple-signature algorithm subroutines to simulate how the routines are used. With the signature system parameters in one file and the public keys in a second file, I am ready to test all the subroutines presented in this chapter. The signature system parameters are critical to the operation of any pairing system. They will also be used in chapter 19 code testing as well. It made sense to create a subroutine to read in the binary file written out in listing 18.21 to simplify all these tests. The code to read in system parameters is shown in the following listing.

Listing 18.24   Signature system parameter file input routine

```
void get_system(char *filename, SIG_SYSTEM *sig)
{
  FILE *sys;
  int i;

  sys = fopen(filename, "r");
  if(!sys)                                       If file not found,
  {                                              exit program because
    printf("can't find file %s\n", filename);    we are hosed.
    exit(-1);
  }
  mpz_inits(sig->prime, sig->cardE, sig->tor, sig->cobse, sig->cardEx,
            sig->coxtd, NULL);
  poly_init(&sig->irrd);                         Initialize SIG_SYSTEM
  curve_init(&sig->E);                           struct space.
  point_init(&sig->G1);
  poly_point_init(&sig->G2);
  poly_curve_init(&sig->Ex);
```

```
mpz_inp_raw(sig->prime, sys);      Input field prime.
mpz_inp_raw(sig->E.a4, sys);
mpz_inp_raw(sig->E.a6, sys);       G₁ curve coefficients
mpz_inp_raw(sig->cardE, sys);      Base curve cardinality
mpz_inp_raw(sig->tor, sys);        torsion and
mpz_inp_raw(sig->cobse, sys);      cofactor
point_read(&sig->G1, sys);         G₁ curve base point
poly_read(&sig->irrd, sys);        Input irreducible polynomial.
mpz_inp_raw(sig->cardEx, sys);     Read in extension curve
mpz_inp_raw(sig->coxtd, sys);      cardinality and cofactor.
poly_point_read(&sig->G2, sys);  ← Input extension curve base point.
mpz_set(sig->Ex.a4.coef[0], sig->E.a4);   Create polynomial versions
mpz_set(sig->Ex.a6.coef[0], sig->E.a6);   of G₂ curve parameters.
}
```

The label on the left of the first block reads: **Read in binary data in same order as written out.**

The main program includes all the structures and linking information with a `#include` header and then lists all the variables, as shown in listing 18.25. After setting up the system parameters structure, the mathematics system is set up using the system parameters with `minit()` for the field prime, `poly_irrd_set()` for the field extension, and `poly_mulprep()` to fill in the polynomial multiplication lookup table.

Listing 18.25   Multi-signature test program variables

```
#include "signature.h"
#include <string.h>

#define EMBED_DEGREE 11

int main(int argc, char *argv[])
{
    FILE *key;
    int i, j, k, m;
    SIG_SYSTEM sig;
    POLY_POINT PK[32], APK;
    mpz_t   sk[32], aj[32];
    unsigned short *msg;
    POINT S[32], Sigma;
    long list[32], nmlst;
    POINT *Sgrp, Ssum;
    POINT *Muvec, *Mumatrix, *Memkey;
    POLY_POINT Pgrpsum;
```

Read in system parameters from previously generated file.

```
    get_system("curve_11_parameters.bin", &sig);
    minit(sig.prime);                   Initialize field prime and
    poly_irrd_set(sig.irrd);            irreducible polynomial with
    poly_mulprep(sig.irrd);             multiplication table.
```

Read in public and private keys for testing signature aggregation.

```
key = fopen("key_data_11.skpk", "r");
if(!key)
{                                               Look for example key file;
  printf("can't find file key_data_11.skpk\n");  exit if not found.
  exit(-2);
}
fread(&k, sizeof(int), 1, key);           Ensure no stupid error
if(k > 32)                                 of not enough storage.
{
  printf("need more space for testing: %d\n", k);
  exit(-3);
}
for(i=0; i<k; i++)
{
  poly_point_init(&PK[i]);                For each key,
  mpz_init(sk[i]);                        read in private key
  mpz_inp_raw(sk[i], key);               and then public key.
  poly_point_read(&PK[i], key);
}
fclose(key);
aj_hash(aj, sig, PK, k);            Compute array $a_j = H(P_j, \{P_1, ..., P_k\})$.
poly_point_init(&APK);
aj_sum(&APK, sig, PK, aj, k);       Compute $A = \sum a_j \times PK_j$.
```

The list of private and public keys is then read into fixed-size arrays. Even though I know the number of keys is less than the array size, I still check for errors. Never hurts to be careful!

The hash of each public key via equation 18.2 ($a_j = H_1(P_j, \{P_1, P_2, \cdots, P_n\})$) and listing 18.7 creates the array aj[]. With this array, the formula for A in equation 18.3 ($A = \sum_{i=1}^{n} a_i P_i$) is computed using the aj_sum() routine from listing 18.8. The message to sign was created using random.org data using short integers. This text was read in and converted to random bytes, as shown in listing 18.26. Some of my random data collections are 8 bits, some are 16 bits, and some are 32 bits. I guess my randomness is a little random.

Listing 18.26 Multi-signature test message input

```
key = fopen("message.dat", "r");      Look for example message.
if(!key)
{
  printf("can't find message.dat\n");   Exit if not found.
  exit(-4);
                                          Space for 16-bit data
}
msg = (unsigned short*)malloc(sizeof(unsigned short)*102);
for(i=0; i<100; i++)
  fscanf(key, "%hd", &msg[i]);          Stuff data into a buffer.
fclose(key);
```

With all the keys available and a test message to sign, the process of testing signature aggregation can begin. Listing 18.27 shows the simulated signing process. Each node has to compute a signature, and then some node has to combine them all into an aggregate. Here, it all happens in the same place because this is just a test.

Listing 18.27   Multi-signatures test signing and verify routines

```
for(i=0; i<k; i++)
{                                    Use each private key
  point_init(&S[i]);                 to create a digital signature.
  sign(&S[i], sig, sk[i], aj[i], (unsigned char*)msg, 200);
}

point_init(&Sigma);                  Combiner takes all signatures
agregat_sig(&Sigma, sig, S, k);      and creates aggregate.
point_printf("Sigma:\n", Sigma);
            Compute Well pairings of
            aggregate signatures and keys
            with base point g2 and message.
            e(σ, g2) ≟ e(H0, A).
if(multisig_verify(sig, Sigma, APK, (unsigned char*)msg, 200))
  printf("e(sigma, g2) matches e(H0, apk)\n");
else
  printf("Signature FAILS verification\n");
```

The output from this part of the testing is

```
Sigma:
▓▶ (1122971341953877016788473253063866977358756337989127408613555436000494578553801,
▓▶ 78553801, 562060647478205699837753954355143586077110983878134497528994
▓▶ 2953401952932440)

e(sigma, g2) matches e(H0, apk)
```

Signature verification is done with routine `multisig_verify()` from listing 18.11. This operation can be done by anyone with access to the public keys, the aggregate signature, and the message. For a blockchain situation, this can be any user.

Because everything is on one computer, it is very easy to ensure the mathematics works as expected. When data must be sent over a network, error correction must be implemented to make sure every node actually signs the same message. It is a good idea to verify a signature the instant it is generated just to make sure it really is valid. Making the mathematics work may be easy compared to the rest of the system.

18.6.4 *Creating subgroup multi-signatures simulation program*

Having loaded the signature system parameters and a set of private, public key pairs, we can create a subgroup simulation with the same data. Figure 18.10 illustrates the steps involved in creating the test program. The main task is to create the membership keys. Then a random list of nodes is selected to sign a message. The aggregation of the signatures and public keys creates the digital signature, which can then be verified. The actual difficulty of transmitting the matrix components to every node is ignored.

Figure 18.10   Test program steps for simulating subgroup signature

Listing 18.28 shows the initialization of the μ matrix and a column vector. The simulation is for each node to compute a column of the matrix using routine `mu_column()` from listing 18.13. The assumption is that each column is distributed to all the other nodes one way or another. Once all nodes have all the other nodes' matrix components for their row, they can compute the membership key (equation 18.15 $M_i = \sum_{j=1}^{n} \mu_{i,j}$) using listing 18.14.

Listing 18.28   Mu matrix column and row calculations

```
Muvec = (POINT*)malloc(k*sizeof(POINT));          | Allocate vector and
Mumatrix = (POINT*)malloc(k*k*sizeof(POINT));     | matrix space.
for(i=0; i<k; i++)
{
  point_init(&Muvec[i]);      | Then initialize GMP variables.
  for(j=0; j<k; j++)
    point_init(&Mumatrix[i*k + j]);
}
```

Simulate each node computing its column data and transmitting all values except diagonal to other nodes.

```
for(j=0; j<k; j++)
{
  mu_column(Muvec, APK, sig, aj[j], sk[j], k);
  for(i=0; i<k; i++)                              | Fill mu matrix
    point_copy(&Mumatrix[i*k + j], Muvec[i]);     | one column at a time.
}
```

After all row components are collected, include diagonal term to compute membership key.

```
Memkey = (POINT*)malloc(k*sizeof(POINT));
for(i=0; i<k; i++)
{                                        Compute all rows;
                                         not possible in reality.
  point_init(&Memkey[i]);
  membership_key(&Memkey[i], &Mumatrix[i*k], k, sig.E);  ◄
}
```

In the previous listing, I compute every membership key for every node. This is not actually possible in reality because the diagonal term is only available for one node. That is, one node can compute a membership key for its own row but none of the other rows because the node only knows $\mu_{i,i}$ for its row. The membership keys do not need to be distributed because they are only used for an individual node's signature.

The setup is complete once every node has its membership key. A message can be signed by a subgroup of all the nodes using listing 18.15. The simulation picks out a set of nodes at random (using another set of values from random.org) and has each of those nodes sign the message. I again simulate the aggregation of the signatures and public keys using subroutine `subgrp_combine()` (listing 18.16). All these steps are shown in the following listing.

Listing 18.29   Subgroup multi-signatures simulated signing

```
list[0] = 5;
list[1] = 2;
list[2] = 17;
list[3] = 10;           Choose a set of
list[4] = 16;           random indexes into key list.
list[5] = 19;
list[6] = 7;
list[7] = 8;
list[8] = 14;
list[9] = 4;
nmlst = 10;
```
**Use list to create a subgroup
of public key and
signature of message.**
```
Sgrp = (POINT*)malloc(nmlst*sizeof(POINT));
for(i=0; i<nmlst; i++)
{
                                        Simulate each node's
  point_init(&Sgrp[i]);                 signature with
  j = list[i];                          a private key.
  subgrp_sign(&Sgrp[i], APK, sig, Memkey[j], sk[j], (unsigned char*)msg,
              200);
}
                            Send all signatures
poly_point_init(&Pgrpsum);  to combiner to create
point_init(&Ssum);          final signature data block.
subgrp_combine(&Pgrpsum, &Ssum, sig, Sgrp, PK, list, nmlst);

printf("subgroup index list:\n");
for(i=0; i<nmlst; i++)
printf("%ld ", list[i]);    Output list, key aggregation,
printf("\n");               and group signature.
printf("subgroup signature:\n");
poly_point_printf("Public Key Aggregation:\n", Pgrpsum);
point_printf("Aggregate Signature: ", Ssum);
printf("\n");
```

The final signature consists of the message, the list of nodes that signed the message, the aggregate sum of signatures, and the sum of public keys on the list. This is fed into the subgroup signatures verification subroutine subgrp_verify() (listing 18.17) as shown in the following listing.

Listing 18.30   Subgroup signatures verification simulation

```
j = subgrp_verify(sig, APK, (unsigned char*)msg, 200,  Verify signature
                  list, nmlst, Pgrpsum, Ssum);         output is 1 or 0.
if(j)
  printf("Subgroup Aggregate Signature Verifies!\n");
else
  printf("Subgroup Aggregate Signature FAILS!!\n");
```

The output from listings 18.29 and 18.30 is shown in listing 18.31. I have removed the modulus, which is repeated for every coefficient, to make it less cumbersome. It still looks pretty messy, no matter how you slice it.

Listing 18.31   Subgroup signatures simulation output

```
subgroup index list:
5 2 17 10 16 19 7 8 14 4              | List of key indexes in order

subgroup signature:                    | Aggregate public key
Public Key Aggregation:                | is polynomial point.
x: 308734027095941801043648138293440102005846759237360993166826506845286990
⇒ 2786196*x^10
+ 273212200056065593756245026360773759080081742681328675765261945316826728
⇒ 052551*x^9
+ 322246917645514957429965308993060676838680721263911632976519780541992229
⇒ 3559149*x^8
+ 760584752500993212526267317146539057825630829777626231748196046598080144
⇒ 524392*x^7
+ 168108570249790268141479112134040509445162533061974180346200494391357303
⇒ 7149470*x^6
+ 134472400115109207558742669593749207007575670214545473137743826979931370
⇒ 8260410*x^5
+ 252262851280186607097181416940012486391095812289355373447132444361555505
⇒ 1031125*x^4
+ 435528634755314760007765975654943489944423073822611819774442468619257248
⇒ 267833*x^3
+ 611134956654561436718818693476633408111697162899828874451657268436690462
⇒ 273227*x^2
+ 101674253509055096647174911633973438707882270057356536605151026710502981
⇒ 9693725*x^1
+ 142775859716672370792408820600112555510239369829989913738050206188040602
⇒ 3408296

y:  270513145912037023647178217539279649863284684432971523215271467990554
⇒ 43876032*x^10
+ 988975539954664249608996954584865067461607598008930160966578820639181828
⇒ 622911*x^9
+ 463197787522181393699884306743777600546025496824591951446233267059418392
⇒ 11378*x^8
+ 192282709108189264341232772903004331377067453252071366255842265988493842
⇒ 9362936*x^7
+ 204923129749669144494757031124257936044361989840503529073612887536220442
⇒ 7813384*x^6
+ 134825276914476597499844132196397874295094721364759444654780348287155945
⇒ 9663517*x^5
+ 253285215225796047962668127984119172414269499889015362622084281201717799
⇒ 0608354*x^4
+ 264292101859039886855810713753941809021815483036315982607919436883368760
```

⟹ `4131872*x^3`

`+   24090447561918171948732372375712341462281610382137675208906320853707 0422`

⟹ `925929*x^2`

`+   8783773876676522118161347154254018837796330633783993396781910376680617 14`

⟹ `128112*x^1`

`+   2187196350558029781662361437995677696410341688014298219533081293215487 57`

⟹ `8458997`

`Aggregate Signature:`   **Aggregate signature is G_1 point.**

`(264442849668561624293476764235549279661221320220098049003355303537454385 58`

⟹ `47657,`

`136592465659166800952109795345022500115300724589906797149366384511212470 370`

⟹ `1079)`

`Subgroup Aggregate Signature Verifies!`

The simulation shows the underlying mathematics works. Getting a system of nodes to communicate is a different problem. Once they do communicate, combining the mathematics should be straightforward.

Answers to exercises

1 For H_0, it is $273 + 128 = 401$ bits. For H_1, it is $259 + 128 = 387$ bits.

2 Three—twice in a_i and once in P_i.

3 g_2 is the base point generator for all public keys, ψ_i is the private key for user i, and m is the message that all users sign.

4 For the left side of 18.26:

$$e\left(\sum_{j\in S} H_2(A,j), A\right) = e\left(\sum_{j\in S} H_2(A,j), \sum_{i=1}^n a_i P_i\right) = e\left(\sum_{j\in S} H_2(A,j), \sum_{i=1}^n a_i \psi_i g_2\right)$$

$$= e\left(\sum_{j\in S} H_2(A,j), g_2\right)^{\sum_{i=1}^n a_i \psi_i}$$

For the right side of 18.26:

$$e\left(\sum_{j\in S} M_j, g_2\right) = e\left(\sum_{j\in S}\sum_{i=1}^n \mu_{j,i}, g_2\right) = e\left(\sum_{j\in S}\sum_{i=1}^n a_i \psi_i H_2(A,j), g_2\right)$$

$$= e\left(\sum_{j\in S} H_2(A,j), g_2\right)^{\sum_{i=1}^n a_i \psi_i}$$

As long as nobody cheats, it all works.

Summary

- H_0 and H_2 convert input data to a G_1 point.
- H_1 converts input data to a value modulo the torsion value r.
- a_j is a hash of all public keys in order with key j placed before the other keys

$$a_j = H_1(P_j, P_1, P_2, \cdots P_n)$$

  which means key P_j is used twice.
- The sum of all keys is

$$A = \sum_{j=1}^{n} a_j P_j$$

- A single node's signature combines a node's private key, a_j value, and a hash of the message

$$s_j = \psi_j a_j H_0(m)$$

- A multi-group signature is the sum of individual node's signatures

$$\sigma = \sum_{j=1}^{n} s_j$$

- Verification of a multi-group signature uses two pairings by checking

$$e(\sigma, g_2) \overset{?}{=} e(H_0(m), A)$$

- A subgroup multi-signature uses a membership key derived from a matrix

$$\mu_{i,j} = a_j \psi_j H_2(A, i)$$

- Each node computes one column of the $\mu_{i,j}$ matrix and sends its value to all other nodes.
- When the matrix is fully distributed, every node computes its membership key as the sum of its row of the matrix

$$M_i = \sum_{j=1}^{n} \mu_{i,j}$$

- Nodes signing a message use their membership key and private key to compute

$$s_i = M_i + \psi_i H_0(A, m)$$

- A subgroup S of nodes creates an aggregate signature with a sum of individual signatures and sum of participating public keys:

$$P_S = \sum_{j \in S} P_j \qquad \sigma_S = \sum_{j \in S} s_j$$

- A subgroup signature is verified using three pairing calculations and checking

$$e(H_0(A, m), P_S) \cdot e\left(\sum_{j \in S} H_2(A, j), A \right) \overset{?}{=} e(\sigma_S, g_2)$$

Proving knowledge and keeping secrets: Zero knowledge using pairings

This chapter covers

- Description of zero-knowledge proofs
- Constructing quadratic arithmetic programs
- Using common reference strings for proofs

In this chapter, I'll get to the edge of cryptographic protocol research by explaining zk-SNARKs. Because this is an active area of research, I'll use a very popular paper, which has over 1,200 citations to explain the concepts. This is complicated, so get a beer and relax. I had to read many SNARK papers a dozen times, so, hopefully, it will only take you a few times through this chapter to understand the ideas.

The chapter starts with a definition of interactive zero knowledge using Ali Baba's cave. Then I'll explain noninteractive zero knowledge and quadratic arithmetic programs. From there, I'll explain the idea of a common reference string, followed by the SNARK mathematics.

19.1 SNARK defined

First, let's look at the origin of the word *snark*. Sometime around 1875, Lewis Carroll wrote in "The Hunting of the Snark":

> They sought it with thimbles, they sought it with care;
>> They pursued it with forks and hope;
> They threatened its life with a railway-share;
>> They charmed it with smiles and soap.
> And the Banker, inspired with a courage so new
>> It was matter for general remark,
> Rushed madly ahead and was lost to their view
>> In his zeal to discover the Snark.

It is a very nice and funny nonsense poem (Carroll, 2010). With the same title as Lewis Carroll's poem, 140 years later Bitansky et al. (2014) wrote

Definition 4.2. *A triple of algorithms $(\mathcal{P}, \mathcal{G}_\mathcal{V}, \mathcal{V})$ is a SNARK if it is a SNARG where adaptive soundness is replaced by the following stronger requirement:*

Adaptive proof of knowledge. *For any polynomial-size prover P^* there exists a polynomial-size extractor $\mathcal{E}_{P^*}$ such that for all large enough $k \in \mathbb{N}$ and all auxiliary inputs $z \in \{0, 1\}^{poly(k)}$,*

$$Pr \begin{bmatrix} (\text{vgrs, priv}) \leftarrow \mathcal{G}_\mathcal{V}(1^k) & (y, w) \leftarrow \mathcal{E}_{P^*}(z, \text{vgrs}) \\ (y, \Pi) \leftarrow \mathcal{P}^*(z, \text{vgrs}) & \wedge \\ \mathcal{V}(\text{priv}, y, \Pi) = 1 & w \notin \mathcal{R}(y) \end{bmatrix} \leq \text{negl}(k)$$

On first reading, this makes less sense to me than the poem!

The acronym SNARK today stands for "succinct noninteractive argument of knowledge." When the algorithm is modified to work as a zero-knowledge proof, the acronym changes to zk-SNARK. For a deeper understanding of zero knowledge in general, Brands's (2000) thesis is an excellent place to start. For a real-world use case, look at Adam Luciano's "zk-SNARKs—A Realistic Zero-Knowledge Example and Deep Dive" (http://mng.bz/QZqR).

The original idea of zero knowledge for cryptographic purposes was to prove that one had a solution to a problem without giving up the actual details of the solution. This involved an interaction between a prover and a verifier. The verifier would ask questions of the prover, and the prover would respond with answers. The odds of getting a wrong answer rose exponentially with the number of questions, so at some point, the verifier could admit the prover did, in fact, have a solution, and the verifier does not know what the solution is.

A simple example of this is called Ali Baba's cave. The cave has two passageways with a magic door blocking the way between them, as shown in figure 19.1. Paul wants to prove to Veronica that he knows the secret that opens the door but does not want to tell her what the secret is.

The scheme Paul comes up with makes Veronica wait outside the cave while he randomly walks up one passageway. Veronica then enters the cave and shouts out a random passageway to come out from. If Paul is on the left side and Veronica shouts

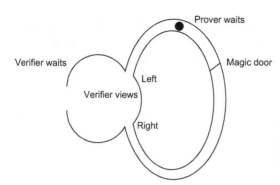

Prover waits

Verifier waits

Left

Verifier views

Right

Magic door

Figure 19.1 Ali Baba's cave illustrates the concept of zero-knowledge proof. The prover knows a secret and the verifier wants them to prove they know it, but the verifier doesn't need to know the secret themselves.

"Right!" then Paul must open the door and come out the right. If he does not actually know the secret, he will come out on the left.

Since both Paul and Veronica are making random choices, the odds of being on the correct side is 50 percent. If Paul comes out the correct side after 10 rounds, the odds, he does not know the secret are only 1 in 1,000. After 20 rounds, it is 1 in 1 million. This is the essence of a zero-knowledge proof. The prover knows something that the verifier wants them to prove they actually know, but the verifier does not need the knowledge themselves.

The rest of this chapter explains how we can compute a zero-knowledge proof with no interactions using elliptic curve points to hide information. The starting point is a replacement for Ali Baba's cave, which is called a quadratic arithmetic program. The secret passage door is replaced by a common reference string. The actual number of points in the common reference string may not seem succinct for a proof of knowledge, but it is at least minimal. Verification uses pairings to combine proofs of knowledge with public information. I use Tate pairings for the actual calculations.

19.2 Concept of the quadratic arithmetic program explained

In this section, I'll introduce the quadratic arithmetic program (QAP) function that acts as the foundation of a zero-knowledge proof. Similar to Ali Baba's secret door, the QAP has secret inputs that only the prover knows.

As described in Groth (2016), the components of the interactive proof are the prover, the verifier, and the function. In the noninteractive proof, the function is expanded to include public and private data. For SNARKs, the function is a QAP. The public input is called the statement, and private data is called the witness.

For an example, I am going to create a reasonable QAP where the inputs are from a medical data record. I use a medicine number, a dose, and a patient number. I want the record to be able to prove that a patient had a specific medicine at a known dose, but the patient is unknown. This is called *witness indistinguishable* in many academic papers because we can prove that one of the patients had that medicine, but you can't figure out which patient.

The QAP consists of wires and multiplication gates. Figure 19.2 shows an example that is used throughout this chapter. I have run across papers that describe QAPs with 20,000 gates, so they can get very large. The purpose here is to get the idea across.

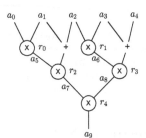

Figure 19.2   Example quadratic arithmetic program

The wires in figure 19.2 are labeled a_j, and the gates are labeled r_j. The inputs to each gate come from the top on both the left and right sides. The outputs from each gate are at the bottom. Each wire has a value either as an input or as a computation. In the figure 19.2 example, equation 19.1 shows we have the following relationships:

$$a_5 = a_0 \cdot a_1$$
$$a_6 = a_2 \cdot a_3$$
$$a_7 = a_5(a_1 + a_2) \qquad (19.1)$$
$$a_8 = a_6(a_3 + a_4)$$
$$a_9 = a_7 \cdot a_8$$

In all the academic papers, variable a_0 is always 1. For my example, I take a_1 as the medicine number, a_2 as the dose (in picograms), and a_3 as the patient number. I chose a_4 to be a random number so the propagation of a_9 backward would not allow an adversary to determine the patient number. While this is a simple, contrived example, it is complex enough to get the ideas across.

To prove equation 19.1 has the a_j values accurately filled in, the form in equation 19.2 is used:

$$\sum_{j=0}^{m} a_j v_j(x) \cdot \sum_{j=0}^{m} a_j w_j(x) = \sum_{j=0}^{m} a_j y_j(x) + h(x)t(x) \qquad (19.2)$$

The $v_j(x)$ functions represent the left-hand inputs to the gates in figure 19.2, the $w_j(x)$ functions represent the right-hand inputs, and the functions $y_j(x)$ represent the outputs of each gate. When the value of x is one of the gates (r_i), we should recover one of the equations from 19.1. The functions v_j, w_j, and y_j in equation 19.2 belong to each wire.

The QAP algorithm takes the r_j values as integers modulo a field prime. To recover the first equation $a_5 = a_0 \cdot a_1$, we have $y_5(r_0) = 1$, $v_0(r_0) = 1$, and $w_1(r_0) = 1$. Since a_5 only comes out of gate r_0, we require

$$y_5(r_1) = y_5(r_2) = y_5(r_3) = y_5(r_4) = 0$$

Notice that a_1 is also an input to gate r_2 on the right, so $w_1(r_2) = 1$. Since a_1 is neither an input to any left gate nor an output to any other gate, we have $v_1(x) = 0$ and $y_1(x) = 0$ for all x. Finally, we have

$$w_1(r_1) = w_1(r_3) = w_1(r_4) = 0$$

The reason we go through this complex description is to choose a value for x that is unrelated and random to the node values. This creates a cryptographic environment that makes it essentially impossible to spoof a_j values. The value chosen for x is secret to both the prover and the verifier. But first, let's see what kind of function gives us what we require.

Exercise 19.1

Why are most function values for v_i, w_i, and y_i equal to zero?

19.3 Lagrange interpolant functions described

In this section, I'll describe a function that satisfies the requirements of the QAP. Using the example from equation 19.1, I give a formula for each node in figure 19.2. The entire QAP for equation 19.1 is described and expanded to a general form.

A function that has the value 1 at one point and 0 at all other points is easy to create using Lagrange interpolation functions. For the gate r_0, we have equation 19.3:

$$l_0(x) = \frac{(x - r_1)(x - r_2)(x - r_3)(x - r_4)}{(r_0 - r_1)(r_0 - r_2)(r_0 - r_3)(r_0 - r_4)} \tag{19.3}$$

At node r_0, we have $l_0(r_0) = 1$, and we also have $l_0(r_i) = 0$ for the other nodes $i = 1, 2, 3, 4$.

Similarly, in equation 19.4, for all the other nodes we have the functions

$$
\begin{aligned}
l_1(x) &= \frac{(x - r_0)(x - r_2)(x - r_3)(x - r_4)}{(r_1 - r_0)(r_1 - r_2)(r_1 - r_3)(r_1 - r_4)} \\
l_2(x) &= \frac{(x - r_0)(x - r_1)(x - r_3)(x - r_4)}{(r_2 - r_0)(r_2 - r_1)(r_2 - r_3)(r_2 - r_4)} \\
l_3(x) &= \frac{(x - r_0)(x - r_1)(x - r_2)(x - r_4)}{(r_3 - r_0)(r_3 - r_1)(r_3 - r_2)(r_3 - r_4)} \\
l_4(x) &= \frac{(x - r_0)(x - r_1)(x - r_2)(x - r_3)}{(r_4 - r_0)(r_4 - r_1)(r_4 - r_2)(r_4 - r_3)}
\end{aligned}
\tag{19.4}
$$

This means we can take

$$v_0(x) = l_0(x)$$

Since a_1 is an input to both the r_0 and r_2 gate on the right, we have

$$w_1(x) = l_0(x) + l_2(x)$$

The output of gate r_0 is a_5, so it looks like we should take $y_5(x) = l_0(x)$. However, this causes a problem because

$$a_0 v_0(x) \cdot a_1 w_1(x) = a_0 a_1 l_0^2(x)$$

This is true of every gate. The inputs are a Lagrange interpolant function, and the multiplication results in the square of the same function. So I use $y_5(x) = l_0^2(x)$.

Figure 19.3 shows a graphical description of the process. On the far left are the functions associated with each gate. The equations from equation 19.1 are expanded to show how each coefficient determines which QAP function the Lagrange interpolant goes into. The square of the Lagrange interpolant goes into the output functions.

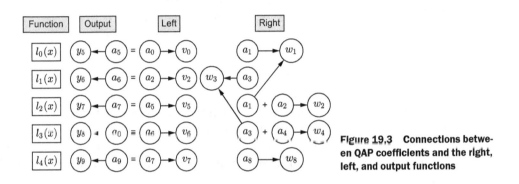

Figure 19.3   Connections between QAP coefficients and the right, left, and output functions

Proceeding this way through all of equation 19.1, the right, left, and output functions are listed in table 19.1. This is all great for x values on gates because the multiplication results in one equation for a particular gate. Since these are functions, the multiplication of the sums of left and right functions results in a lot of cross terms.

Table 19.1   QAP example functions

j	v_j	w_j	y_j
0	$l_0(x)$	0	0
1	0	$l_0(x) + l_2(x)$	0
2	$l_1(x)$	$l_2(x)$	0
3	0	$l_1(x) + l_3(x)$	0
4	0	$l_3(x)$	0
5	$l_2(x)$	0	$l_0^2(x)$
6	$l_3(x)$	0	$l_1^2(x)$
7	$l_4(x)$	0	$l_2^2(x)$
8	0	$l_4(x)$	$l_3^2(x)$
9	0	0	$l_4^2(x)$

Notice in equation 19.2 there is an additional term $h(x)t(x)$. In equation 19.5, the $t(x)$ function is defined as the product of all the gates:

$$t(x) = \prod_{i=0}^{n-1} (x - r_i) \tag{19.5}$$

The degree of $t(x)$ is the number of gates n. The degree of each Lagrange interpolant function is $n-1$. The degree of $h(x)$ then has to be $2(n-1) - n = n - 2$. Let's take a look at the cross term $l_0(x)l_1(x)$ in equation 19.6:

$$
\begin{aligned}
l_0(x)l_1(x) &= \frac{(x-r_1)(x-r_2)(x-r_3)(x-r_4)}{(r_0-r_1)(r_0-r_2)(r_0-r_3)(r_0-r_4)} \frac{(x-r_0)(x-r_2)(x-r_3)(x-r_4)}{(r_1-r_0)(r_1-r_2)(r_1-r_3)(r_1-r_4)} \\
&= \frac{(x-r_0)(x-r_1)(x-r_2)^2(x-r_3)^2(x-r_4)^2}{(r_0-r_1)(r_0-r_2)(r_0-r_3)(r_0-r_4)(r_1-r_0)(r_1-r_2)(r_1-r_3)(r_1-r_4)}
\end{aligned}
\tag{19.6}
$$

This is a huge mess at first sight, so let's create a new function for the denominator in equation 19.7:

$$p_i = \prod_{\substack{j=0 \\ j \neq i}}^{n-1} (r_i - r_j) \tag{19.7}$$

Using equation 19.7 for $i = 0$ and $i = 1$ in equation 19.6, and pulling $t(x)$ out using equation 19.5, equation 19.6 converts to equation 19.8:

$$l_0(x)l_1(x) = t(x) \frac{(x-r_2)(x-r_3)(x-r_4)}{p_0 p_1} \tag{19.8}$$

Noticing the pattern in equation 19.8, a form that is useful for programming is shown in equation 19.9:

$$l_i(x)l_j(x) = \frac{t(x)}{p_i p_j} \prod_{\substack{k=0 \\ k \neq i,j}}^{n-1} x - r_k \tag{19.9}$$

The $h(x)t(x)$ term in equation 19.2 is then the combination of all the cross terms with the assumption that the squared terms are taken care of by the sum over $y_j(x)$. As long as the values for the a_j are legitimate, this is true. If a_j does not satisfy the QAP, then equation 19.2 will not be true.

If there are n gates in the QAP, there are $n(n-1)/2$ cross terms. A QAP with 20,000 gates has 200 million cross terms! Keeping track of all the coefficients of those cross terms requires a lot of programming. For the example in figure 19.2, there are five gates, so we have $5 \times 4/2 = 10$ cross terms. Using Mathematica to keep track of the terms, I found the cross terms to have the coefficients as shown in table 19.2.

Suppose we pick a value $x = z$ along with specific values for $a_1, a_2, a_3,$ and a_4. From the formulas in equation 19.1, we can compute the remaining coefficients a_j, and from these, the coefficients of the cross terms in table 19.2. However, the prover does not know the value of z, so we have to expand equation 19.9 as a polynomial. We also can do this same expansion for the Lagrange interpolation formulas because they are also a product of $(x - r_j)$ terms.

Table 19.2 $h(x)$ cross terms coefficients

l_0l_1	$a_1a_2 + a_0a_3$
l_0l_2	$a_0(a_1 + a_2) + a_1a_5$
l_0l_3	$a_0(a_3 + a_4) + a_1a_6$
l_0l_4	$a_1a_7 + a_0a_8$
l_1l_2	$a_2(a_1 + a_2) + a_3a_5$
l_1l_3	$a_2(a_3 + a_4) + a_3a_6$
l_1l_4	$a_3a_7 + a_2a_8$
l_2l_3	$a_5(a_3 + a_4) + a_6(a_1 + a_2)$
l_2l_4	$a_7(a_1 + a_2) + a_5a_8$
l_3l_4	$a_7(a_3 + a_4) + a_6a_8$

To see the pattern, let's multiply the factors in the numerator of equation 19.8 to get equation 19.10:

$$x^3 - (r_2 + r_3 + r_4)x^2 + (r_2r_3 + r_2r_4 + r_3r_4)x - r_2r_3r_4 \tag{19.10}$$

The highest power has coefficient 1. The next-lower power of x has a coefficient that is the sum of all the roots. Following that is the sum of all combinations of two roots. This pattern repeats for as many factors as there are. When given a list of roots, we can compute all the coefficients for the expanded polynomial by taking sums of combinations of one, two, etc., up to the degree of the polynomial of the roots in the list. We use this to expand every $l_i(x)l_j(x)$ cross term as well as every $l_i(x)$ in the v_j, w_j, and y_j formulas.

> ### Exercise 19.2
> Given a QAP with the following set of gates:
> $a_0 \cdot a_1 = a_4$
> $a_2 \cdot a_3 = a_5$
> $a_4 \cdot a_5 = a_6$
> What is the cross term function $t(x)h(x)$? Assume you know the Lagrange interpolants $l_0(x)$, $l_1(x)$, and $l_2(x)$ for each gate.

19.4   The common reference string

In this section, I'll explain the common reference string (CRS). The CRS is common to both the prover and verifier. It is a reference that all users can access. The CRS consists of many bytes of data, which computer science defines as a string. The CRS depends on the QAP, but every individual record uses the same CRS data.

The purpose of a CRS is to give the prover and verifier a way to prove knowledge without leaking information to each other. The problem with a CRS is that somebody has to know the secret values used to generate it. These values are called toxic waste in the cryptographic literature. State-of-the-art cryptographic protocols are finding ways to make the CRS updateable. These methods are called structured reference strings (SRS). The basic idea is the same though: there are a set of points on an elliptic curve and its extension field that contain information about the QAP that allow a prover to create a proof for a record of data using some of the data as a public statement and the rest as a private witness.

Since Groth (2016) uses a CRS, I will explain how a CRS works. The idea of the reference string is to make it impossible to compute the witness values from the public statement values and to ensure the prover can not alter the QAP function to create a fake record.

I first explain the points that make up the CRS, then describe the prover formulas, and finally describe the verifier formulas. Then I break down how the verifier formulas work by expanding the equations.

The prover creates points on G_1 and G_2 using combinations of the CRS points along with the values of a_j for a specific record. The verifier only knows the public a_j values. Everyone has access to the QAP formulas and the CRS, so every record can be independently proved and verified. Any attempt to change a formula or fake a CRS point breaks the proof.

I take the point G to be the base point on G_1 and the point H to be the base point on G_2. I make the assumption that we are on a pairing-friendly curve with cryptographically secure torsion level and reasonable field size. The CRS generator chooses five values at random with respect to the torsion value, which are labeled $\alpha, \beta, \gamma, \delta$, and z. The value of z can not be one of the r_j values. The odds of that are small, but one should check, especially if there are thousands of gates.

To simplify notation, I'm going to create a variable that is not in the CRS directly but is computed by the CRS generator. In equation 19.11, let's define θ_i as

$$\theta_i = \beta v_i(z) + \alpha w_i(z) + y_i(z) \tag{19.11}$$

So we can write the CRS listed in Groth (2016) as equation 19.12:

$$\alpha G, \beta G, \delta G, \{z^i G\}_{i=0}^{n-1}, \left\{\frac{z^i t(z)}{\delta}G\right\}_{i=0}^{n-2}$$
$$\left\{\frac{\theta_i}{\gamma}G\right\}_{i=0}^{l}, \left\{\frac{\theta_i}{\delta}G\right\}_{i=l+1}^{m}, \tag{19.12}$$
$$\beta H, \delta H, \{z^i H\}_{i=0}^{n-1}$$

The points αG, βG, and δG are the random values times the G_1 base point G. The points βH and δH are random values times the G_2 base point H. The term $\{z^i G\}_{i=0}^{n-1}$ is the set of points created when taking powers of z^i times the base point G, which gives n points total. The set of points $\{z^i H\}_{i=0}^{n-1}$ is similar but they are on G_2 with base point H. The set of points $\left\{\dfrac{z^i t(z)}{\delta} G\right\}_{i=0}^{n-2}$ are $n-1$ points that combine $t(z)$, δ, and

powers of z^i with the base point G. The two groups of points $\left\{\dfrac{\theta_i}{\gamma} G\right\}_{i=0}^{l}$ and $\left\{\dfrac{\theta_i}{\delta} G\right\}_{i=l+1}^{m}$

split up statement and witness values using the base point G. The random values γ and δ ensure they stay isolated from each other.

Within the CRS, we see that two terms are broken up at the point l. The values from $\{0..l\}$ are the public statement terms, and the values $\{l+1..m\}$ are the private witness terms. In my example, I use a permutation of the a_j's to make this work out.

For each record, the prover creates two random values, r and s. These are combined with the CRS to create three points. While the first two look similar, the first is on G_1, and the second is on G_2 as shown in equation 19.13:

$$A = \left[\alpha + \sum_{i=0}^{m} a_i v_i(z) + r\delta\right] G$$
$$B = \left[\beta + \sum_{i=0}^{m} a_i w_i(z) + s\delta\right] H \tag{19.13}$$

The third point looks really complicated and horrible. Given the CRS, it is not that hard to actually compute, as shown in equation 19.14:

$$C = \left\{ \left[\frac{\sum_{i=l+1}^{m} a_i \theta_i + h(z)t(z)}{\delta}\right] \right.$$
$$\left. + s\left(\alpha + \sum_{i=0}^{m} a_i v_i(z)\right) + r\left(\beta + \sum_{i=0}^{m} a_i w_i(z)\right) + rs\delta \right\} G \tag{19.14}$$

The verifier can then take the public data along with the previous three points to verify the record does have a witness value that uses the QAP. To do that, in equation 19.15, they first compute the point:

$$V = \frac{\sum_{i=0}^{l} a_i \theta_i}{\gamma} G \tag{19.15}$$

With the point V, the CRS, and the points A, B, and C from the prover, they then check equation 19.16 is true:

$$\tau(A, B) \stackrel{?}{=} \tau(\alpha G, \beta H) \cdot \tau(V, \gamma H) \cdot \tau(C, \delta H) \tag{19.16}$$

If the statement and witness values for the a_j are consistent, then this should be true. Let's see why by using the properties of pairings. The first calculation is

$$\tau(A, B) = \tau\left(\left[\alpha + \sum_{i=0}^{m} a_i v_i(z) + r\delta\right] G, \left[\beta + \sum_{i=0}^{m} a_i w_i(z) + s\delta\right] H\right)$$

We can take the factors multiplying each point into the exponent of the pairing to get equation 19.17:

$$\tau(A, B) = \tau(G, H)^{\left[\alpha + \sum_{i=0}^{m} a_i v_i(z) + r\delta\right] \cdot \left[\beta + \sum_{i=0}^{m} a_i w_i(z) + s\delta\right]} \tag{19.17}$$

Expanding the right-hand side of equation 19.16 the same way, we find equations 19.18, 19.19, and 19.20:

$$\tau(\alpha G, \beta H) = \tau(G, H)^{\alpha\beta} \tag{19.18}$$

$$\tau(V, \gamma H) = \tau(G, H)^{\dfrac{\sum_{i=0}^{l} a_i \theta_i}{\gamma} \cdot \gamma} \tag{19.19}$$

$$\tau(C, \delta H) =$$
$$\tau(G, H)^{\left\{\left[\dfrac{\sum_{i=l+1}^{m} a_i \theta_i + h(z)t(z)}{\delta}\right] + s\left(\alpha + \sum_{i=0}^{m} a_i v_i(z)\right) + r\left(\beta + \sum_{i=0}^{m} a_i w_i(z)\right) + rs\delta\right\} \cdot \delta} \tag{19.20}$$

Examination of the exponent in equation 19.17 shows all the terms appear in the exponents of the equations in 19.18 to 19.20. This is what is meant by "working in the exponent."

Figure 19.4 is a high-level view of the process involved with proving both sides of equation 19.16 are equal. At the top of the diagram are the two factors within the left-hand side of the equation. The multiplication results in the nine terms shown in the middle of the diagram. Each row includes the three terms: β, Σw, and s. At the bottom of the diagram are the right-hand-side terms from equation 19.16. There is one box for the left-side pairing, which is the multiplication of two factors with three terms each. There are three boxes for the right-hand-side pairings.

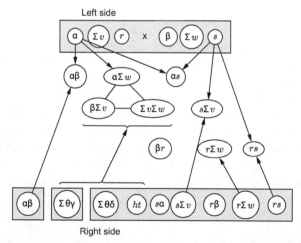

Figure 19.4 Illustration of exponent multiplication showing how all terms combine to prove equality

Each factor in the exponent of equation 19.17 has three terms. The first two terms in each factor, when multiplied, give $\alpha\beta$, which is equation 19.18. In equation 19.19, we see that the γs cancel. In equation 19.20, one δ cancels, and the last three terms gain an extra δ. Equating just the exponents of both sides of equation 19.16 gives equation 19.21:

$$\left[\alpha + \sum_{i=0}^{m} a_i v_i(z) + r\delta\right] \cdot \left[\beta + \sum_{i=0}^{m} a_i w_i(z) + s\delta\right] \overset{?}{=}$$

$$\alpha\beta + \sum_{i=0}^{l} a_i \theta_i + \sum_{i=l+1}^{m} a_i \theta_i + h(z)t(z) \qquad (19.21)$$

$$+ s\delta\left(\alpha + \sum_{i=0}^{m} a_i v_i(z)\right) + r\delta\left(\beta + \sum_{i=0}^{m} a_i w_i(z)\right) + rs\delta^2$$

I hope it is clear that there are identical terms on both sides that are "obvious." The $\alpha\beta$ term, $r\delta\left(\beta + \sum_{i=0}^{m} a_i w_i(z)\right)$ term, $s\delta\left(\alpha + \sum_{i=0}^{m} a_i v_i(z)\right)$ term, and $rs\delta^2$ term should all be clear from the multiplication of the factors inside the brackets of the first line in equation 19.21. Subtracting those terms from both sides leaves us with equation 19.22:

$$\alpha \sum_{i=0}^{m} a_i w_i(z) + \beta \sum_{i=0}^{m} a_i v_i(z) + \sum_{i=0}^{m} a_i v_i(z) \cdot \sum_{i=0}^{m} a_i w_i(z) \overset{?}{=} \sum_{i=0}^{l} a_i \theta_i + \sum_{i=l+1}^{m} a_i \theta_i + h(z)t(z)$$

$$(19.22)$$

The first thing to notice is the sums over θ_i can be combined into one sum. Doing that combination and putting the definition from equation 19.11 in for θ_i gives us equation 19.23:

$$\alpha \sum_{i=0}^{m} a_i w_i(z) + \beta \sum_{i=0}^{m} a_i v_i(z) + \sum_{i=0}^{m} a_i v_i(z) \cdot \sum_{i=0}^{m} a_i w_i(z)$$

$$\overset{?}{=} \sum_{i=0}^{m} a_i \left(\beta v_i(z) + \alpha w_i(z) + y_i(z)\right) + h(z)t(z) \qquad (19.23)$$

Notice that the first two sums in equation 19.23 match the first two terms in the sum after the equals sign. This leaves us with the definition of the QAP from equation 19.2. As long as nobody tries to fake any values, the verification will work.

Another item to notice is that the prover uses the witness values, and the verifier uses the statement values with the points C and V, respectively. These combine to create the QAP function. The "toxic waste" variables α and β hide the a_j coefficients in the sum over the left and right inputs to the QAP. The random values r and s chosen by the prover allow for zero knowledge when the verifier executes the proof.

Exercise 19.3

The high-level diagram in figure 19.4 is missing arrows to make the diagram readable. Which terms on the top (left side) are missing arrows to the middle terms? Which terms on the bottom (right side) are missing arrows to the middle terms?

19.5 zk-SNARK example code

In this section, I'll describe the programs that simulate a SNARK proof of knowledge. These programs model a real-world application in a very simple manner. Real-world zk-SNARK code is going to be far more complex than the examples shown here because they are attached to higher-level projects. The dimensions of the arrays are larger, but the basic ideas are the same. There is going to be a fixed QAP with public statement variables and private witness variables. There may be thousands of witness values for each public value. This makes creating the proof slow but the verification very fast.

The example code consists of five files. One is called snarkbase.c because it contains common subroutines for the other four programs. Figure 19.5 shows how these files are related.

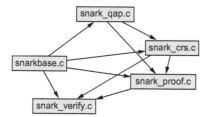

Figure 19.5   SNARK example code subroutine relationships

The programs are snark_qap.c, snark_crs.c, snark_proof.c, and snark_verify.c, and they are executed in that order. The snark_qap.c program outputs the data necessary to implement the QAP of figure 19.2 and table 19.1. The snark_crs.c program uses the same pairing-friendly curve from chapter 18 to output the CRS points listed in equation 19.12. Program snark_proof.c inputs the data from those two programs to create the three points in equations 19.13 and 19.14. Finally, program snark_verify.c inputs the CRS data and the record from the proof to compute equation 19.16.

19.5.1 Common subroutines in snarkbase.c

In this section, the fundamental SNARK code is described. These subroutines could be used in any real-world application. The subroutines that could be used in any SNARK program, rather than the specific examples contrived here, are placed in file snarkbase.c with their prototypes placed in snarkbase.h. There are a total of eight subroutines. Most are related to Lagrange polynomial construction, so the $v_i(x)$, $w_i(x)$, $y_i(x)$, and $h(x)$ functions can be created for the QAP.

I break down the Lagrange polynomial into two parts. The denominator is given by equation 19.7 ($p_i = \prod_{\substack{j=0 \\ j \neq i}}^{n-1} (r_i - r_j)$). The numerator is similar to equation 19.5 ($t(x) = \prod_{i=0}^{n} (x - r_i)$). The difference between $t(x)$ and $v_i(x)$ is that one factor $(x - r_i)$ is missing. For $h(x)$, two factors are missing. In all these cases, a combination of roots r_k is used to compute each coefficient in the expansion of the product.

The first subroutine computes the denominator p_i and is shown in listing 19.1. The input is a list of primes that represents the gate values of the QAP. The subroutine uses the modulus built into the modulo.c file. Because the calculations are done modulo point order and not on the field prime, care must be taken to set the modulus to the torsion value of the base points on the curve. We'll see that in later listings.

Listing 19.1   Lagrange multiplier denominator routine

```
void p_i(mpz_t p, int i, mpz_t *list, int n)    ← Number of primes in array
{
  int j;                              ↑ Array of primes representing gates
  mpz_t term, rslt;        | Index of gate being referenced

  mpz_inits(term, rslt, NULL);
  mpz_set_ui(rslt, 1);            | Start at 1.
  for(j=0; j<n; j++)
  {
    if(j == i)      | Skip reference gate ...
      continue;                | ... and multiply each
    msub(term, list[i], list[j]);  | term into a result.
    mmul(rslt, rslt, term);
  }
  mpz_set(p, rslt);
  mpz_clears(term, rslt, NULL);
}
```

The next two subroutines are used to compute the values for Lagrange polynomials and their combinations. The form is similar to equation 19.10, where each coefficient of a power is computed separately using the rules of possible combinations. The first subroutine builds a table that lists the starting and ending index for each factor required in a coefficient. Figure 19.6 shows how the table is built up with the starting indexes incrementing by 1 and then working backward from the end, decrementing indexes by 1. The table ensures every possible combination of r_j value is used.

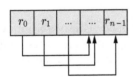

Figure 19.6   Index generation for l_i coefficients

An example would be an array with seven entries with all the combinations for three r_j values. That means there are three rows with the limt value of 7. The output k has the values shown in the first box of figure 19.7. The first column is an index to the root used in the multiply. The second column is the last root index needed for that slot.

Figure 19.7   Example table for root indexing

The process multiplies $r_0 r_1 r_2$ for the first term, $r_0 r_1 r_3$ for the second, and proceeds as shown in figure 19.7. When the last index goes over the limit in the second column, the previous row is incremented. Since no roots are duplicated, the following row then starts one past, as shown in the last box of the figure. This repeats until the last term, $r_4 r_5 r_6$. Thus, every possible combination of three terms out of seven in a list is found.

The code to build the initial table is given in listing 19.2. The output is an array that is input variable `rows` long by two columns wide. The first entry in each row is the starting index, and the second entry is the ending index. The input `limt` is the length of the array being worked on.

Listing 19.2   Permutation table routine

```
void startk(int *k, int rows, int limt)
{
  int m, index;

  index = 0;
  for(m=0; m<rows; m++)
  {                              Start each row
    k[2*m] = index;              one step from previous row.
    index++;
  }
  index = limt - 1;
  for(m=rows-1; m>=0; m-)
  {                              End each row
    k[2*m + 1] = index;          one step before next row.
    index--;
  }
}
```

The algorithm to compute all the coefficients of a Lagrange function is shown in figure 19.8. The list of roots, the number of roots n, and which indexes to remove are inputs. For the QAP polynomials, I use $i = j$ because it is the same process. The test for `except i & j` works for both cases.

A counter is used to keep track of which coefficient is being worked on. The counter value is the same as the number of roots in the table. The computation of each term within a coefficient is simply pulling each root out of the list and multiplying them. That term is then added to the coefficient.

The rest of the algorithm increments the first column of the table shown in figure 19.7. It looks complicated because of all the bookkeeping.

The computation of coefficients is shown in listing 19.3. The inputs to this routine are the complete `list` of prime roots of the Lagrange polynomial and the number n of them as well as the two subscripts for $l_i(x)l_j(x)$. To get the coefficients for $l_i(x)$, I set both i and j to the same value. The variable `cflimt` is set to $n-2$ for $l_i(x)l_j(x)$ and $n-1$ for finding coefficients for $l_i(x)$. The factors for $l_i(x)l_j(x)$ are the product terms from equation 19.9, without $t(x)$.

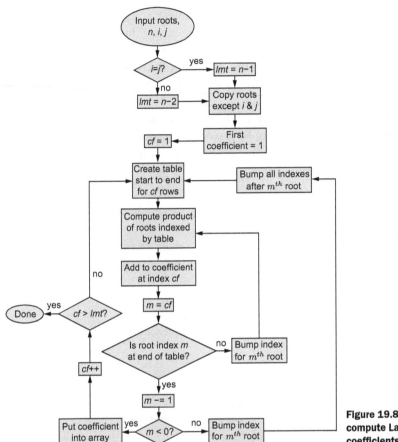

Figure 19.8   Algorithm to compute Lagrange polynomial coefficients

The routine then makes a sublist of the roots included in the polynomial, leaving out the i and j roots. This makes creating the combinations of roots using the previous table very simple. The table is held in array k.

Listing 19.3   Finding all coefficients for Lagrange polynomial

```
void li_lj(mpz_t *coef, int i, int j, mpz_t *list, int n)
{
    int *k, m, cfdex, done, bmp, r, cflimt;
    mpz_t sum, term, *sublst;

    if(i == j)                    If indexes are the same
        cflimt = n - 1;           compute l_i(x);
    else                          otherwise compute l_i(x)l_j(x).
        cflimt = n - 2;
    sublst = (mpz_t*)malloc(sizeof(mpz_t)*cflimt);
    r = 0;
    for(m=0; m<n; m++)
    {
```

```
  if((m != i) && (m != j))
  {                                    Copy roots to new list
    mpz_init(sublst[r]);               removing input index
    mpz_neg(sublst[r], list[m]);       values.
    r++;
  }
}
k = (int*)malloc(sizeof(int)*n*2);    Make space for indexing table.
mpz_set_ui(coef[0], 1);                First coefficient is always 1.
mpz_inits(sum, term, NULL);
for(cfdex = 1; cfdex < cflimt+1; cfdex++)   Loop over all coefficients.
{
  mpz_set_ui(sum, 0);
  startk(k, cfdex, cflimt);    ←—— Create combination lookup table.
  done = 0;                     Use a flag to mark
  while(!done)                ←—  reaching end of table.
  {
    mpz_set(term, sublst[k[0]]);   Pick up first root to multiply ...
    for(m=1; m<cfdex; m++)                    ... then use all rows
      mmul(term, term, sublst[k[2*m]]);       from index table.
    madd(sum, sum, term);         ←—— Add to this coefficient.
    m = cfdex - 1;   ←—— Start at the end of the index table.
    bmp = 0;
    while(!bmp && !done)    Use flag to exit checking sequence.
    {
      if(k[2*m] != k[2*m + 1])
      {
        bmp = 1;                This row is not
        k[2*m]++;               yet finished.
      }
      else
      {
        while(!bmp)    Check as many rows as needed.
        {
          m--;
          if(m < 0)
          {
            done = 1;        No more rows;
            bmp = 2;         all done with coefficient
          }
          else
          {
            if(k[2*m] != k[2*m + 1])    Is this row done yet?
            {
              k[2*m]++;          No, keep going.
              while(m < cfdex-1)
              {                            For all following rows,
                m++;                       start at next
                k[2*m] = k[2*(m-1)] + 1;   possible index.
              }
              bmp = 1;       Use index list for next term.
```

```
                }
              }
            }
          }
        }
      }
    }
    mpz_set(coef[cfdex], sum);      | Save coefficient in array.
  }
  mpz_clears(sum, term, NULL);
  for(m=0; m<cflimt; m++)            | Clean up stack.
    mpz_clear(sublst[m]);
}
```

The first coefficient is always 1, so that is set directly. The variable cfdex keeps track of each coefficient after that in the main loop. The index table k is created using the startk subroutine, and then the table is used to keep track of each combination. I do this with the index m, which starts on the last entry in the k table.

The first column in the k table is a list of indexes for creating the combination of roots to multiply. After multiplying these together, the result is summed into the coefficient. For the second coefficient, cfdex = 1, so no other terms are multiplied. The loop just sums all the roots one at a time, which is what we see in equation 19.10 for the second coefficient. The variable bmp is used to determine whether I have figured out the next combination correctly. If the first index in the mth row does not equal the last index, then the first index can be incremented, and the routine multiplies the next set of roots.

When a row is finished, I then attempt to go to the previous row in the table. At some point, m goes beyond the first row, and m goes negative. That is the point where the coefficient has been fully computed, and it can be saved into the output array. If the number of combinations is not finished, the index for row m is incremented, and then each following row is set to the index 1 greater than the previous row.

For QAP sizes of tens of thousands of gates, there is probably a more efficient way of doing this, especially on a parallel processor. It only needs to be done once for every QAP. With the general coefficient routine in listing 19.3 and the denominator routine in listing 19.1, the subroutines to compute $l_i(x)$ and $l_i(x)l_j(x)$ coefficients are straightforward. The following listing shows the former routine.

Listing 19.4 Calculating coefficients for $l_i(x)$

```
void liofx(mpz_t *coef, int i, mpz_t *list, int n)
{
  mpz_t pi;
  int j;
                                     | Get coefficients,
  li_lj(coef, i, i, list, n);        | expanding (x − r_j).
  mpz_init(pi);
  p_i(pi, i, list, n);      | Get denominator for (r_i − r_j).
  minv(pi, pi);
  for(j=0; j<n; j++)                 | Invert denominator
    mmul(coef[j], coef[j], pi);      | and modify
                                     | all coefficients.
```

```
    mpz_clear(pi);
}
```

The same process is followed in listing 19.5, which computes the coefficients for $l_i(x)l_j(x)$ cross terms. The only difference is there are two values in the denominator rather than just one.

Listing 19.5   Calculating coefficients for $l_i(x)l_j(x)$

```
void liljofx(mpz_t *coef, int i, int j, mpz_t *list, int n)
{
    mpz_t pi, pj;
    int k;
                                    | Get coefficients,
    li_lj(coef, i, j, list, n);     | expanding (x - rⱼ).
    mpz_inits(pi, pj, NULL);
    p_i(pi, i, list, n);
    p_i(pj, j, list, n);            | Get denominator for (rᵢ - rⱼ).
    mmul(pi, pi, pj);
    minv(pi, pi);
    for(k=0; k<n-1; k++)            | Invert denominator
        mmul(coef[k], coef[k], pi); | and modify
    mpz_clears(pi, pj, NULL);       | all coefficients.
}
```

An important task is to create the $h(x)$ cross terms table similar to table 19.2. Since we do not know the hidden values of z^i, the construction of an array similar to that shown in table 19.3 is required. Each cross term in $h(x)$ includes an expansion of $l_i(x)l_j(x)$. Every coefficient in the expansion is then multiplied by the $h(x)$ coefficients. A routine to create the initial $l_i(x)l_j(x)$ table is shown in listing 19.6.

Table 19.3 $l_i(x)l_j(x)$ Cross terms

i	j	x^{n-2}	x^{n-3}	$\cdots$	x^0
0	1	c_{01}^0	c_{01}^1	$\cdots$	c_{01}^{n-2}
0	2	c_{02}^0	c_{02}^1	$\cdots$	c_{02}^{n-2}
$\vdots$				$\vdots$	
$n-2$	$n-1$	$c_{n-2\,n-1}^0$	$c_{n-2\,n-1}^1$	$\cdots$	$c_{n-2\,n-1}^{n-2}$

The first calculation is the total number of coefficients in the table. The easiest way to see how this comes about is to note we have $(n-1)$ terms with $l_0(x)l_j(x)$ and $(n-2)$ terms with $l_1(x)l_j(x)$ down to one term with $l_{n-1}(x)l_n(x)$ cross terms. This is just the sum from 1 to $n-1$. Each cross term contains $n-1$ coefficients, so the total number is

$$k = (n-1)\sum_{i=1}^{n-1} i = n\frac{(n-1)^2}{2}$$

The routine to create each individual $l_i(x)l_j(x)$ array of coefficients is called for each possible combination of i and j. This is a rare routine that creates the space rather than expecting the calling program to create the space, so don't forget to clear the table and free the space from the calling program.

Listing 19.6   Computing table of $l_i(x)l_j(x)$ for all i and j

```
mpz_t* all_lilj(mpz_t *list, int n)
{
  mpz_t *table;
  int i, j, k;

  k = n*(n-1)*(n-1)/2;                           Allocate space
  table = (mpz_t*)malloc(sizeof(mpz_t)*k);       for all coefficients.
  for(i=0; i<k; i++)
    mpz_init(table[i]);
  k = 0;
  for(i=0; i<n-1; i++)
  {
    for(j=i+1; j<n; j++)
    {
      liljofx(&table[k], i, j, list, n);    One row for every
      k += n - 1;                           combination of i and j
    }
  }
  return table;   ← Don't forget to free table!
}
```

The operation of multiplying every coefficient in a row by the coefficient in $h(x)$ for that cross term is shown schematically in figure 19.9. On the left is the vector of coefficients computed as in table 19.2. The matrix in the center is the coefficients computed by the all_lilj() subroutine. The columns are summed to get an output vector that has the same number of coefficients as each row in the matrix. The output set of coefficients is what allows us to use the CRS points z^iG and z^iH.

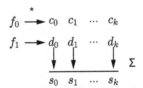

Figure 19.9   Matflat function operation

The index in figure 19.9 refers to the power of z^{n-2-i} in a polynomial expansion of the Lagrange interpolant functions and their products. When the term $\sum a_jw_jG$ is actually computed, we use the coefficients from the vector a_jw_j which are the values s_k in figure 19.9 times the z^iG computed in the CRS. This is how neither prover nor verifier knows the value of z, but can compute polynomials using the points which hide the powers of z^i.

Listing 19.7 implements the schematic of figure 19.9. The inputs are the coefficient matrix table mat with the number of coefficients in each row labeled as width and a vector of coefficients coef of length elements, which is the same as the number of rows in matrix mat. The output is vector that has width entries.

> **Listing 19.7   Multiplying the matrix row by a single value**

```
void matflat(mpz_t *vector, mpz_t *mat, int width, mpz_t *coef, int length)
{
  int i, j;
  mpz_t *cmt;

  cmt = (mpz_t*)malloc(sizeof(mpz_t)*width*length);
  for(i=0; i<length; i++)
  {
    for(j=0; j<width; j++)
    {
      mpz_init(cmt[i*width + j]);                        Multiply each row
      mmul(cmt[i*width + j], mat[i*width + j], coef[i]); by one coefficient.
    }
  }
  for(j=0; j<width; j++)
  {
    mpz_set_ui(vector[j], 0);
    for(i=0; i<length; i++)                              Sum down each column
      madd(vector[j], vector[j], cmt[i*width + j]);      for one final coefficient.
  }
  for(i=0; i<length*width; i++)
    mpz_clear(cmt[i]);
}
```

The last two routines in snarkbase.c are used in the snark_crs.c program to compute $l_i(z)$ and $t(z)$ for a specific value of z. The function lcalc() is shown in listing 19.8. The inputs are the value z, the coefficients for $l_i(x)$ found from listing 19.4, and the degree of the coefficient vector. Technically, these outputs are toxic waste, which should never be known by any prover or verifier.

> **Listing 19.8   Computes $l_i(z)$ for one value**

```
void lcalc(mpz_t rslt, mpz_t z, mpz_t *coef, int deg)
{
  int i;

  mpz_set(rslt, coef[0]);    Start at the highest
  for(i=1; i<=deg; i++)      power of z.
  {
                             Multiply one power of z
    mmul(rslt, rslt, z);     for each coefficient.
    madd(rslt, rslt, coef[i]);  Add last coefficient to finish.
  }
}
```

The last routine in snarkbase.c is the calculation for $t(z)$ from equation 19.5 ($t(x) = \prod_{i=0}^{n-1}(x - r_i)$). The inputs are the gate root primes, the number of roots, and the value of z. The following listing shows this simple routine. The routine name `tofz()` was already used in the pairing_sweep.c program.

Listing 19.9   Computes $t(z)$

```
void tofzgrth(mpz_t t, mpz_t z, mpz_t *list, int n)
{
  int i;
  mpz_t tmp;

  mpz_init(tmp);
  mpz_set_ui(t, 1);          Set result to 1.
  for(i=0; i<n; i++)
  {
    msub(tmp, z, list[i]);     Difference of z and root
    mmul(t, t, tmp);           Multiplied into result
  }
}
```

19.5.2 *Program to compute QAP parameters*

In this section, I'll describe a program that computes QAP parameters. It is specific to the example chosen in this chapter. Your own situation will require rewriting this program to your specific problem.

With the subroutines in snarkbase.c, we can create the data for a specific QAP problem. The problem I'm going to solve is shown in figure 19.2 and table 19.1. Listing 19.10 shows the beginning of the program in file snark_qap.c, which includes the entire pairing-friendly math structure.

Listing 19.10   snark_qap.c program setup

```
#include "signature.h"        Include all routines
#include "snarkbase.h"        and structures for pairings.

int main(int argc, char *argv[])
{
  FILE *qap;
  mpz_t list[11];
  int i, j, sw[10], l;
  mpz_t *htable;
  mpz_t *vj, *wj, *yj;
  SIG_SYSTEM sig;
                                              Read in pairing-friendly
  get_system("curve_11_parameters.bin", &sig);   curve data.
  minit(sig.tor);           Use torsion prime
                            for modulus.
  for(i=0; i<11; i++)
    mpz_init(list[i]);
```

```
mpz_set_ui(list[0], 31);
mpz_set_ui(list[1], 37);          Pick five primes
mpz_set_ui(list[2], 41);          for gate root values.
mpz_set_ui(list[3], 43);
mpz_set_ui(list[4], 47);
```

Listing 19.11 shows the code construction of table 19.1. Space is created for each of the wire variables vj, wj, and yj. These are two-dimensional arrays with one row for each wire and five columns, one for each of the Lagrange function coefficients. The wire variable coefficients are initialized, and then the coefficient values are computed using the liofx() routine. The last line of the listing creates the cross terms table for $h(x)$ needed in the CRS program.

Listing 19.11   Creating QAP functions

```
vj = (mpz_t*)malloc(sizeof(mpz_t)*10*5);
wj = (mpz_t*)malloc(sizeof(mpz_t)*10*5);
yj = (mpz_t*)malloc(sizeof(mpz_t)*10*5);
for(i=0; i<50; i++)
{
  mpz_init(vj[i]);
  mpz_init(wj[i]);
  mpz_init(yj[i]);
}
liofx(vj, 0, list, 5);                          | v0 = l0
liofx(&wj[5], 2, list, 5);
for(j=0; j<5; j++)
  madd(wj[5 + j], wj[5 + j], vj[j]);            | w1 = l0 + l2
liofx(&vj[10], 1, list, 5);                     | v2 = l1
liofx(&wj[10], 2, list, 5);                     | w2 = l2
liofx(&wj[20], 3, list, 5);                     | w4 = l3
liofx(&wj[15], 1, list, 5);
for(j=0; j<5; j++)                              | w3 = l1 + l3
  madd(wj[15 + j], wj[15 + j], wj[20 + j]);
liofx(&vj[25], 2, list, 5);                     | v5 = l2
liofx(&yj[25], 0, list, 5);                     | y5 = l0
liofx(&vj[30], 3, list, 5);                     | v6 = l3
liofx(&yj[30], 1, list, 5);                     | y6 = l1
liofx(&vj[35], 4, list, 5);                     | v7 = l4
liofx(&yj[35], 2, list, 5);                     | y7 = l2
liofx(&wj[40], 4, list, 5);                     | w8 = l4
liofx(&yj[40], 3, list, 5);                     | y8 = l3
liofx(&yj[45], 4, list, 5);                     | y9 = l4
                                                Create li(x)lj(x)
htable = all_lilj(list, 5);                     cross terms table.
```

The values shown on the right:
- $v_0 = l_0$
- $w_1 = l_0 + l_2$
- $v_2 = l_1$
- $w_2 = l_2$
- $w_4 = l_3$
- $w_3 = l_1 + l_3$
- $v_5 = l_2$
- $y_5 = l_0$
- $v_6 = l_3$
- $y_6 = l_1$
- $v_7 = l_4$
- $y_7 = l_2$
- $w_8 = l_4$
- $y_8 = l_3$
- $y_9 = l_4$

Create $l_i(x)l_j(x)$ **cross terms table.**

Listing 19.12 creates a permutation vector used to make equations 19.14 and 19.15 operate as advertised. We know that $a_0 = 1$, so I take a_1 and a_2 to be statement variables. Looking at the QAP formulas in equation 19.1, we see that both a_5 and a_7 only depend on a_0, a_1, and a_2. So these are also statement variables and can be public. The remaining variables are part of the witness.

Listing 19.12   Permutation vector setup

```
sw[0]  =  0;
sw[1]  =  1;
sw[2]  =  2;
sw[3]  =  5;                    Statement variables
sw[4]  =  7;
sw[5]  =  3;
sw[6]  =  4;
sw[7]  =  6;                    Witness variables
sw[8]  =  8;
sw[9]  =  9;
l  =  4;
```

The value of l is set to 4 because entries `sw[0]` to `sw[4]` are statement indexes while `sw[5]` to `sw[9]` are witness indexes. The value of m is therefore 9, and the value of n is 5 because that is the number of gates. I save the number of a_j rather than the last index as in the equations, so I take $m + 1 = 10$ as what is saved for the QAP parameters.

Listing 19.13 shows how the data is saved to a file. While a real-world case is much more complex, the QAP for a specific record only needs to be computed once.

Listing 19.13   Saving QAP data to disk file

```
qap = fopen("snark.qap", "w");
i = 5;
j = 10;
fwrite(&i, sizeof(int), 1, qap);      n = number gates
fwrite(&j, sizeof(int), 1, qap);      m = number QAP coefficients
fwrite(sw, sizeof(int), 10, qap);     Permutation vector
fwrite(&l, sizeof(int), 1, qap);      l = split for statement/witness
for(i=0; i<5; i++)
  mpz_out_raw(qap, list[i]);          Root values for all gates
for(i=0; i<50; i++)
  mpz_out_raw(qap, vj[i]);            QAP coefficient matrix left inputs
for(i=0; i<50; i++)
  mpz_out_raw(qap, wj[i]);            QAP matrix right inputs
for(i=0; i<50; i++)
  mpz_out_raw(qap, yj[i]);            QAP coefficient matrix outputs
for(i=0; i<40; i++)                   l_i(x)l_j(x) cross terms
  mpz_out_raw(qap, htable[i]);        coefficient matrix
fclose(qap);
```

19.5.3 Common reference string creation

In this section, a program to create the common reference string is described. It is also tailored to the example in this chapter, so your own situation will require rewriting this program.

Similar to the QAP generation, the first thing done in the CRS creation is to read in the paring-friendly curve parameters and start with the field modulus set to the point torsion value. The list of variables and startup are shown in listing 19.14. The reading of the snark.qap file requires creating space for the correct number of parameters and initializing each one before inputting them from the file.

Listing 19.14   CRS program variables

```
#include "signature.h"          Entire paring-friendly curve
#include "snarkbase.h"          list of subroutines
int main(int argc, char *argv[])
{
  FILE *qap, *crs;
  mpz_t *list;
  int i, j, k, m, n, *sw, l;
  mpz_t *htable;
  mpz_t *vj, *wj, *yj;
  mpz_t alpha, beta, gamma, delta, z;
  mpz_t *zpow, *theta, tmp, tdlta;         Variable names
  SIG_SYSTEM sig;                          similar to
  POINT aG, bG, dG, zG[5], thtaG[10], ztG[4];   mathematical
  POLY_POINT bH, gH, dH, zH[5];            descriptions
  mpz_t r, s;
  POINT A, C, Tmp, V;
  POLY_POINT B, P, R;
  POLY eab, eVH, eCH, eAB;

  get_system("curve_11_parameters.bin", &sig);   Read in pairing-friendly curve.

  minit(sig.tor);        Set initial modulus to torsion value.

  qap = fopen("snark.qap", "r");
  if(!qap)
  {
    printf("can't find file snark.qap\n");
    exit(-2);
  }
  fread(&n, sizeof(int), 1, qap);       Read in number of gates
  fread(&m, sizeof(int), 1, qap);       and number of lines in QAP.
  sw = (int*)malloc(sizeof(int)*m);
  fread(sw, sizeof(int), m, qap);
  list = (mpz_t*)malloc(sizeof(mpz_t)*n);
  fread(&l, sizeof(int), 1, qap);
  for(i=0; i<n; i++)
  {
    mpz_init(list[i]);
    mpz_inp_raw(list[i], qap);
  }
  k = n*m;
  vj = (mpz_t*)malloc(sizeof(mpz_t)*k);
  wj = (mpz_t*)malloc(sizeof(mpz_t)*k);    Create space for all variables.
  yj = (mpz_t*)malloc(sizeof(mpz_t)*k);
```

```
for(i=0; i<k; i++)
{
  mpz_init(vj[i]);
  mpz_inp_raw(vj[i], qap);
}
for(i=0; i<k; i++)
{
  mpz_init(wj[i]);                    | Initialize all variables . . .
  mpz_inp_raw(wj[i], qap);
}
for(i=0; i<k; i++)
{
  mpz_init(yj[i]);
  mpz_inp_raw(yj[i], qap);     | . . . then read in data from file.
}
j = n - 1;
k = n*j*j/2;
htable = (mpz_t*)malloc(sizeof(mpz_t)*k);
for(i=0; i<k; i++)
{
  mpz_init(htable[i]);           | Same for cross terms
  mpz_inp_raw(htable[i], qap);   | table, which is huge
}
fclose(qap);
```

To begin creating the CRS, a set of random values is chosen which are within the size of the torsion value of the base points. An example is shown in the following listing, where the variable names follow the convention in equation 19.12.

Listing 19.15   Creating toxic variable values

```
mpz_inits(alpha, beta, gamma, delta, z, tmp, NULL);
mrand(alpha);
mrand(beta);          | Toxic waste variables
mrand(gamma);         | modulo torsion size
mrand(delta);
mrand(z);
```

With the value of z chosen, the next set of toxic waste are the powers of z^i for the number of gates. The maximum power of z is $n - 1$.

Listing 19.16   Generating powers of z^i

```
zpow = (mpz_t*)malloc(sizeof(mpz_t)*n);  | Create space for n values.
for(i=0; i<n; i++)
  mpz_init(zpow[i]);            | Initialize all elements.
mpz_set_ui(zpow[0], 1);    ← The first element is z⁰ = 1.
for(i=1; i<n; i++)                        | Every element is
  mmul(zpow[i], zpow[i - 1], z);  | z times previous.
```

With the powers of z and the inputs for the QAP coefficients, the values of θ_i can be computed as in equation 19.11. This is shown in listing 19.17. The value of j was set in listing 19.14 to be $n - 1$.

Listing 19.17 Computing hidden values θ_i

```
theta = (mpz_t*)malloc(sizeof(mpz_t)*m);
for(i=0; i<m; i++)
  mpz_init(theta[i]);

for(i=0; i<m; i++)
{
  lcalc(tmp, z, &vj[i*n], j);        |j = n - 1
  mmul(theta[i], tmp, beta);         |β * v_i
  lcalc(tmp, z, &wj[i*n], j);
  mmul(tmp, tmp, alpha);
  madd(theta[i], theta[i], tmp);     |+ α * w_i
  lcalc(tmp, z, &yj[i*n], j);
  mmul(tmp, tmp, tmp);
  madd(theta[i], theta[i], tmp);     |+ y_i²
}
```

The θ_is are split into two groups. The statement values are divided by γ, and the witness values are divided by δ, as seen in equations 19.14 and 19.15. The value l determines the split point. The following listing finalizes these values for the CRS.

Listing 19.18 Final θ_i and $t(z)/\delta$ calculation

```
for(i=0; i<=l; i++)
  mdiv(theta[sw[i]], theta[sw[i]], gamma);  |l is split point for statement.
for(i=l+1; i<m; i++)
  mdiv(theta[sw[i]], theta[sw[i]], delta);  |Remaining values are witness.

mpz_init(tdlta);
tofzgrth(tmp, z, list, n);                   |Compute t(z)/δ.
mdiv(tdlta, tmp, delta);
```

All the computations in listings 19.1 to 19.18 are done in the exponent, which means they use the modulus of the torsion value of the curve. To use the values as multipliers of points on the elliptic curve, I need to flip the modulus from sig.tor to sig.prime. Then the irreducible polynomial field can be initialized as well. I added the routine mset(prm) to the modulus.c file, which just copies prm to the static modulus variable without attempting to re-initialize it. The following listing shows switching to elliptic curve mode and the calculation of three points: αG, βG, and δG.

Listing 19.19 Elliptic curve point calculations

```
mset(sig.prime);          |Switch back to
poly_irrd_set(sig.irrd);  |elliptic curve parameters.
poly_mulprep(sig.irrd);
```

```
point_init(&aG);
elptic_mul(&aG, sig.G1, alpha, sig.E);    |αG
point_init(&bG);
elptic_mul(&bG, sig.G1, beta, sig.E);     |βG
point_init(&dG);
elptic_mul(&dG, sig.G1, delta, sig.E);    |δG
```

Listing 19.20 has the loops that create the powers of z^i in the CRS list of points (equation 19.12). There are gate number n of points $z^i G$, QAP line number m of points $\theta_i G$, and $n-1$ points $z^i t(z)/\delta\, G$. Between listing 19.19 and 19.20, these are all the G_1 points in the CRS.

Listing 19.20 Vector points on G_1 in CRS

```
for(i=0; i<n; i++)
{
  point_init(&zG[i]);                 |Create z^i G points.
  elptic_mul(&zG[i], sig.G1, zpow[i], sig.E);
}

for(i=0; i<m; i++)
{
  point_init(&thtaG[i]);              |Create θ_i G points.
  elptic_mul(&thtaG[i], sig.G1, theta[i], sig.E);
}

point_init(&ztG[0]);
elptic_mul(&ztG[0], sig.G1, tdlta, sig.E);   |First compute t(z)/δ G.
j = n - 1;
for(i=1; i<j; i++)
{
  point_init(&ztG[i]);               |Create z^i t(z)/δ G points.
  elptic_mul(&ztG[i], ztG[i-1], z, sig.E);
}
```

Listing 19.21 shows the computations for G_2 points that go into the CRS. There are the three single points βH, γH, and δH, along with the gate number of $z^i H$ points.

Listing 19.21 Calculation of G_2 CRS points

```
poly_point_init(&bH);
poly_elptic_mul(&bH, sig.G2, beta, sig.Ex);    |βH
poly_point_init(&gH);
poly_elptic_mul(&gH, sig.G2, gamma, sig.Ex);   |γH
poly_point_init(&dH);
poly_elptic_mul(&dH, sig.G2, delta, sig.Ex);   |δH
for(i=0; i<n; i++)
{
  poly_point_init(&zH[i]);                      |z^i H
  poly_elptic_mul(&zH[i], sig.G2, zpow[i], sig.Ex);
}
```

Listing 19.22 shows the writing of CRS values to a file. This only has to be done once for a particular QAP. All the random values and intermediate values computed with them should be destroyed and lost forever. This is an area of ongoing research to deal with this as a leakage point for security. Understanding the purpose of the CRS and how it is used helps with updated versions of this process.

> **Listing 19.22   Saving CRS data to file**

```
crs = fopen("snark.crs", "w");
fwrite(&n, sizeof(int), 1, crs);
fwrite(&m, sizeof(int), 1, crs);       Same data as QAP
fwrite(&l, sizeof(int), 1, crs);
point_write(&aG, crs);
point_write(&bG, crs);                 Save single G1 points.
point_write(&dG, crs);
for(i=0; i<n; i++)
point_write(&zG[i], crs);
for(i=0; i<m; i++)
  point_write(&thtaG[sw[i]], crs);     Save multiple
j = n - 1;                             G1 points.
for(i=0; i<j; i++)
  point_write(&ztG[i], crs);

poly_point_write(&bH, crs);
poly_point_write(&dH, crs);            Save single G2 points.
poly_point_write(&gH, crs);
for(i=0; i<n; i++)                     Save multiple
  poly_point_write(&zH[i], crs);       G2 points.
fclose(crs);
```

19.5.4 *Creating the proof for a record*

In this section, a program to generate a record that contains a proof of knowledge is described. The example code described here is very contrived to get the idea across of how to compute the proof parameters for a single record. Figure 19.10 gives a schematic idea of how a record is converted into values used in the QAP. The statement values are public, so I am going to take the variable a_1 to be the medicine number and a_2 as the dose in picograms. Looking at figure 19.2, we see that both a_1 and a_2 directly affect a_5 and a_7. So these values must also be public. The variables a_0, a_1, a_2, a_5, and a_7 are thus the statement, and the remaining variables are the witness and depend on the patient number. This reordering is installed in the variable sw[] to permute the order so indexes 0 to l are the statement as required by the CRS.

The program snark_proof.c inputs the QAP parameters, the CRS values, and the pairing-friendly curve parameters. Using chosen values for the statement and witness, the program uses two subroutines to compute the remaining wire values in the QAP as well as the coefficients in the cross terms. These are formulas in equations 19.1 and table 19.2.

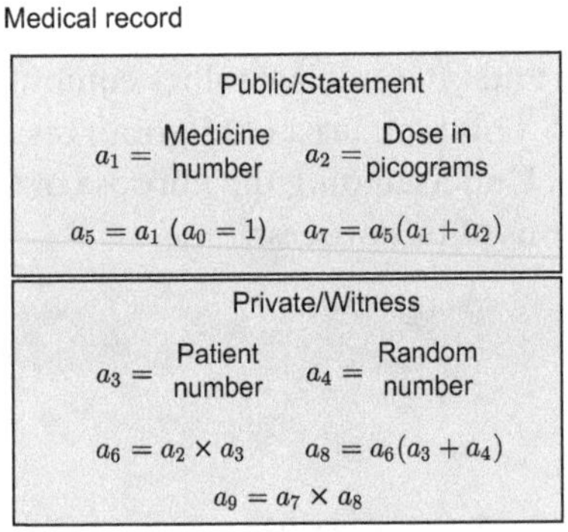

Medical record

Public/Statement		
$a_1 = $ Medicine number	$a_2 = $ Dose in picograms	
$a_5 = a_1 \ (a_0 = 1)$	$a_7 = a_5(a_1 + a_2)$	

Private/Witness		
$a_3 = $ Patient number	$a_4 = $ Random number	
$a_6 = a_2 \times a_3$	$a_8 = a_6(a_3 + a_4)$	
$a_9 = a_7 \times a_8$		

Figure 19.10   Assignment of values for each record in QAP example

Using the `matflat()` routine from snarkbase.c, the proof combines the computed function coefficients with the QAP parameters to multiply the CRS points to create points A, B, and C as in equations 19.13 and 19.14. The statement data and points are then saved to a file. This represents a single record in a SNARK-style proof. One would expect hundreds to thousands of these records in a real system.

The subroutine in listing 19.23 takes the three record values a_1, a_2, and a_3 to create all m line values using equation 19.1. The output is a vector for use in all other subroutines that require a_i values.

Listing 19.23   Computing line values for QAP

```
void wires(mpz_t *aj, mpz_t a1, mpz_t a2, mpz_t a3)
{
  mpz_t tmp;

  mpz_set(aj[1], a1);
  mpz_set(aj[2], a2);            Copy inputs to
  mpz_set(aj[3], a3);           corresponding locations.
  mpz_set_ui(aj[0], 1);    ← Set a₀ to 1.
  mpz_set(aj[5], a1);       a₄ is a random number
  mrand(aj[4]);             to hide witness.
  mmul(aj[6], a2, a3);         a₆ = a₂ · a₃
  mpz_init_set(tmp, a1);
  madd(tmp, tmp, a2);
  mmul(aj[7], tmp, a1);        a₇ = (a₁ + a₂)a₅
  mpz_set(tmp, a3);
  madd(tmp, tmp, aj[4]);
  mmul(aj[8], tmp, aj[6]);     a₈ = (a₃ + a₄)a₆
  mmul(aj[9], aj[8], aj[7]);   a₉ = a₇ · a₈
  mpz_clear(tmp);
}
```

With the vector of a_j from the `wires()` routine, the cross terms from table 19.2 can be computed. Listing 19.24 shows this subroutine. This is specific to the QAP, so it should be public. Only provers have access to all the values, but the cross term coefficient calculations are public. This is why I added a random value for a_4 to ensure any leaked information from the higher-level lines could not be used to determine the patient number.

> **Listing 19.24** Computing $l_i(z)l_j(z)$ **cross term coefficients**

```
void crossterms(mpz_t *crscoef, mpz_t *a)
{
  mpz_t t0, t1, t2, t3, t4, t5;

  mpz_inits(t0, t1, t2, t3, t4, t5, NULL);
  mmul(t1, a[1], a[2]);
  mmul(t2, a[0], a[3]);                    l0l1 : a1 · a2 + a0 · a3
  madd(crscoef[0], t1, t2);
  madd(t0, a[1], a[2]);
  mmul(t1, t0, a[0]);
  mmul(t2, a[1], a[5]);                    l0l2 : (a1 + a2)a0 + a1 · a5
  madd(crscoef[1], t1, t2);
  madd(t1, a[3], a[4]);
  mmul(t2, t1, a[0]);
  mmul(t3, a[1], a[6]);                    l0l3 : (a3 + a4)a0 + a1 · a6
  madd(crscoef[2], t2, t3);
  mmul(t4, a[0], a[8]);
  mmul(t5, a[1], a[7]);                    l0l4 : a0 · a8 + a1 · a7
  madd(crscoef[3], t4, t5);
  mmul(t2, t0, a[2]);
  mmul(t3, a[3], a[5]);                    l1l2 : (a1 + a2)a2 + a3 · a5
  madd(crscoef[4], t2, t3);
  mmul(t2, t1, a[2]);
  mmul(t3, a[3], a[6]);                    l1l3 : (a3 + a4)a2 + a3 · a6
  madd(crscoef[5], t2, t3);
  mmul(t4, a[3], a[7]);
  mmul(t5, a[2], a[8]);                    l1l4 : a3 · a7 + a2 · a8
  madd(crscoef[6], t4, t5);
  mmul(t3, t0, a[6]);
  mmul(t4, t1, a[5]);                      l2l3 : (a3 + a4)a5 + (a1 + a2)a6
  madd(crscoef[7], t3, t4);
  mmul(t2, t0, a[7]);
  mmul(t3, a[5], a[8]);                    l2l4 : (a1 + a2)a7 + a5 · a8
  madd(crscoef[8], t2, t3);
  mmul(t2, t1, a[7]);
  mmul(t3, a[6], a[8]);                    l3l4 : (a3 + a4)a7 + a6 · a8
  madd(crscoef[9], t2, t3);
  mpz_clears(t0, t1, t2, t3, t4, t5, NULL);
}
```

The snark_proof.c program starts out with a list of variables that includes the QAP file and CRS file. The record data is created within the program because this is just an example. The following listing shows the variables and initialization of the pairing-friendly curve.

Listing 19.25   Proof program initialization

```
int main(int argc, char *argv[])
{
  FILE *qap, *crs;
  mpz_t *list, *coef;
  int i, j, k, m, n, l, *sw;
  mpz_t *htable, *hxcoef;
  mpz_t *vj, *wj, *yj, *aj;
  SIG_SYSTEM sig;
  POINT aG, bG, dG, *zG, *thtaG, *ztG;    Same variables
  POLY_POINT bH, gH, dH, *zH;             as CRS with additional
  mpz_t *av, *aw, r, s;                    points for proof
  POINT A, C, Tmp, V;
  POLY_POINT B, P, R;

  get_system("curve_11_parameters.bin", &sig);
  minit(sig.prime);               Sets up pairing-friendly
  poly_irrd_set(sig.irrd);        curve parameters
  poly_mulprep(sig.irrd);
```

The QAP data is read in exactly the same as in listing 19.14. The CRS data is read in similarly, as shown in listing 19.26. Every point is initialized before being read in. Space for vectors of points is created before the loop that reads in each point.

Listing 19.26   Reading in CRS file data

```
  crs = fopen("snark.crs", "r");
  fread(&n, sizeof(int), 1, crs);
  fread(&m, sizeof(int), 1, crs);    Same values from QAP
  fread(&l, sizeof(int), 1, crs);    are overwritten.
  point_init(&aG);
  point_init(&bG);
  point_init(&dG);            Read in $G_1$
  point_read(&aG, crs);       single points.
  point_read(&bG, crs);
  point_read(&dG, crs);
  zG = (POINT*)malloc(sizeof(POINT)*n);
  for(i=0; i<n; i++)
  {
    point_init(&zG[i]);       Read in $z^i G$ points.
    point_read(&zG[i], crs);
  }
  thtaG = (POINT*)malloc(sizeof(POINT)*m);
  for(i=0; i<m; i++)
  {
    point_init(&thtaG[i]);    Read in $\theta_i G$ points.
    point_read(&thtaG[i], crs);
  }
  j = n - 1;
```

```
ztG = (POINT*)malloc(sizeof(POINT)*j);
for(i=0; i<j; i++)
{
  point_init(&ztG[i]);                      | Read in z^i t(x)/δ G points.
  point_read(&ztG[i], crs);
}
poly_point_init(&bH);
poly_point_read(&bH, crs);
poly_point_init(&dH);
poly_point_read(&dH, crs);                   | Read in G_2
poly_point_init(&gH);                        | single points.
poly_point_read(&gH, crs);
zH = (POLY_POINT*)malloc(sizeof(POLY_POINT)*n);
for(i=0; i<n; i++)
{
  poly_point_init(&zH[i]);                    | Read in z^i H points.
  poly_point_read(&zH[i], crs);
}
fclose(crs);
```

To compute the coefficients for the cross terms as well as the wire values, I flip back to the torsion prime for the modulus in the modulo.c file. Listing 19.27 shows the execution of these steps. Once the cross term coefficients are computed, they are combined with the $l_i(x)l_j(x)$ matrix, which was called `htable[]` in the QAP file. The final vector is called `hxcoef[]`, which are the $h(z)$ coefficients.

Listing 19.27 Computing QAP wire values and $h(z)$ cross term coefficients

```
mset(sig.tor);                | Back to torsion value
aj = (mpz_t*)malloc(sizeof(mpz_t)*m);
for(i=0; i<m; i++)
  mpz_init(aj[i]);
mpz_set_ui(aj[1], 2036);       | Medicine number
mpz_set_ui(aj[2], 1700000);    | Dose in picograms
mpz_set_ui(aj[3], 49);         | Patient number
wires(aj, aj[1], aj[2], aj[3]);  | Compute all wire values.

coef = (mpz_t*)malloc(sizeof(mpz_t)*m);
for(i=0; i<m; i++)            | Create vector
  mpz_init(coef[i]);         | for all cross term
crossterms(coef, aj);        | coefficients.
hxcoef = (mpz_t*)malloc(sizeof(mpz_t)*j);
for(i=0; i<j; i++)                | Multiply cross term
  mpz_init(hxcoef[i]);           | coefficients with
matflat(hxcoef, htable, j, coef, m);  | h(x) table.

mpz_inits(r, s, NULL);           | Get random values
rand_rs_get(r, s, sig.tor);      | modulo the torsion size.
```

I also have a subroutine to pull random values r and s from a file I downloaded from www.random.org. These values should change for every record to ensure zero knowledge is maintained for all records.

To compute points A and B, the prover must first compute the sum of left and right QAP functions times the wire values. As with the $h(x)$ coefficients, the tables created in the QAP program for $v_i(x)$ and $w_i(x)$ need to be flattened after multiplication by the a_j vector. This is the same process as shown in figure 19.9; the code is shown in the following listing.

Listing 19.28   Sums over $a_j \cdot v_j$ and $a_j \cdot w_j$

```
av = (mpz_t*)malloc(sizeof(mpz_t)*n);      │ Create space
aw = (mpz_t*)malloc(sizeof(mpz_t)*n);      │ for vectors.
for(j=0; j<n; j++)
{
  mpz_init(av[j]);                         │ Initialize vectors.
  mpz_init(aw[j]);
}
matflat(av, vj, n, aj, m);                 │ Multiply each row
matflat(aw, wj, n, aj, m);                 │ and sum each column.
```

With all the preparations finished, we can now compute the three points A, B, and C, which are the zero-knowledge proofs for the record. Listing 19.29 shows code to accomplish all of equation 19.13. The coefficient tables are in decreasing power order, but the points in the CRS are in increasing power order. The indexing for the points is backward because I loop in coefficient order.

Listing 19.29   Computing proof points A and B

```
mset(sig.prime);                   ┌ Switch back to
point_init(&A);                    │ field prime modulus.
point_init(&Tmp);
point_copy(&A, aG);                │ Start with αG.
j = n - 1;        ← Backward indexing starts at n − 1
for(i=0; i<n; i++)                 │ zⁱ powers backward
{                                  │ from coefficients.
  elptic_mul(&Tmp, zG[j - i], av[i], sig.E);   │ Multiply ∑ aⱼvⱼ coefficients
  elptic_sum(&A, A, Tmp, sig.E);               │ with zⁱG points.
}
elptic_mul(&Tmp, dG, r, sig.E);
elptic_sum(&A, A, Tmp, sig.E);     │ Add in δG times r.
point_printf("A: ", A);

poly_point_init(&B);
poly_point_init(&P);               │ Initialize G₂ variables
poly_point_copy(&B, bH);           │ Starts with βH.
for(i=0; i<n; i++)
{
  poly_elptic_mul(&P, zH[j - i], aw[i], sig.Ex);   │ Multiply ∑ aⱼwⱼ coefficients
  poly_elptic_sum(&B, B, P, sig.Ex);               │ with zⁱH points.
}
poly_elptic_mul(&P, dH, s, sig.Ex);
poly_elptic_sum(&B, B, P, sig.Ex);     │ Add in δH times s.
poly_point_printf("B: ", B);
```

Listing 19.30 shows the calculation of equation 19.14. The first step is to duplicate the $\sum a_j w_j$ for B but do it on the G_1 curve. This is then multiplied by r. The next value is to multiply point A by s and add that into C. The sum of $l+1$ to m of $a_i \theta_i G$ is computed and also added to C. Finally, $h(z) \cdot z^i t(z)/\delta G$ is summed over all coefficients and added to C.

Listing 19.30 Computing proof point C

```
point_init(&C);
point_copy(&C, bG);              | Start with βG.
for(i=0; i<n; i++)               | z^i powers backward
{                                | from coefficients.

  elptic_mul(&Tmp, zG[j - i], aw[i], sig.E);   | Multiply ∑ a_j w_j coefficients
  elptic_sum(&C, C, Tmp, sig.E);               | with z^i G points.
}
elptic_mul(&C, C, r, sig.E);     | Finish with r(βG + ∑ a_j w_j G).

point_copy(&Tmp, A);
elptic_mul(&Tmp, Tmp, s, sig.E); | Add in sA ...
elptic_sum(&C, C, Tmp, sig.E);

for(i=l+1; i<m; i++)
{
  elptic_mul(&Tmp, thtaG[i], aj[sw[i]], sig.E);  | ... then add in ∑ a_i θ_i G
  elptic_sum(&C, C, Tmp, sig.E);                 | for witness only values.
}
j = n - 1;                       | h(z) has degree n - 1
for(i=0; i<j; i++)               | Backward from j - 1
{
  elptic_mul(&Tmp, ztG[j - 1 - i], hxcoef[i], sig.E);
  elptic_sum(&C, C, Tmp, sig.E);                 | Finally, add in h(z)t(z)/δ G.
}
point_printf("C: ", C);
```

With the proof points finished, the record can be saved to a file. Listing 19.31 shows how I saved this example. The statement values are saved but not the witness values. In a real system, the witness values would be saved in some encrypted form where the prover has access to them but no one else does. The points A and C are saved first, followed by B, and the proof process is finished (other than cleaning up the stack).

Listing 19.31 Saving proof points to file

```
qap = fopen("snark_record.0", "w");
fwrite(&n, sizeof(int), 1, qap);
fwrite(&m, sizeof(int), 1, qap);    | Same data as QAP, CRS
fwrite(&l, sizeof(int), 1, qap);
for(i=0; i<=l; i++)
  mpz_out_raw(qap, aj[sw[i]]);      | Only save statement values.
point_write(&A, qap);
```

```
point_write(&C, qap);              | G₁ points first
poly_point_write(&B, qap);         | G₂ points last
fclose(qap);
```

19.5.5 *Zero-knowledge verification of a record*

In this section, the verification code to check a proof of knowledge record is described. The last step in a zk-SNARK process is verification. The program snark_verify.c reads in the CRS data along with the record file and computes equation 19.16 using Tate pairings. The following listing shows the standard opening similar to the three previous programs with similar variable names.

Listing 19.32   SNARK verify program startup

```
#include "signature.h"
#include "snarkbase.h"

int main(int argc, char *argv[])
{
  FILE *crs, *qap;
  int i, j, k, m, n, l;
  mpz_t *aj;
  SIG_SYSTEM sig;
  POINT aG, bG, dG, *zG, *thtaG, *ztG;
  POLY_POINT bH, gH, dH, *zH;          | Variables from CRS
  POINT A, C, Tmp, V;                  | Variables from proof record
  POLY_POINT B, P, R;
  POLY eab, eVH, eCH, eAB;             | Computed pairings

  get_system("curve_11_parameters.bin", &sig);
  minit(sig.prime);
  poly_irrd_set(sig.irrd);             | Read in paring-friendly
  poly_mulprep(sig.irrd);              | curve parameters.
```

The CRS data is read in exactly the same as in listing 19.26. Then the record data is read in as shown in listing 19.33. As with all previous imports, the GMP variables are allocated and then initialized.

Listing 19.33   Importing record data for proof

```
qap = fopen("snark_record.0", "r");
fread(&n, sizeof(int), 1, qap);
fread(&m, sizeof(int), 1, qap);          | Duplicate of QAP data
fread(&l, sizeof(int), 1, qap);
aj = (mpz_t*)malloc(sizeof(mpz_t)*(l+1));
for(i=0; i<=l; i++)
{
  mpz_init(aj[i]);                       | Input only statement
  mpz_inp_raw(aj[i], qap);               | number of line values.
}
```

```
point_init(&A);
point_read(&A, qap);
point_init(&C);
point_read(&C, qap);          Input two G₁ points
poly_point_init(&B);          and one G₂ point.
poly_point_read(&B, qap);
fclose(qap);
```

The verify point V from equation 19.15 is then computed using the statement a_j values from the record with the CRS values for $\dfrac{\theta_i}{\gamma} G$. This is shown in the following listing.

Listing 19.34   Computing point V for verification

```
point_init(&V);
for(i=0; i<=1; i++)   ← Include only statements from record.
{
  elptic_mul(&Tmp, thtaG[i], aj[i], sig.E);   Multiply aᵢ with point
  elptic_sum(&V, V, Tmp, sig.E);              θᵢG and sum into V.
}
```

The Tate pairing calculations of equation 19.16 are shown in listing 19.35. The first requirement is a reference point not related to any of the inputs. A random point has an exceptionally high probability on a large field of accomplishing no relationship.

Listing 19.35   Tate pairing computations for verification

```
poly_point_init(&R);                        Select random point
poly_point_rand(&R, sig.Ex);                on G₂ for reference.
poly_init(&eab);
poly_point_init(&P);
tog2(&P, aG);                      Move αG to G₂.
tate(&eab, P, bH, R, sig.tor, sig.Ex);   Compute τ(αG, βH).

poly_init(&eVH);
tog2(&P, V);                       Move V to G₂.
tate(&eVH, P, gH, R, sig.tor, sig.Ex);   Compute τ(V, γH).

poly_init(&eCH);
tog2(&P, C);                       Move C to G₂.
tate(&eCH, P, dH, R, sig.tor, sig.Ex);   Compute τ(C, δH).

poly_init(&eAB);
tog2(&P, A);                       Move A to G₂.
tate(&eAB, P, B, R, sig.tor, sig.Ex);    Compute τ(A, B).

poly_mul(&eab, eab, eVH);                   Multiply
poly_mul(&eab, eab, eCH);                   τ(αG, βH)·τ(V, γH)·τ(C, δH).

if(poly_cmp(eab, eAB))                 If multiplication equals
  printf("Record verifies!\n");        proof, then all is well.
else
  printf("Record falsified!\n");
```

The Tate pairing subroutine requires both points to be on G_2. The subroutine `tog2()` described in section 18.3.4 converts a G_1 point from field prime structure to polynomial structure. This is done for all four pairings. The proof is then verified by multiplication of the first three components and comparing with the proof points pairing $\tau(A, B)$.

Using the QAP example shown in this chapter along with the input values from listing 19.27, the four programs write out and read in the QAP, CRS, and record data to report `Record verifies!`

Let's end this book with a quote from Lewis Carroll (Carroll, 2010):

> They hunted till darkness came on, but they found
> > Not a button, or feather, or mark
> By which they could tell that they stood on the ground
> > Where the Baker had met with the Snark.
> In the midst of the word he was trying to say
> > In the midst of his laughter and glee,
> He had softly and suddenly vanished away –
> > For the Snark *was* a Boojum, you see.

Answers to exercises

1 Most function values are zero because a line value can only come out of one gate. A line value can only go into a gate on the right or left once per gate.

2 We can write down the output, left, and right functions directly from the QAP:

$$y_4 = l_0^2 \qquad v_0 = l_0 \qquad w_1 = l_0$$
$$y_5 = l_1^2 \qquad v_2 = l_1 \qquad w_3 = l_1$$
$$y_6 = l_2^2 \qquad v_4 = l_2 \qquad w_5 = l_2$$

And all other functions are zero.

We have $\sum a_i v_i = a_0 l_0 + a_2 l_1 + a_4 l_2$ and $\sum a_i w_i = a_1 l_0 + a_3 l_1 + a_5 l_2$. We then multiply these together

$$(a_0 l_0 + a_2 l_1 + a_4 l_2)(a_1 l_0 + a_3 l_1 + a_5 l_2) = a_4 l_0^2 + a_5 l_1^2 + a_6 l_2^2 + t(x) h(x)$$

to get on the left-hand side:

$$a_0 a_1 l_0^2 + a_0 a_3 l_0 l_1 + a_0 a_5 l_0 l_2$$
$$+ a_2 a_1 l_1 l_0 + a_2 a_3 l_1^2 + a_2 a_5 l_1 l_2$$
$$+ a_4 a_1 l_2 l_0 + a_4 a_3 l_2 l_1 + a_4 a_5 l_2^2$$

Because of the QAP equations, the squared terms cancel, and we have

$$t(x)h(x) = a_0 a_3 l_0 l_1 + a_0 a_5 l_0 l_2 + a_2 a_1 l_1 l_0 + a_2 a_5 l_1 l_2 + a_4 a_1 l_2 l_0 + a_4 a_3 l_2 l_1$$

3 On the top, $\Sigma v \times \beta$ to $\beta \Sigma v$, $\Sigma v \times \Sigma w$ to $\Sigma v \Sigma w$, $r \times \beta$ to βr, and $r \times \Sigma w$ to $r \Sigma w$. On the bottom, $s\alpha$ to αs and $r\beta$ to βr.

Summary

- A zero-knowledge proof convinces a verifier that a prover knows a secret without divulging the secret. This is useful in financial and medical environments where amounts or ailments are not an issue for access to private information.
- Ali Baba's cave is an interactive zero-knowledge proof. The first zero-knowledge cryptographic algorithms were interactive.
- Succinct noninteractive arguments of knowledge (SNARKs) are a noninteractive proof of knowledge. This eliminates the communication problems associated with interactive proofs.
- A quadratic arithmetic program (QAP) consists of sums and multiplications, with each multiply being a gate. It forms the basis for a noninteractive proof of knowledge.
- Each gate in a QAP is represented as a unique prime in the torsion field of a pairing-friendly curve. The unique prime allows the construction of functions which replicate the gate equation when a prime for that gate is the input to the QAP.
- Left, right, and output functions to each gate are Lagrange interpolant functions, which are 1 at a specific gate and 0 at all other gates. Every equation of the QAP can then be verified as having correct inputs or rejected by not being equal as required by the QAP.
- Inputs and outputs to gates are called wires. They must have values modulo the torsion field size. The values are specific for each record being verified.
- Output functions are squared to match the input left and right multiples to form the QAP. The QAP will not verify without this difference between inputs and outputs.
- The cross terms $h(x)$ are formed by removing all squared terms in the fundamental QAP formula:

$$h(x)t(x) = \sum_{i=1}^{m} a_i v_i(x) \cdot \sum_{i=0}^{m} a_i w_i(x) - \sum_{i=0}^{m} a_i y_i(x)$$

- $t(x)$ is the product

$$t(x) = \prod_{j=0}^{n-1} (x - r_j)$$

where r_j are the primes for each gate.
- To compute a proof, all Lagrange functions are multiplied out to find the coefficients of each power x^i. This reduces the size of the common reference string (CRS).
- The CRS is created with random values which must be lost. These are called toxic waste in the literature. An adversary could create a proof using arbitrary inputs if these values became known.

- Public wires are called statement variables, and secret wires are called witness variables. The verifier only knows public information. The prover knows both public and secret information. The proof of knowledge will fail if any of the values do not satisfy the QAP formulas. This is why the verifier can trust the prover does know all the information.
- The prover knows both statement and witness values. The prover creates a proof for a statement using these values with the CRS. The prover also uses two random values to prevent information from leaking through multiple records. In this way, every record is a unique proof.
- The verifier only knows the statement values. The verifier uses the CRS and proof points to verify or reject a proof. The verifier's task is much easier than the prover's task because they only compute four pairing values for each record. The difference in difficulty is the essence of the SNARK concept to help ensure security.
- A SNARK *is* a Boojum!!

appendix A
Code and tools

This appendix tells you where to find the GNU Multiple Precision Arithmetic Library and how to compile it on a Linux system. I'll describe how to install the PARI/gp interactive tool and library from the source. The compilation from the source of the library KangarooTwelve is also covered.

A.1 GNU Multiple Precision Arithmetic Library

The whole point of elliptic curve cryptography is to use numbers that are too large to solve the logarithm problem in a reasonable amount of time. As pointed out in the preface to the book, we require 160-bit numbers for an 80-bit level of security. With 8 bits to a byte, that's 20 bytes. Since a long, long type in C is 64 bits or 8 bytes it is too short for what we want. And at the 512-bit level size of number, we require 64 bytes for each number.

Handling this level of problem requires a lot of work. Fortunately, we can use a multibyte numerical library that already has the low-level crunching done for us. While there are many such libraries available, I chose the GNU Multiple Precision Arithmetic Library (GMP library) because (a) it is free and (b) it is updated on a regular basis.

You can get the latest GMP library on its home website at https://gmplib.org/. There is an online HTML version of the documentation as well as a PDF version you can download. To get the latest version, on the right-hand side of the page, you can just click the first link to the right of Download or scroll down a bit to the Download section, where you have a choice of Compression or Location. Once you pick a version, you can unpack it with the command

```
tar xf gmp-x.y.z.tar.*
```

where * is one of `gz`, `lz`, or `zst`. Then switch to the directory that was unpacked

```
cd gmp-x.y.z
```

For all Linux systems, the fastest install method is standard:

```
./configure
make
sudo make install
```

You can also run

```
make check
```

to double check all the subroutines were compiled correctly.

As with all large projects, GMP has a huge number of options. Look in chapter 2 of the GMP documentation for "Build Options" and "Notes for Particular Systems." On my system (Ubuntu 18.04), the default compilation worked fine.

Once the GMP library is installed, the subroutines are found in the header:

```
#include <gmp.h>
```

The `#include` first appears in listing 2.1 for finite field math in chapter 2.

Most of you are probably wizards with makefiles. I am not. I prefer brute-force listing of each program. For example

```
test_mod: test_mod.c modulo.o poly.o
          gcc -o test_mod test_mod.c modulo.o poly.o -lgmp
```

This assumes `#include <gmp.h>` is included in each of the `*.c` files, and the linker knows where to find the `libgmp.a` in the system directory. On my system, it is located in `/usr/local/lib`.

The GMP library has a lot of advantages for embedded systems developers. For the low-level routines, you have a choice of the standard API calls or the "secure" API calls. The idea behind the secure versions is to run in constant time independently of the inputs. Obviously, these are slower than the standard calls. Since an embedded system can be monitored by an adversary while it is running, using the secure version makes it much harder for them to determine what inputs are being used in each different section of code.

This monitoring is called a "side channel attack." By looking at the power consumption of a device, it is possible to learn what sections of a processor are running and which chunk of code is running (see Kocher, 1996). For Internet of Things devices, power is a critical problem, and that might override the security issues. Power use, timing, and security are system-level choices. As you implement your system, make sure you think about other constraints. Make it work first and then modify what works to have better survivability in the real world.

A.2   *PARI/gp*

PARI is a mathematical library, and gp is a command-line interface to the library. We link to PARIlib; we run gp from a terminal. Mathematicians use both because programming in C and making API calls is sometimes easier than programming in gp. While the library is very sophisticated, we only need a few things in this book that are specific to the elliptic curve problem over finite fields.

You can get a copy of PARI from https://PARI.math.u-bordeaux.fr/. It is free software and maintained by mathematicians all over the world. The French government helps support it through CNRS (https://www.cnrs.fr/en) and INRA (https://www.inria.fr/en). PARI has been available since 1983, so it is really well debugged.

The main use of PARIlib and often gp is to check our programming in C using GMP calls. I *know* PARI/gp is right, and if I don't get the same answer with my code, I have a bug to find.

The manuals for PARI can be found at https://PARI.math.u-bordeaux.fr/doc .html. The installation guide is found in both its own document and in the User's Guide. As usual for Linux-type systems, it is very easy to install. First, download the latest version and unpack it:

```
tar xf PARI_x.yy.z.tar.gz
```

Next, switch to the directory that was unpacked:

```
cd PARI_x.yy.z
```

To accept all defaults, simply type

```
./Configure
```

and finally compile and install the whole library and calculator:

```
sudo make install
```

After waiting a while, the compilation and install will finish, at which point just type gp. You should see

```
GP/PARI CALCULATOR Version x.yy.z (released)
```

so the tool is ready to use.

When we use the PARIlib API calls, we have to include the standard header for PARI:

```
#include <PARI/PARI.h>
```

The makefile for PARIlib is copied from `PARI_x.yy.z/examples/Makefile`. This will link in the proper libraries (math and PARI) as dynamically loadable. This default configuration works every time for me, but if you have problems, you can also force static linking.

Inside the makefile we find these lines:

```
# change this TARGET to compile your own programs
TARGET = extgcd
```

So copy the examples/Makefile to your own working directory, create your C file that will include the PARI.h, edit the TARGET line in Makefile, and type make. Your API calls to PARIlib will be linked in, and you will have your own special mathematics calculator. We put this to work in chapter 7.

A.3   *Building KangarooTwelve library*

KangarooTwelve unpacks into a directory called K12-master, but I prefer to create a directory so the zip file is separated from all my other files. I issued the command

```
mkdir K12
```

and cut and paste https://github.com/XKCP/K12/archive/refs/heads/master.zip into a browser, which I then direct to save into the K12 directory. The next step is to change into the K12 directory and unpack the download with

```
cd K12
unzip K12-master.zip
```

This creates a directory K12-master. Change to that directory and type make:

```
cd K12-master
make
```

The makefile lists many options to build. The simplest and most direct for 64-bit machines is the generic64/libk12.a static library. That's what I'm using for the examples in this book.

Building is very quick, and then we can copy the library into a standard location. The commands are

```
make generic64/libk12.a
sudo cp bin/generic64/libk12.a /usr/lib/libk12.a
```

The k12.header directory in the example source code contains files copied from the K12-master/lib and K12-master/lib/Optimized64 directories. There is more there to explore.

appendix B
Hilbert class polynomials

This appendix gives the code that creates the Hilbert class polynomials used in the book to find pairing-friendly curves. In chapter 14, I introduce the method of complex multiplication for finding pairing-friendly curves. The process of finding a correct curve involves solving for the *j*-invariant using Hilbert class polynomials.

The discriminants α are all equal to 3 mod 4 and range from 7 to 163. While that is sufficient for this book, there is no reason to stop at 163. The output file is listed after the program.

B.1 *Generation code*

The program to create the list of Hilbert class polynomials is simple in PARI. Listing B.1 shows a loop over the α values 7, 11, 15, 19, 23 + a * 20 for $a \in \{0, 1, \cdots 7\}$.

> **Listing B.1   Hilbert class polynomial generation**

```
/*************************************************************
 *                                                          *
 *    Print out Hilbert Class Polynomials of j(tau) using   *
 *   pari/gp function polclass().  The values of D come      *
 *   from the values used as alpha in the GMP routines       *
 *   which look for pairing friendly curves.                 *
 *                                                          *
 *************************************************************/

#include <pari/pari.h>

int main(int argc, char *argv[])
{
  FILE *hlbrt;
  GEN D;
```

```
    long atab[5] = 7, 11, 15, 19, 23;

    int i, j;
    pari_sp av;

    pari_init(2*1024*1024*512, 5*1024*512);

    hlbrt = fopen("Hilbert_Polynomials.list", "w");
    for(j=0; j<8; j++)
    {
      for(i=0; i<5; i++)
      {
        D = stoi(-(atab[i] + j*20));
        pari_fprintf(hlbrt, "%Ps : %Ps\n", D, polclass(D, 0 , -1));
      }
    }
    fclose(hlbrt);
}
```

B.2   *Hilbert class polynomial file*

As seen in the code listing, the output is a file that contains the polynomials. These are not modulo anything yet. Once we know the prime we are working with, then the formulas take on meaning.

Listing B.2   File Hilbert_Polynomials.list

```
-7 : x + 3375
-11 : x + 32768
-15 : x^2 + 191025*x - 121287375
-19 : x + 884736
-23 : x^3 + 3491750*x^2 - 5151296875*x + 12771880859375
-27 : x + 12288000
-31 : x^3 + 39491307*x^2 - 58682638134*x + 1566028350940383
-35 : x^2 + 117964800*x - 134217728000
-39 : x^4 + 331531596*x^3 - 429878960946*x^2 + 109873509788637459*x +
➡ 20919104368024767633
-43 : x + 884736000
-47 : x^5 + 2257834125*x^4 - 9987963828125*x^3 + 5115161850595703125*x^2 -
➡ 14982472850828613281250*x + 16042929600623870849609375
-51 : x^2 + 5541101568*x + 6262062317568
-55 : x^4 + 13136684625*x^3 - 20948398473375*x^2 + 172576736359017890625*x
➡ - 18577989025032784359375
-59 : x^3 + 30197678080*x^2 - 140811576541184*x + 374643194001883136
-63 : x^4 + 67515199875*x^3 - 193068841781250*x^2 +
➡ 455845124329502343750*x - 62569039542622536621093750
-67 : x + 147197952000
-71 : x^7 + 313645809715*x^6 - 3091990138604570*x^5 +
➡ 98394038810047812049302*x^4 - 823534263439730779968091389*x^3 +
➡ 5138800366453976780323726329446*x^2 - 425319473946139603274605151187659*x
+
```

➡ 737707086760731113357714241006081263

-75 : x^2 + 654403829760*x + 5209253090426880

-79 : x^5 + 1339190283240*x^4 - 6366718450945836*x^3 +

➡ 17934414241780934830698339*x^2

➡ - 5859423003994491322155950334*x + 5458041030919737322344464663391

-83 : x^3 + 2691907584000*x^2 - 41490055168000000*x + 549755813888000000000

-87 : x^6 + 5321761711875*x^5 + 85585228375218750*x^4 +

➡ 2832109057867936148437500000*x^3

➡ + 49757773388437263873559570312512*x^2 + 43218120225761639283828735351562512*x

+

➡ 54980643020486449015781021118164062512

-91 : x^2 + 10359073013760*x - 3845689020776448

-95 : x^8 + 19874477919500*x^7 - 688170786018119250*x^6

➡ + 39501357586714451925820312512*x^5

➡ - 13089776536501963407329479984375*x^4 +

➡ 3521633228586647267627252282949218751*x^3

➡ - 14374159398715735745728390109712480468751*x^2

➡ + 21106316391166752679539154247640568847656251*x

➡ + 1077896945765400100029767719961771486816406251

-99 : x^2 + 37616060956672*x - 56171326053810176

-103 : x^5 + 70292286280125*x^4 + 85475283659296875*x^3

➡ + 4941005649165514137656250000*x^2

➡ + 13355527720114165506172119140625*x +

➡ 2882661293701402906746615600585937512

-107 : x^3 + 129783279616000*x^2 - 6764523159552000000*x +

➡ 33761878920396800000000012

-111 : x^8 + 236917342626795*x^7 + 12257744369763349962*x^6

➡ + 561297001274616272980442066191*x^5 +

➡ 2987537813865962860773420720531252*x^4

➡ - 25675269514993965918445147228203062874*x^3

➡ + 88953282358528708595648019437144660946708*x^2

➡ - 647739954031047207028640913754030358554427611*x

➡ + 275247938158191914108618311671972505565108944171

-115 : x^2 + 427864611225600*x + 130231327260672000

-119 : x^10 + 764872171216961*x^9 - 70241355662808988599*x^8

➡ + 585035810262130969538043606647*x^7 -

➡ 52855712468679496581065487695942573*x^6

➡ + 4794937071328670764609540039796857947016*x^5

➡ + 1248061125580954568962714454232920307637387312*x^4

➡ + 2949402292050789631376660131337128565472278044312*x^3

➡ - 2922239288308487110110226377908965676741020403786171*x^2

➡ + 34648562621856173929218117272992393771129500446065423412*x

➡ - 116699204423738000315134782086796630250645876359016898871

-123 : x^2 + 1354146840576000*x + 14880959417548800000012

-127 : x^5 + 2375421230598750*x^4 - 30614197896114609375*x^3

➡ + 5642626198092219066070054687500*x^2 -

➡ 64331030949386896516600669921875000*x

➡ + 31973067147883366749127367367553710937512

-131 : x^5 + 4130485792112640*x^4 - 6711771218292244480001*x^3

➡ + 10720548428383845409305395212*x^2 - 60354680538951673475558801408*x

+ 14453063839469022407515532636 9792

-135 : x^6 + 7122306993287625*x^5 + 77686119211324699125*x^4

+ 50727257383070661992492657625000*x^3 +

6287358207316396508331268293987 18750*x^2

+ 432122386821367459504553400606 1857421875*x

+ 328452743924211931124295775034 6113869140625

-139 : x^3 + 12183160834031616*x^2 - 53041786755137667072*x +

67408489017571610198016

-143 : x^10 + 20680840776413625*x^9 - 6152626465680933171875*x^8

+ 42769886496072855434764384179 6875*x^7

- 126605537475340807363556327903 076171875*x^6

+ 347566867620018255645304528640 79986572265625*x^5

- 669600645730781825539256319987 784782409667968750*x^4

+ 603983906559183104116023978233 55987582206 72607421875*x^3

- 798349057751305578167824766612 3524158120155334472656250*x^2

+ 172938678455959890794097467818 75312506407499313354492 1875*x

- 146892619386926916220452018018 596212706528604030609130859375

-147 : x^2 + 34848505552896000*x + 1135680038948044800 0000

-151 : x^7 + 58309232586862950*x^6 + 110701821929 6858557941*x^5

+ 33999666164675336642484091553 53722*x^4

+ 696051331532443897373341805353 77491802*x^3

+ 779394774943277357155375818745 718823538863*x^2

+ 271248134304567044479896903675 912851345002767*x

+ 326920034037900090245872011325 7045278788199227087

-155 : x^4 + 96905542950912000*x^3 - 444778710963574 53824000*x^2

+ 20396251654725321097216000000*x + 3742586002846485628479078400 0000

-159 : x^10 + 16004137022342145*x^9 + 80544826577049275346921*x^8

+ 256013206178624027636386371124 00617*x^7

+ 129255746983938282302189755288 96357700901*x^6

- 500195761724247829095994019904 150074287948239*x^5

+ 913762736386278962009828554433 3489602867649370969*x^4

- 524825455503595921093730052259 4699105450465645 9581968*x^3

+ 131220647466890593981458207559 99068176177994167765889 1350*x^2

- 125380849804846892558943693244 057944355284981734410556485821*x

+ 492138841632124759442683677426 834911521489075988588 79501540753

-163 : x + 262537412640768000

appendix C
Variables list

In this appendix, I'll list all the variables used in the book in order of appearance. Many of the variables in this book have the same meaning in every chapter. An example is the use of capital letters to signify points on an elliptic curve. Some variables have different meanings in each chapter because they come from different references. The major example is a_j, which is a generic coefficient in some places and a very specific representation of a formula in others. The following list of variables is by chapter and in order of appearance within the chapter.

Chapter 2

a	arbitrary integer	e	number of zero bits in $p-1$
p	prime modulus modulus	q	odd value in $(p-1)/2^e$
x	square root of a	y, r, b, t	square root algorithm variables

Chapter 3

x, y	coordinates of 2D point	λ	slope of line between two points on elliptic curve
P, Q, R	points on an elliptic curve	k	integer multiplier of points
a_4, a_6	ordinary curve coefficients	$f(x)$	right-hand side of elliptic curve equation
0	point at infinity		

Chapter 4

E	specific elliptic curve	$\text{avf}(x)$	associate value function
G	generation point with prime order	s_A	implicit signature
A, B, S, P, U	multiples of G	z	shared secret
$\#E$	cardinality of curve E		

Chapter 5

B	base point	s_p	private key
P, Q, R, U, V	multiples of B	s	digital signature (Schnorr)
e	hash of message	k	random value
n	field prime modulus	c	x component of point (for signature)
M	message	d	digital signature (ECDSA)
		h, h_1, h_2	verify signature values

Chapter 6

E	elliptic curve	p	field prime modulus
$\#E$	cardinality of elliptic curve	t	trace of Frobenius
x, y	coordinate on elliptic curve		

Chapter 7

p	field prime modulus
a_k, b_k, c_k	polynomial coefficients mod p
x	polynomial variable

Chapter 8

p	field prime modulus
x^j	polynomial variable
t^j	polynomial variable of irreducible polynomial
a_i, b_i, c_i	polynomial coefficients modulo field prime
a, b, c	polynomial sum
prime polynomial	same as irreducible polynomial

Chapter 9

x^k	polynomial variable / polynomial sum
x^{p^i}	polynomial power modulo irreducible polynomial

Chapter 10

r	remainder	a, b	polynomial sums
q	quotient	$irrd$	irreducible polynomial
$lc()$	leading coefficient of polynomial	u, w, t, y, ρ	gcd algorithm variables
$deg()$	degree of polynomial		

Chapter 11

p	field prime modulus
x	polynomial variable
a_k	coefficients modulo field prime p
f, g	polynomial sum

Chapter 12

p	field prime modulus
a, b, x, y	polynomials modulo prime polynomial
q	value mod p
e	number zero bits in $p - 1$ square root algorithm
	(and) exponent in pseudo division algorithm
f	irreducible polynomial
$res(f, a)$	resultant of polynomials f and a
$cont(a)$	content of polynomial a
A, B, g, h	polynomial sums in resultant algorithm
Q, R	polynomial quotient, remainder
	pseudo divide algorithm
$lc()$	leading coefficient of polynomial
$deg()$	degree of polynomial
q, d	constants modulo field prime

Chapter 13

r	large prime in cardinality
p	field prime modulus
$\#E_k$	field extension cardinality
t_k	trace of Frobenius for field extension
k	degree of field extension
λ	polynomial slope of line between field extension points
x, y	polynomial coordinates on field extension curve

Chapter 14

r	large prime in cardinality
p, q	field prime modulus
ρ	ratio of bits in p to bits in r
α, D	discriminant of a quadratic equation
t	trace of Frobenius on base curve
j	j-invariant of elliptic curve

h	cofactor to cardinality
$\#E$	cardinality of base curve
a	multiplier for discriminant
k	embedding degree
$r(z), t(z), q(z)$	functions to find pairing-friendly curves
z, x	inputs to find pairing-friendly curves
c	coefficient for elliptic curve
f	quadratic non-residue for twist curve
$H(x)$	Hilbert class polynomial
$h(x), hc(x), A(x),$ $B(x), P(x)$	polynomials in factoring algorithm
d, e, x_1, x_2	solutions to factoring polynomial
a, b	quadratic equation coefficients

Chapter 15

Z	ring of integers
Z/nZ	ring of integers with $n\times$ all integers removed
E_{F_q}	elliptic curve over field q
P, Q, R, S, T	points on field extension curve
$e_m(\cdot, \cdot)$	elliptic curve pairing of two points
μ_m	m^{th} root of unity
0	point at infinity
$h_{P,Q}(R)$	function that is core of Miller algorithm
λ	slope of line between polynomial points
ν	y intercept on line between polynomial points
$f_P(R)$	Miller algorithm result

Chapter 16

P, Q, R, S	polynomial points on extension field curve
$e(\cdot, \cdot)$	Weil pairing of two points
$f_P(R)$	Miller algorithm result
$\#E$	cardinality of base curve
p^k	dimension of extension field
p	field prime modulus
t_k	trace of Frobenius on extension curve

Chapter 17

P, Q, R, S	polynomial points on extension field curve
$\tau(\cdot, \cdot)$	Tate pairing of two points
$f_P(R)$	Miller algorithm result
$E[m]$	points of order m on curve E
E/mE	points on E with points m times E removed
μ_m	m^{th} root of unity

Chapter 18

H_0, H_1, H_2	hash functions
G_1	points on field prime curve
G_2	points on extension field curve
r	large prime in cardinality
M, m	message or document
p	field prime modulus
b, t, h	values in hash functions
P_i	public key person i
ψ_i	private key person i
g_1	base point on field prime curve
g_2	base point on extension field curve
$\{P_1, P_2, \cdots, P_n\}$	set of keys for n users
a_j	hash of public keys to value mod r
A	sum of all public keys
s_i	person i signature of document
σ	aggregate of all signatures
$e(\cdot, \cdot)$	Weil pairing of two points
$\mathfrak{P}$	fraktur font P - list of all public keys
μ	matrix of membership keys
$\mu_{i,j}$	one entry in matrix of membership keys
M_i	membership key for person i
P_S	sum of subset public keys
σ_S	aggregate of subset signatures

Chapter 19

a_l	integer value of wire l
r_k	integer value of gate k
$v_j(x), w_j(x)$	input functions of all gates
$y_j(x)$	output function of all gates

$h(x)$	cross terms of gate functions
$t(x)$	product of all gate terms
$l_k(x)$	Lagrange interpolant associated with gate k
p_i	product of differences between r_k
$\alpha, \beta, \delta, \gamma, z$	random values, turn into "toxic waste"
θ_i	sum of input/output functions
G	base point on field prime curve
H	base point on extension field curve
A, B, C	proof points for specific record
V	intermediate point in proof operation
$\tau(\cdot, \cdot)$	Tate pairing of two points
k, n	integer numbers, not modulo anything
c_i, d_i, f_i, s_i	arbitrary coefficients of polynomials

selected bibliography

Barreto, P. S. L. M., B. Lynn, and M. Scott. "Constructing elliptic curves with prescribed embedding degrees." In *Security in Communication Networks*, Cimato, S., Persiano, G., and Galdi, C. (Eds.), pages 257–267. Springer Berlin Heidelberg, 2003.

Bitansky, N., R. Canetti, A. Chiesa, S. Goldwasser, H. Lin, A. Rubinstein, and E. Tromer. "The hunting of the snark." *Cryptology ePrint Archive*. Paper 2014/580, 2014.

Blake, I., G. Seroussi, and N. Smart. *Elliptic curves in cryptography*. Cambridge University Press, 1999.

Boneh, D., M. Drijvers, and G. Neven. "Compact multi-signatures for smaller blockchains." In *Advances in Cryptology—ASIACRYPT 2018*, T. Peyrin and Steven Galbraith, editors, pages 435–464. Springer International, 2018.

Brands, S. *Rethinking Public Key Infrastructures and Digital Certificates: Building in Privacy*. MIT Press, 2000.

Carroll, L. *The Hunting of the Snark*. Melville House, 2010. Illustrated by M. Singh.

Cohen, H. *A Course in Computational Algebraic Number Theory*. Springer-Verlag, 2000.

Diem, C. "On the discrete logarithm problem in elliptic curves." *Compositio Mathematica*, 147, 75–104, 2011.

Doliskani, J., and É. Schost. "Taking roots over high extensions of finite fields." *Mathematics of Computation*, 83, 435–446, 2011.

Faz-Hernandez, A., S. Scott, N. Sullivan, R. S. Wahby, and C. A. Wood. "Hashing to elliptic curves." Internet Engineering Task Force, 2021. http://mng.bz/M1Rn.

Freeman, D., M. Scott, and E. Teske. "A taxonomy of pairing-friendly elliptic curves." *Cryptology ePrint Archive*, paper 2006/372, 2006. https://eprint.iacr.org/2006/372.

Groth, J. "On the size of pairing-based non-interactive arguments." In *Advances in Cryptology—EUROCRYPT 2016*, M. Fischlin, and J.-S. Coron, editors, pages 305–326. Springer, 2016.

Koblitz, N. *A Course in Number Theory and Cryptography*. 2nd edition. Springer, 1994.

Koblitz, N., and A. Menezes. "Pairing-based cryptography at high security levels." In *Cryptography and Coding*, N. P. Smart, editor, pages 13–36. Springer, 2005.

Koblitz, Neal, and Alfred Menezes. "A riddle wrapped in an enigma." Cryptology ePrint Archive. https://eprint.iacr.org/2015/1018.

Kocher, Paul C. "Timing attacks on implementations of diffie-hellman, rsa, dss, and other systems." In *Advances in Cryptology — CRYPTO '96*, Neal Koblitz, editor, pages 104–113. Springer Berlin Heidelberg, 1996.

Lidl, Rudolph, and Harold Niederreiter. "Finite fields." In *Encyclopedia of Mathematics and Its Applications*. Cambridge University Press, 2nd edition, 1997.

Menezes, A. "An introduction to pairing-based cryptography." In *Contemporary Mathematics*, volume 477, pages 47–65, 2005.

Menezes, A., M. Qu, and S. A. Vanstone. "Some key agreement protocols providing implicit authentication." In *2nd Workshop on Selected Areas in Cryptography (SAC '95)*, pages 22–32, 1995.

National Institute of Standards and Technology. *Federal Inf. Process. Stds*, November 2001. http://mng.bz/AdOe.

National Institute of Standards and Technology. *NIST Special Publication 800-185, SHA-3 derived functions*, 2016. http://mng.bz/ZExN.

National Institute of Standards and Technology. *NIST Special Publication 800-56A revision 3*, 2018. http://mng.bz/RZqRf.

National Institute of Standards and Technology. *Federal Inf. Process. Stds*, February 2023. https://doi.org/10.6028/NIST.FIPS.186-5.

Riesel, H. *Prime Numbers and Computer Methods for Factorization*. Birkhäuser, 2013.

Roetteler, M., M. Naehrig, K. M. Svore, and K. Lauter. "Quantum resource estimates for computing elliptic curve discrete logarithms." In *Advances in Cryptology—ASIACRYPT 2017*, T. Takagi and T. Peyrin, editors, pages 241–270. Springer International, 2017.

Rosing, M. *Implementing Elliptic Curve Cryptography*. Manning Publications, 1999.

Silverman, J. H. *Advanced Topics in the Arithmetic of Elliptic Curves*. Springer-Verlag, 1994.

Silverman, J. H. *The Arithmetic of Elliptic Curves*. Springer-Verlag, 2nd edition, 2009.

von zur Gathen, J., and J. Gerhard. *Modern Computer Algebra*. Cambridge University Press, 1st edition, 1999.

Wong, D. *Real-world Cryptography*. Manning Publications, 2021.

index

Q